C000264314

"Rose MacFarlane's memoirs are a delightful [...] Jennifer Worth's Call the Midwife series. T[...] attractive Rose in 1968 in the Jordanian capita[...] hospital in Jordan as a United Nations Assoc[...] country shortly after the Six-Day War of 1967. As the [...] was welcomed as *Sitt Malaki* (Miss Queen) and immediately promoted to the position of matron. This chapter of her life, lived in the fast lane, is a particularly fascinating read that I can imagine being made into a film or TV series.

The book begins with Rose's early family life in Derbyshire and Cornwall, and nurse training at Sheffield's Royal Hallamshire Hospital. She writes about the ups and downs of her life and work in London in the 1960s, two marriages, divorces, childbirth, and nursing in the NHS and independent sector. The book concludes in Kent in 1985, at the end of Rose's nursing career ..." **Helen Sullivan** (SRN Retired), Hove, Sussex. [Full review in the Nursing Standard 28 April 2014 issue.]

"I too trained in the 1960's Now retired and having suffered current nursing care I believe that if the sound elements of the old SRN course had been kept and built on, nursing would not be in the mess it is in today. A good read, provoking many forgotten (good and bad) memories!!!" **E A Hyde** (SRN Retired)

"Enjoyed this book a very accurate account of nurse training in the 50s & 60s." **Chris Mackay**

"Could not put it down. A brilliant read from start to finish. Brought back many happy memories of my days in nursing." **Michael Regan**

"Hi Rose, thank u 4 book. Congrats I cudn't put it down it's fab. Lottsa luv Sheri. xx" **Shirley Beard**, Chatham. [Shirley is remembered with affection in the book.]

"Well done Sis, you certainly have a page-turner here! June burst out laughing many times when she read it." **Neil Murphy,** Sheffield. [Rose's brother's book **Neil's War: One boy's story of his evacuation to Ireland at the outbreak of WWII** covers the family period 1939-1945.]

"Fantastic! What an achievement. I can't remember what happened last year in my life. I just kept reading it, sometimes long into the night." **Nikki Lawrence**, Chateaubriant, France

Naked Nurse

My Life in Nursing

Rose MacFarlane

RoseTintedSpecs Imprint

COPYRIGHT MATTERS

Copyright ©Rose MacFarlane 2013
Published in the United Kingdom by
RoseTintedSpecs Imprint April 2013. This printing with minor corrections
August 2015.

This book and illustrations are copyright and there should be no
reproduction without permission from the publisher. All rights reserved.

It is sold subject to the condition that it shall not, by way of trade or
otherwise, be lent, resold, hired out, or otherwise circulated without the
publisher's prior consent in any form or binding or cover other than that
in which it is published and without a similar condition including this
condition being imposed on the subsequent purchaser.

Naked Nurse: My Life in Nursing is autobiographical. The author
trained as a nurse at the Sheffield Royal Hospital in the middle 1960s and
gained medical experience in the UK and Middle East. All incidents are
real. Names and some locations have been changed. The author extends
her thanks and appreciation to all those school friends, nursing friends,
colleagues and family who helped in telling the story.

Front cover image "Rose in Alex's E-Type Jaguar, Amman 1968." All
images courtesy of the author, her family and Rose Photo Archive (RPA).
Font licensing correct at time of publication.

ISBN 978-0-9544518-9-9 (paperback)
ISBN 978-0-9571686-0-2 (e-book/ Kindle)

RoseTintedSpecs Imprint
Publisher: David G. Rose
Butchers Farm, Molash, Kent, United Kingdom
www.rosetintedspecs.com
email: publisher@rosetintedspecs.com

Printed in the US. British-English spelling is used in this book

DEDICATION

To My Two Lucky Eggs

I have fallen below zero.
I sit with my cat cradling an empty universe.
The Faerie Queen looks old now and her handbag empty.
I sit and worry about my death
And whether some Roman-nosey vicar
Will creep in to steal my last words from life.
And will my girls sit, like two still harps,
Either side of me
Trying to cheat for me a spit of life?
And the door will open
As nice Nurse Squint brings me my syringe of gin
In her brown and crepe-soft soles.
Remember:
All breeze is breath of me
Singing Love to You.
Remember that and soon smile,
For you are my Two Lucky Eggs

Rose MacFarlane

INTRODUCTION

I trained as a nurse within the National Health Service in the middle-1960s. In those day autocratic Matrons and spinster Sisters used their absolute power to shrivel every student nurse's fragile ego, to re-mould her into someone as dedicated and as single-minded as they were.

Early television series gave some idea of British hospital life. Emergency, Ward 10 that ran from 1957 to 1967 was rather soppy. A more accurate portrayal of the harsh regime was Britain's most popular film of 1954, Doctor in the House. This and later Carry On films reminded me of our allying with fellow medical students to get us through the terror and indignity of our training days.

At Sheffield's Royal Hospital in the North of England where I trained, Matron was an awesome figure who connived with the senior consultant to run a tighter than tight ship. Matron's two deputies roamed the hospital corridors during the day ensuring their combined wishes were complied with. From eight pm to eight am a senior Night Sister and her two deputies also kept us toeing the line. Total obedience to Matron and Sisters created a seamlessly efficient, immaculately-run hospital.

Patients fell in line also, so to speak but they were the point of all of us being there and were cared for to as high a degree as Florence Nightingale revered her casualties of the Crimean War.

Our indoor uniform was a grey dress with starched white apron, cap and cuffs, black stockings and long cape. We wore the cape with pride because for most of us, becoming a nurse was a long-cherished dream. We could only be seen outdoors with a bottle green gabardine coat and hat over our uniform. This was considered more a penance as we would hurry back and forth between the Nurses' Home in leafy Fulwood and the Victorian hospital buildings in West Street in the centre of the city.

Some of us undertook a six-month induction in hospital ways as pre-entry cadets nicknamed Green Girls because of the mucous green overalls that looked like sack cloth and indicated we were without status. The first three months at Nursing School was a theory and practice induction. After this we were "Student Nurse" for three years. If we failed Hospital Finals or did not pass the State Finals we were downgraded to SEN (State Enrolled Nurse) status. If we passed these two final exams we were Nurse with SRN (State Registered Nurse) status. Passing Finals marked the next difficult phase, the transition from eager-to-please student to responsible Staff Nurse.

Chapter One
#Sister of Night ...# (Gore/Lee)

"Good evening Student Nurse MacFarlane. Welcome to Pye-Smith Ward. Night Sister Low has only just rung to say our regular Staff Nurse is off sick this evening. This is most unsatisfactory. What are they thinking of, putting a Second Year in charge ..."

Pye-Smith Ward's biro-thin matriarch Sister Grey tutted. She was clearly pained at having to commune with a dim junior nurse like me at Sheffield's prestigious Royal Hospital.

"And to add to our woes Student Nurse, we're running very late because a critically-ill gentleman has just been brought up from Casualty," Sister Grey continued in her Northern bark. "I will go through my report with you as soon as it's finished. Now, run along and hang your cape in the cloakroom."

"Thank you, Sister," I replied shaking, now I was actually on the ward.

Who wouldn't be in *status panicus* from being re-routed at the last minute to take charge of the hospital's senior ward? It is March 1964, two weeks after my eighteenth birthday and at the beginning of my second year of training as a nurse. I had been snatched from a much cosier night-duty assignment on Women's Geriatric where we could get away with some larking about with our favourite barmy auxiliary, a real pantomime dame with red pom-pom slippers, plenty of slap and pencilled-in eyebrows that could have scared the Grim Reaper.

Sister Grey's immaculate Pye-Smith Ward by contrast was the hospital's thirty-bedded critical care ward for male patients. Many would be on death's door. This is also the age before the cardiac resuscitation facilities of the NHS's smaller Intensive Care Units (ICUs). We had learnt during our training that if a patient's heart arrested it was likely to be *kaput* for the unfortunate soul.

"Ee, Rose! I've just 'eard they've sent you up to death-watch alley to take bloody charge!" yelled Manic Myrtle minutes earlier as we'd hurtled past each other in opposite directions along the old hospital's gloomy corridors. "Rather thee than me with old Granite Chops Grey!"

Manic Myrtle was a Barnsley Whippet and my ultra-skinny room mate at Tapton Court Nurses' Home on nearby Fulwood Road. She could have been an understudy for Audrey Hepburn except she was a firecracker. Though juniors, both of us were already night-duty ward-floaters, filling in for our student pals on their nights off. We could also be dispatched at a moment's notice as an extra pair of trembling hands in various witching-hour emergencies. As rooky no-nothings we had only been entrusted thus far to take brief charge of low-key wards when the Staff Nurse was on one of her two meal breaks. I say her, as there weren't any male nurses at The Royal, at any NHS hospital as far as I know, in those days.

The prospect of being in charge of thirty or so patients through the night even for a few minutes with no Staff Nurse present terrified us, as it would a new air stewardess asked to take over the controls of an airliner. Any dozy moth could tell our gormless forms tiptoeing around the beds of the very poorly patients expected to pop off, willing them to hang on until the Staff Nurse returned.

To non-medical people, determining if someone is dead may seem a no-brainer. This is how it seems in death scenes on television and film. Cardiac arrest is an easy one to determine as the unfortunate pegs out very quickly. For patients in slow decline it can be as though they are having the last laugh by stopping breathing for an age, then shuddering back to life like a wheezy old steam engine. This could go on for hours and is very upsetting for the relatives.

Now I was walking-the-walk. I was flying solo. Sister Low, our senior night-time *commandant* may as well have delegated Mad Mave Bolsover who tramped endlessly around Sheffield's city centre, to run Pye-Smith Ward. Haunting memories of my older brothers' merciless mocking as Nurse Twitty-Toes whenever I wore my childhood nurse's uniform floated into my *hippocampus*.

As I turned towards the cloakroom I felt Sister Grey's ferret-brown eyes bore into me through her *pince-nez* spectacles.

"You have worked on my ward before, on days, as I recall, Student Nurse MacFarlane?"

"Yes, Sister," I nodded grimacing, hoping she wouldn't link me with the recent Prize Ward-howler.

"Hmm ... I trust and pray you'll have an uneventful night tonight Student Nurse. Now let me finish the report. And do tidy your hair off your collar, you look a fright."

Such sniping at trainee nurses was now almost music to our well-tuned ears. It was rash to think of ourselves as anything above cockroach droppings. The hospital's punitive training regime was ring-fenced to keep us obedient and ever desperate to please. Whatever we endured, be it low pay, no social life, constant exhaustion, scowling sisters and a complete lack of self-esteem, we were still privileged and proud to be Sheffield Royal Hospital nursing students. Add this to being brought up in the God-fearing, self-denigrating 'Fifties and of course, we were putty in their immaculate hands.

The howler had happened a couple of weeks earlier on the ward when I had been feeding a cachexic 'Jack Tar' suffering from insane paralysis, the last stages of syphilis. Our miniscule but muscular Deputy Matron, Sister Foggart on her daily stomp asked my syphilitic patient a tad too unconvincingly how he was feeling. He waited until she had walked on a little way before spitting out his milk, raising his 'skull' from the pillow, curling his little finger and yelling in a clear Cockney voice,

"An I bet 'er 'ole's only that big!"

A silence descended on the ward, as after a huge natural catastrophe. Staff and patients were aghast. Ex-Sergeant-major Foggart froze, her koala-brown eyes spinning like Catherine Wheels. Thankfully, she marched off the ward without uttering a word leaving the staff barely able to contain themselves with mirth. Those were the patient's final words. He died that night, his skeletal body curled like a Pompeii victim.

Hanging up my comfort blanket in Pye-Smith's tiny cloakroom, my full-length cape with blood-red woollen lining, I tidied my frizzy mop in front of a sliver of mirror. Were the broken mirror and my fear-induced migraine a twin omen goading me into calling it quits? Could I dare jack it all in and flee to London to join my Catholic school pals living the high-life in Hippy Land, so they had me believe?

As I fantasised about jumping ship before I'd even sailed, a willing moron serving in an overheated edifice, images of my stern mother came to mind instructing me to do the right thing for Queen and Country. In true passive style, Nurse People-pleaser MacFarlane trooped back to the ward and the discomfort of a lengthy report to get to grips with.

Sitting in a Ward Sister's hallowed office for the first time is as disquieting as being called in to the Headmistress's study. Observing Sister Grey with her permed, fading ginger hair and repaired hair-lip gave me a glimpse of her as a vulnerable old stick more to be empathised with than feared. For five seconds, anyway. The longer she spun out the day's report on her thirty patients, the more jittery I became, a mouse being toyed with.

She went through the report in painstaking detail allowing me time to underline in my notebook specific care requirements and to note especially the patients who might not last the night. The thought there might not be any patients left in the morning crossed my mind. Seeing the harassed woman's tired face matching her name I hadn't the nerve to whimper like a witless nitwit.

Sister Grey, unwittingly perhaps, left the *coup de grâce* to the end.

"And we are a little behind tonight Student Nurse because the critical admission you have just underlined is His Worship the Lord Mayor. He had an acute asthma attack and requested a bed on main ward rather than a side room, Labour through and through, you know!" she whispered respectfully. "He is in the last bed by the side wards. He was very tired on admittance and best you leave him to sleep. He is critical but stable but he could go into a bronchial spasm which would be, as you are well aware, life-threatening."

Did she say the Lord Mayor of Sheffield was on my ward, on my first night in charge ... that he could spasm and die? Headlines flashed before my eyes,

LORD MAYOR PERISHES, IDIOT NURSE BLAMED

"The duty doctor is Doctor Smythe," Sister Gray concluded, "your auxiliaries tonight are both sterling ladies. Senior Night Sister Low will have the drug cupboard keys and will be in at ten. Let us hope you have a quiet night ... Nurse!"

I thanked Sister, almost curtseying, preening for a moment on her addressing me as "Nurse." We couldn't call ourselves Nurse until qualified. Until then we were addressed as "Student Nurse" or more likely "brainless idiot ... stupid moron ... excuse for a simpleton ..." There would be no pantomime dame activity that night. Maybe just witches stirring a cauldron on the staircase cackling "bubble, bubble, toil and trouble for you, this full moon, nitwit nursie ... *hah, hah, hah!*"

After Sister Grey's departure at about eight-thirty that chilly March night, Naked Nurse gathered up the report book in which the nurse-in-charge on all wards entered a synopsis of each patient's progress through the shift. Sister Grey's first entry was typical:

Day Report: 03/03/1964
Patient: Mr. Reg Sweeney, aged 76
Diagnosis: Hypothermia

Slept poorly, a little agitated. Temperature: F102.00, 2 am. Dr.
Wilson called. Penicillin injections commenced as per chart. Fluids
encouraged, pressure-areas good. Please encourage fluids, turn 4
hrly. when in bed and ambulate if possible. Record 4 hrly. TPR.
He's worried about his wife and feeding his racing pigeon Harry ...

As Nurse-in-charge I would have to put my skates on and rush
around the ward meeting and greeting, hoping to absorb all the
patients' names, ages, diagnoses, medication and concerns. It was said
Night Sister Low always knew every one of the Royal Hospital
patient's details, even on a first night back on duty. She, the Ancient
One, as she seemed to us at eighteen, expected all her junior and
senior nurses to know their stuff by the middle round at two am. If
you failed in this task you were marked as a *klutz*. Demotion was
subtle, taking the form of subsequent night duties as outcasts on
wards like Ear, Nose and Throat (ENT) where nothing ever happened
except for the midnight stroll of the 'White Lady.'

Tonight has to be a good night, Naked Nurse prayed, as Sister
Grey's black court shoes clacked off into the distance. She now had
to run for the Sisters' bus back to their designated Virgin's Retreat,
also in leafy Fulwood. I wouldn't have left me in charge of this
precious ward with its impeccable reputation, I thought, still shaking
a little.

Adjusting her starched white cap, smoothing her pristine apron
and patting her frilly white cuffs for luck, Naked Nurse took a deep
breath and entered Pye-Smith Ward as self-conscious as John Wayne
when he was made to walk across camera. The *compos mentis* patients
turned to stare.

"Smile for the nice gentlemen," I urged myself. "Go cure or kill,
Honey!"

Introducing myself to my ward auxiliaries was my first priority as
they would be my backbone for the night. One was serving the old
faithfuls Horlicks and Ovaltine. The other was on the urine bottle
round chatting away to the male patients about 'owt and nowt.' Their
seasoned eyes clocked my brand new second-year belt as they greeted
me with a polite welcome.

"I'm Missers Mac," announced the chubbier one with a kindly face that resembled a pickled walnut.

"And I'm Martha. Welcome Luv, looks like we're in for a reet 'ard neet. But we'll 'elp yer. Won't we Missers Mac?" chirped her sidekick.

"'Course we will! But you'll need a special dispensation to get through t'neet, Luv. Wot with our VIP admission, 'n' all!"

"Thanks ladies. It'll be a breeze I'm sure," I lied.

Before introducing myself to our Lord Mayor dozing at the far end of the ward, I had to attend to two moribund gentlemen feverish with end-stage cancer, lying as still as stricken angels on a mini death row close to the ward entrance and morgue. As they lived, so they were dying, circumspect and uncomplaining in their neat-as-ninepence beds. None of Dylan Thomas's "rage, rage against the dying of the light" here.

I had a vision of my own brother Damien laid out, enshrouded, labelled and carted off on a metal trolley to the same soulless hospital morgue a year earlier. He was now at my shoulder reminding me to treat all dying patients as I would a loved relative. My two terminal patients in Pye-Smith that night would need their Brompton Cocktails four-hourly on the dot. No social drink, this. It was a gin-based concoction of morphine and cocaine that would need Night Sister's authoritative touch.

Student nurses were not allowed medicine cupboard keys or to do ward round medicines on their own. All opiates and sleep or relaxation medications were double-locked away. Items could only be checked out by a nurse with at least one other nurse or auxiliary present. Usage of all medicines was recorded on a patient's prescription sheet, entered in a ledger regarded as a legal document and signed for.

I moved on to introduce myself to the two other critically-ill but by contrast, hyperactive gentlemen Billy and Fred. These desperadoes were sitting bolt upright next to each other in oxygen tents, distressed from laboured breathing and cruel deprivation of the Capstan and Senior Service cigarettes that had caused their demise. Breathless Billy managed a smile and drew my attention to a note he had scrawled,

'Elp, fech Copper, I am Billy, bin eld prisner. Gi US A FAG'

With nicotine junkies a sharp eye is needed for any sympathetic mobile patient or visitor who might slip cigarettes and matches into an oxygen tent. Fag hags can be as wily as alcoholics. One match strike, however and we could all be victims of the habit. Oxygen tent patients can become confused and hostile due to their confinement and a build-up of carbon dioxide in the brain.

Many patients like these desperadoes came from the poor areas of Sheffield and their pathetic plight was upsetting. Former grafters in the city's steel works or "down't' pit" from thirteen or younger, their work was all they knew. Typically, they had pinched faces, tinged blue extremities and spoon-shaped finger nails. Their anguish couldn't be alleviated with sedatives or opiates as this risked depressing their breathing even more. It was a harsh way to go and we couldn't comfort them with any physical contact inside their zipped-up tent. Anyway, a reassuring handhold up here in the North of England would probably have been spurned with a "gerroff, ye daft booger!"

The Angel of Death could collect any of our five very sick patients that night and my concern was how I could also keep an eye on the remaining flock of poorly men. I felt particularly for three emaciated lads of my age with serious bowel problems. Ulcerative colitis tends to occur in younger people and I was to administer slow-release steroid enemas to them at bedtime in the hope it would help keep them off their commodes by forestalling frequent and embarrassing bouts of bloody diarrhoea.

My other patients were a fascinating mix of complex diagnoses. They included two dangerously unstable diabetics, four chronically ill kidney and liver patients, three recovering double pneumonias, one rheumatic fever and one polio case, as well as our VIP asthma patient.

There was much to do before lights out at ten o'clock. Mrs. Mac and Martha, ward fixtures of many years were a dream team settling the patients and I really appreciated their support. Their presence enabled me to visit each patient to say hello at least and check their notes, even if some were giving my youthful countenance and beginners' uniform the Third Degree. I only recognised this wary eye years later when I found myself looking over doctors or police officers who looked as though they would have preferred being out on Pogo Sticks.

My VIP in the last bed in the ward was sitting propped up with an oxygen cylinder by him and a mask over his nose and mouth. His chest rose and fell with the effort of a very poorly asthma patient. As I removed his mask to check his tongue was not drying up I noted he was gorgeous and not the elderly whiskered worthy I had envisioned. His Worshipful, Mr. J. S. W. "call me Jack, please, Nurse," was a forty-something Alan Bates with a grin as wide as the River Don.

While I was checking his blood pressure, temperature and pulse we had a brief chat. He promised he would be on his best behaviour! The elderly gent next to him was busy emptying his heavy glass urinal onto the floor, set on throwing it at our VIP. With a pared-down night staff it can be a conjuring act getting everything done before lights out and my first night on this ward was already building up to being a true test. Once lights are out, ward activities can take on a surreal atmosphere. Heaven help me if it turned into a 'full moon night' when the moon can actually trigger bizarre nocturnal activity, particularly among seriously ill patients.

Tonight, four patients including my two in oxygen tents, were already chattering gibberish. This was not a good sign. Billy the breathless tent-scribe had managed a second note,

Elp - the Boogers ave captured me - fech Bobbies

Sister Low arrived at ten o'clock on the dot for her first round and to oversee the giving out of medicines. If all the senior staff were getting on in years, Sister Low was truly vintage. She was an awesome thickset matriarch who tramped miles of hospital corridors with an aura of Cruella de Ville. If Jane Eyre had a grandmother it could have been her. We viewed her as a cool operator who never lost her temper and who always spoke quietly, unlike most of the daytime Sisters who were arguably certifiable in their behaviour. Sister Low was unnervingly calm and feared and respected by nurses and doctors alike.

As we began the Papal tour, Naked Nurse's memory bank of the hastily learnt patients' details blanked as her hypersensitive ears detected the terrifying sound of desperate wheezing and laboured breathing at the end of the ward. His Worship the Lord Mayor was turning a delicate shade of grey-blue as a major asthma attack caused his breathing to spasm and constrict. We were there in a flash.

"We'll manage alright won't we, Nurse?" he gasped, winking at me, trying to reduce my poorly undisguised anxiety.

Sister Low drew his curtains calmly and told me to call the houseman and tell him it was an emergency call. Minutes later, after an intravenous injection of Theophylline to calm the patient's breathing his condition stabilised. A side-effect of this drug, however, can be over-stimulation of the heart and cardiac arrest. This was a worry in the days before the routine use of ECG monitors to check a patient's heart beat. Sister Low instructed me to stay with the Lord Mayor. She would finish the ward round on her own.

Saved by the Mayor that night from memory blanking, some

blagging and the Evil Eye, Night Sister had also reassured him I was one of the most competent young nurses she had and he was in safe hands. I didn't learn this until later and would really have appreciated hearing it at the time.

Of five terminal patients that night, four lived for another day, another shift. It was for me as a Second Year the best and worst of nights. The Lord Mayor was wonderful and he became adept at ducking stuff thrown at him by his confused neighbour. Aggravating patients are moved but when emergency admissions occupy all spare beds this becomes impossible.

Thankfully, I also managed my first ward death competently having been alerted to it by my new friend, Jack. It was Billy in the adjacent bed who had expired. Saddened as I was at not being able to spend more time at his bedside, it wouldn't have made much difference. A last fag wouldn't have done him any harm either, though his time left would have been even shorter out of the tent. I supervised Martha with the itemising of the contents of his locker, laying him out and labelling him ready for the porters to take him down to the mortuary.

On my first night in charge it was not only my late brother Damien who came to mind. Maverick older brother Billy had contracted Rheumatic Fever in the late 1940s and was in Pye-Smith Ward for weeks. As he got better, he said, the fitter among them organised a syndicate betting on who would be the next to croak.

My two auxiliaries shone the long night. Martha's only little quirk was her refusal to enter the sluice between midnight and one o'clock in the morning when yet another 'White Lady,' according to her, sometimes appeared. Bizarrely, at midnight exactly when the good ladies had gone to supper, I had to fetch a bedpan from the haunted sluice. Timidly switching the light on, I grabbed a stainless steel pan only to drop it on the concrete floor as the light went out of its own accord. Martha was wide-eyed with joy at the vindication of her foible.

As ever on night duty, a night of pandemonium evaporates at daylight, just as Day Staff come breezing in. It may have been my own tiredness but even the most recalcitrant and aggressive patients were sitting up fresh as daisies, smiling and sane.

My VIP boosted my self-esteem more than I could have imagined when taking over Pye-Smith Ward, despite the fact he must have felt pretty awful on admission. He could easily have spent the night being cosseted on the detested private wing instead of spending a sleepless night on an open ward. I went to say goodbye to him and he promised an invitation to the mayoral parlour for tea. I must bring a friend, he insisted. The mayoral Rolls-Royce would pick us up!

A few days later my mate Ditzy Delia and I were chauffeured through the streets in our well-pressed, bottle green outdoor uniforms. The citizens of our good town gawped as we waved imperiously, giggling. Tea was a grand affair and I thanked the Lord Mayor for helping me through what might have been a night to forget rather than a night to remember.

He was my first 'person of power' patient and his tangibly giving temperament was calming. Such people never abuse their status. Instead, they go out of their way to make you feel good. The best of men, women and children I met during my career were modest, encouraging, kind and fun to be with whatever their circumstances. I have witnessed people from babies to centenarians bear intolerable suffering with astounding dignity.

The fact that I'm writing these words shows this night on the ward was a seminal moment in my early nursing and one that would make my forty-plus years as a nurse worth every moment. Before I go any further, I realise I should actually start at the beginning with my childhood in Sheffield and tell you firstly, about some of the incidents from the year dot to my teenage years that compelled me to become a nurse.

Chapter Two
#From the moment I could talk, I was ordered to listen ...# (Cat Stevens)

We were seven in our family when the war in Europe ended. I was the second to last, delivered by my father in March 1945 in a Nursing Home in Dronfield. Mother's last child brother Simon was born in December 1946.

My eldest siblings by a decade were Morris, Jane and Billy. Pre-war infants, they spent the War years as evacuees with father's relatives in Cork in Southern Ireland. Each returned to a cherished image of "home, sweet home" that was no longer. Morris came home early because he was depressed. Billy rose to the challenge perhaps too successfully and was ordered back to England in 1943. Jane loved Ireland and stayed the course. When she returned, the cosy family of four children had morphed into a demanding brood of seven.

"It was a shock," Jane, told me years later. "We left as spoilt kids with servants and came back to a new and unfamiliar home with unknown brothers and sisters. I was suddenly Nanny helping war-weary parents. There was sickness too with Morris and Pascal contracting diphtheria, then haemorrhagic measles. And Billy nearly died of an asthmatic condition in Ireland."

"The only time I saw your father break down and cry," Mother also told me years later, "was when we were nursing two very sick children. He was on call throughout the War and running a slum area

practice night and day single-handed. Combine that with our scrambling to the air-raid shelter night after night and fitting in visits to Ireland to see the older kids ... poor man. And we weren't always paid in full for patient consultations. I had four more pregnancies to manage while assisting your father, all without the help of our five pre-war maids. It was hell, but no different to everyone else's ..."

What an adjustment also for my mother coming from a well-to-do background to running a large family under those conditions in the days without fridges, washing machines, central heating, convenience foods, credit and the like.

From 1944 she also grieved deeply for her twice-decorated pilot brother, Bill, often referring to him as her twin because they were so close. Uncle Bill was shot down over northern France in May 1944 on a double mission dropping equipment and an SOE (Special Operations Executive) agent during D-Day preparations ten months before I was born. Brother Billy wrote a book about his experiences in Ireland and dedicated it to Uncle Bill. Mother became pregnant with me two months after this traumatic loss.

The last time my mother mentioned Bill was when recalling her father's death just after the War. As Grandfather took his last breath her sister Margaret whispered "Brother Bill's come to fetch Father ..." and fainted.

Auntie Margaret confirmed years later that their recently deceased brother appeared at the foot of Father's death-bed. He was in uniform with his cap under one arm, exactly as he had stood at their mother's death-bed in 1941. An Australian cousin researching my mother's Scottish family recently sent me a copy of Grandmother's 1941 Death Certificate. Uncle Bill's signature showed he was present.

A pregnancy with the end of war in sight should have made for a happy birth but it wasn't so because of Mother's grief for her beloved brother.

"I don't know why," she would muse, nattering away to Little Me as if I was an inanimate object "but while carrying you I craved cigarette after cigarette for the first time in my life! I smoked everything stacked in the cupboard, the unwanted gifts to your father. And you, you little pest, you took three days to arrive. It must have been the thatch of hair you were born with ... Visitors would peer in your cot and comment on my wee monster! And to cap it all Child, you cried non-stop for your first six weeks ..."

Was it any wonder, suffering from nicotine withdrawal, I remarked when an adult. It might explain why I puffed away on Woodbines from the tender age of twelve, when I could get away with it.

Caring genes were clearly transfused to me within Ma's knackered womb regarding the way I responded to her post-war melancholy. Assuming a caring role for her from a very early age, I became her unwitting confidante. "A woman's place is in the home" was a cultural decree until the late 'Sixties and my intelligent and talented mother was no different from millions of other women who had to repress any notion of finding fulfilment or independence through a career or creativity.

Watching a newsreel footage of top-hatted, grim-faced post-war politicians reminded me recently how forbidding the patriarchy was. A man's power base was clearly in the external world. A woman's, my mother's domestic power base certainly, was configured to feed her frustration and misery.

Noting how much my two spirited older sisters irritated her I determined to become her cheery little minder. Suffering from an undiagnosed underactive thyroid, even with a GP husband, she would sit in front of the fire year-round moaning about being the cold. Becoming a precocious Mummy-pleaser was my way of being tolerated by her. Surely she would love me one day, wouldn't she? If I kept on doing all I could to soothe away her troubles.

Animals do not brood after a fight or other set-back and neither do kids. They survive emotional neglect, if this is the case, by fantasising. My underwhelming and worn-out parents clearly favoured chosen siblings. My mother favouring Billy, Damien and Simon and my father Sulky Sis.

#Mother you had me, but I never had you
I wanted you, but you didn't want me ...# John Lennon

"You, Ro, were independent from the age of five," Sister Jane observed as she gradually took on the role of surrogate mother. It was true. I remember a summer's evening when I was determined I wouldn't show that I minded being overlooked. What else is a spirited and bold young girl to do to survive in a large brutish family?

As clear outsiders, Jane and I became each other's champions. With her reputation as the naughtiest girl in the school (Notre Dame, Sheffield), then naughtiest nurse ever at the Royal in Sheffield, she was a hard act to follow! A Joyce Grenfell hilarious kind of girl, I loved listening to her escapades. She seemed so brave. Us younger ones viewed grown-ups as terrifying "though shalt not" spoilsports whom we dare not disobey as she did.

Pa bought his first practice just after the Wall Street Crash of 1929. It was in one of the worst slum areas of inner Sheffield. He had to bob under thick rubber "Johnnies" pegged up on back yard lines with the daily washing, he said. Unsurprisingly many of his worn-out female patients suffered from "nerve trouble." These desperate women would return repeatedly for their bottle of the calming herb Valerian, their "Mothers' Little Helper."

My parents survived the war and their very busy life with an occasionally-glimpsed rich sense of the absurd. My Cork-born father's Achilles' Heel was that he was an intellectual and social snob. This may be because he had to work harder to fit in with his English-born colleagues' social status.

"Say but, not bu' ... say it, not i' ..." he would interject, correcting us at the meal table in his received pronunciation in an attempt to have us all speaking properly. It was a maddening habit from a gentle man whom I otherwise idolised. Manners and good form were sacrosanct, to the extent that he pulled up in the car one Summer evening and knocked a bag of chips out of my hands on the street. I was ordered home for a time-honoured "always remember you are a doctor's daughter, lecture."

He had an impeccable taste for the good things in life and retained a sense of style all his life. At eighty he could still wear the dapper Savile Row suit he wore when he married my mother in 1929. On many an evening he would teach us to tap dance or he would hide playing cards up his sleeve and perform one magic trick after another. The poor man must have been running on empty for most of the time, yet he exuded a calm presence.

During my first year of life, 1945, we lived in rural Greenhill over the practice. A still-expanding and rapidly growing brood needed a bigger home. As hard up as my parents were, they were fortunate in securing a much more majestic Fanshawgate House in the exquisitely bleak countryside on the Sheffield-Derbyshire borders. It was rented from one of Pa's eccentric land-owning patients Poll Hattersley.

Despite her riches she lived like a character from a Grimm's Fairy Tale by a spit-black range in a darkened hovel about a mile away from

us on the edge of the meagre village of Holmesfield. When we called to see her she would invite me to fetch a jar of threepenny bits from her damp scullery and would give us one each.

Fanshawgate House was originally the dwelling of the owner of the farm next us. In the late Nineteen-Forties when I was still a wimp of a child, blood-soaked local people would frequently knock on our farmhouse door.

"Ist' Doctor 'ome, please Missus?" a toothless relative would squeak, anxiously seeking my beleaguered father to patch them up, hopefully for free.

Trekking out to us on the edge of the moors however inclement the weather was a preferred option to having to travel miles to the Emergency Room in Sheffield. Few owned a car, some had a motorbike and sidecar. If father was out on his rounds my capable mother would deal with them if she could, with me hovering in my little nurse's outfit asking if I could stick one of my plasters on them. If they were too sick or injured she would call an ambulance.

In pre-NHS days most GPs owned their practices. They usually worked on their own, underpaid and on call day and night. Pa became so overworked running surgeries at Greenhill and Totley he developed a duodenal ulcer. Realising her husband was a breakdown waiting to happen, Mother insisted he took at least half a day off a week. Doctor William Joseph MacFarlane worked far harder than today's pampered, over-paid GPs just to make ends meet. He had a wife, eight children, a car, two surgeries and two practice housekeepers to support.

Mother helped by running the dispensary when they lived over the surgeries. She would add the Valerian, for example, to the inert liquid of green, yellow or red that made the medicine more palatable. Patients would be most upset if the colour they liked ran out, even though the dose of Valerian was the same.

"Ee, Missus, that there green medicine what you gi' me, it weren't 'alf as good as the red stuff what Doctor gimme afore!"

It was a perfect example of the placebo effect. Herbal medicines and preparations were prescribed by GPs because there were so few pharmaceutical drugs available apart from M & B's sulphur-based compounds and good old aspirin. I wish I had learnt more about them from both my parents.

Penicillin, the first of the post-war wonder drugs must have made a huge difference to my father's efficiency and his patients' health. On Pa's return home from work one evening when I had a painful ear infection I was brought downstairs.

"Rose," he informed my miserable three-year old self, "here is a wonderful new medicine that will take your nasty earache away and there's a special glucose sweet for you, if you are a good girl."

Mother held me firmly and taking out a ready-prepared glass syringe and hypodermic needle Pa injected me in my plump upper arm. Shocked tears at this perceived assault were pooh-poohed, as they were for the next five evenings when he continued to inject me with his miraculous Penicillin.

The placatory sweet was usually reserved for emergency diabetic patients. Post-war sweet rationing in 1948 permitted us children only two gold-dust sweets a week. Screaming my head off each time I was injected meant the longed-for sweet did not come my way. Mother would shoo me up to our ghost-cold bathroom to wee from my shivering from fear and upset when all this little girl wanted was a cuddle. The treatment worked but for a long time I feared Pa's return home which before had been my favourite time of day.

Having lost their pre-war army of domestic staff, this Great Gatsby-era couple dealt with the harsh reality of war and austerity of post-war years as pragmatists. Mother could have organised the British Armed Forces as well as run a home efficiently.

"When I had my five servants before the war, although I happily helped your father by running the pharmacy, I still had time to draw and paint and play golf. We had a gay old time!" she would reminisce. "I could only find one part-time cleaner afterwards as they had all moved on somewhere. To better jobs, I think, I don't know."

When in a happy mood reflecting on better times, Mother would do the Charleston and Father would tap dance. Fred Astaire was his idol. War-time food shortages were a dire experience for these 'Twenties high-life people. They told of being given a present of a bottle of whisky, a rare occurrence for civilians during the war years, only to drop it accidentally on the stone kitchen floor.

"We were so desperate to save it we used gauze from the surgery to try and soak it up!"

Part of Pa's eight days a week workload was the war dance around the old Morris on freezing winter mornings and before many a winter night-time call-out around Derbyshire. Many of these would be to home births where problems had developed. Most mothers gave birth at home. He was also called out to do what he could for critically-ill children suffering from a catalogue of life-threatening diseases. Diphtheria, rheumatic fever, polio, scarlet fever and whooping cough were commonplace. They are a rarity now thanks to decades of vaccination programmes.

When I had my first daughter in 1971 I dithered over whether to have her vaccinated.

"You must," Pa urged. "There is a no more distressing sight than a child sick with whooping cough or diphtheria."

"Yes, and remember my Uncle David," added Mother. "He lost two children to diphtheria and the shock of their deaths caused him to emigrate to New Zealand, to warmer climes than Glasgow."

Brought up in an age in which they accepted their fate before their elders and betters, war-weary families like mine developed a 'put up and shut up' mentality. They were aware also of millions worse off around a shattered Europe. There were so many people stateless, homeless, penniless, sick, injured, without families, work or hope. Tortured prisoners from the Far East in particular, returned home deeply traumatised to receive little or no help with their psychological problems. The fate of Concentration Camp victims and survivors introduced a moral despair at how human nature and so-called civilised peoples could descend to such depths of evil and depravity.

In more comfortable times the television series All Creatures Great and Small about a country vet during the 'Forties and 'Fifties paralleled my father's life as a country GP. His practices were only a skip and a jump away from the Yorkshire Dales of the television series. However grim the call-out, whether of doctor or vet, people just got on with it. Could most people today cope with the stress endured by our families during the Blitz, for example, or during white-out winters? 'Stress' didn't exist in the early 'Forties, whereas "just gerronw' it," did.

In our family, my older Brute Brothers Placid Pascal and Demonic Damien were constantly exasperated by us useless girls. We soon realised they were far too preoccupied with fighting the Nazis to have time for our nonsense games. Except, that is, when we were required as dumb extras for their derring-do.

Reading became my real world from the age of four, my escape. Passionate about Noddy, Rupert Bear, Br'er Rabbit, Peter Pan (with Lucy Atwell's iconic pictures drawing me in) and Grimm's frightening fairy tales, the daily challenge offered in these pages made home life tame by comparison. I loved the I-Spy series too and we took them with us when we were out in the wilds of Derbyshire.

Life was brutal, except when Father came home at lunchtimes and in the evening. Surviving sibling bullying and teasing in exchange for the occasional honour of taking part in some wartime re-enactment was the order of most days.

The adjacent farm's wooden-seated double loo became a chapel for Sulky Sis and I into which we could withdraw from the boys if necessary. While sitting warming our bums on the tactile wood we would read the cut-out squares of local newspaper strung together as toilet paper for the farm workers, as opposed to the more expensive Bronco roll we had in the house. We found Bronco too crisp but it did have the right toughness to wrap around a comb, allowing us to hum through family singsongs. An art surely lost forever with the softness of the toilet rolls we couldn't do without today.

While we were sitting on our hidey-hole lavatory, Ma once overheard me declaring "they stink fru their bottoms, don't they?" referring to Pascal and Damien's sadistic behaviour towards us. She didn't understand what it was like being constantly dismissed for being a useless twitty girl.

Incredibly, we were free to swoop into the farm at the side of the house. MacFarlane scallywags need only open the kitchen door, walk five paces to the gate and unless Farmer S. had locked it for safety reasons, roam anywhere they wished. Here was more escapist fantasy, our own Disneyland. We were already lucky living in wild and windy countryside, ferocious in tooth and claw. Pushed, pulled and chased around gardens and farm buildings by energetic siblings was second-by-second heaven, or it was hell. It would not suit everyone but even just a taste would surely be better for today's couch-potato, games-console kids?

Farmer S. was a six-foot two-inch wellingtoned, cockerel red-faced workaholic. He had his own take on what are known as Health and Safety issues today that would have made our childhood tractor and trailer-riding jaunts, for example, a no-no.

"Joost shut alt' gates and barn doowers, me Ducks and don't do 'owt daft," he would bawl as we scrambled on or off the trailer bouncing back and forth between farmyard and fields. He didn't mind and even seemed happy letting our own permanently-wellingtoned feet wander freely through a cow pat festooned, urine-soaked farmyard and fields.

Lame Daisy was my favourite cow on the farm, my own pet patient whom I was allowed to walk to and from the fields each day. It was a laborious task for a five-year old but I convinced myself she was too weak to walk by herself. When the sun was high and the grass sweet in the meadow I would wander down to chat to ever-patient Daisy. Her loomy eyes showed she was always waiting for me.

Visiting the cow shed ("'t cowarse," as Farmer S. would say) taking in wafts of warm perfumed straw and cow poop while stroking our favourite cows or petting a new calf, was a daily routine. As was hearing the satisfying 'squirt, squirt' of warm jets of milk from the cow's rudely plump udders hitting the bottom of a gleaming bucket. It hit all the senses, including the palate, as we were always given a mug of Mama Cow's freshest of milk shakes.

So evocative is the smell of a cow house that sixty years on when my husband and I were in Denmark re-visiting his childhood Summer haunt, my infant self was suddenly watching cows being milked by hand by Farmer S. balanced on his three-legged stool, cap set front-to-back and head pressed against the cow's flank as he worked. It evoked the same feeling for my husband about his *morfar* sitting on a stool in the same manner but wearing a black beret and wooden clogs.

We would then march on to inspect the smellier pig-sty, then the hen-house to seek out bum-warm eggs, finally climbing up to the hay loft above the cowshed where we'd squeal if the Brute Brothers were lying in wait threatening to throw a dead mouse or rat at us.

At fruit-picking and potato-gathering times we would help Mrs. S. "our Beattie," carry lunches and jugs of ale to the workers feeling "reet proud" of ourselves. On rare occasions we would be invited to watch her, dressed in cassock-white overalls and natty hairnet making butter and cheese in her pin-shiny dairy. Also rare and a great treat was an invitation into her kitchen whenever boxes of fifty or so baby chicks arrived.

"Our Beattie" was one of the few kindly souls soothing us through our Boot Camp upbringing when, on even the coldest days, we were forbidden to re-enter our house until the dot of mealtimes. Wherever we lived, third eldest brother Placid Pascal would ingratiate himself with the lady of the next door house enjoying being indulged by bosomy, busy-bee 'mother figures.' Never one to make a fuss, he realised early on that Ma was 'in love' with asthmatic Damien, a five-star bully loathed by us younger siblings because he knew he could do no wrong in Ma's eyes.

And so, Placid Pascal and his imaginary friend Amos would creep in to toothless Beattie's warm kitchen, happy to listen to her nattering about this and that while she slaved away preparing real grub for her ravenous farm workers. We envied Pascal's diplomatic prowess while we were obliged to remain outside in all weathers, unless invited by nearby farmer's kids to play in their house or barn.

Our Beattie and Farmer S. were a heroic double-act who never told us to vamoose. Their elder daughter Lanky Sonia would even lead us around like a helpful shepherdess happy to show us her pet frog or new piglet. She was always much kinder to me than Sulky Sis, who, unlike older sister Jane, acted as though I was invisible. I did my best to repay the neighbourly kindness by being present and correct, ready to accompany Farmer S., striding off with him over three or more fields to bring the cows in.

"Joost keep aht of way o' Doris, the lively booger int' middle. She's got a reet sharp kick on her, me Ducks," he would remind me, a glistening dewdrop on his wind-sail of a snout.

He couldn't manage without me as 'back man' behind Lame Daisy and I knew she wouldn't kick me. He led, crook in hand, growling weird cow talk, like my husband's grandfather's, to keep them in line. Although Little Nurse Twitty-Toes longed to be a tomboy to gain a whisker of respect from Pascal and Damien she was a healer, cleverly diagnosing Lame Daisy was sad-eyed because the other cows ignored and even despised her for being a disabled cow. I would frequently suffer chronic arm ache from pulling up grass for her to eat while the others chewed their cud quietly, looking on as though I was as sad a case as Daisy. The beastly Brute Brothers would sometimes emulate Lame Daisy to see if I would tend them as well.

We moved to Fanshawgate House in 1946 as a family of ten and by 1950 only the youngest five were still at home. Morris, the eldest, opted out of middle-class life to become, "horror of horrors," a coal miner. This was in an era when the local physician was a pillar of a fawning community along with the vicar and 'squire.' A Freudian memory recall of Ma throwing Morris's lunch box at him confirmed our parents suffered from selective snobbery, an amnesia, since their eldest son's choice of profession linked directly to the immediate ancestral past. What was so abhorrent to my parents?

Mother's grandfather was a colliery manager in Kilsyth until the colliery closed because of strikes. Later, in the 1881 Scotland Census he records himself as a Glasgow Dockyard Labourer. Her father is listed in the same census as Apprentice Iron Forger, aged twelve. This was not bad for a man who ended up as managing director of Cammell Laird's Steel Works in Sheffield.

Grandfather Russell was by all accounts a gentle giant of a man, a champion caber tosser and mean Scottish dancer. He could recite all of Rabbi Burn's works. He read the St. James' Bible three times in his life, so it was said. His expertise as a steel master in the manufacturing of big navy guns (one is on display outside the Imperial War Museum in Greenwich) was the reason he was called upon to advise on problems Harland and Wolff were having with the hull of the ill-fated Titanic. Writing this reminded me of the poster-sized sepia photograph we once had of Grandfather and Queen Mary walking side by side down a street in Sheffield.

Grandfather built his own mansion, Gartmore, in Lodge Moor, Sheffield. He had an extra long bath installed to take his six-foot four inches. All eleven of his children, including Mother, were privately-educated, with three sons going up to Cambridge, one of them achieving a Triple Blue. As a child I was fascinated by their 'jolly hockey sticks' mannerisms and accent. My flummoxed ears would ache comparing their P. G. Wodehouse 'top ho!' utterances with the gritty language of Farmer S. and his family.

"Oh, I say! This is mop-haired Ro. How absolutely splendid!"

"Ee, by gum, lass, th'art got a reet bush of curls on thee 'an't tha'?"

Pascal, Damien and Sulky Sis were manic in utilising every precious daylight hour re-enacting scenes from their favourite film and comic-book heroes that included Billy the Kid, Davy Crockett and Robin Hood. Adolph Hitler was lampooned and the youngest "bit-player siblings" would hang around awaiting inclusion as extras however slavish or demeaning our roles were.

When they returned to school after the holidays I was soon bored being left with whiney baby brother Simon to play with. Lagging behind in not being at school was seriously affecting my sibling credibility and I began a campaign of begging my parents to let me start school early. The battle was won and Mrs. Eyre, the local infant teacher agreed an early start date. At long last, my four-year old brain reasoned, I would soon not be told to go away and play with a baby rattle. Little did I know how detestable and traumatising the reality of school life was. I had made a big mistake and soon began to loathe being cabined, cribbed and confined within a crowded classroom.

Trekking our little bodies across miles of scary, boggy terrain to and from Holmesfield Primary School, my disgruntled brothers would yell at me to hurry up or would simply drag me along, sometimes by my hair. Try as I would, my pint-sized legs kept slithering in the mud or slipping on ice. I would falter in deep snow trying to keep my gravity-defying cotton knee socks with frayed elastic garters up, endeavouring to keep warm and keep my puny legs from being scratched by gorse and blackberry and stung by nettles.

Sulky Sis sniggered, happy with me being the new weakling.

"If you cry like that, your fat face will freeze forever in this wind. So there, Cry Baby Bunting!"

Damien didn't help, hissing in my face, yanking me along by my plaits.

I had imagined my first day at school mid-term would be as exciting as Christmas Day. The dream was demolished, hour by slow hour, the day swirling down the plughole of my illusory dreams from the moment Mrs. Eyre sat me at my tiny desk and left me to "look and listen."

Looking and listening became excruciating as the rest of the class chanted away counting in indecipherable adding-up games in no-nonsense Northern twang. Feeling utterly exhausted from the slog to school, I crumpled in silence through my imprisonment with these serious kids and rote learning. Desperate to jump up and run away, Dozy Rosy drifted through playtime, lunchtime and back to class as if on autopilot. At going-home time, Mrs. Eyre helped me with my gabardine and led me outside to my aloof siblings already sullen with the prospect of the homeward march with me in the failing light of a freezing cold November afternoon.

As we crossed the road to the fields, two boys suddenly caught hold of skinny, asthmatic Damien, dragged him down and rubbed his face in the road before Pascal pushed them off. Sulky Sis shared my angst and clutched my hand for the only time I can recall just as I leant over and wretched up my greasy mince and turnip school dinner over her new sandals. Pascal, to his credit, tried to soothe us with the promise he would bring his catapult to school the next day and bring the Foreman boys to submission. Damien wept all the way home, running ahead to inform a startled mother of the ruck.

When Father called at the Foreman house on his way home from surgery to discuss the incident, only their mother was at home. Later that winter's night both parents came up to our house and insisted it had happened because Damien had stolen a Dinky Toy from one of their boys. Hearing hushed but angry exchanges Sulky Sis and I prayed that Jesus would cut the Foremans' legs off.

Even though we weren't enamoured with Damien's general behaviour, the episode scared us and we missed the reassuring presence of older Morris, Jane and Billy. We were subdued again a few weeks later when Pa was called out to the Foreman house. Their young mother had fallen down the stairs and cut her throat on a bucket. The boys never came back to the school.

While Morris was underground in nearby Chesterfield bringing coal up to keep wheels turning and the country warm, my second eldest brother Billy was away with the RAF training to be a pilot. Jane was in the big city training to be a nurse. All three had suffered teenage difficulties because of their wartime evacuation.

Jane now lived-in at Sheffield Royal's Nursing Home and would come home by bus on her days off. Cherished visits, as she was especially kind to me, she would bring spare farthings because she knew I collected the ones with the robin on. Once a week we would go into the sweet shop next to our Primary School after being met by Jane who would bring along our ration books. A halfpenny would buy a single Black Jack and give a farthing change. She said I had a long way to go before I had a pound's worth, 960 farthings.

Sometimes Jane would draw mischievously anarchic fairies for me to colour.

"That's daring Doctor Daddy with his stethoscope," she would

31

whisper, starting him off with red underpants and golden wings. "And that's Mummy, 'Crikey Christina,' a feared Boudicca Fairy in a kilt in her chariot with us all on board quaking!"

Soon after I had started school she came home in her smart, outdoor nurse's uniform, asking me to go up to the nursery with her while winking at Mother. I told her about the scary Foreman boys who had bashed Damien and about Sulky Sis rowing with the girls in her class.

"All the girls in our schoolyard lined up in a chain against Sulky Sis ... and she grabbed hold of me just as I was about to join the 'nemy gang against her. I was frightened until Mrs. Eyre came out and told them all off ..."

"I know but don't worry. Just you try this dress on," Jane smiled, "and if it fits, you can be Princess to my May Queen in two weeks' time and all those horrid school kids will be green, yellow and pink with envy when they see you being crowned!"

My pretty, slim sister then put on a long white silk dress covered with a net skirt dotted with raised violet buds. Ma said she looked like Scarlett O'Hara in Gone with the Wind. It made me wonder if she would be gone with our strong wind across the moors in such a flimsy dress! Mine was a white Alice in Wonderland-style design with short bunched sleeves and embroidered violet pinny with an ermine-style bordered cape.

"There! It fits fine and Wousie (a spinster patient and devotee of Pa's) is going to bring you a beautiful pair of shoes!"

"Will you wear a crown like the real Queen and will I wear a chiara?"

"Yes, Sweetie, a crown when I am crowned. We'll be tying a maypole of ribbons in your lovely curly hair then you'll be crowned with a t-i-a-r-a."

"Who will c-crown us?"

"Oh, I expect it'll be a very important person in the village, Ro."

"More important than Daddy?"

"Well, yes ... and no. And you'll have to be on your best behaviour and smile for England."

Another patient of Pa's sent an open-top car to pick us up on a brilliant Darling Buds of May day with only one last-minute nail-biter. Wousie hadn't appeared with my shoes. Mother drove pell-mell to nearby Totley to pick her up. A flustered Wousie ran out of the car gasping. In her hands was a shoebox with a Cinderella-perfect pair of jade green velvet sandals with new-smelling leather soles.

Mother flapped a lace hankie sprinkled with *eau de cologne* under Wousie's nose. She was a fussy, well-meaning spinster who loved and spoilt me. Seeing me dressed as a princess in shoes she'd chosen, combined with her spending the day with Dr. MacFarlane's Sound of Music family made it a special day for her also.

That day Little Dozy Rosy could happily have flown straight to Narnia with her favourite older sister looking prettier than any of my scrapbook photographs of Princesses Elizabeth and Margaret. Waving all the way up Fanshawgate Lane as if we were royalty, we even waved to the dopy cows and brain-dead sheep as well as to the straggle of villagers outside The Robin pub before rumbling into the fête with Jane making me cry with laughter mimicking with "ee by gums."

Our coronation was to take place on Holmesfield's mangy sports field where Morris and my Casanova brother Billy played village cricket matches on summer weekends. Giggly girls would flock to flirt with them, viewing the doctor's tall sons as home-grown James Deans. Knockout Billy got special attention with his come-hither green eyes and mop of dark curly hair. Morris was more discriminating and somewhat too shy to take advantage of the situation.

To my chagrin, Jane had a regal throne to sit on whereas I had a crummy velvet cushion on the grass. The newly-crowned May Princess was about to go into a sulk when the Queen whispered it was also my role to keep the throne warm while she had a secret ciggy. Thrilled to be doing my duty I also put her gift of a bracelet on my wrist, slipping my present of a boring ABC book under my cushion. I was already a star reader.

Jane had to be back at the hospital next morning but she left her exquisite dress on a hanger in the nursery for Sulky Sis and I to parade in. We did this for the whole day, replaying every regal moment of the previous day's ceremony until the Brute Brothers burst in, deciding it was too girlie for words. We were soon soaked through with water pistol fire and deafened by cap gun explosions. Cowed in a corner they threatened us with imprisonment unless we handed over any presents or money we had been given at the fête. This included Jane's precious crown and my tiara.

Girlie pursuits went on the back burner when we were obliged to play out passive roles in the boy's macho escapades. They rarely allowed us to fire their cap guns, shoot their bow and arrows, play with their prize marbles or dress up in their cowboy, soldier and Indian outfits. They were resolutely mean and mardy with us. How I longed to be an only child, except for a sister like Jane, that is.

In the pecking order of who mattered most in the MacFarlane clan's rowdy world, we three youngest accepted ourselves as on a par with earwigs. If it was too wet and cold to play outside, Pascal and Damien would commandeer an old shed as Biggles' Secret Spy Den. We were allowed into the den only if we knew their ever-changing password, didn't speak and came with slices of bread and jam sneaked from the kitchen.

Even then we were told we smelt, were not allowed a crumb of the plunder and were too stupid or scaredy-cat to be real spies or Indian squaws. Ordered to scram we'd snivel away to build our own pathetic, damp, insect-ridden den in the front garden hedge making sure we did not trample any precious flowers being nurtured for the village Flower Show as Doc MacFarlane's potential triumphs.

The newly-landscaped gardens at Fanshawgate House became a therapeutic heaven for Pa. He would invite us to follow him around on instructional nature walks from which we would bring back specimens to dry, name and store on the nature table in the nursery. Doctor Green Fingers' spacious front garden, rear vegetable garden and orchard were well looked after by two of his patients.

Gentle George was 'head gardener' and glad to have gainful employment on his return from war duty. His lisping, mentally-impaired brother, bespectacled Freddy, was his assistant. Watching Freddy lick his lunch plate clean in gratitude for one of "Mithuth Mth's luvverly din-dins," was a wicked pleasure for us wishing we could do the same.

George and Freddy were the first non-brusque younger men we encountered. They were painstaking and kind in teaching us about flowers and butterflies and lots of "God's other little critters," as they put it. Salt of the earth stalwarts who, like Puck in A Midsummer Night's Dream cast a spell on me, making me fall in love with nature's gentle men thereafter.

Chapter Three
#Four Strong Winds# (Neil Young/Ian Tyson)

During famously harsh Derbyshire winters, raw punishing winds would brew up over the surrounding moors howling and moaning like a Banshee trying to get into the house. Rickety sash windows offered little protection in the days before central heating and double-glazing. Our tough-love upbringing ensured we endured the winter weather without a whimper, roaming the moors like the Bronte's at Hayworth. The nearby Holmesfield's inhabitants also shrugged off the cruel conditions with hardy Northern grit.

Edie, our home help enjoyed frightening us pointing to the patterns on the frosted glass, telling us that the wicked Jack Frost had drawn them. It was a sign he would come on winter nights to steal our noses and we would half suffocate under flannel sheets rather than wake snout-less. As silly as we were it never dawned on us the designs were etched in the glass. Any cheeky faces we might pull when out with her would stay that way should the North Wind blow, the usually kindly Edie also taunted. And we must never, ever pick common cow parsley, otherwise known as Mother-die ...

All five bedrooms at Fanshawgate were without heating. Icicles would hang from the gutters and frost would form on the inside of the upstairs window panes when North-easterlies found their way in through every crack and crevice. Being scolded for wetting the bed was sometimes the preferred choice to risking hypothermia in our cruelly cold bathroom, or even getting out of bed and using a chamber pot.

"Who wet the bed, then ..." Ma would demand at breakfast staring coldly at my forlorn face, much to the delight of my smirking siblings. To wet the bed was the sin of childish sins since we were all potty-trained by three months.

"I couldn't be fagged with washing and drying nappies without a laundry maid," she would remind us, rather pleased with herself. "I put you on your potties with your bottles in your mouths and you were done in no time."

Ma MacFarlane's autocratic reprovals at mealtimes both shamed and ensured, through the Brute Brothers' relentless mocking, we would be back in line in an instant. Our parents' united approach to no-nonsense discipline was calculated and seamless. Their experience with their three wilful older children meant us five younger ones were reigned in as tight as a drum skin.

Sunday evenings during the winter was tin bath time in front of a glowing range in the kitchen because the bathroom was as cold as an Eskimo out-house. Sulky Sis would take first turn, sitting even more sulkily with Ma scrubbing her as if she was a freshly-dug spud. When it came to my turn, Silky Sis and Simple Simon would chorus "pot-belly frizz bush" as Ma flannelled me down with my week's worth of muck sploshing round the greying water, unless saved by the telephone. Then there would be some defensive splashing with the risk of a clout on Ma's preoccupied return.

"NO ... you mustn't ... hurry up ... you idiot ... stupid ... she's only a girl ... because you aren't old enough ... cry-baby ..."

Most children are bombarded with negatives from stressed parents, teachers and hostile grown-ups than ever they are showered with positive encouragement. Day-dreaming was my way of escaping a world full of portent and discomfort. Small children skip alongside their distracted parents chattering away to invisible friends in their parallel world with as much earnestness and with far more joy than they experience in irksome reality.

Winter time would have us longing for the coming of monster snowfalls in Derbyshire swathing bleak moors and steep Lows, with drifting against endless dry-stone walling six feet and more. At "snoworama" breakfasts Mother would try and quieten us with bowls of warming, treacle-smothered porridge, muttering that true Scots put salt on theirs. There would be gobbling in our collective rush to leave the table and grab the warmest mittens, scarves and hats. Wellington-ready we would slither and slide up and down Fanshawgate Lane with the boys pulling the sledges seeking out the steepest toboggan runs. It was the only time we came together without the usual "know thy place" sibling rivalry, happily ignoring our freezing wet mitts, raw red finger-tips and wet bottoms as we endeavoured to stay out as long as possible.

Then, lovely Edie would appear with a Thermos of cocoa and squares of parkin.

"Oo er, jus look at your blue little hands, Ro. They'll drop off for Jack Frost to eat if you don't put on these dry mitts."

Those happy memories of playing together on the moors and lanes sometimes with kids from nearby, snowballing and tobogganing then traipsing home frozen with faces as red as a robin's breast are of their time. Our parents let us wander for miles around the countryside Winter and Summer as long as we were back home on the dot for lunch and tea. In those days bogeymen and scary creatures were in our ancient copy of Grimm's Fairy Tales, not out there in a Big Bad World.

During the worst of those harsh Derbyshire winters, snowdrifts confined us indoors for days. The 1946-1947 winter is still the worst post-war on record. From December 23rd to St. Patrick's Day, March 17th, 1947, my father slept at the surgery leaving Mother to look after seven of us on her own at Fanshawgate. From two-day old baby Simon wrapped in six shawls, to fifteen-year old Morris, all of us lived in the kitchen because it was the only room she could keep warm. Farmer S. was our saviour sledging milk to the village and returning with essential supplies when they were available. Without the farmers' help many inhabitants of Upland Britain would not have survived the winter of '47. The only outside assistance was from very occasional aircraft drops of hay and coal.

Mother hadn't been able to leave the house until she made it to the St. Patrick's Day Ball in Sheffield. Her friends were alarmed at her emaciated appearance and black eye from colliding with the back door. Pascal loved it, three months off school, when "he-men" were out daily searching for wood for the fire. How must it have been for Mother incarcerated, immured even, with six young children and a new-born in one room with the rest of the house frozen?

Although I can't remember the notorious Winter of 1947 I do recall a year or two before we left Fanshawgate being woken on Christmas Eve because of a surprise visit from Father Christmas.

"Children, arise you sleepy heads, there's someone to see you!" Pa called up from the kitchen.

All five of us tumbled down the stairs with Dozy Rosy last as she couldn't find one of her red pom-pom slippers given to her by Wousie as an early Christmas present. Hopping sleepily over the cold lino to where Father Christmas was sitting on our rocking chair by the door she felt woefully undressed for such an awesome occasion.

"Ro, sit on Father Christmas's knee. He's flown a long way to see you all," my bemused father said, pleased as Punch that one of his patients had been kind enough to oblige for the occasion. I sat on one of the plump gentleman's knees while Sulky Sis sat on the other. My seven-year old self scrutinised his face through his white whiskers.

"You've got a big red nose like my Daddy's!" I pronounced.

There was silence except for my father clearing his throat and Father Christmas's leather boots squeaking as he bounced us gently up and down. Our Christmas stockings hung motionless over the kitchen range and our scrawled letters begging for presents were still on the hearth with a glass of milk and two biscuits for our distinguished visitor.

After reeling off a list of hoped-for presents ... a Noddy car, Noddy Annual, marbles, a skipping rope, a party dress, gold crown, sweets ... Pa asked us to sing We Will Rock You for our honoured guest before we climbed the stairs back to bed. Damien naughtily, we learned many years later, sang "I saw Mummy Kissing Santa Claus."

As hard as it was to fall asleep that night, we knew we had to sleep otherwise the reindeers wouldn't land on our roof and we wouldn't be left any presents. I must have cried out from a bad dream because Billy who was home for Christmas, sauntered into my room.

"Shut your peepers Ro and get back to sleep or Papa Christmas will take your pressies to Little Orphan Annie instead!"

I slept only fitfully with the agony and ecstasy of that Christmas Eve. Awoken again in the early hours, actually by our parents returning from Midnight Mass, I heard my giggly mother shushing just outside the bedroom door. Sliding under the covers with my rag doll Minnie, both of us in a panic should we be caught awake, I couldn't stop myself giggling when I heard a crash and Father Christmas mutter "Oh, Christ ..."

"Is she kissing Santa Claus, Minnie?" I whispered, trying to figure out what was happening until a weight on my feet on the end of the bed and silence told me that Santa had been and hopefully gone. When everything was really quiet, perhaps after I had dozed a bit more, Minnie and I listened for the reindeers flying off but heard nothing.

Now my big problem was resisting opening the bulging pillow case at the foot of my bed. I couldn't and quietly retrieved packages, opening them one at a time under the bed covers. Just as I was thinking how wonderful Santa was, the first presents were a mouldy prayer book and red and grey jumper with fluffy things on it. I knew they were from my Godmother Auntie Peggy, the new owner of the Bakewell Pudding Shop.

Thinking I had remained undiscovered, Stinker Billy returned.

"Listen Ro," he whispered as a 'plane passed overhead, "that's Santa's Old Dad! He flies behind as he's too old to sit in the sleigh now. He stashes all the presents taken back from brats like you who open them too early ..."

Billy left the room as quietly as he had entered and I reasoned there was only one way out of the dilemma. I would open the rest of the presents, put the worst ones back in the pillowcase and hide the best under the sheet with me and Minnie guarding them!

After an uncomfortable night shared with presents and wrapping paper that made a noise every time I moved, I went bleary-eyed into Ma and Pa's bedroom where there was already a lot of noise and activity. This is where we brought, or were supposed to bring our little sack of presents on Christmas morning and open them. A grinning Billy winked at my guilty face as Jane gently asked me to show my presents.

"Big Mouth Billy told me you opened them early!" she said. "Silly girl. You have no surprises now, do you?"

I shook my head pitifully and she started undoing the ringlet rags Edie had tied my hair up with before I went to bed.

"Oops a daisy," she said as my curly waist-length hair tumbled, "you'll just have to have these things from Billy, Morris and me!"

My face was a picture, Jane said, as she held up a matching set of pearl hair-slide, necklace and bracelet and a beautiful white party dress.

"Cheer up, Ro," Billy teased again, "I radioed Father Christmas's Dad last night. I'm a pilot too, don't forget and told him everything was tickety-boo in the Mad MacFarlane house. Merry Christmas Sis!"

I told Ma and Pa in a hushed voice I heard Father Christmas swear. They and my older siblings cried with laughter that Christmas morning.

Spring and early Summer were also wonderful times for us. One beautiful June morning my sister and I were called out of our junior school class by the head teacher and told we must meet our parents at the school gate. Twizzling round and round on one leg, like lopsided barley-sugar sticks, we waited until our spanking new Morris Oxford pulled up. Mother hissed for us to jump in. Sulky Sis gave me a hefty push as she went for the front passenger seat, leaving me to get into the back.

As Mother zoomed off, I realised I was sitting next to a strange old woman in a navy and white spotted dress and floppy sun hat bent over in a most peculiar fashion. Because we often gave lifts to wounded and weary patients I thought she must be a sick patient of Pa's.

"We're off to Bridlington for the afternoon, children," announced my unusually light-hearted mother as we sped out of Holmesfield village. A very special treat, of course as we usually only got away on annual trunk-laden holidays to Barmouth or Looe, when Ma and Pa were relaxed and smiling and not talking shop.

"But why has the Lady got such hairy hands?" I asked loudly with genuine concern. My Mother spluttered but answered me nay.

When we were well away from Pa's surgery boundaries of Totley and Greenhill the 'hairy-handed lady' threw off her hat to reveal my

father crying with laughter. I was startled even more by his uncharacteristic quivering, like an apoplectic fish.

"Oh, God in Heaven, child, you will be the death of your Daddy!" Doctor Pa rasped, struggling to undo the dress. A short-sleeved shirt and rolled-up linen trousers gradually appeared.

"Your Father's taking an extra half-day off," mother

explained. "We had to disguise him as Dame Trollop in case any of his patients spotted him leaving town!"

Some "do you remember when Ro said ..." *faux pas* reeled off my mother's tongue. The trouble with having me in on such a mission was that I was pathologically indiscrete. Throughout childhood I asked constantly inappropriate questions in a loud voice. My mother said she would have to cross the road if she saw a war veteran, for example shambling along with a peg leg knowing something like "what has that man got a tree leg for?" would issue from my big mouth.

My indiscretion took many forms. On one winter Sunday morning we went into Mass and the church was so brightly-lit I exclaimed in wonder "Oh, they'll be able to see my sins!"

When Wousie visited us for tea one afternoon Placid Pascal, trying his best to be polite asked, "will someone pass the booter, please?"

Mother corrected him.

"It's not 'booter', Pascal Dear, it's butter."

"And it's not 'booger', Pascal, its bugger!" piped up my sparkly four-year old self. It didn't help either when I was invited to sit on elderly Wousie's bony knees. Enveloped in the sickly scent of violets I exclaimed "pooh, you smell!" My aghast mother ordered me to my room as poor Wousie sniffed into her embroidered hanky.

Summers rolled by too quickly but as autumn leaves and deeper skies arrived Pa made more time away from a relentless work schedule. His evening priority would be to earmark potential prize specimens of fruit and vegetables in the garden ready to be picked and plucked for various village competitions. Produce was also reconnoitred for preservation and storage in sealed glass jars in our pantry and cellar as well as for Mrs. MacFarlane's famed fruit pies.

Under Pa's exacting directions we would wrap unblemished apples and pears singly in old newspapers that, by 1950, featured endlessly picture-perfect royal princesses, the 'celebrities' of the day. The fruit was stored on racks under our beds and would last us through Winter. Our reward for bringing in these fruits was being given our own hyacinth bulbs to pot and place in our dark cellar to be ready, magically for Christmas.

Pa never needed to raise his voice for us to jump and do his bidding. We youngest three were easily persuaded to pick off culprit caterpillars from his cabbages. We would drop these into jam jars with

41

wax paper covers with holes for the little wrigglers to breathe but not escape. It would also cost Pa a princely penny per child to motivate us into picking dandelion heads off his pristine lawn on dry summer evenings.

Pascal and Damien would be put to bigger boys' work in the orchard on autumn afternoons, picking the mass of ripe fruit in the half-acre of fruit trees. The Brute Brothers naturally didn't take long to work out short cuts. They were soon sawing branches from the cherry and apple trees, commanding their well-trained skivvies below to hurry with the actual picking from the fallen branches.

Pa would be snoozing blissfully upstairs as he did each afternoon. Angst-ridden mother would be wringing her hands, afraid of him waking before the boys had disposed of the branches and boot-blacked the sawn ends on the tree. The boys would proudly display 'their' labour, piles of apples, plums and cherries, triumphantly pocketing sixpence a box before Pa took off for evening surgery.

Forever one step behind our older siblings we would never learn. As with the brutal massacre of our pet chickens and hens, for example we three would dumbly stand watch all morning at Pascal and Damien's behest, scanning Farmer S.'s fields for the cursed fox who would, of course, never show. The boys would be doing boys' things out on the range practising with their pellet shotguns for when we gave word of having sighted the killer.

Pascal couldn't wait to boast one fine day how he had been 'blooded,' chopping off the head of poor Prudence who had been sacrificed for dinner. He had bravely done the deed but didn't tell us he nearly passed out on seeing headless Prudence flapping around the garden until she finally laid to rest.

"Poor Pascal, he went as white as a sheet. I thought he had seen a chicken being killed and would know of the after-effect," Mother laughed, as she took Prudence's still warm body to show me how to pluck her.

She promised I could have one of the hen's feet to scare the others with by making her claws open and close. It didn't get this far. Quietly terrified this young hen would revive as I pulled at her feathers, I recoiled with each tug, finally slipping and hitting my head. Poor Prudence, from whose generous bottom I had proudly collected warm eggs each morning. I was happy to be judged a useless chicken plucker and retired.

Slaughter was the name of the game in the countryside, from

following the local hunt across the fields from our upstairs windows, to our pleading to watch the demise of cherished Gloria our home-fattened porker when she was judged porky enough for dinner. Strapped to a trestle her throat would be slit. Farmer S. would make us hide around the corner before poor Gloria gave out an unearthly scream. Her carcass would be hung so the blood drained and Mother and Beattie would chop and slice her into joints, spare ribs, chops and other things still lipstick pink, ready to feed her hungry family.

It didn't worry us that one minute she was Gloria and the next a succulent roast served with home-grown vegetables and followed usually by a delicious fruit pie.

Becoming immune to the remorseless animal activity in the countryside and around the farm may have made us a little bloodthirsty as kids. There was a certain amount of pushing and pinching for pole position before a slaying or major copulation. X-rated by the grown-ups the latter activity was the one we most wanted to see, though we were unsure why as the "birds and the bees" were only half understood. We were still totally innocent to where babies came from.

Peeping on those banned days through the old kitchen gate that led into the farmyard was the equivalent of a ring-side seat. Watching some of our favourite and not so favourite cows being forced into cattle trucks abattoir-bound was not considered that scary. Most fun would be on days we were repeatedly served with a dire warning not to "cum through t'farmyard on't pain of a slapped arse ..." On our way back from school Pascal and Damien, knowing what the ban meant, would drag us across the fields in time to catch the action. I didn't have a clue what it was all about but tuned into their lascivious excitement nevertheless.

If Farmer S. caught sight of our bobbing heads over the kitchen gate on insemination day he'd scowl like Harold Steptoe and yell, "stay out'ta bloody farmyard, lasses and lads, while t't friggin' bull hast bin and buggered 'em all and buggered off! You could be killed ye sen! And take young 'uns indoors, d' y' hear?"

The younger, healthiest cows were harried into place ready for some disconcerting hanky-panky with the imported Romeo we naturally called *El Toro*. This great muscular beast would stagger around determined to mount every one of them, with a puce-cheeked Farmer S. yelling and directing his crook like a demented Dervish until all the young females had been done.

The one thing that did upset us and cause brother Simon and I to wonder if we might be next, was witnessing the drowning of mewling kittens in the water trough. Living in a medical family where emergency telephone calls or bloodied people on the doorstep had long been the norm did not prepare us for innocent kittens being dispensed with. What I said about my real world being in my books held good where elements of brutality introduced slowly and surely through Hansel and Gretel, Red Riding Hood and the Grimm's Fairy Tales were absorbed by our innocent selves.

They were a preparation that failed for a real horror event one unforgettable day when I was four. I happened to be by our kitchen door when someone knocked. I opened it to a little boy before me, mute with shock with an arrow through his eye. Frightening dreams for weeks afterwards caused me to dread the sound of the doorknocker in case a headless man or woman was at the door as Demonic Damien had convinced me could happen.

Not long after the arrow trauma, Ma was driving near our Totley surgery when in front of our eyes, a middle-aged patient of my father's slipped and fell face down on a patch of wet grit. Mother helped the shocked woman into the back next to me and I cringed at her grit-embedded facial injuries. I was doing my best to feel for this poor woman while feeling deeply ashamed at wishing she wasn't there, terrified I would once again be tormented by frightening dreams.

Crying out during nightmares meant our risking being pilloried as mardy brats, or sissy at our boisterous breakfast table the next morning. Mother's Scottish upbringing had been an emotionally Spartan one, if well-to-do. Her reading on child-rearing, I discovered early on in my own quest for things to read, was that of the no-nonsense Guru of the 'Forties and 'Fifties, Dr. Truby King.

To show one's emotions was not the done thing. Feelings were to be contained. In my early days, the patron saints of this emotional desert seemed to be the Royal Family, particularly Queen Mary, a ghostly, ramrod-straight statue of a woman. To this day I have not seen a picture of her with a facial expression other than utterly expressionless. It is hardly surprising that in later life my own daughter chides me for hiding my real feelings when upset. My worry is that should I ever break down and "cry me a river" I would be unable to control it.

That day in the car the gritty woman apologised profusely to my mother for the trouble she had caused. Why couldn't I be brave like my father who dealt with the maimed and mutilated with such ease? The question troubled me even at this tender age of four. Was I brave enough to be a real nurse? It felt good making my dolls feel better but I hadn't yet worked out how to deal with real physical trauma. It troubled me because a nurse I wished to be, like my sister Jane and my Aunt Agnes who was the youngest Matron in the country at the time.

It did not help my anxiety when one afternoon Damien fell out of a tree and broke his arm. He had to go to hospital to have it set. I didn't mind him being banned from tree-climbing because I hated bird-nesting. Sometimes my brothers would take the eggs for their collection, other times they would prick each end with a briar or blackberry thorn, suck out and swallow the contents.

Then, my younger brother tripped over a pile of logs we were playing on in the farmyard and gashed his mouth. Screaming his little head off was bad enough but my mother's worried face convinced me he was going to die and that I would be blamed. All I could do when she took him inside was to run round and round at the back of the farm until exhausted, convinced my world had ended and Simon was dead.

It was Lame Daisy's mournful mooing that wrenched me out of my misery. After creeping into her far end stall and telling her about Simon's accident I fell asleep on a pile of straw beside her.

A woman's screams and cries for help woke me.

"Our Beattie" was up in the hay loft collecting stray eggs and had almost fallen through some dodgy planking into the cow shed. It was impossible to miss her lower half poking through the ceiling. As the distraught woman was stuck fast like a thief in village stocks, her Lyle-stockinged wellied legs and long pink bloomers in full view, I called up politely asking if she was alright.

"Go and get bloody 'elp, me Ducks ..." she bellowed.

Elated that I could be of some use, my brain went into overdrive and I bunched some straw under her in case she fell through. I then bolted across the yard to our house trying not to giggle at seeing a lady's under-garments for the first time. Beattie was soon hauled back into the loft where she waited until Pa came to suture a gash in her leg with him also worrying about her getting a horrible disease called tetanus. From being chastised over my brother's accident I was now the heroine of the moment.

We hadn't a clue how adults looked undressed but we did have a healthy Freudian curiosity about our own "naughty bits." One summer evening we were up in a neighbour's field where we'd go to play with the two Pepper boys. On this occasion we had a pile of dressing-up clothes with us, including an exotic pink tutu we girls were desperate to try on.

Sulky Sis and the oldest Pepper boy, both aged about seven decreed we show our naughty bits to the opposite sex of our own age. Only then would we get to wear the tutu. Sulky Sis had to show hers to the elder boy and me to the younger boy and vice versa. It was also decreed we go down the hill to keep the deed private. I was about five and knew what we were up to was not quite right. Curiosity and the longing to wear the tutu, however, were over-riding all else.

We went down to the neighbour's field a couple more evenings, as I recall, inventing more peek-a-boo games, enjoying breaking the law away from the Brute Brothers and parental eyes.

Or so we thought.

Soon afterwards when I was alone in the kitchen, Demonic Damien twisted my arm threatening to tell Mother about our little games. His sneering made my legs wobble with fear and his sinister tone implied that what we had done was a grievous sin.

Did he have secret spying powers, as we were miles from anywhere? How did he know? His nastiness upset me more than anything. From then on he would thump us younger three at will, subjecting us to Chinese burns when he was sure no one was looking. We never said anything but we knew he was taking advantage of the fact he was Mother's favourite because of his asthma. Needless to say 'biology' classes were discontinued and the tutu disappeared without any of us girls getting to wear it.

What I thought was really unfair was the obviously naughty interest the Brute Brothers and their friends had in the new and glamorous neighbour who lived down the lane. There were no children in their beautiful house but we were allowed to play in the barn on the rare occasions we were not allowed to play in Farmer S.'s barn.

A reputed beauty queen, she was the local eccentric artist's pretty wife. She had short black hair and would sometimes come to the door in the daytime in her nightie. The boys sometimes went down there with Pa's racing binoculars and sniggered about this. Billy even wrote a poem but didn't give it to her.

One morning when we were playing down that way they dared us to walk up the drive and knock on her door. Sulky Sis thought it was silly and refused. They just wanted to see her pretty face, they said. We were still close by when the cake van pulled up at the end of her drive. The cake van, butcher's van and coalman called every week at Holmesfield and farms round about. When the cake man disappeared inside the house the boys ran down and whisked up the van's roller door indicating which cakes they wanted. I was to do the deed because I was small enough to clamber in. Besides, they had to keep watch although they seemed to know the cake man would be a while.

Cakes were grabbed out of my hand as quickly as I took them off the shelves as we were always hungry from playing high-energy games all day long. Stuffing these exotic pirated buns and tarts into giggling mouths was the nearest experience to Heaven I could recall. The equally satiated driver appeared an age later and drove off. The boys just laughed as they walked up the lane munching their spoils.

"Why is nobody hungry?" Mother queried as we pushed our paste sandwiches around the plate at tea time.

"Erm, Auntie Beattie gave us some freshly-baked bread with her home-made butter ..."

Rumour has it, I heard my mother repeating to someone much later, the artist's wife has run off with the butcher's boy.

With the constant brouhaha around us at Fanshawgate House flowers became a passion. From an early age I saw them as things to cheer you up and to talk to. Canterbury Bells, peonies and snapdragons, lavender, Sweet Alyssum and big bright African Marigolds I found endlessly fascinating. Arriving home for lunch with my father in the crinkly heat of Summer after accompanying him on his rounds, I would step out of the car, nose-high to his prize bed of Tea Roses, their exotic colours, petal textures and scents spinning my head as we passed. It was wonderful being outside. Being a medical man, Pa always included the formal names of the plants as if we were *bona fide* Latin scholars.

The garden at Fanshawgate was in complete contrast to the dank, musty interiors of many of the houses we entered on Pa's home visits. The main rooms of his wealthier private patients were wood-panelled and station waiting-room brown or jaundice yellow from coal fires and nicotine smoke. Furniture was "don't touch" polished Victorian cabinets, fussy tables, potted plants and magic carpets from China or Persia making the rooms austere and claustrophobic. I would feel like Alice in an oversized world. Gasping sometimes from an overpowering scent of lavender, heavy cologne or beeswax polish I would tiptoe around after my father or sit stiffly in a rough-fabric old armchair. To this day the smells of such houses reminds me of Mother's "always remember you are a doctor's daughter ..."

I did try to be polite but hunger occasionally got the better of my manners and morning house calls could drag on. It was unfortunate one morning that one of Pa's adoring, upper-crust lady patients clutched me to her *crêpe de Chine* blouse and heaving bosom. Her perfume was overpowering and the words "pooh, what a pong," left my lips. Pa was furious and it was no use protesting my innocence.

The only other time I remember disgracing myself was being sick over another of his posh patient's prize Aspidistra, unable to contain the clumpy, mushy peas I had been forced to eat at school.

The far friendlier over-crowded, sometimes untidy houses of poorer families were always preferable, even though they could be as dark and as cold as a witches' coven and smell of boiled cabbage and urine-soaked nappies. Ugly patterned carpets or cold lino under-foot tended to make the back-to-back houses look like Pa's surgery or an undertakers. Those in the middle social spectrum favoured, or tolerated heavy flock paper, tasselled port-wine coloured velvet curtains, embroidered cushions and crocheted toilet roll covers. Every house seemed to an Aspidistra on a *jardinière* and a piano. Refrigerators, radiograms and telephones were still a rarity and the items most prized for those wanting to keep up with the Joneses. All had pristine net curtains that made the rooms crisp and gloomy at the same time.

For those of us who remember the early episodes of Coronation Street, Hilda Ogden was the stereotypical housewife scurrying around cleaning, cooking, washing, ironing, baking, shining the brasses and giving the front doorstep a daily scrubbing or whitening. The front room, sometimes called the Sunday room, was reserved for receiving visitors, special occasions and for viewing newly-deceased relatives. The family Bible had pride of place here. The "cleanliness is next to Godliness" ethos was still all-pervasive.

Monday was wash day everywhere. This was the day our own Mrs. Overalls next door would look fit to melt, labouring over a steaming copper tub, pushing and pulling, lifting and dropping her husband's heavy blue overalls with wooden tongs. Her hands would turn blister red as she dragged them to the washboard to scrub and pummel as if bashing the devil's backside. Through all this she would chat, finally wiping her hands and fetching me some tasty bread and dripping or slices of black pudding for my help. My help was probably just accompanying her through this weekly ordeal.

As children, we observed life and how best to fit in with the *status quo*. Our inner lives, however, were where we dwelt when left alone. I spent as much time as possible out playing or in my room reading in peace or in the nursery running my 'hospital ward.' I dutifully joined in with the rough and tumble of family life as required while keeping my core self apart.

The day I made the decision to go it alone came about when it became clear I would never be a favourite of either parent, as other of my brothers and sisters clearly were. I also determined that no one would know how much this gutsy, good-hearted little girl minded being repeatedly passed over.

"I will make my own way from now on," became 'Orphan' Rose's Independence Day mantra.

Placid Pascal and I made similar decisions when we both cottoned on to who was in and who was not in the dynamics of this one-way Family Favourites. My favourite family figure was my late grandfather who was loved and admired by everyone. At times of strife I would chat away to Jock Russell's family photo. He was Big Bird in a kilt with a huge heart and huge wings in which he enfolded his eleven-strong brood and troop of grandchildren.

Grandmother first saw this giant of a man in Glasgow dancing reels on a wooden stage. Tiny Jeannie MacFarlane was sitting in the audience turning the heel of her sock, uncomfortable with such frivolity. Jock's thoughts had gone further on sighting the serious blue-eyed lassie.

"A good home-maker here, I'll be bound ..." he mused. They married on New Year's Eve 1890 in Glasgow.

The feeling at five years old that I had to soothe and heal anything with a pulse was gathering pace. It was the only way I could counter the fear I was experiencing listening to my doctor father's war chest of stories of his injured and dying people on an almost daily basis.

"Did you have a good surgery, Bill?"

"Not too bad, Chris. Called out to do an emergency tracheotomy on Shearer's youngest who was choking to death as I arrived."

"With diphtheria?"

"Yes. She's not out of the woods, yet ..."

"Didn't they lose five sons in the War?"

"Mmmh! Have to save this one. She's in Lodge Moor Sanatorium now. I'll call in there after evening surgery. What's for lunch, Love?"

I wanted to shout at my parents not to talk about this constant human misery in so matter-of-fact a way but daren't because of scorn from the Brute Brothers. I would rush upstairs instead to our old nursery where I would wave my stethoscope and thermometer and a healing hand over my injured dolls and wounded stuffed animals. These were the real patients, not the replicas my parents chewed over at mealtimes.

I also believed that if I prayed hard enough I might be able to perform the Lazarus-type miracle we'd heard about in church, whether the walking wounded was Lame Daisy or one of my nursery toys. Whenever I wore my tiny blue-check Super Nurse's uniform with fake fob watch and white apron with red cross on the bib I was Nurse Rose and felt as grown up as my nursing student sister.

My treasured uniform would often have to be forced off me at bedtime. I thought if I kept it on in bed I would be on call like my father and could accompany him on any night emergencies. On mornings I didn't go with him on his rounds, I would do my own in my nursery ward checking on sick and dilapidated dolls, Gollies and teddy bears. Often they were victims of Brute Brother torture, flung about or torn apart whenever they were bored or frustrated from being incarcerated on bad weather days. Teased as Nitty Nora the School Nurse I only had some status when called upon to bandage their ketchup-splodged war wounds.

When Pa returned from morning surgery, this frequently exhausted man would graciously do his rounds in Nursery Ward before his snooze. His warm cushiony hands made me feel safe and happy whenever I held them. Prior to my Independence Day, my attempting to gain his approval took much of my time as I adored everything about him. Memories of him being funny and gentle with us when we were small made it all the harder to equate with the man, who, as we grew older, became ever more emotionally detached.

Maybe the good doctor coped with the manic demands placed upon him by drifting off as the *alter ego* of his heroes Humphrey Bogart and Fred Astaire. They were the style icons of his day. Their cool 'Forties cinema tilted trilby trench-coated super-sleuth look was not lost on him. I have a photo of him dressed and looking the same way.

Every Thursday afternoon on Pa's half-day off a week, because locums had to be paid for out of his barely sufficient budget, my parents would go to the cinema. Doc MacFarlane, who resembled Astaire with his slight frame and immaculate presence would practise tap dancing routines when his last patient had departed and we were waiting in the waiting room. This was surely his way of letting off steam from the stress of the day. He would even thank his Totley Surgery housekeeper while tapping his way down the stairs.

On what must have been their most eventful Thursday night at the cinema hundreds of German aircraft began bombing the city. That was the beginning of the Sheffield Blitz of December 1940, five years before I was born. Ma was directed to seek shelter from the firestorm in the public toilet opposite. Father had to accompany a policemen who broke into Boots near Cole's Corner for Pa to grab emergency medical supplies for the casualties of the bombing.

Ever the artist Ma, meanwhile, sketched a picture of the incendiary scene that night. She painted it over with brilliant orange and reds the next day. The dramatic "fire storm" painting ended up in a drawer along with a stack of other sketches and paintings she did over the years. I didn't know the details of that night until reading about the incident in brother Billy's book seventy years after the event.

Witnessing how revered my father was within our local community was not a surprise to me as he had a distinguished aura about him as a quiet well-mannered gentleman. In our innocent apple-pie world where deference prevailed and the King was happy in his counting house, everyone as they say, knew their place.

Vicars, priests and ministers harangued their obedient congregations with threats of purgatory and eternal damnation should they stray from the path of righteousness. "Remember you are a doctor's daughter" was the meaningful yet meaningless mantra I grew up with. All part and parcel of our boringly predictable world where the cloth-capped working man whistled his way to work and giddy girls tumbled out of their factories with hair rollers clearly visible under the head scarves. They wanted to look nice when they went out in the evening. Not much changed until university-educated trouble-makers dared to begin to examine the *status quo*.

Large families like ours are considered freakish today but were more common in the '50s, although most of my school friends with younger parents had only one or two siblings.

"Children should be seen and not heard" meant we happily skulked around tongue-tied whenever our posh relatives visited, patting us on the head and very generously slipping a pound note into our probably grubby hands. They were clearly treating their younger sister as if she was a charity case like the mindless Old Woman Who Lived in a Shoe. There was occasionally some sighing over her decision to quit the Presbyterian Church and become a Papist and for having so many children as a consequence when it was no longer the "done thing." For other people decades before, large families had been "for Empire."

Ma's sister had also converted and married a medic from Cork like Pa. Aunty M. had five children. They lived on the edge of a large Sheffield Council Estate where Uncle G. had his surgery. Their youngest, Connor, was two weeks older than me. My first memory of easy-going Connor was him letting me ride his tricycle, a little gentleman from the age of three! We played outside their house on the pavement near shops. It was an odd feeling when we had green fields and moors around us

Fortunately, the adult world and our world in which we were free to roam without close supervision were two different spheres about which each knew nothing.

Chapter Four
#In and Out the Windows ...# (Maypole Song)

Our rumbustious Little House on the Prairie existence in Derbyshire ended in June 1953 when I was eight years old. The process must have begun at the end of 1946 when Ma said "enough" after the birth of her eighth child, brother Simon. Her insistence on some form of contraception was anathema to my Irish father. Catholicism loomed large and the inevitable happened.

For the gentleman of the house to seek solace with a family servant under such circumstances was undoubtedly more common in yesteryear. Two female friends in my adult life told me their fathers ran off with the housemaid after impregnating the poor girls because of sexually repressed wives rather than religious diktats. Pa did not run off with Edie after impregnating her, he went away to sea on his own.

It is perplexing that a highly intelligent man should break up his family and marriage because of a change in a sexual pattern, one long overdue in my mother's eyes. Women have a litany of requirements, mostly emotional and including the need to feel loved and appreciated. Their part in a marriage is not just one of sex for the male and being relegated to birthing machine.

All the Church offered my parents was that they should adhere to the traditional practice of unsafe "safe sex." Ma was no longer prepared to have marital relations on this basis or in the contraceptive-free way my father was insisting on. The Church, feared more in those days, exercised its power and excommunicated her. It doesn't do it today, with countless Catholics practising some form of reliable birth control methods, including vasectomy, that are a mortal sin.

Excommunication for Pa would have had more serious consequences. He must have thought about and even confessed his misgivings about the morality of what he was doing with a young unwed woman under his wife's nose and must therefore have reasoned it was less sinful to impregnate her than use a condom with his wife. To add to the tragedy, Edie's illegitimate child died soon after birth with congenital problems. I remember Pa visiting her after surgery one morning and saying "don't tell your Mammy that I visited

Edie." I had to stay in the car.

I cared less about not telling Ma than not seeing Edie. I missed her deeply, our kind and fun nanny. Our busy mother had little time for cuddles or play or to read to us. She had even less time now, deprived of domestic help.

Secretly selling his practices and side-stepping his marital, ethical and financial problems, Pa ran away to sea. He just disappeared. A few weeks later Ma didn't tell us she was driving down to Southampton to pick him up after his first stint as ship's surgeon on the SS Asturias. She disappeared too. When she was stressed she became ill. This situation stressed her so much she succumbed to double pneumonia on the drive down and was hospitalized. Adding to Ma's and probably Pa's worries was Billy in hospital with Rheumatic Fever.

For the two weeks of our mother going missing along with the trauma of a disappeared father who must have gone back to sea without ever leaving Southampton, the five of us, Little Simon and I, Sulky Sis, Damien and Pascal were taken in by Farmer S. and his wife. Our once happy family was disintegrating.

My memories of that bewildering time are bleak like the weather. School finished early one afternoon because of a snowstorm and we were faced with the trek of a mile or so home in semi-darkness unable to see more than a foot in front of us. I was little Orphan Rose of my own fairy tale, snivelling with despair as the boys did their best to guide Sulky Sis and I home. Kindly Farmer S. came out to meet us raft-less orphans. Beattie sat me on her knee in front of the fire in their cosy kitchen rubbing my freezing knees chattering away until I revived. I was very happy, while also very sad. Beattie cuddled me as if it was the most normal thing in the world.

This was my first experience of grown-ups' business and might explain why Early One Morning and similarly poignant folk songs of the plight of maidens are favourites from as far back as I can remember.

Sadly for teenagers Jane and Billy they were home during the goings on and had witnessed Pa canoodling with Edie when he thought they were in their beds. Mother refused to believe the gossip. The pregnancy must have been "nympho" Edie and one of the village lads. She went into denial and the pneumonia she went down with eventually was a psychosomatic reaction that set a pattern of reactive behaviour that became familiar to all of us in later years.

As a teenager I began wondering why the Church hadn't excommunicated my father for making Edie pregnant when she wasn't his wife. Or, indeed, for being unfaithful to his wife. "No sex before marriage" was drummed into us from our hormonal years. "No sex outside marriage" didn't feature. When I heard it was because the Church didn't like women it was as clear as daylight, if members of the Church wanted to see it. The girl's misfortune and her child dying must have been a harder one to bear than our situation yet she was completely ignored by the Church.

Over the next few years Pa was like a locum Father Christmas. He came home regularly and continued to provide for his family. His presents were always carefully chosen and expensive. Sulky Sis and I received miniature dressing tables and a mini tape-recorder from Japan, elephant-hair and opal bracelets from Mombasa, castanets and Spanish dancer's *mantillas* from Seville and grass skirts and garlands from Hawaii. He posted dozens of postcards to me and brought home beer mats and matchboxes for my collection.

When, at the age of six or seven I feared he had gone away for good because he was away longer than usual, he just appeared one afternoon at Fanshawgate with a big smile on his face. My present on that occasion was a wind-up walking doll. This brightly-coloured metallic Japanese doll strutted her spellbinding stuff in pre-Louboutin red platform boots with wheels. A later observation was how incredible it was that Japan recovered so quickly after the Second World War to design and produce such *avant-garde* toys and gizmos when equivalent toys did not exist in austere post-war Britain.

Our most prized collective present was a View-Master, a square-eyed viewer box in which a picture disc was inserted to show brilliant, full-colour 3-D photographs of Disney tales and exotic pictorial scenes. Our childhood was distinctly monochrome with the occasional sepia and silver. I didn't see a film at the cinema until I was ten years old and that was black and white.

Mother coped with austerity and her own bleak period after the War organising a large family with big expenses and her husband leaving her, according to her, with a drawer full of bills.

"I was traumatised," she confided. "He never said a word about selling the surgeries or that they were going to cut off the electricity at home. He was not a practical man and I finally realised I would have to take charge if we were to survive."

Pa's actions could also have been a *cri de cœur*. He had reached fifty years of age, his work and home life were probably tougher than he ever imagined. Two World Wars and in his case, the Irish Revolution of 1919 to 1922 would have taken a toll on him. It was a painful few years for General Practitioners after 1945 with many of them, including my father, valiantly resisting the march of the National Health Service.

Although Mother came from a well-off family she was competent and capable. She had to work things out for herself from an early age. "We bought our own, you know ... monthly pads ... out of our pocket money. Such things were never talked about at home in Scotland ..." she said.

She frequently recalled her own mother's melancholy, her constant keening for Scotland after fifteen pregnancies and eleven children and I think she was rapidly going the same way after eight of her own and a disappointing marriage. Pa's dramatic change of lifestyle to one of relaxation and luxury, greater status and a far lighter workload suited him well.

I have no idea what his thoughts were on leaving his wife behind to the same never-ending chores, a hum-drum existence and single-handed responsibility of bringing up the family. Her thoughts on the matter she made known endlessly.

Ma did at least have the Morris Oxford. On the last occasions I did rounds with Pa in the old Morris I was afraid it wouldn't start, or worse, wouldn't stop. It had a personality that caused my mother anxiety and my father stress. Fear manifest itself one afternoon when we were blackberrying outside the house. Ma came down the lane from an errand in the village with the engine screaming. We waved cheerily as she flew past, not recognising terror in her face. The brakes had finally failed. Ma and the car ended up in the ditch opposite the local artist's driveway.

The new one, the Morris Oxford, was the first in Sheffield in 1948, so the boast went. Pa was chuffed with it and we felt like royalty. It was shiny and black and had no starter handle and it was a thrill to see and smell in the garage.

Over the next few years, Hong Kong, Singapore, Madeira, Lisbon,

Montevideo, Buenos Aires, Mombasa, Sydney, Hawaii, Las Palmas and Nairobi became familiar exotic names to us with Pa on South American routes and six-week, around-the- world cruises. This Sheffield GP became a true globe-trotter, a voyager. His last tour of duty was on the luxurious RMS Andes, billed as the only liner on the South American route with stabilisers.

He had reached the rank of Commodore Surgeon. He had entertained royalty at his table along with many a rich widow. One of these, my mother later remarked with her eyebrows raised, sent him a brace of pheasant and silk pyjamas every Christmas for years.

Mother cared less and less about such things as time passed but was happy her husband had a job he liked. His absence was a blessing, she said once. Damien became his substitute, the "little man around the house." It was a change us younger three hated as Damien evolved into a sadistic, sneering monster who could do no wrong.

Billy survived his hospitalization and at the age of eighteen in 1951 continued with his passion of following our family hero, Uncle Bill, in getting his Wings. He would occasionally buzz Fanshawgate in his little RAF aeroplane, no doubt without permission and off course. At least once he almost gave Mother a heart attack with acrobatics that were a little too low for comfort. This child put her hands to her ears.

I was also resolute in my intention of becoming a nurse, as was Placid Pascal in becoming a police officer. When I was a student nurse I looked at other gawky medical students on the wards and wondered how anyone can decide a career at seventeen, let alone four years of

57

age. Chosen careers, part of a wish list or day-dreaming, come and go unless the child is being pushed. Prancing about on the wards as a student nurse eventually, thinking nursing was about looking good in a smart uniform and making people feel better was a fantasy quickly shattered by sniping Sisters. We were soon made to feel dolts, unfit even to clean bedpans. Nevertheless, I was proud of that idealistic child who would not be dissuaded.

The end of the first part of my childhood as I say at the beginning of the chapter, was the day after Queen Elizabeth's Coronation on June 2nd, 1953. Mother departed wild Derbyshire with her remaining brood for the tiny 12th-century village of Lostwithiel in Cornwall. We left our school, friends and extended family to become "Emmets." Ma waxed on about its history, the Black Prince, castles, smuggling, tin mines and even a place where silver coins had once been stamped. She showed us pictures a few days before we left. She at least was full of hope it would be a healthier climate for Damien's troublesome asthma. The attraction for us was the beaches and the notion we would be on a perpetual Summer holiday. I don't know when she went down to see the house but she did, on her own, to secure the purchase of Lostwithiel's Old Vicarage for the princely sum of £300.

All five of us piled in to the comfy Morris Oxford that Wednesday morning with Ma. Beattie and a pale Lanky Sonia with whom we'd shared many a drama on the moors and around the farm, waved tearful farewells. Ma found space for their parting gift of a bag of sugar and three jars of home preserves (there was still rationing on) and we were off!

Goodbye Lame Daisy, Farmer S. and Aunty Beattie; goodbye Nanny Edie, Fanshawgate House, gardens and orchard, tin baths in front of the fire and warm wooden lavatory seats; goodbye my waist-length thick, curly hair, rags for ringlets; *au revoir* older siblings and ration books; goodbye maypole dancing and fairy rings, hand-stands and hopscotch, Aunty M. and Uncle G. and cousin Connor and family; cheerio family holidays in Scarborough, Looe and Barmouth and "first to see the sea!"; goodbye kind patients, country life, tadpoles and blanketing snow drifts, miserable cold, chapped knees, zooming down hills on our sledges; goodbye Old Daddy, Father Christmas, Holmesfield Juniors and smelly Sheffield city.

Chapter Five
#Kernow# (Matt Crocker)

When Ma, Pascal, Damian, Sulky Sis, Little Simon and I set off we didn't have any notion of what the change downwind from wild, Heathcliffian countryside to a sleepy Cornish backwater would mean. Mother was not forthcoming, though she had tried to whet our appetites without winding us up. She didn't even tell us we would have our own castle to play in. It was much later we learned she couldn't really tell us anything because she had only spent one afternoon in the village, probably most of it with the estate agent.

Our departure was delayed by a day so we could watch the Coronation on Uncle David's television set in Sheffield bought especially for the occasion. The Queen appeared to us as a tiny sombre figure drifting along in her robes with only the weight of the crown preventing her from floating away.

I became bored stiff with hours of ceremony on the grainy black and white screen. A deeper reason for my disinterest was that it had prevented me taking part in our school's red, white and blue-ribboned maypole extravaganza. I loved "trippy, tripping up and down," making those wonderful maypole ribbon patterns as we wove in and out of each other's space. Missing this last event, this last day at school, upset me for a long time. Mother assured me every school had a maypole and that I would be able to "trippy trip" in Cornwall. This was not so. When we discovered our new school in the most pagan county in England didn't have one I was bereft.

The six-bedroomed, three-hundred-year old vicarage, in a town, was a shock after our rural isolation and wide open spaces. It was in narrow Fore Street with houses either side of us and a church and graveyard directly behind. The church, St. Bartholomew's, was built in the 12th Century on a site sacred for six hundred years before that. There were some 'olde' village stocks by the church door. Opposite the house were auctioneers Rowse, Jeffrey and Watkins.

Our house felt haunted and I was glad we all went in together. The servant's room at the back overlooking the graveyard was dark and very creepy. A postage stamp-sized front garden and blip of a back yard with decrepit out-house and shed would never endear itself to us like Fanshawgate and the moors beyond. It was noisier too, with the church almost on top of us. My poor mother didn't know we would have to get used to sleeping through quarter-hourly chiming from a set of noble bells twenty yards away.

I was missing my old house badly even before entering the new one. I missed Pa not being there too and not going out with him on his rounds. He was still a kind and generous man, though we were by then used to him being at sea, returning as a semi-detached part-timer.

On my first morning in Lostwithiel I sat on the garden wall in the sunshine rather than mope around the house. It was far more interesting watching the removal men wobbling in and out with our familiar furniture with my exhausted mother fussing and fretting. The

60

town had surely seen nothing like it since Cromwell was supposed to have tied his horse, named Charles after the king, to the font in St. Bart's three hundred years earlier.

Other non-Cornish immigrants slipped in to town quietly. Not us. Our massive removal van held up traffic for most of the day, its contents paraded before main street shoppers and street corner gossips. The invasion of the MacFarlanes as weird Catholics sent ripples through the town. It was touch and go for a while apparently, as to whether us 'Emmets' would be accepted.

I was agog at so many buildings and so much activity a hairsbreadth away from us. It was intimidating at first and my ears craved the melodious birdsong my father always alerted us to, rather than the Surround Sound of a busy little village. We had already heard "they be Emmets, they be!" 'Emmets' being an appellation used of anyone from the other side of the River Tamar. The old boys chit-chatting outside the Working Men's club had aired the second standard observation,

"'nd Virgin Mary worshippers 'n' all, as Oi've 'eard!"

After about an hour of musing on the wall a dark-haired girl of my age with a determined air about her came up to me and asked in a soft Cornish brogue "do 'ee want to play?" Once I had deciphered her kind invitation and gained my distracted mother's permission we skipped down the road together.

We passed a real chip shop and it was as exciting as going on a first date! My new friend Jenny was eight like me but smaller with the inscrutable eyes of a street-smart fox cub. I was much taller than all the kids of my age down in Cornwall I soon discovered, topped as I was with a thick bush of curly hair. It took me a while to understand Jenny's 'brrs' and how soft the accent was, whatever was said. Yorkshire by comparison can be softly blunt when spoken kindly as, "hello luv!" but no messing when barked, as "shut tha face, or I'll shut it for tha. Gerrit lad ..."

Jenny was also miles brighter than any of the local kids and the majority of the grown-ups as well. Nothing fazed her. She knew what she wanted and would stand up to her parents and the Devil if needs be if she thought they were being stupid or unfair.

Discovering my new Primary School did not have a maypole, when Cornwall is steeped in history and pagan mythology, was a big letdown. Fearing walking home after school in my first week, however, became a greater concern. I was immediately picked on by the Rundall brothers who kept punching my arm, sneering "Frizz Bush" and "Gollywog" until Jenny quietly ordered them to leave me alone. They did but one day when she was not around I was threatened again and was frightened enough to take a different route home after school. I ran so fast down a back lane I smashed into a wall and bloodied my nose.

We soon got used to each other and their tormenting eased. It was replaced by a constant and lusty "we'll take you to ... if you ..." or "I'll give you ... if you show ..." We were eight. The boys were always trying to make extra pennies, usually for marbles, while the girls wanted more sweets. The Rundalls had a tooth ruse going that year, offering some token in exchange for teeth that had, or were about to come out. Their household, as most, was visited by the Tooth Fairy who left a then substantial silver sixpence under the pillow in exchange. They must have made a few bob from disbelievers, or those who remained afraid of them. I did get friendly with one of them when we were young teenagers, when we couldn't find anyone better.

My middle brothers Pascal and Damien had no problems with their new school, Bodmin Grammar. They were cock-a-hoop at having moved far away from Sheffield and the loathed De La Salle Catholic Grammar School. The Brothers there were renowned for their sadistic use of the strap in order to maintain discipline and instil good Christian ideals. The Bodmin headmaster, affectionately known as 'the Boss,' was a reserved and kindly man who did not condone the beating of his pupils.

The Boss did have a cane for his war-wound limp. He would place it symbolically on his desk before errant boys. At all other times it was kept in the umbrella stand and he would lob his battered trilby onto it each morning.

Aware of being an incomer and not a *bona fide* Lostwithielite I quickly became Jenny the Tribal Chief's shadow. If we rowed, we would soon seek each other out. Other kids would trundle along with us when invited to do so as we sometimes needed extras for our dressing up or den games. Who wouldn't be happy in the top team of benign tearaways? If Jenny wasn't around I'd wander off and dawdle with other friends. Annie was one, a simple girl who would show her glass eye and seeping eye socket if you asked her.

Ma never allowed us to have our friends in to play, whereas I was always welcome in Jenny's house on Quay Street. Her house was more interesting anyway, located behind her grandfather's butcher's shop front. She was sandwiched between the oldest building in Cornwall, the Duchy Palace and the town's similarly ancient dairy.

We would play hopscotch or five-stones in the dairy yard which was part of a two-acre site constructed by Edward the Black Prince, the first Duke of Cornwall, who elevated the status of the town and became immensely rich from tin dues. The Palace was a Great Hall modelled after that at Westminster and completed in 1300.

Jenny would spook us with talk straight out of a Daphne Du Maurier novel, of the bones of dead smugglers beneath our feet jangling like wind chimes at Halloween. These men would land contraband at the nearby quay on the Fowey spiriting it through a mile-long tunnel, so legend and Jenny had it, to the Black Prince's abandoned Restormel Castle up the hill and out of sight of the town. The lane leading up from Lostwithiel to the castle is steep and winding, through thick woodland. Duchy-owned fields lead down to the River Fowey. This lane and the tunnel, if it existed, must have seen many a n'er-do-well through silent nights. Smuggling took over as tin-mining declined with the silting up of the river from mine workings.

No one apart from us kids seemed interested in the legend and folklore. No one seemed to care about its historic structures either. "There is history in every stone in the borough of Lostwithiel," wrote John Betjeman but it was many years before I could catch up with it beyond Jenny's tales. The town was founded by the Normans but the

mining of tin, copper and zinc on Bodmin Moor is pre-Roman. The Celts traded it with Phoenicians, the River Fowey was the key to getting this valuable material to the sea. Lostwithiel, six or seven miles inland became the most important stannary town in England. Tin dues earned the Duke of Cornwall £2,000 in 1338, making him one of the richest men in Europe. Not surprisingly he spoke of the town as the Lily of the Valley.

Learning about the rich local history, the daily doings at Restormel Castle when inhabited by princes and nobles, or the English Civil War's Battle of Lostwithiel would have been riveting compared with the endlessly rehashed Bible stories we had to daydream our way through at Lostwithiel Primary School. What better place could there be to haggle over the price of rum, brandy and tobacco with eyes, teeth and sharp knives glinting in the moonlight than a ruined castle? And what better place to feed the imagination of a child?

I did experience problems understanding the thick Cornish accent when it was spoken with a deep burry sound. On our second day in Lostwithiel, Ma asked me to go to Liddicote's, the butcher in Fore Street.

"I would like a pound of lamb's liver, please."

"Wot d'ee want, my 'andsome?"

"Er, er, a pound of liver, please."

"A pound of what ..." asked the blue-bearded butcher with hairy hands like the wolf in Red Riding Hood.

I stood there dumfounded.

"Oh, for goodness sake ... the little girl wants a pound of liver, Arnold!" a prim and proper voice echoed behind me. I turned to face Mrs. Liddicote, the swarthy pirate's unlikely wife and Lady Mayor. She was sitting bolt upright properly attired, with a hat, in her smart glass-screened box. Her role was to take the customers' cash or, as jesting locals implied she was there "to keep her eye on Arnold, in case he bolts with the cash or flirts with a filly!"

"There you are, My Dear," Doris smiled. "How are you settling in? I do hope your mother will become a satisfied customer with us."

"Thank you, Madam," I faltered, walking out backwards as if she was the Queen of Lostwithiel, clutching the disgusting cold soft liver, colliding with the door.

Relatives coming and going soon made us regulars at Lostwithiel's railway station kept impeccably tidy by a kindly Mr. Station Master. He lived in a picture-post card cottage by the station. The Cornish Riviera from Paddington would steam by on its way to Penzance and I thought how nice it would be to be born and spend your life in one nice place, like Lostwithiel. In the early 'Fifties the furthest local people travelled was to the seaside a few miles away and big town, Plymouth. That was a twice-yearly undertaking for new Sunday-best clothes and Christmas presents. It was an hour away on the train or a hitched ride on a milk lorry from the factory in Lostwithiel.

My sister Jane would sashay down from Sheffield with her nursing friend Sigrid for her holidays. They were slim sexy girls who would leave the locals open-mouthed when out dressed as Betty Grable or Mitzi Gaynor look-alikes in hot pants and high heels. Eldest brother Morris would visit when on leave from the RAF. Auntie M. and our uncles David, Alec and even Gordon from Australia made pilgrimages to Lostwithiel to check on their younger sister "with so many babies she didn't know what to do ..." Brother Billy would visit every Summer with his wife Nuala and daughter Polly.

Nuala was a charming, dippy Irish girl who looked like the author Edna O'Brian. She had also trained as a nurse with Jane and Sigrid at Sheffield's Royal Hospital. On her first visit she walked to the wool shop to buy some tapestry wool for Mother. The gently-mannered owner was fondly known as Queenie, though not addressed as such. Everyone 'knew' he was 'gay.'

"Oh, thank you so much Mister Queenie!" she gushed in her entrancing Irish brogue!

It is just as well the locals treated those who were different with a teasing humour, rather than by denigrating them.

Ninety-nine per cent of Lostwithiel's population was made up of indigenous Cornish people. People travelled little and rarely moved house. Newcomers were mostly professional, such as solicitors or doctors. Who didn't enjoy beautiful Cornwall with its slow pace, exquisite scenery and unique charms if lucky enough to have holidayed there in the 1950s?

Children maximise disappointments and disruptions but can minimise them quickly if there are compensations. Lostwithiel's advantages were many with us free to roam around the ancient village and beyond. Nearby Bodmin Moor, Brown Willy the highest point in

Cornwall on which we found bits of a Second World War aircraft, and Dosmary Pool in which the Lady of the Lake caught King Arthur's sword, were all a disappointment. Really exciting were the endless beaches and coves we explored during our holidays. I hardly remember rainy bad-weather days all the time we lived in Cornwall. There seemed only warm, sunny Continental weather days we didn't know in Derbyshire.

In Yorkshire and Derbyshire's bleak and God-fearing realms, folk braved raw winds, snow or filthy fog seemingly without enjoying life. By contrast Hardy's books and the Poldark tales portray the South-West as a vivid landscape with extraordinary light and fields swaying with wild flowers enclosed by primrosed hedgerows and edged with a breathtaking coastline.

Moving to the heart of a village soon became our own Enid Blyton adventure making up for living in a mouldy, haunted vicarage. Having friends nearby meant we were no longer at the beck and call of the Brute Brothers for their war and vampire games. Damien had taken over the backyard shed and was constructing amazingly detailed model planes and warships while continuing to bully us younger ones with ritual thumpings and Chinese burns whenever we were alone. We were frightened of him but he knew Mother would never believe her treasured son had such sadistic inclinations. Favouritism is the last

un-named abuse with the 'unfavoured' often suffering greatly.

Once again, Placid Pascal virtually moved in with our neighbours, "the Ds." Jenny's aunt and uncle. He had quietly accepted Ma's preference for Damien. Actually, we would all have liked to move next door. Mrs. D., also known as Flo, was plump and generous and I can still hear her exploding laughter that made everyone feel they had imbibed a glass or two of scrumpy. Aden, her stick-thin workaholic husband was also full of good-natured gusto.

After finishing his lorry driving at the milk factory, Aden would go to the cider farm until dusk, often allowing us to sit on his trailer, speeding around local farms collecting apples or returning flagons full of cider. Hanging on to bales of straw or boxes of fruit was as thrilling for us as a ride at Alton Towers is for today's kids. Flo was constantly baking perfect pasties, caraway seed cake, Madeira cake and butterfly buns while Mother would be baking apple pies and Bakewell tart. Any mother found to have an empty cake tin risked the stocks.

We would fall in and out with their youngest daughter, plump Titian-haired Junie who, on an off day would stand in the narrow alleyway between us firing off searingly insensitive taunts.

"'Ee be Beans on Toast ... Beans on Toast 'ee be ...'" referring to Ma's penchant for industrial-size tins of the beans we had for breakfast, year in and year out.

In retaliation we would stand on our garden wall shouting "tiddy oggy for brains ... tiddy oggy ... tiddy oggy ... for brains. *Nah, nah ni, na na* ...'" referring to the best-tasting meal in England, the home-cooked Cornish pasty.

It was the Cornish accent that fascinated us above all for its charm and ease on the ear. It never grates, even when voices are raised, as with the soft Southern Irish accent that amuses rather than offends.

"'Ow 'r 'ee, moi 'andsome? You look boodiful, dun'ee?'"

In a village of about two thousand inhabitants, people knew who to meet and greet and who to avoid. People cared more about each other and loneliness wasn't a social problem. We did hear of suicides. The whole village was very upset when our jolly District Nurse put her head in the oven. It was after her hysterectomy, Mother said. A friend's dad also shockingly, hanged himself. Another ageing shopkeeper shot himself. Children we knew also died in the Post-war period including one from diarrhoea and vomiting and another of leukaemia. In those days people would remove their hats respectfully when a funeral cortège passed.

There were "kiddie ticklers" in the village but they didn't bother us. We occasionally played with a gauche girl who had been impregnated by her simple dad. Some of the older boys might give chase for a bit of fun before losing interest and returning to their catapults and marbles or fishing in the river. It was Reds Under the Beds in this early Cold War period that we were quietly made to fear, not local people. And sin, of course.

People were more content with their routine and with their lot, more so perhaps than today. I don't remember any of us going away on holiday while we lived in Cornwall because we had a pretty village, a choice of beautiful beaches and lovely drives near us. We made more trips to Par beach than people who had lived in the village all their lives. Mrs. D. said she couldn't remember the last time she was there, so Ma promptly hauled her in to the car with us one Summer day with no excuses being accepted.

It was almost entirely women on the streets then, as the men would be working. Shopping at a trusted butcher and quality greengrocery shops was a relaxed, almost gentle affair with time to chat with friends and make pleasantries with less well-known neighbours. The wives would return home to cook and clean. In the afternoon they would listen to the wireless or read. Evenings were for tea, parlour games, singsongs and perhaps watching a programme or two on the television if you had one. Hardly anyone owned one until the end of the 1950s. My cousin Jock Russell rowed for Cambridge in the 1956 Oxford and Cambridge Boat Race. A school friend's mother invited me in to watch it. Cambridge won and it was very exciting!

Coming to terms with our uprooting, new house and Pa being away was hard to adjust to. His new role as a part-timer was strange. He had been happy having us around at Fanshawgate but now he was living a bachelor life at sea he seemed to find it difficult to communicate. He even stopped small talk. He would chat away, however, at twenty-to-the-dozen to Ned, the South American opera-singing parrot he brought back after one of his early trips. The fact that he chose our presents from abroad with such thought meant he still cared but I still pined for the rhythm and pace of family life when our dad was the local GP and had star billing.

Ma would fill him in about our doings in her weekly airmail letters but he never followed through, asking us about our lives. But then, none of my friend's dads did. It was the women who chattered and gossiped with each other while the head of the household would reserve his chat for the British Legion, or pub, where ladies weren't welcome.

Mother now acted as father's ventriloquist's dummy for familial imperatives, or it was a tactic to show a united parental front and hold the family together.

"Your father says you ... your father wouldn't be pleased if ..."

It left her with all the grotty roles of parenting and negative associations. He literally sailed in and out of our lives as a benign Daddy Christmas. I suppose it was inevitable we responded to Ma's more significant presence while easing Pa out of our lives, though we were still happy to welcome him home every few weeks.

Being a doctor's wife ranked well in the early 'Fifties when there was still much emphasis on "one's status," when class division was still prevalent across society. Different classes still did not mix socially. Mother was steeped in this.

"One should never get familiar with one's servants," she would say, as if there had been no war and servants had not all but disappeared in Britain. She also claimed she held on to her five servants before the war because of her fair but firm rules of employment. Children pick up on such things, of course, wondering why this "fair but firm" was not applied to more pertinent things such as her treatment of her children. In urban Lostwithiel, with her doctor-husband mostly absent there were no status life rafts to which Mother could cling. I still had to remember I was a doctor's daughter but it carried little currency.

When she decided she needed a cleaner, she had no choice. It had to be Mad Maisie. A plump, careworn woman, Mad Maisie would regale my unprepared mother with stories about her umpteen children turning up from time to time from various orphanages.

"This latest kiddie that turn up, he be black, Missus M.! I forgot all about 'ee!" she informed my astonished mother one day when asking for the day off so she could get to know him a little better. Rumour had it she had serviced the GIs based nearby during the War and had forgotten how many kiddies she had put away.

"She must have had twelve or thirteen," a neighbour informed us, without any moral judgement. Whatever scandals happened, they were tutted over by the community for a short while, then accepted, even forgotten.

My parents had been fussy about whom we mixed with in Sheffield. In Lostwithiel, however, they had little choice but to accept our choosing our friends from all backgrounds. They never understood that going through a state school, as opposed to one of

their private schools, meant we would pal up with other children from state schools. It was not a question of riff-raff *versus* 'suitable' friends. Were we really supposed to consider our non middle-class friends as lesser mortals than ourselves?

It was a ridiculous notion when my friend Jenny was smarter than I was, better dressed and had loads more toys than I ever did. Okay, so her parents didn't hold their knives 'correctly' but this is sliding into the seamy end of snobbery.

Thank goodness instructions such as checking if the bottom button of a man's waistcoat was left undone, or who held his or her knife like a pencil and other instances of a silly hoopla of social niceties one had to learn in order to keep *mater* and *pater* happy was on its way out from the moment we hit Lostwithiel.

Mother did become more relaxed and less concerned with Middle Class "ought" and "must" but Father would still correct our manners and speech and go bonkers if he caught us slavering over a fourpenny bag of scorching chips in the street.

Finding out later about my mother being of generations of proud Kilsyth mining families makes me realise where my Labour leanings originated. My father too, came from a lowly Cork family that collectively funded him through medical school because he was the bright one. Proof that it only takes a generation to change from peasant to toff. Toff as he saw it anyway.

When rationing ended in Britain in the 'Fifties and there began the steady climb to Harold Macmillan's "you've never had it so good" times I was well aware of my friends' younger mums spending freely. In a more thrifty Yorkshire it was more about saving for a rainy day, with most children I believe, receiving one toy plus an orange for birthday and Christmas. Down in Cornwall parents bought their children clothes, prams, bikes and toys for Christmas and birthdays. They dressed them impeccably in bright dresses and hand-knitted cardigans and jumpers. Sunday School was a fashion parade for Sunday Best outfits. Easter Sunday saw the grand parading of children in brand new top-to-toe outfits.

I felt like a Bag Lady's child in my sisters' cast-offs. Even then, toe ends would be cut out of my shoes with a razor blade as my feet grew. Fortunately, we had to travel several miles to either Par or Fowey Catholic Church on Sundays and Sunday Best did not seem so important among people you didn't know. Such a notion was for "common people" Mother would say, "not for us." Once back home after Mass it was grin and bear it in my hand-me-downs, or stay indoors. Jenny was always tactful and shared her new doll's pram or bike with Orphan Rose with great generosity.

The showdown came when I was given a seventy-year old neighbour's cast-off Cuban-heel lace-ups to wear to school. To be made to wear granny shoes was the final insult when brothers Damien and lately, little Simon because he was the youngest, had almost everything they asked for. Sulky Sis handled Mother differently, in making a huge fuss until she got what she wanted. This left Pascal and I as the passive mutts.

On her way home from school that day Miserable Rose ran like the wind in her socks to The Parade and slung the Old Duck's Cuban heels into the river. Mother didn't say a word about my returning from school shoeless with blackened socks and I went back to wearing my old sandals with the toes cut out.

Simon took the opportunity to flaunt his squeaky new lace-ups and new racing bike, making me want to run away at the time. I had a vintage 1930s crate with worn tyres and suicide brakes, sold to me by our ancient Guiding Commissioner. Several of us young Guides had recently grumbled our way to our commissioner's rural abode on a Guide Badge-gaining hike of six miles. We found her country pile on a July day with tar melting on the road. Our sleeping bags were arranged in her hayloft and we were left alone for the night terrified of rats and field mice sneaking in to nibble ears and toes.

71

She asked thirty shillings for the bike, even though it needed a complete overhaul. Wounded pride aside, I had great fun peddling miles around Lostwithiel's glorious countryside, free at last!

I learned later from research, comparison with other family finances and knowing from my own experience of holding the family purse strings that shortage of money was not the issue. Pa made sure his wife and family were well-provided for. Eighty pounds a month from him in 1953, wasn't bad pay for my mother. The fear of being left destitute made her the strict "keeper of the purse," so much so, that we would push Simple Simon forward to plead for our sixpence pocket money if we needed it a day or two in advance.

Because of issues like these in my childhood I developed a lifelong awareness and concern for the less advantaged and would not wish to be a parent's favourite. It doesn't mean to say that not being one didn't hurt at the time. The favoured ones grew up to be self-centred and less gracious than those of us who were overlooked.

Between the ages of eight and sixteen I had to sleep in the same bed as Mother when Father was away at sea because she didn't like sleeping alone. Sulky Sis refused to oblige. It was a bizarre experience at a time when we viewed everyone over twenty as remote and boring beings who controlled our lives from afar. I was embarrassed at having to sleep with my mother and I was also in fear of her.

Listening to her frequent moans about money and the strife her wretched urchins caused her burdened me also. She would harp on that she had never wanted children. Her disenchantment with my father was also upsetting and I would cover my ears like an autistic child who hates noise. It also bugged me that I gained no perks whatsoever for my loathed night-time incarceration with my depressed mother.

This was how I heard about grown-up issues. Things like, "oh, what am I to do, Billy's got a girl pregnant ..." and "never get married, Ro, sex is awful ..." Happy family events became few and far between.

We all groaned when Jane announced her engagement to an RAF officer with a Terry Thomas 'tache and accent to match. Sulky Sis and I hated the bridesmaids' dresses Ma had made and were secretly pleased when the Wing Commander broke it off. Sulky Sis had already refused to wear the Shocking Pink seersucker creation with matching pink open-toed shoes. Jane was not happy at being jilted and had a breakdown that caused her to be given the heave-ho from the RAF.

I did work hard at making Ma laugh whenever she suffered an attack of the glooms as she had a touchingly young giggle once she relaxed. My caring role for this needy Boudicca became a lifelong one. When I tell youngsters my generation never cheeked our parents, they laugh. We obeyed our parents from fearing their wrath, whereas today's kids thankfully, tend not to feel so intimidated. It was a shock hearing Iron Jenny stand her ground against her parents, just the fact she was contradicting them. Invariably she won, which made me wish I could do the same.

Children react to their lot in life generally without question. Although I found Ma's relentless

pessimism distressing, I listened as well as I could without ever thinking to tell older Jane or Billy or Morris. They might have realised she was depressed and that it needed sorting. Staying outside the house as long as possible was also a preferred option, as was losing myself in books. To this day I feel almost desolate without a book to drop into.

The consequences of Mother's doom and gloom balanced by an upbeat 'Sixties philosophy determined me to go for optimism any day. I understand why she felt trapped and bear no malice. I just wish she had enjoyed a happier life.

"And don't you look just like your mutherr!" Jenny remarked in her soft Cornish accent, fifty-five years later. My husband and I were touring Cornwall and stopped in Lostwithiel. I popped into the Post Office and there she was.

"We were good together, weren't we?" she said later that evening, with a mischievous look in her sharp eyes. I commented there were so many cars now and the village had expanded with many new estates. We went for a little walk and smiled at the kids of fourteen years of age or so, sitting flirting on the Drill Hall wall, just as we had done in the late 'Fifties.

Meeting Jenny after so many years was a Madeleine Moment as warm and wicked memories streamed forth. As they say, the longer in the tooth you become the more your mind wanders back to childhood. Jenny, now a pillar of her community, was just the same, as droll and self-deprecating as I remembered her. We are in regular touch now. What she really thought of our barmy family, I have yet to ask. She will surely say there was never a dull moment with the MacFarlanes down the road.

Chapter Six

#As Tears go By ...# (Marianne Faithfull/Jagger-Richards)

Our new environment was soon an ever-changing adventure playground with the village and surrounding woodland a haven in which we could wander at will. The freedom to roam beyond the eagle eye of the family was unnerving to begin with but it didn't take us long to become thoroughly familiar with our new territory.

After the aconites and bluebells of winters milder than us Northerners could have imagined came crocuses, primroses, warming sunshine and the first batches of delectable Cornish clotted cream ice-cream. In some years we were organised into picking bunches of primroses for the Spring flower market in Covent Garden in London. We received threepence a bunch for our labour and it was a welcome supplement to meagre pocket money.

In the Summer, Jenny and I and other friends would take a picnic with us up the mile-long meander to Restormel Castle. It was the perfect stage for us to play out our Black Prince adventures. The local lads took the macho roles. Girls were only permitted to look after the 'wounded' and do the domestic things. We didn't want to do any fighting anyway, except fire their cap guns, preferring pretend-dressing as Maid Marian, Guinevere or Indian Squaws.

Restormel Castle, a circular Norman shell with moat was ours to play in and around as we wished. It was mostly unattended and there wasn't anyone to stop us from feeling our way up crumbling staircases, straddling ancient walls and creeping carefully along treacherous narrow parapets pretending to fire arrows below or escape being tagged.

We loved skipping, especially the marathons in the street with two of us holding a long rope and everyone taking turns jumping in and out singing rhymes to keep up the momentum. Ball games were a daily activity. These included rounders, piggy-in-the-middle, throwing it against a wall and clapping before catching it, or throwing it around your back to the wall and clapping before catching it. We got good at three-ball juggling, hopscotch, five-stones and rolling beautifully patterned marbles. We also walked, skipped, ran about, cycled and roller-skated our way through perfect Summer days. No one directed us. We thought up our own play agenda.

Children have a natural survival instinct if left to find safe levels of "can and can't do." Children today who are molly-coddled and ferried everywhere by car, even 200 metres to school if Mum or Dad have to go off to work, I call Legless Children. Our generation do question whether such tight parental control is a form of deprivation. How can kids gain confidence without venturing into the wide world? The thought of parents in those days clocking their children's movements as it is done today via Facebook and Smartphone and so on is unimaginable.

Jenny and I and sometimes her timid sister Carron and cousin Julie would travel on the train from Lostwithiel to nearby Par Beach two or three times a week during the Summer holidays. The beach was huge and the water by the little harbour milky from china clay workings. We would swim when the tide was in, build sand castles, play ball games and walk on the cliff top towards Fowey. We were a group of girls on our own all day, though I was mindful of Mother's words about tides, current and cliffs and "never go out above the waist ..."

The high point of any trip to the seaside was an ice-cream. We had money for one each. At the end of the afternoon we would trek with our things back up to the railway station tired and happy.

We also joined in succession, Brownies, Girl Guides, St. John's and local drama groups. We spent many hours in Coulson Park, bumping up and down on its see-saws and suffering being hard-bumped by rogue boys. The well-used swing was where we would bicker and banter with other girls and share tart sherbet, barley sugars, aniseed balls and gobstoppers. Our weekly pocket money bought us little more than a quarter (four ounces) of pineapple chunks from the tiny step-down sweet shop in Fore Street.

Coulson Park lay between the River Fowey and the railway line to Fowey on the coast. On most days the park would be deserted except for birds and squirrels and we wished a meteorite would drop out of the sky to liven things up. Occasionally, time just stopped and cabin fever would loom. Just when it was about to take hold, something would come to the rescue, even if only the annual invitation to become one of Jesus' soldiers. It wasn't a Summer holiday without the Barmy Army, the itinerant Holy Joes and Joannas parked-up by the river inviting us to sing Jonah and the Whale or recite Hell and

Damnation literature for a free colouring book.

We did have a 'flea pit' in the town that poor Mother would have a fit about when we wanted to go. Warm Cornwall hosted flea epidemics, she said. If she was feeling generous we would be given the ninepence for an afternoon show of Disney and Doris Day films. I loved the cockerel announcing Pathé News. We could not often put news clips into context even as young teenagers but they showed there was a big bright, colourful and sometimes worrying world beyond our small town. The cockerel symbolised the cinema of the period, along with J. Arthur Rank's gong, MGM's lion, RKO's radio mast, the lady with the lit-up tray of ice-cream tubs and little wooden spoons ...

I remember being impressed with the life story of John Phillip Sousa, the American March King, who wrote many tunes we knew and hundreds we didn't. It would have been lovely to have his magnificent marching band knock the stuffing out of the town. Pascal liked the film as well and saw it every day for a week because he helped out in the projection room. He was a proud horn player in Lostwithiel's marching band before he picked up a clarinet. The cinema's owner, a quiet, bearded man was known as 'the professor' because he knew every word in the English Dictionary. Nobody had the temerity to test him on this.

Skipping up the garden path after school one day, Ma opened the door with a face that would have frightened thunder.

"Can I go and play at Sadie's?"

"No. You must come in and get straight into the bath!"

"But we have a bath on Sunday evenings ..."

"I know, Ro but the flea problem is getting worse. I've been all round the house again today with a bar of soap and I don't know where they are coming from. Leave your clothes in the bin in the hall and I'll deal with them."

This went on for a couple of weeks and we became seriously stressed and bitten. Ma came the closest I saw to a breakdown. Mattresses and carpets were thrown out, sulphur candles were burnt in every room and still the little critters hopped, skipped and jumped into our beds. Demonic Damien's idea of turning them into a flea circus got short shrift. Eventually Aden and an exhausted Ma located the nest under her bedroom floorboards. Sulky Sis's pet rabbit brought inside occasionally got the blame.

In our early teenage years the park's shabby old shelter was a great draw and well-frequented for innocent kissing with lads, especially on winter nights or when it was raining. We felt as daring as bungee jumpers and tingled, knowing we would be punished with a lockdown and turned into pariahs of shame if caught. This shelter was a magnet for innocent trysting. It should be entered for the Turner Prize as it stands! And yes, fifty years on, it is still there, probably similarly frequented.

People joked a Sexual Revolution has always been ongoing in Cornwall. "It's a man's place to try and a woman's to deny" was almost written in the sky as a warning we should keep ourselves "tidy" as Princess Diana later expressed it. How shocked we were when our tiny younger class mate Terry gave birth in her bed one night, poor girl. How traumatised she must have been, thinking she just had a bad stomach ache. The father, also aged twelve was our goody-goody class monitor, quiet and proper.

We might have expected it of randy Jo Roper who spent his last year at Primary School looking for maidens who had an idea of what it was to "go all the way." He got as far as kissing me. He resembled a young Robert Mitchum and over the next few years was actually temptation on a stick. The shelter became his hunting ground to which we would traipse on winter evenings. Fighting him off was difficult as he was gorgeous. He had a double difficulty with us in that reputation was all and we were still amazingly ignorant about the birds and the bees.

Was I shocked and horrified at being grabbed by Jo the Lad? No. Was I a Lolita in the making? Yes and no. Temptation was all around but strict instructions had been dinned into all us girls at home and by the Church.

Second only to the shelter in popularity for us youngsters on the loose was the tiny window at the top of the Old Malt House steps. There was a direct view into the bedroom of the one son Mad Maisie had at home with her.

"... they ain't got no clothes on!" might come the shocked commentary from whoever had reached the window first. "His head's 'down there' and hers ... is 'down there' the other way!"

When one local girl began dating a lad who lived nearby, Flo tut-tutted at what must have been a village hazard.

"She can't go with him, 'ee's 'er half-brother!"

Mrs. D. laughed out loud when, not long after we had moved into the village I told her I knew where babies came from.

"Do ee, moi 'andsome?"

"Yes," I blushed as I pointed to her generous cleavage. "They come out of there! There's a hole between your er, things and the baby pops out between your, er, boobies?"

"You'll be the death of me, Child!" she said, giving me a large piece of Madeira Cake. "Now go out and play before I bust moi guts and garters!"

Once I overheard my mother talking to our handy man Adam, who was setting up his ladder to do some painting on the house. Opposite us was the estate agents and auction house part-owned by the town's portly mayor. Adam had just reached the top of the ladder when he was on his way back down.

"Sorry, Missers M. Oi 'ad to get down fast as Oi could," a panicked Adam spluttered.

"Dearie me, Adam, you look as if you've seen the Devil Incarnate!"

"No, Missers M. Oi dun't knows 'ow to tell ee ..."

"Oh, come, Adam, I helped run my husband's surgery for more years than you've had hot pasties ..."

"Well ... Oi just spied Mister Mayor and Gertie P. on the settee in the top floor office ... you know ... Oi nearly fell of my perch, I can tell ee. Oo'd 'ave thought them two at it, like rabbits?"

Mother tried to keep a straight face. The vision of the balding, pot-bellied mayor doing hanky-panky with middle-aged Miss P., chapel organist and infant teacher was too much for me. She used to be my teacher. We didn't know what it was all about, just that it was "goings on," of which there seemed to be plenty around the village. Catholic Sheffield was puritanical by comparison as I was to find out on my return as an older teenager.

Later that evening Jenny and I sloped off to the park shelter to talk about the incident and puff and cough our way through our packet of five Woodbines. These were an improvement on the paper cigarettes Damien had taught us how to roll, light and smoke. Those burnt our throats and smarted our eyes. What was a bad asthmatic doing smoking anything? It shows how determined teenagers can be to defy sensible edicts from parents.

In my early teens and told nothing about the facts of life, I began reading Pa's forbidden medical books kept in a locked cupboard in the lounge. Here were pictures of breasts, the adult penis and vagina, some with pubic hair, some without. It was unfortunate the pictures, many in lurid colour, were there because they showed deformities, tumours and cankers and the effects of herpes and end-stage syphilis. Many of the pictures were gross and I was not to know for many years what a normal penis, for example, looked like.

Pa also brought home gruesome murder weeklies from America in colour. You didn't see such things in newsagents in England. They detailed real murders, sexual, sadistic and violent and offered an analysis of the killers' behaviour. I had to be feeling very strong to flick through one of these. Sulky Sis couldn't resist them and would have screaming nightmares. Presumably Pa's interest was medical.

The meteorite never arrived in the park but I do recall a young Death in Venice Adonis with curly golden hair appearing in a canoe floating lazily down-river, one Summer evening. We kept pace with him as he told us he was off from boarding school and staying in the family house on the misty reaches of the other side of the river. He was from the family of the famous war poet, Siegfried Sassoon. Jenny and I decided he looked lonely and vied with each other to be his date. We hadn't a prayer, of course and had to make do with mooching with the local lads.

To be thought of as "fast" or as "easy meat" with virginity still the required state for marriage, was tantamount to being covered in gold sequins and paraded around the village. The thought of being unwed and pregnant, even though we didn't know how girls got pregnant, was as big a fear. Nevertheless, once awakened, many a night through our virtuous but hard-pressed teenage years was spent hoping to bump into lads of our age as frisky as we were.

Also awakening with appetites whetted, were older teenagers looking for possibilities. There were even some day-dreaming damsels who had married too young seeking liaisons with young men they may have yearned for at school, or who just got their juices flowing. For them it was the greater privacy (as if no one knew it went on) of the St. Blazey cinema or a bumper car ride in a fair out of town.

In winter months the dingy church hall in Lostwithiel was our "Cavern." Old-time dancing classes were the front but at least it was warm, actually the only warm place in the village. It must have been sheer desperation driving us there to strut the Valeta, the Gay Gordons and the waltz with our hesitant string bean of a vicar doubling as Dance Master.

We were "apple scruffs," as George Harrison would later sing, when we became Jo Roper's Skiffle Group groupies, privileged to be invited to watch them rehearse, also in the church hall. It was so exciting jigging about to that new raw sound from tea-chest bass, washboard and thimble and Jo's cheap guitar coming together with a recognizable Dream Lover. Afterwards, we would brew tea in a big silver pot and Jo would smooch with us in the kitchen. We were "made up," as they say in Liverpool, feeling as if we were the only ones in town having fun.

After one winter evening dance at the Drill Hall, Jo Roper offered to walk me home. I should have known this was playing with fire. He hauled me into the Parade shelter in the dark and I had to fight him off. At thirteen years of age I was frightened because he was trying to put his hand up my skirt. He was willing to go out with me at the weekend, he said, if I would let him have his way, meaning "having sex," I presumed. We knew he was already having his way with a flighty hussy, Gemma Potts. Was it because she was adopted, we wondered, as we knew her genteel parents hadn't a clue about what she got up to. She had bragged that she and Jo had spent a night in her parents' beach hut at Par Beach!

My awkward moment with my dastardly heart-throb was ruined by three local Teddy Boys wearing luminous socks who did a 'surprise' from behind the shelter where they were having a quiet smoke. One of them was Mrs. D.'s son, Benny. They were older and Jo Roper had no option but to disappear. Never was I happier to see my neighbour.

At the end of the year we would look forward to kisses under the mistletoe and playing spin the bottle at the church hall Christmas parties, hoping for a kiss with a gorgeous boy in the room behind the stage. Jo Roper remained top dog as his kisses were divine I have to admit, not wet and sloppy like those from the less experienced oiks.

By the time we started grammar school we had moved on to 'illicit' corset-rippers and illustrated romantic novellas, swapping them surreptitiously on the school bus into Bodmin. Our days of reading Girls' Crystal Annuals and Bunty were over.

I passed the Eleven Plus, just, as I hated arithmetic but was a good reader, well-read also and not shy to converse. I started at Bodmin, rather than the less prestigious Fowey Grammar as one of four local children with a connexion (Damien and Pascal were there). Sadie, Jenny and Wendy were the other three. Sadie started her period that day and we were upset she kept it secret for ages through fear and shame. The poor girl thought at the time in class she was dying because she had no idea what was happening to her.

Grammar School as I was growing up, did not thrill me. In our overcrowded classroom my brain shut down as fearsome teachers in black gowns marched in, disgorged words and notions that might as well have been in a different language and marched out again. Mrs. Fry on the other hand, our formidable French teacher, used cartoon-like pictures to introduce French vocabulary beginning with *maison*.

I didn't mind English and for a time was our history teacher, Mr. Webster's, pet. Maths was utter gobbledygook. I am sure I was innumerate, even maths dyslexic as is now being postulated as yet another syndrome. This was a great pity as I found physics and chemistry fascinating. Boredom in many of the classes was the main problem, I recall, being uninspired by the teacher or teaching methods of the day.

In some classes I copied shamelessly off the class swat but could even fail at this, as when our maths teacher Mr. James said wearily "if you are going to copy off Owen, Miss MacFarlane, at least try and copy correctly."

It was a sad moment when, soon after leaving Cornwall, Jenny wrote to say that Mr. James had committed suicide.

Some time in the mid-'Fifties, Sulky Sis befriended a teenage girl named Sybil. She fascinated us because she spent most of her time in a Plymouth orphanage, coming down to Lostwithiel to stay with a reclusive foster mother for a few weeks in the year. One lunchtime she came running to our house clearly distressed crying, "my Foster Mum's choked on a banana and isn't breathing."

The poor woman died, leaving Sybil once again with the orphanage as her home.

She was a naturally happy-go-lucky, worldly young teenager who could have played Nell Gwynne. To us she was amazingly upbeat for a girl who spent most of her time in a lousy home for abandoned kids. Sulky Sis was always mean to me, whereas Sybil would happily chat away. Sulky didn't like it, clearly resenting I was ever born.

The fascination lay in the girl's stories of naughty goings-on at the orphanage, as if it was absolutely normal. It was for her, we soon realised. We were chuffed and a little surprised when Mother agreed to take her in rather than have her return to the orphanage at the end of the holidays. Unfortunately Sybil and Sulky Sis started staying out late and began returning home after the witching hour. Daring to defy Mother was akin to telling Frankenstein to take a walk.

When Sulky Sis returned very late one Saturday night alone, Mother pelted downstairs to confront a teenage daughter who had taken one too many liberties. Sulky must have cheeked her as I heard Mother slap our petulant sister across her face. She returned to our shared bed fuming.

"That is it," she said firmly.

Nobody heard Sybil return that night and the next day she was told she would be going back to the orphanage. Mother was not having Sinner Sybil leading her daughter astray. To us it rather looked the other way around.

Sweet Sybil told me everything she got up to and that kissing was lovely. I wished I had defended them both, reassuring Mother I knew they weren't really misbehaving. I missed Sybil a lot when she left, wishing she had been my older sister and Sulky Sis had been sent packing.

Sybil's banishment must have affected my sister seriously also. She became ever more difficult at home, more withdrawn and later, seriously anorexic. It didn't help that the local Teddy Boys and Elvis look-alikes with their shocking pink or lime green socks and dodgy drainpipes called her Titless Sis. Their mono-celled brains were tuned to Cornish lasses developing curves much earlier than us Northern girls.

On many a Saturday we would do our duty at weddings at St. Bart's waiting in the churchyard. Quizzical pairs of eyes would fix on the bride's tummy and someone would begin quietly "here comes the bride, all fat and wide/ forty inches wide/ buttered on both sides ... with a bun in her ov-en ..." or whatever was thought appropriate.

As Catholics the MacFarlanes had to observe strict rules about non-attendance at other church services, religious lessons at non-Catholic schools and even school assembly. Because we were the only Roman Catholics in the village I would be asked vexing questions by the other kids like "ee worship the Virgin Mary, dun'ee?" and "ye worships ghosts and not God, Oi've 'eard!" or "is it true ye drinks Jesus' blood, then?"

Who could blame them for thinking we were odd when our parish priest Father Bernard came up with the bright idea of hearing our confession in a wardrobe in a games room above a Lostwithiel pub? This was to save us travelling six miles to his little church in Par. When word got around, it was as though we were practising witchcraft at Salem. That the same priest could be spied through our window saying the occasional Mass in our lounge, using our ornate Jacobean sideboard as his altar, must have looked like pure Pagan or Wicca practices to passers-by.

This is where the early Catholic Church gleaned most of its rituals anyway, in the hope of making pagan converts. The early Sixth-century Catholic Church in Lostwithiel would have practised a mishmash of pagan and Roman ritual making them New Age at the time. Sometimes I felt we were the pagans. We were certainly outsiders in Lostwithiel being Emmets, Catholics and Middle Class. Living right in the middle of town and mixing freely with local children helped our being accepted into the village fold I'm sure. It was different for the other children of the town's well-to-do professional families who were sent to private schools and barred from mixing with kids on the street.

I had already made many deals with the Father, Son and Holy Ghost if they would straighten my frizzy mop, replace my brain with one of a high IQ and making me multi-lingual into the bargain. Oh yes, and if they could possibly arrange a little more pocket money and Ma to stop favouring gloating Damien and snivelling Simon, that would be good to.

I don't know what Pa made of it all down in Cornwall. As I say, he talked less and less. With mother having bought the house in the village and organised the entire family down to Cornwall he must have known his control over the family was slipping. There may even have been a deal somewhere between my parents.

He wrote a book about hygiene at sea after an outbreak of food poisoning on one of his trips. He then began his memoirs, an erudite work sprinkled with Latin and literary quotations. Mother and I helped by one-finger typing out his scripts when he was at home working on it. She would frequently shake her head about the book standing no chance of being published, it being completely out of touch with post-war Britain. He wrote one about making cocktails too. These manuscripts are now lost.

We had got used to him coming home from sea and going off again a couple of weeks later. He liked to spend his mornings and evenings fishing when home and Dozy Rosy was the one commanded by Mother to keep him company. This was not fair since Sulky Sis was his favourite. The fact she refused point blank to accompany Pa down to the river made no difference.

"Just be a good girl and keep your father company," Ma would implore. Wringing her hands meant she wanted him out of the way. I didn't like it and I felt sad for Jenny because she would be at a loose end during those weeks, especially if we were on school holidays.

First thing in the morning Pa would bring out some elegant, hand-crafted Japanese fishing rods and a box of exquisite hand-made flies which he taught me how to tie to the hooks. We would walk through the park to the wilder banks and mud flats of the Fowey. In the afternoons, after his snooze we would walk further down-river, as far as Golant. My job was to dig for lugworms. Pa never fished with other

anglers because his catching nothing at all became a joke. They would haul fish in non-stop on their basic rods but would always be polite to Pa.

These were difficult days for me with him ever more introverted. Hours could pass on the river bank without him speaking. It did nothing for my confidence as a child and young teenager and probably explains why to this day I am uncomfortable when people fall silent. I also like background noise, whatever I am doing.

On our return home for lunch he would prepare cocktails based on tonic, lemon and Merrydown Cider as he wanted us to become used to drinking gradually in the way French children learn.

Dinner was in the dining room rather than the parlour. Mother would lay the table with white damask and their wedding present gold-rimmed china plates. I would surreptitiously pour Pa's evening gin and vermouth cocktails into the carpet as they were gruesome. Ma never caught on. She did find dozens of Halibut oil capsules squished under the kitchen chair cushion and I was told off. It was either that or I gagged.

While we were 'enjoying' our drinks before dinner Pa would play his treasured operatic arias as well as new finds like Eartha Kitt or the Danish comedian Victor Borge on the gramophone. Ma and Pa were great raconteurs and always sounded like best buddies when reminiscing together about lighter incidents at the surgery and during the War. We would remain respectfully quiet and careful of keeping our elbows off the table and chewing our food as slowly as Pa did.

After dinner we would play Ludo or Snap or gambling games, including Poker and Sevens. The stakes were a halfpenny a hand. Sometimes I won the kitty and this supplemented my pocket money for extra chews that still cost only a farthing a piece. Sulky Sis played to win. If she didn't, she played up.

Pa's greatest listening pleasure was the great opera classics sung by Callas and Sutherland. Those wonderful arias and choruses are part of my growing up. Ned the parrot would rock slowly from side to side on his perch, singing along. Full-throated, in tune and as ecstatic as Pa, he knew the entire repertoire.

My yearning to become a nurse strengthened while we lived in Lostwithiel. At nine I was a St. John Ambulance Cadet and proud as Punch to be wearing the emblematic uniform. It was a grey dress with puffball cuffs and white pinafore apron. I wore it weekly at First-Aid sessions. We learnt First-Aid and Home Nursing to a rigorous degree taking frequent tests and doing live demonstrations and competitions at local and county shows. Most years I would be on duty with our group at Lostwithiel's carnival and regatta.

Competition was fierce among the St. John groups and our determination and will to win would have outclassed the ferocious rivalries at a Crufts Dog Show. My father, however, wasn't at all encouraging when he saw me in this uniform. Whenever he was called out to attend a road accident he dreaded a St. John's zealot, as he called them, pushing through the crowd.

"They'd even bring their own bloody stretchers," he would lament. "I'd have to boot them out of the way before I could attend to the casualty!"

One year at the carnival I was dressed in a genuine *hula* skirt and *lei* garland Pa had brought back for me from Hawaii. Another time I was presented as the Old Woman in a Shoe. We would then dance the 'Flora' with our champion Brass Band which Placid Pascal belonged to. He, Billy and I were the musical ones. At our annual Regatta, antics on the greasy pole over the river were our favourite. Youths would sit astride the pole swinging sacks with soot in them at each other. No one lasted long before falling into the water.

Brother Damien and his friend John never wanting to be outdone, lashed a raft of wood and empty oil drums together one year. Their engineering incorporated a bicycle that would enable them to propel the 'Nautilus' at a fair speed along the river. It didn't get very far before capsizing, dunking them into the cold water. They drew a good round of applause and cheers for their efforts.

Undeterred by Pa's pessimism, my unfailing attendance at St. John's paid off with another step up the nursing ladder at the age of thirteen as a St. John Volunteer Helper in the Cottage Hospital at Fowey. I'd never been as happy as when helping real nurses at patients' bedsides. I could have flown back home to Lostwithiel as Super Nurse when a kind nurse let me wear her cape at tea time.

The biggest annual event for our St. John group was the Royal Cornwall Show. Ecstatic to be invited as a First-Aider one year I ran out of our tent to receive a smile from the Queen Mother as she was driven past a few feet away. I have also seen the Queen, her sister Margaret and young daughter Anne while on duty at the Show. We were all struck by their petal-luminous skin. Rumour had it they washed in Champagne.

Moving up from Brownies to Guides helped Jenny and I gain credibility, though we didn't think much of fire-lighting, knot-making, semaphore and tracking. Whenever I sew a button on though, I still wind the thread around the back of the button on completion as forgetting to do this caused me to fail my needlework badge first time. I also tie bin bags in a perfect left-over-right and right-over left reef knot.

When Guides were no longer "hip," we joined the local drama club for a lark and were catapulted to stardom. My first role was playing the heroine in a forgotten Noel Coward play, I'll Leave it to You. My stage fiancé Bobbie was the son of the local Mayor. BJ was handsome and polished in a Jeeves and Wooster way. He was about twenty and took himself very seriously, clearly loathing playing opposite a tall, gawky fourteen-year old. To me, he was the epitome of sophistication compared to younger bumbling, mumbling local lads. Jenny played Bobbie's brattish, schoolgirl sister and was a star even with a Cornish, rather than an upper-crust, accent.

My mother, who rarely attended any of our doings since she'd "been there and done that" with my older siblings, said my acting debut was something she would not miss for the world. She sat in the middle of the front row with Mrs. D., whose laughter during the play would have been recognised across the village. This was part of the trouble! All went well until my 'fiancé' began playing and singing an interminable, mawkish three-verse song at the piano at the back of the stage. I was sat on a settee facing the audience, flicking through a magazine.

"The sweetest name that ever I heard, is Faith ..." he gushed in a cloying, posh voice, through to the chorus,

"I drink all day on its delights ..."

We are a family of uncontrollable gigglers, once triggered and it was excruciating having to cope with Mother and Mrs. D. before me, crying with laughter. Their hysterics meant I had to depart from the direction and keep walking back and forth to a pretend window where I could turn my back to the audience and wipe my own eyes. It was agony, corpsing on my debut, made all the worse by my stage love being distinctly unamused.

BJ had to kiss me lightly at the end of the play which made this budding actress the happiest in the business. I was, of course, in total denial about his complete disdain at having to take the stage with me. I fell for him during rehearsals and after the play finished began stalking the poor boy. Every evening I would sit on Gwynne's front step on lower Bodmin Hill waiting for five minutes to six when BJ would drive down Bodmin Hill after work in his light green Morris Minor. The fact that he grimaced rather than acknowledge me mattered not a jot. He was shy and didn't know how to be unshy. All he needed was ... a girlfriend.

Gwynne would take me into the house laughing, treating me like a younger sister. I was there quite a lot helping look after her three young children as a change from the line of lifeless dolls along my bed. She was a free spirit, always laughing as if nothing bothered her. We all loved her as she never talked down to us. She happily enlightened us about the birds and the bees too, when no one else would consider it. Apart from these occasions with Gwynne and to an extent with Sybil when she lived with us, sex was invariably associated with negative connotation, threatening imperatives, innuendo and put-downs.

"Don't you bring trouble 'ome, moi girl ... they won't respect you ... just say NO ... she's a tease ... they don't marry 'used goods' ... she's 'easy' ... don't let her lead you on ..."

After the Coward play I returned to volunteering at Fowey Hospital most weekends when not on away days with the St. John Ambulance at competitions and jamborees. During holidays I helped my sister Jane as well at the Cottage Hospital in Perranporth where she was a Nursing Sister. It was a lovely hospital with open views across gardens to the sea. Jane would give me an apron and sometimes a cap and I would help with meals and things like changing the water in the flower vases. Matron was lazy, however and sloppy regarding patient care, I was told.

One example was in her not allowing sheets to be changed if any of the patients wet the bed and she considered there was no excuse for it. Jane threatened to expose these practices to the News of the World and I agreed with her until Mother had the vapours, saying it would only bring us shame and notoriety. In those days this newspaper was read only by riff-raff. Jane soldiered on with little backing from her seniors. The local MP stood behind her until

changes were introduced and she was fortunately supported by her new fiancé, a physiotherapist at the same hospital. He was a handsome lad with an athletic build and was surfing champion of Perranporth. Eventually she became so dispirited she felt forced to hand in her notice.

Becoming a real nurse would be a walk in the park, I assumed. My St. John training was actually very good and I thought there would be a seamless transition after all my pre-nursing and first-aid experience. When I did walk on to my first ward, it felt as it did on my first day at infant's school and I wanted to faint with nerves. Only the thought of all those years of longing to be a "real nurse" from the age of three kept me there.

We lived in Lostwithiel until 1960 when I was sixteen, eight years in total. Jenny and I remained firm friends throughout that time. My class mates at Bodmin Grammar School, Jenny, Winnie and Sadie along with Pascal, Damien, Sulky Sis and later, Simon, would catch the special bus to school. It was laid on specially for us Chosen Few. We would frequently torment our Billy Bunter bus conductor, sometimes debagging him and dressing him up as a Bodmin Grammar School girl. Actually, he probably loved it!

Simon joined us for our final two years and set off a fire extinguisher on his first day. I vowed I would run away to an orphanage if any of my brothers or sisters did something like that in public just once more.

They did, of course. Probably the most embarrassing MacFarlane sibling episode occurred when Mother was local Tory Party Secretary at the time of the 1959 General Election. Eldest brother Morris was visiting on RAF leave and decided he would visit Jane in the hospital at Perranporth as well. Morris took Pascal and Damien along with him. The three of them returned home at around one o'clock in the morning somewhat inebriated.

"What'sh thish?" demanded Morris, pointing to a traitorous Labour Party poster someone had dared to paste over our local Tory MPs' grinning face on our garden gate. The boys crept around the house to Damien's shed in the back garden as quietly as they could and picked up paintbrushes and a tin of blue paint.

"Hi ho ..." began Morris.

"... it's off ... hic ... to work we go," continued Demonic Damien.

With only a cuspate moon to light their way around the village through shadows and back streets, the Booze Brothers systematically painted over every poster of the leery Labour candidate's poster face they could find. None were spared, from the elderly widow's parlour window on Fore Street to the Working Men's Club, over the 12th-century bridge and back along all streets from the station. It was an accomplished feat of malicious poster-daubing.

Why were the boys sniggering at breakfast, I wondered, with blue paint on their hands? Sulky Sis grassed on them on our walk to the station forecourt where the school bus waited. She pointed out every act of vandalism on the way, every messy blue daubing and I wished I wasn't there.

"Your brothers are idiots," said a rarely disgusted Jenny. "Mrs. P. is only an old widow. Now she'll have to get a chair out to stand on to clean up her window ..."

She was really cross with me for the only time I can remember. I was an innocent in the matter and red with shame.

That evening the village Bobby, the one we occasionally saw canoodling in mufti in the rushes along the mud flats, stopped at our garden gate and rocked back and forth gazing at the new Tory poster pasted on it.

"Time for the Inquisition," said Mother to her hung-over sons at the rat-a-tat tat at the door. They made themselves scarce.

"Oh, good evening Officer," she began, "can I help you?"

"Good evening to 'ee Missus MacFarlane. Er ... oh yes ..." he paused to remove his helmet. "It has come to moi attention that three tall gentlemen was witnessed by the signalman walking over Lostwithiel's bridge, hin the hearly hours of the morning. And Oi is wanting to ask you, Madam if the said gentlemen were your sons?

Because only tall personages could have damaged private property by deliberately painting over Labour posters around the town."

"Oh, no, Officer," Mother insisted, "my sons were away yesterday with my daughter in Perranporth."

While they were talking she noticed a trail of blue paint under the policeman's feet leading into the house. She stepped outside and began edging PC Plod back down the path.

"Well, we'll have to leave it for now, Madam," he said, taking the hint, "Oi do 'ave a darts match at The Monmouth in half an hour."

"Thank you, Officer. Dreadful business," Mother proffered. "All the more reason for The Tory Party to stay in power and sort out this worrying increase in hooliganism. Good night, Officer."

As Cornish folk tend to be pocket-sized, Ma MacFarlane's tall sons were a giveaway but we heard no more on the topic. Pascal was a police cadet at the time and mortified it would get back to his superiors in Sheffield.

It was only weeks later I again wished I was an only child. Damien and his mad friend John decided they would make their own lead weights for their fishing lines. The ideal supply they worked out, was on our doorstep, on the church roof in fact. It prompted yet another visit from the constabulary.

Jenny commented on my crazy family on one other occasion only, when she accused Sulky Sis of stealing one of her hard-to-find film star cigarette cards. She was very near to completing the set. It was a glamorous picture of Elizabeth Taylor I had admired but she knew I wouldn't have taken it. Ma and Jenny's mother had a 'pistols at dawn' as they were both as tough as they come and the missing cigarette card magically re-appeared. On the whole, there was a grudging approval of the antics the MacFarlanes got up to, livening up the town in the process.

It was fortunate the D.s were particularly good natured with what Damien and Jane had in mind for them next. Damien had just started experimenting with wire, batteries, speakers and microphones and things in his shed and decided one full moon it was time for a 'happening' in the churchyard. He managed to place a speaker from an old wireless set under Flo and Aden's bed next door and trail the wire out of the window and down to the shed. At about midnight, when their bedroom light had been off for a while, he began a solo performance, moaning into a microphone in a bucket accompanying himself with a tormented clanking of chains.

Flo couldn't wait to speak to Mother that morning.

"What is it, Florence?" Mother enquired of our unusually pale neighbour.

"Well, Oi never ... didn't you 'ear it in the noight, the noises from the graveyard? It put the fear of God into moi Aden and me ..."

Mother had words with Damien when he got back from school.

Jane was not averse to similar antics. She had become very interested in drama and performance, something to do with her nursing training maybe. When down one weekend visiting she told Aden she had a commission to interview him as a model worker, to be known as Comrade Adenski, for the BBC 'Russian Service.' Using one of the miniature tape recorders Pa had brought from Japan, Damien and she recorded the interview about his life at the milk factory as a model worker. It seemed to escape Aden's notice the interview was conducted with Jane speaking in a strong foreign accent.

Damien worked on the recording and the following week put the tape recorder inside the 'special' overseas radio set we lent them to listen to the broadcast in their living room. Flo and Aden listened in wonder as the 'broadcast' began.

"Well, Oi thinks that's smashing," said Aden afterwards, well-impressed with the interview going out across the Soviet Union. "Oi don't know how to thank 'ee. Oi've been telling them about it at the factory all week ... now we're roit famous ..."

Damien and Jane did come clean in the end and fortunately our neighbours loved the whole practical joke.

Placid Pascal was the first of us younger ones to leave Bodmin Grammar and then home. He returned to Sheffield to become a police cadet and boarded with Billy and Nuala. I also spent part of the Summer each year at their flat in Nether Edge.

Nuala was a warm Irish girl with an endearing humour. She was a benign rebel in contrast to Five-star Jane. Nuala would offer me the odd puff of a Nelson and teach me essential Gaelic like *pogue me hone!* ('kiss my butt!'). She had primed Billy with this phrase for his first meeting with her mother in Waterford saying it was a classic expression of welcome! She was the third grown-up to treat me as an equal, happy to let me help look after her picture-perfect little daughter Polly. She loved nattering about her and Jane's nurse training days at the Royal and the hell-raising they got up to. It ran in the family and was probably a reaction to our strict, or rather stifled, upbringing. Demonic Damien and Sulky Sis soon followed Pascal. Mother realised it would not be long before the house in Lostwithiel was empty and made arrangements for she, Simon and I to return to Sheffield at the end of my fourth year at senior school. It would not be too much of a wrench for me, much as I loved my friends. Village life for this teenager was beginning to be claustrophobic. In any case, I was getting closer to the start of nurse training which I had no doubt would commence at The Royal.

Damien's departure from Bodmin Grammar will doubtless never be forgotten. In his last term, our last year in Cornwall, he and other sixth formers managed the impossible, sneaking into the staff room on April Fool's Day and spiriting away the staff's very large, seasoned Brown Bess. The staff were incensed at the disappearance of their irreplaceable teapot and gated the whole school after lunch while chosen pupils went on a frantic search.

I don't think I imagined the evil eye us MacFarlanes got from our teachers for the remainder of our final term.

A theatre production marked the end of the Summer Term. Damien had written a priceless sketch for it that he and a group of Sixth Form friends performed, The Case of the Missing Teapot. The skinniest lad in the school appeared on stage in a loincloth and, in slow motion, struck a tiny dinner gong hanging centre stage. The lights dimmed and the curtain rose to the very teapot under spotlights. During the play the staff were represented with gowns and mortar boards and thumbs in their lapels with some blatant parodying of the more eccentric teachers.

The production was hilarious and very well received. I got several comments of approval from my teachers and was relieved that I might yet be able to leave town with this last performance having quashed all other MacFarlane deeds over the years in Lostwithiel and Bodmin that were best forgotten.

Jenny had been a loyal and tolerant friend, standing up for me whenever the going got tough. My family's background was so different from hers, yet she never remarked on it, nor about my being a weirdo Catholic. She was the wisest of friends.

We were now old enough to wear stockings and small heels as well as foam petticoats under our skirts to make them swirl and stand out

for Saturday night jigs in the Drill Hall and it was probably a good time for a change. 'Fifties pop music had reached Lostwithiel with Bill Haley's Rock Around the Clock and evil gyrating Elvis scandalising mothers of teenage girls. Mrs. D. liked Tommy Steele and Singing the Blues. Cliff's Living Doll was my favourite. Times they were a-changing. A social explosion had begun, fuelled by a new and vibrant popular music.

It looked as though it would take some time to sell the Old Vicarage but we left Lostwithiel anyway so Simon and I could start at our new schools in Sheffield in the Autumn term of 1960. Mine was Notre Dame High School. Our new house, a 1930s corner semi in Banner Cross Road, Ecclesall was close to Billy, Nuala and little Polly. It was a cold and soulless abode despite our artistic Mother's attempt at making it home. We were back in Sheffield after eight years in Cornwall, in exile it had occasionally felt.

My classmates at Notre Dame were a bunch of down-to-earth sweeties. Elaine, a quiet switched-on brown-eyed girl had an older heart-throb brother Mick at De La Salle College and we would be invited to parties with his pals. As luck would have it, Mick only ever teamed up with Robina, the prettiest girl in our year. Generally, the girls' brothers and friends, good Catholic boys, were there to chaperone us. This included my cousin Connor whom I had grown up with. He and his pal Phillip would bring their mates and our social life in the short time I was at this school was good. I just wished Jenny could have come along with our wonderful Cornish beaches!

I stayed on into the Sixth Year in September 1961 to re-sit two O-levels to get better marks and to take a new subject, Anatomy and Physiology. I wouldn't be doing A-levels because my pre-entry nursing cadet training was starting the following March. Having fewer lessons allowed me to join the drama club in which I secured star billing as Eliza Doolittle in Shaw's Pygmalion and Christy Mahon in Synge's The Playboy of the Western World.

My acting was lousy but the school buzzed about the Nuns forbidding me to utter Eliza's line "Not bloody likely!" It caused a sensation in 1912. Even Fishwives at the time were mortified with the suggestion this kind of language could be heard at Billingsgate. It was still a problem in 1961 at Notre Dame High and had to be substituted with "ruddy." Bets were on as to whether I would disobey our Upper Orders. I didn't know what I would do either!

When the moment came "Not *cough* bloody *cough* likely!" emanated from my mouth. Sister Monica was outraged and I saw her exit with her nose in the air. For a moment I didn't know if I would burst out laughing. I would have if my mother and Dear Flo had been there!

The school was doing well with the second play also. The Dublin audience rioted at its first performance in 1907 because of the mention of women's undergarments. As Christy, I had to wear a pair of men's working boots. I kept these in the classroom during rehearsals but they disappeared and I had to report it to my form teacher because they were symbolic to the play. This teacher was the one who invariably discovered magazines and cigarettes and things we should not have had in our desks through, she said, "divine visitation" to her on such matters.

During her next class everyone was tittering not because the boots had been located by the Holy Ghost but because Susan May, our Sophie Loren look-a-like was sitting quietly at her desk wearing them. What a contrast they were to her model-perfect pins! It was the funnier because she had never shown a sense of fun all the time we were at school. She was normally too svelte and sophisticated for that.

At our end of term musical concert I was also booked to do a turn. Damien had long owned a banjo and shown me easy chords. Jane's husband, Bernard the surfing champion and wannabe folk singer, had taught me Gone are the Days, a mournful negro spiritual.

Elaine and her best friend Val were my backing singers.

And so, a Star was born! Not me, of course, as my playing ability was about the same as my acting. It was Val's beautiful soprano voice that hit the rafters and bounced back to steal the show. She was lead soprano in the choir when the BBC recorded us singing unusual arrangements of The Lord is my Shepherd and *Ave Verum Corpus*.

Val was also a star in being the only person in the school who had a copy of Penguin's newly-published unexpurgated edition of Lady Chatterley's Lover. She daren't bring it to school in case the Holy Ghost nuked it. Instead, she invited Elaine and me back to her house in posh Dore in West Sheffield. Before we could read the sexy bits, Val had to shoo her hospitable mum into the kitchen so we could concentrate on our homework. We then sat on the stairs so we could see all comers. It was the 'daisy chain' bit we needed to read, apparently and pages were slowly turned. We were so ignorant about a sexual relationship like this one we understood almost nothing and could only titter as though we were well informed.

Our pronouncement, as was probably that of the jury in the recent trial about the book, was that it was all a bit tame! D. H. Lawrence I had found thoughtful but stilted so it was odd seeing the "f" and "c" words in print in a work of literature. It made us wonder what the Nuns would have made of Mellor's little daisy chain if they were having trouble with Shaw's "b" word!

Au revoir Jenny and family, the D.s next door, Gwynne and family, Wendy and Sadie; goodbye Par, Polkerris and Fowey beaches, Perranporth, Cornish pasties, Cornish ice-cream and clotted cream, liquorice laces and forbidden bubble-gum, Lostwithiel to Fowey train rides, five-stones, pick-up-sticks, Ludo and Snakes and Ladders, Monopoly, the Floral Dance, the Gay Gordon's, Guy Fawkes' Night, cigarette card collecting of 1950s Hollywood stars, Restormel Castle, Coulson Park, The Shelter, see-saw bumps, hopscotch and skipping, Girl Guides and St. John Ambulance, Lostwithiel Primary School and Mr. Kindly 'Dewdrop' Hawkins, Bodmin Grammar, step-sister Sybil, sherbet dips, roast chestnuts, 'Rock-around-the-clock,' foam petticoats, lime green socks, the beloved flea-pit, the annual carnival, the annual travelling fair, fishing with Pa and returning home smelling of lug-worm bait and eels and never catching anything over eight years!

Goodbye above all, to Jo Roper for stealing my first kiss and Michael Cole for my first disgusting French Kiss! And to Michael 'Elvis' Penhaligon for being a good pal, Mrs. Fry my French teacher who would undoubtedly have been French Fry had we known what they were, Lostwithiel floods, "'ello moi 'andsome!" my first bicycle and all those long, lazy Summer days.

Chapter Seven
#Thief# (Our Lady Peace)

My longed-for career as a fledgling nurse began in March 1962 with my being offered a place as a pre-entry nursing cadet at the esteemed Royal Hospital in Sheffield. After pre-entry nursing my SRN training would begin the following May. I was in the first year of the sixth form at Notre Dame High so I would be leaving half-way through A-Levels. Abandoning my Highers didn't worry me as I had passed the all-important Anatomy and Physiology GCE. A looming family crisis meant I wouldn't have been able to concentrate on schooling anyway.

It was made quite clear at my primary interview that I had better not emulate my mischievous sister Jane who had trained at the hospital thirteen years earlier. Her infamy was Olympic Gold, unsurpassed and immortalised by the time of my interview. It was not my imagination that Matron and her coven of Old School Sisters on the interview panel twitched at any reference to Jane, however oblique.

Ma confirmed she had been a reprobate at Notre Dame High as well as during her training at the hospital.

"What did she get up to at Notre Dame ..." I asked idly over breakfast.

"Oh, she was awful, Ro. We were forever being called up to the school. She once put a mouse in her form teacher's shoe. That was Sister Ursula. The poor woman fainted."

I asked if it was anything to do with her being an evacuee in Ireland during the War years.

"Oh, possibly, Ro, Dear. All three of them, Morris, Billy and Jane came back wild, filthy and lice-ridden. Billy was actually deported for running errands for the IRA."

Ma saw my interest and continued.

"He was six when he went and nine when they sent him back. He was a precocious little devil. We don't know exactly what he got up to but there was an incident with a U-boat. He was interviewed by the Prime Minister, de Valera and deported under Ireland's Emergency Powers Act."

My jaw dropped. This had been a well-kept family secret.

"And Morris?"

"Oh, Morris was a pain too. We had to fetch him home early. He was eleven but refused to go back to school because of some principle or other. Then he nearly died of diphtheria. Then Pascal caught it after they had a spitting competition. Billy nearly died of an asthmatic condition in Ireland and got diphtheria back in Sheffield as well. Pascal and Damien also went down with haemorrhagic measles. These were the worst times of our lives as parents, Ro. The war caused so much grief. It just never ended."

She agreed I had always behaved though I reminded her of the time I went swimming in the Fowey against her wishes. She reminded me I was silly enough to hang my wet costume on the line.

"Thank goodness you're not a prankster.," she said smiling. "May you restore the MacFarlane good name Child. Now you had better get along to school ..."

The looming crisis that was to take over the rest of the year was a rare and aggressive form of bone cancer, a Ewing's Tumour. Demonic Damien apparently ignored a lump in his thigh for some months until about the time of my pre-entry acceptance letter. His GP referred him to hospital for a biopsy on a now egg-sized bulge. I did not know that certain cancers progress slowly through older patients but roar through young bodies. Damien was twenty-one years old.

Because Pa was back at sea when the Ewing's Tumour diagnosis was confirmed it fell on my second oldest brother Billy to break the news to Ma that the son she cherished most was possibly going to die.

"It's as bloody hard as telling the Pope that God himself has cancer ..." moaned Billy after we'd sounded out every which way of telling Ma. The other three older siblings had left home and were part of the MacFarlane Diaspora in London. Following suit, eager to be cool after our Cornish backwater, Damien had joined them briefly after being dismissed from the Navy for covering up his asthmatic condition. He had set his heart on a career in the Royal Navy as far back as I can recall.

Because Jane was pregnant and away from Sheffield it was decided, secretly from Mother, I would take charge of Damien's care at home while he underwent the crude treatments on offer. In the 'Sixties, patients were not told they had cancer and our resorting to lies, lies and more lies soon became as stressful as having to manage Damien's unrelenting physical deterioration. People feared the word 'cancer' more than the word 'death,' perhaps because treatment was barbaric and mortality high. At least I had Billy, Nuala and my Sheffield police officer brother Pascal on hand.

It was make or break for Naked Nurse. Her training had not even begun.

Although Mother had helped Father during the Blitz and dealt with a steady flow of injured and wounded at our back door and brought us up almost single-handedly in Cornwall, there was the strong possibility she would lose the will to live over this matter of her favourite son. How was I meant to cope with my brother possibly dying and watch my majestic mother go quietly over the edge? So overpowering was this last concern Damien's cancer was almost a side issue.

We had all witnessed her raging episodes of frustration ending with her fainting as if dead. Recent rows were almost always triggered by my dumbfounded father being confronted with "how do you expect me to carry family responsibilities while you're living the life of Riley on cruise ships ..."

On the day Billy saw Damien's consultant, Ma arranged to come over to Billy's house. I was already there feeling sick with the anticipation of what would happen when the beans were spilt about the concerning lump. I was cleaning the cupboards in Nuala's tiny kitchen as a diversion when the doorbell rang. Nuala and I clung to each other, listening at the living room door.

"Um, you know I had a meeting with Damien's orthopaedic consultant this morning ..." Billy began.

"Yes, of course."

"Um ... it isn't good news. It's a Ewing's Tumour."

"Oh, God! Not ... no ..."

"They hope it hasn't spread but ... anyway ... they want to try radium first. And see how it goes. We just have to hope ..."

Nuala and I waited for the scream.

To her credit Ma didn't scream. She wept openly for a moment then fell calm. This was too serious a situation for any acting and as we came in and sat down she looked at each of us with a sadness in her eyes I will never forget. It was at this moment toddler Polly came carefully down the stairs from the bathroom, burst into the living room and announced,

"Granny, I've done a 'hardy' as big as a wardrobe!"

Damien was in the Jackson Orthopaedic Ward at the Royal recovering from his biopsy surgery. Mother said she couldn't see him just yet so Nuala and I went to the hospital that evening. This was the first occasion we had to lie as we decided to tell him he had a bone infection. Nuala did the talking and was wonderful, full of smiles and reassurance but when we left the hospital the strain showed on her face.

"This is going to be hard," she said squeezing my hand.

Back home in Banner Cross Road Ma had gone into damage limitation mode. She was absolutely insistent that nurses – and she included me – or not, we were never to divulge the fact her son had cancer. We had to be careful in public too, lest anyone should overhear and it got back to him. Damien was relatively fit and would be leaving the ward the following day. He had already said he wanted to do several things, including go out walking and see friends while undergoing treatment. This top secret aspect was surely part of Mother's denial. If she didn't hear it, it wasn't there. Damien would certainly not hear of his terminal condition from hospital staff. It was much later we learned that he knew about the cancer from the beginning.

I was too overwhelmed to cry after the ward visit, until I got off the bus. It was the lying I found hardest; lie after stupid lie that had already undermined the dignity my brother should have been accorded. My friend Pamela meeting me outside our house so we could do our homework together was the trigger and I began bawling. Eventually I told her what was wrong. I felt better but was now a traitor and urged Pamela to keep it secret. She was the only friend I told and it enabled me to leave the House of Horrors behind over the coming months and pretend that life was normal.

The initial comfort I felt after confiding in Pamela lasted until assembly next morning. Our formidable headmistress, Ice-pick Sister Monica appeared clasping the end of the long wooden Rosary she wore around her waist, doubtless a visible indication of her virginity. She immediately began beseeching that we pray for a young man with leg cancer who could die at any moment but who had turned his back on the Church.

Tired as I was from having been awake two nights comforting Mother, I thought for a moment that Sister Monica must have a direct line to God. My brother was surely still the handsome, six-foot two-inch lad I had seen in the ward the previous evening who would shortly be out and about. I rushed off after assembly without permission and knocked on her door.

"Oh, my D-e-a-h, I had no idea," Sister gasped on learning Damien would be out of hospital the following day.

Her pinhole eyes enlarged by pebble glasses showed some distress as she explained that Father Murphy, a friend of Billy and Nuala, had sent out a communiqué asking that his co-priests, local nuns, the staff at Notre Dame High and the Christian Brothers at De la Salle pray for Damien's lost and possibly damned soul. I accepted the excuse and felt slightly better in that my older brother or Nuala had also told 'someone else' of the cancer.

It was inevitable the spectre of religion would loom large in a Catholic family especially with me at a Catholic School. In exchange for praying to every saint going over the coming months all the Church offered was suspension of belief and hollow promises. We existed in two universes, one surreal, the other deluded, right up until the day Damien died.

Catholicism didn't seem to have taken a hold down in Cornwall so my experience of a Catholic school was a late one. On my first day at Notre Dame High the nuns welcomed my sixteen-year old soul as if I was so spiritually deprived it had shrivelled and all but gone to the Devil. The fact that I was changing schools and Examining Boards a year before my GCEs bothered them not a jot. It was my Catholic indoctrination that had to be brought up to speed with special lessons, extra homework, careful study of hagiologies and a closer reading of the New Testament. I was also piled up with outside reading the Church deemed essential, including a not particularly uplifting book, Against Communism.

To be fair, the nuns were very kind to me knowing about my brother. I'd had a bad time at the beginning of the year being treated as a fast girl in need of salvation because I had varnished my toenails. I was reported to the nuns by our gym mistress Miss Wayne and wasn't allowed to forget my admonishment over tempting sin and attracting the type of boys who "walk around with the Pill in their pocket."

The contraceptive pill became available for married women at Family Planning centres in several cities in the UK in 1961 and throughout the country from 1962. Moral and medical argument raged over it but the Sisters were fighting a losing battle. By 1969 more than a million women in Britain, married and single, were in control of their fertility and by extension, their sexuality.

I was a good teenager in 1962, trusting and noble and so used to being put upon I had no notion of there being a Me. I wasn't alone in feeling that home, school and Church were united in quashing even the tiniest rasp of thinking we might matter in our own right. The nuns fussing over me and hauling me off to every religious gathering was oddly comforting despite the ribbings from my more daring jive-mad, hair-do flouncing classmates.

In April 1962, just after his cancer diagnosis, Damien met Anne, a newly-qualified paediatric nurse from the local children's hospital. They took to each other instantly. Despite her knowing he might die she committed herself to comforting him. I had already learned that children's nurses are a race apart even among nurses. Anne was of this mould, optimistic, fun and deeply caring. She never wavered through Damien's rapid decline.

Damien began his treatment in June for radium therapy and guinea pig Mustard Gas chemotherapy. There was no obvious deterioration in his health for the first three months and it gave us the false hope that treatment was working. Mother insisted Father remain at sea so Damien would believe his illness was only an acute bone infection. Though nasty, it was curable. Neither Damien nor the household were strangers to hospitals. He had endured many bouts of life-threatening asthma since childhood. This was on top of the other war-induced illnesses Mother mentioned.

Ma and Pa bought David a Morgan, a sports car he was passionate about. They could only do this with a loan from the family's 'rich uncle,' Uncle David, Mother told me later. He loved it but it was soon parked outside the house unused and a very visible reminder his strength was waning. I felt very sorry for my parents and this desperate act.

Near the end of my final term at Notre Dame High I was called out of chapel at school and urged to hurry home as an unspecified emergency had arisen. The flustered old nun did her best to comfort me as I wailed this was surely the end. I set off on the two-mile walk home through Ecclesall Woods with my head full of the hushed tones that surround cancer and its prognosis as a plague hinted at through Jane and Nuala's medical mutterings of greedy gobbling metastasising growths with terminal pain beyond measure.

The emergency was a new lump on Damien's upper arm. The poor sod had taken Billy into the garden shed to show him. Billy was white as a sheet and Mother and Jane were on the sofa sobbing. David had taken himself out for a spin in his beloved car.

What did they want from me, I puzzled, until it clicked. They were looking at me to do something, to be the grown-up ... The best I could at that moment was make a pot of tea.

After confirmation the cancer had not been contained there was a visible deterioration in my brother's health. Each week a new lump indicating secondary cancer developed in his lungs, spine and brain. Harsher treatment at hospital only sapped his strength making him anaemic and needing regular blood transfusions. Well-meaning priests and nuns remained determined to kid us to the end while chiding us for not having faith. Lies and pretence were now really ramping up.

It didn't help that Billy had a breakdown during the Summer severe enough for him to be admitted to a psychiatric unit where he stayed for several weeks. Damien was puzzled.

"Grown men don't blub," he remarked, unable to see it in terms of his brother watching him die.

When Billy returned from the psychiatric clinic he was banished to the attic bedroom of our house to get a grip on himself because he could not stop weeping. Nuala was visiting her own sick mother in Ireland and came home early to a wreck of a husband.

In the family now, along with the denial of cancer, I was witnessing punitive treatment of a bereft Billy condemned for letting mother down. Sulky Sis had packed her bag weeks before and disappeared to London after announcing it was my job to look after Damien and Mother. We didn't see her again for years. Clearly battling mental health problems she became an anorexic recluse. Her brother's demise was simply another situation she couldn't handle after walking out on her nurse training at St. Mary's in Paddington and being sacked from the RAF because of her anorexia.

I tried to understand the suffering of both my brothers and would take Billy his tea in the attic and sit with him as he wept. I did the same for Damien but seeing one adult male crying inconsolably and another losing his hair with his skin stretching across his bones only strengthened my feeling that my world was about to collapse.

At seventeen, most of me wanted to get back to the teenage world of youth clubs and innocent parties my school pals were hopping off to. Life was moving on all around. Trad Jazz stomps had been rejected in favour of back-combed hair, loopy fashions and the new and exciting sound of electric guitars.

My relationship with Damien changed as I spent more time with him, even though he had been an unforgivably sadistic bully to his three younger siblings for years. It was only when I began nursing I realised his behaviour could have had something to do with the stimulant drugs he took daily to keep his asthma under control.

Religion had also caused much guilt over the years because I believed my earlier hatred and anger towards him was sinful. Our priest at Par in Cornwall had notched up many confessions on the matter from when I was seven onwards. Although feeling compassion now, I still had to battle resentment at Damien bringing grief home with the cancer. Psychotherapists tell us we can think what we like but it is actions we are responsible for. Catholic admonishment told us we are accountable for every thought, word and deed.

Part of the bullying had been Damien's sexual abuse for two or more years in Cornwall when I was at an age I believed babies were found under gooseberry bushes. It wasn't penetrative sex, as far as I am aware, more 'messing about.' I hated him doing such things but did experience ambivalence as it was preferable to the pain and angst of being hit. I knew what he was doing was wrong but didn't know why. On the day he stopped because I "might get pregnant" he gave me the family facts of life book to be read, almost as a guilty secret. It was written by a nun and I was none the wiser about pregnancy after poring over it. It remained one big puzzle.

On the very same day in Coulson Park in Lostwithiel an off and on pal, Jilly Crow, was on the swing surrounded by her faithful little gang. She called to me in her thick Cornish brogue,

"Have 'ee 'ad it, yet then, Rose?"

Her friends tittered. I went bright red because of things Demonic Damien was doing to me when Ma was not around.

"Had ... what?" I stuttered, terrified she actually knew about it.

"Your period!"

"What's that, then?" I asked cautiously, trying to remember if I had seen the word while flicking through Pa's medical books. *Menses* I would have understood.

"Well, if 'ee dun't know. I ain't gonna tell 'ee then!"

My way of coping was to rise at six every morning to attend Mass. I also offered a thirty-day prayer to the Virgin Mary in exchange for a promise of a miracle. Walking to my local church on those bright summer mornings did give me a sense of purpose. Saint William's priest Father Keegan was a towering, unassuming middle-aged man with the look of a young Brando. I developed an innocent attachment to him as he was such a calming influence. The Big C was now on free reign at home rendering everyone useless and everything hopeless. Father Keegan was a constant presence offering unremitting kindness and encouragement to me.

It also hit hard when my lifeline school friends Elaine and Pamela told me of their plans to be away for the Summer earning money for their Autumn start at college. Mother said a definite no to my going away as well. The entire family were destined for Golgotha. My designated 'sack cloth and ashes' reading was a Thomas Kempis book The Imitation of Christ and The Lives of the Saints. I found their austere lifestyles and faith in the supernatural appealing. Damian was suffering beyond belief and I could only hope he would be guaranteed a happy afterlife in God's navy as Admiral-in-chief.

The mind copes as best it can when pitched into a nightmare scenario. Counselling and support was non-existent and as I couldn't talk about it to anyone except Anne, the Catholic Church came a good second. Suffering, was after all, their game.

I left my haven, Notre Dame High School, for the last time in July 1962 with a deep sense of despair. Walking home through Ecclesall Woods I began tearing up my hymn book watching the crumpled paper float off in the wind. It was not much of a comment on the end of my schooling.

"On Margate Sands, I could connect nothing with nothing," wrote T. S. Eliot during his breakdown.

My rage lapsed into a bleak sobbing in dappled sunlight under Horse Chestnut trees.

"'Ere Duck, you dropped these ..." a little Thora Hird said, scuttling after me with some torn hymnody. "Don't take on, so, Luv. It'll all cum reet int' morning. Was you tearing up ye luv letters, then?" She walked with me to the bus station at Temple Bar talking quietly about her family and losing her sons in the War, perhaps trying to cheer me up. I couldn't concentrate.

Mother did her utmost to cope and held up much of the time. She had long taken barbiturates to help her sleep. These were Tuinal and Seconal, the only sedatives available at the time. It was understandable that her insomnia had come from the war years with eight babies to look after and constantly broken routines. The dose she was taking was sufficient to knock a horse out as I discovered months later when she offered me Seconal one morning to help me sleep when a run of night duty finished and I needed to get ready for days.

Anne, Father Keegan and Nuala remained stalwarts regarding Damien's deterioration. My favourite cousin Connor also showed great empathy and introduced me to his sixth-form school pals at De La Salle College. One of his friends, Phillip, I had already met at a Saint Vincent's Catholic youth club where Jo Cocker played in his early days. Both Connor and Philip were lively characters who would come over to cheer Mother up. Philip would take me for drives around Derbyshire. He was the eldest in a family with an invalid dad so he knew how it was. For me, meeting a genuinely considerate person who adored his long-suffering mother was a giant leap in understanding that males could be non-macho and openly kind.

Philip's background was one of poverty and the impetus for his demonstrating a work ethic and determination to do well. For now, his badge of honour was the carrying around of a new LP, as it was for Mick and Keith of the Rolling Stones when they were at school. Girls tended to buy soppy singles with their pocket money until Beatles albums went on sale. Philip introduced me firstly to John D. Loudermilk whom he revered, then to other artists. He would also write hilarious letters to me with 'Kilroy' drawings.

Early in August, a bald and Belsenesque Damien asked to return to Cornwall for a week with me, Ma and Pa. He wanted to see his long-time school friend John Debenham with whom he had collaborated on many whacky projects. All went reasonably well, though John and others, not knowing of Damien's illness were visibly shocked by his appearance. I was happy to see my childhood friend and 'twin' Jenny again but remained silent about my brother's condition.

On our return to Sheffield Damien could barely walk. Unbelievably, he was involved in a car crash as a passenger and not in his Morgan and was taken to hospital with a head injury. It happened on the one weekend my exhausted parents went away for a break. Jane and Nuala had come to the house to take over. My parents' recall was the lowest point for all of us at the time. Listening to them debating it might have been better if he had died in the crash, I had to get out of the house.

He was by then guzzling tubes of Veganin, an over-the-counter analgesic mix of paracetamol, codeine and caffeine. In the 'Sixties morphine was only available for the cancer sufferer's last days. He began confiding in me over more personal matters. He was fond of Anne but did not love her, he admitted. To my great discomfort he told me he had been unable to make love to her recently. He was also still smarting at having been thrown out of the Navy because of his asthma, as it was all he'd ever wanted to do. I was too inexperienced to be of any help other than to sit quietly listening.

When I undertook a Marie Curie course two decades later I felt wretched not having the skills when sitting with my brother. I could have eased his fear and angst considerably by being open and gently up front. The course showed how questions should be fed back to the patient.

"Have I got cancer, nurse ... is that what is worrying you? I'll ask the doctor to talk to you ... How long have I got? Perhaps I should get my affairs in order ... I am not one who favours time limits but it isn't a bad idea to do this anyway, don't you think ...

It was Anne breezing through the house that saved us all. She would kiss Damien's ghostly face and stroke his bald head. She would sponge his profuse cold sweats as necessary and calm his anxious, laboured breathing. Such tasks would have repulsed most non-nurses and some nurses too. Anne went beyond this. She would lie on his bed and cuddle him, doing her best to make him feel like a normal twenty-two year old.

She often invited me to the flat she shared with other staff nurses to get me out of the house. With my training about to start it felt good being with girls who would be my seniors being so kind at the time. I felt privileged to be Anne's friend.

When Damien came home from care at the hospital to be with his family for a short while he began weeping, just as Billy had during his breakdown. He told me he now understood why Billy had cried and that he was truly sorry for having berated him.

Father came home on compassionate leave to oversee Damien's pain control. We were now unable to reach Damien, even with humour. He was out of it most of the time, thankfully sleeping for ever longer periods with the quantity of Brompton Cocktail (an equal mix of gin, cocaine and morphine given to terminal patients) he was requesting.

He didn't want be left alone after Extreme Unction. Mother had to go elsewhere during this, the last sacrament. God might yet intervene, Father Murphy insisted to the end and make Damien well again.

Damien requested he return to The Royal on the weekend of October 20th. 1962. The day after, Jane, Nuala and I sat outside orthopaedic Arthur Jackson Ward opposite Matron Welburn's office, waiting for afternoon visiting time. We managed to smile at the many hilarious escapades this beguilingly eccentric character had been involved in during his twenty-two years of life. There were things Nuala had not heard from Billy.

My brother was a complex character touched with a vital creative and inventive energy. He and Pascal would cry with laughter at the silliness of the Goons and brilliant comic timing in Hancock's Half-hour. If he was not making exquisite model ships and aeroplanes he would be scripting plays for radio, including one with Cornish John about an infamous and fictitious Battle of the Tiddy-Oggy (Cornish pasty). He could have been Peter Cook's doppelganger. He looked like him and had a similar surreal sense of the absurd.

When a teenager he had taken over old Bodmin Prison, then a derelict building and opened a Beatnik jazz club. Brother Pascal played clarinet and became a good jazzer in his own right. Beatniks were about in darkest Cornwall in the late 'Fifties along with artist and sculptor communities, annual carnivals, the Padstow Hobby Horse and the Helston Floral dance. Ma believed her side of the family was related to both Alexander Graham Bell and Robert Louis Stevenson and this surely was the reason for Damien's precocious inventive and creative personality.

His last weekend on Earth was spent in a side ward in Arthur Jackson Ward. Matron Welburn came breezing out of her office while I was sitting with Jane and Nuala in the corridor waiting again for visiting time on the ward. Jane and Nuala fell uncomfortably silent.

"Hello, my Dear," tall, elegant Matron began, ignoring her former miscreant nurses, "I understand you are to start with us this Monday as a cadet nurse. I think it best you take a week off before you begin. Goodbye."

Not a caring word about Damian did she utter. It was a foretaste of this God-like woman's cold *hauteur*. What was I doing signing up to years of this sort of thing I wondered just as Nuala and Jane began spluttering like naughty schoolgirls. At least it was the first time in months we had giggled.

Two nights later my three older brothers who had gone to sit with Damien returned at two in the morning, their Thermos flasks unopened, to tell us he had died. Between us we had kept Damien company day and night because he said he didn't want to be alone. Now my tall, slim brother with tawny wavy hair, dark eyebrows and intelligent, slate-green eyes was gone.

Father woke Mother with the news that their son was now at peace. She let out a heart-stopping scream as she had apparently done when her brother Bill died after his plane was shot down in May 1944. Pa sedated her. When the hospital rang later that morning to say flowers had arrived on the ward for him and what should they do with them, I went upstairs to ask. Mother was still in bed and Father was up and dressed in his immaculate Savile Row suit, staring out of the window. He let out a choking sound I had never heard, before blowing his nose. This was my lowest moment.

In my subsequent nursing career I experienced many reactions to death. Most people react with a resigned sadness and go onto autopilot, getting to grips with the fact they will never speak or laugh or cry with their loved one ever again. Relatives have also screamed at me, hit out, fainted, laughed or become hysterical. Seeing my brother's lonely coffin 'lying in' at St. William's Church, Ecclesall was harrowing but he had company to the end, with my three older brothers keeping a vigil. I sobbed, finally, when he was lowered into the ground at Abbey Lane Cemetery.

Mother later told me Father blamed himself for not being in theatre at the time of Damien's first biopsy. The consultant had apologised for not applying a tourniquet to Damien's leg and requesting an immediate biopsy report. If Damien's leg had been amputated at that stage to prevent secondaries being released into the blood stream he may have survived. What had happened was a "letting the cat out of the bag" one oncologist explained. It was a death sentence by default. Ewing Tumours only affect young people and still today, I read of heroic youngsters who do not make it. Edward Kennedy's son survived because his leg was amputated early.

The Church had its way to the end with Damien 'dying in Grace.' It was more for Mother's benefit that she and I fretted how we could get him to wear a Miraculous Medal as he became increasingly dismissive about the Catholic faith over the months. When we visited him in hospital in his last week we saw a visiting nun had 'miraculously' persuaded him to wear one. He had also agreed to Extreme Unction, the final guarantee of Grace in the Church's eyes, and to giving his last confession to Father Murphy.

"Look boy, you are going to die ..." the priest said.

"I know, Father, I've always known," Damien responded.

The priest passed this information on to us, that Damien had read hospital notes left inadvertently on his bed and secretly gone to Sheffield's main library to look up his prognosis. He knew from the very beginning he was likely to die but didn't let on, most probably to spare Mother's feelings.

It was repugnant having freckle-faced 'Ryan O'Neil' look-a-like Father Murphy involved with family matters in this way. He had abused me when I was eleven years old, pinning me against the back wall of the church trying to go further than just kissing me. He was later thrown out of the Church for years of sexual impropriety.

I thought long and hard about many things in the months afterwards. I decided it was far less harmful to believe in fairies than in the overwhelming and impersonal machinery of the Catholic Church in the matter of a drawn-out death. It had caused our family to self-destruct on the one hand while also preventing me from self-destructing on the other. Thirty years later I was grateful for counselling that made me realise I wasn't able to deal with my brother's death at the time. It enabled me to feel sadness for that used-and-abused little girl of long ago and understand the naïve seventeen-year old who, like anyone else of that age caring for a dying relative, should not have had to muddle through so many raw emotions and memories.

Thankfully, Dame Cicely Saunders and her remarkable hospice movement are persuading medical staff that patients have a right to know, changing the notion that Dr. Daddy knows best. If a hospice's insightful help had been available they would have worked with Mother to show how lying about his terminal diagnosis cancelled out any prospect of an open, honest dialogue with Damien. It would have lessened the pain on both sides had we all been able to share the truth with dignity.

Years later Mother told me that after her brother Bill was shot down in 1944 over occupied France, Damien became the person who mattered most to her. She made no apology in saying she had to love someone, nor for her bald statement she had fallen out of love with Pa years before.

"You would only understand if you went through a war, Ro," she intimated. "I fell for one of brother Bill's pals, an Australian bomber pilot. He was so much like Bill. Sadly, he was shot down as well as Bill. I didn't know at the time if I would be able to cope with it all."

I was shocked at Mother opening her heart late one night when the third great love of her life, Damien was dying. I had always sensed her inner despair and tried to respond as best I could by not causing any trouble, unlike my needier older sisters. Then, as a teenager I felt for her but I was also angry internally that she had no insight, or even seemed to care, at how her traumatic life had affected us younger ones.

Many things fell into place, including the reason when Pa was away, our family GP had insisted Damien rest from his chronic asthma attacks at Truro Sanatorium rather than at home. It was to give them a rest from each other. I also began to understand Damien's seemingly omniscient powers in being able to lift her moods and why she smiled when he entered the room. Even if she knew he had been spiteful to us moments before she would have made some excuse on his behalf.

It was shortly before his death he told me it had been a burden through his teenage years knowing Mother was in love with him. It was the reason, he said, he wanted to leave home and travel the world. It is a pathology I have seen many times since in other mothers' obsession with a treasured son. It never came to sex in my family example but there were elements of a Jocasta Complex.

Damien lies in the family grave in Abbey Lane Cemetery with Ma, Pa, beloved sister Jane and sadly in 2013, brother Pascal. Much loved Nuala lies nearby.

Chapter Eight
#First Day at Work ...# (Daniel Johnston)

On my first day as a Green Girl at that most prestigious nursing coalface, The Royal Hospital, Sheffield, I went in the back gate and reported to the Deputy Matron, Sister Foggart. The reputation of this ex-army dynamo was fearsome and I stood to attention quivering. What unnerved me more from the start of my interview was the glimmer of sympathy, even concern, in her cow-sad eyes. Holding back a Lady Bower Dam-full of suppressed sadness a week after my brother's death, the last thing I wanted was anything that would trip off a session of inconsolable bawling.

Fortunately, Sister's eyes quickly hardened as she settled into the hospital's Commandments of Dos and Don'ts and the many things that were and were not expected of me through my six months of pre-nurse training. When she had finished grilling she escorted me at speed to the laundry room where I picked up my shapeless, bilious green uniform and was pointed in the direction of the Nurses Changing Room. I was then to report to Women's Surgical, Edgar Allen Ward.

That was it, my introduction to real nursing. I was now a Green Girl in sack-like, passion-killing attire more associated with a penitentiary feeling the lowest of the low in the nursing hierarchy. Nevertheless, I managed a smile on entering the ward feeling mighty privileged to be in the Holy of Holies of British hospitals.

My first ward allocation, Women's Surgical, was on the ground floor by Jackson Ward. Those early days passing the ward in which my brother spent his last days were hard. Each time I passed on lunch or tea breaks or on ward errands I wanted to see that he really was not there, that I might yet take him home, fit and well. My mind had yet to process the fact he was gone for good.

It didn't help that I didn't know a soul at the hospital, not even the only other two Green Girls on the premises. I was an invisible 'gofer.' I also missed my school friends badly. It was some compensation being number seven in my merciless family in that I was long used to being seen and not heard. It was anyway, worth enduring now I was on my way to becoming a real nurse.

115

The Sister in charge of Edgar Allen Ward, Sister Froggart (not Deputy Matron Sister Foggart) shared top billing at the hospital with Sister at ENT (Ear, Nose and Throat) in causing nurses to lose sleep and pounds of weight. I had been primed by my sister Jane about Sister Froggart's domain, Edgar Allen. She was a ferocious Old-school perfectionist with the nickname Aunty Girty, one of Matron's Rottweilers and one of the hospital's Spinsters from Hell. She resembled a kindly Thora Hird, until she lost her temper. If any of us were not giving one hundred per cent we risked public slaughter.

I soon learned that the speedy clack-clacking of her highly-polished court shoes was the warning she was glowing like an incendiary and that one of her student nurses was the likely target. Our Thora Hird would then morph. I became almost used to being as tense as a cocked pistol when she was on duty.

"Call yourself a student nurse?" she bawled at this frozen blob of Green Girl even before her very first morning break. "Yer couldn't bootter a buttercup the right way up, yer useless mess of a Miss ..."

So lowly were Green Girls, my first day's induction was actually left to the cleaner, Grace. She was Sister Froggart's trusted ally and the power behind the mops. Her companion was a thumb-sized, roly-poly, twizzle-eyed Minnie Mae who had a voice like a door squeak and took the world on her shoulders. This loyal duo could almost handle Aunty Girty. When they did manage to placate Sister after an incident her oak-brown eyes would soften and she would smile, revealing slightly buck teeth.

At the end of my first day, I went to request permission to make my way home.

"So you're Jane MacFarlane's sister ..."

Sister Froggart leaned on the ward cupboard looking me up and down with a "nowt but trouble, 'er," look, all over her face.

"Er, yes, Sister."

"'Ay, well I'm watching you. Just remember, you'll cop it if you take after 'er. Off you go now and you'd better not drop any more trays ..."

I winced, remembering the look from her during the doctors' rounds that morning that would have melted the Devil's horns. Pitying looks from every corner of the ward shrivelled my virgin soul as the fortunately empty metal tray hit the ward's speckled stone floor just as the senior surgical consultant Mr. Anderson walked in.

"You're Bill MacFarlane's lassie, aren't you?" he asked kindly in the shattered silence that followed.

"Yes, Sir."

"Give him my regards and my condolences to your family, won't you, Dear Girl."

"Thank you, Sir," I spluttered.

I had never seen him before but had heard my parents mention him as a colleague of my father's when a GP. Pa had now been at sea for thirteen years and how this eminent man knew who I was remains a mystery. He saved my fragile confidence over that blunder. He saved me from a roasting as well.

It was fortunate I got on well with Sister from the start and soon wanted to give her a hug. Her generation did not 'do' physical contact and I felt her occasional outburst during the week could have been due to something lacking in her personal life. There were whispers of a wartime love interest. Her ward cleaning team were very supportive and once I had proved I was reliable and not 'posh,' I was welcomed into their tight universe.

Ward sisters had complete control over their territory in those days. Wards were efficiently run and the devoted, long-term domestic staff were zealous about keeping them spick and span. This regime didn't just rest with the Sisters. Matron or her deputies would carry out twice-daily rounds. All were obsessive about high-calibre patient care and cleanliness. Customs and practices were many and included daily dressings being changed only after dust had settled after bed-making and cleaning. Patients were only permitted two visitors at a time for one hour a day. Visitors could sit on bedside chairs, never on the patient's bed. Nurses stood at the door to count visitors in. There was zero tolerance to sloppiness from staff.

I spent most of my Green Girl ward time learning these things, along with scrubbing, cleaning, airing, fetching and carrying and disinfecting everything used by the patients. I took orders from the cleaners and other nurses on duty as well as Sister. I would polish bedpans if asked by the cleaners, if they were pushed for time. They had the authority on Sister's nod to keep trainee nurses in line and make sure we learned the ropes. Once I was part of Sister Froggart's clique and knowing I could calm her when she was on the rampage, nervous students allied with me.

Sister did make Grace and Minnie Mae's lives difficult on occasion, usually at mealtimes on doctor's round days. She would preside over the trolley issuing instructions and serving meals so quickly we had to run like rats around the ward with the trays. There was no room for error, a forgotten fork or water glass. You had one chance with the salt pots. It was not the time to buckle under a tongue-lashing.

"Nah, Nursie," Minnie Mae hissed at me once in the corner of the ward, "don't let Sister catch you booing. She'll 'ave your guts for starters!"

Mae's pea-green headband had slipped down over one eye from her running back and forth.

"Now, 'oo put the lettuce on the hot trolley? Can't you see it melting ..." Sister barked, a little more friendly than she had just been to me. "It'll be Nero, here, no doubt!"

On these fraught days if everything had gone according to schedule Sister Froggart would be calmer when the puddings had been served. This was the time Minnie Mae would consolidate gains.

"Ee, yer 'air looks loovly today, Sister Fwoggart. Pure pewter."

Sister would sigh, patting her softly-permed hair, her brown eyes reminding me of Lame Daisy's at Fanshawgate. Only at such moments could we relax.

As nurses-to-be we were well aware that Old School Sisters had given their life to their work. We did occasionally make derogatory remarks about demonic spinsters, spinster being a term of dread for us young singles, reasoning that this partly explained their occasional blowing up. On the whole, it was a seminal experience working under a dying breed of nurses from Matron down who belonged in thought, word and deed to the Florence Nightingale tradition of absolute vocation. Nightingale died in 1910 and our seniors in 1963 could have been trained by nurses who may have known, or even worked with the *Grande Dame* of nursing.

The Royal Hospital enjoyed its excellent reputation because of the dedicated hierarchy of Matron Welburn, her deputies and her dedicated team of Ward Sisters. Consultants had little to do with the day-to-day running of the hospital, though an irascible 'Sir Lancelot Spratt' could be found in every training hospital. For these Doctor Gods at a time when the NHS was still esteemed around the world for its pioneering free care from cradle to grave it must have been a celestial existence. No one, especially us underlings questioned the authority of these people.

Student nurses understood they were incidental to a system that demanded the highest calling. A few younger Sisters were married and had a life. The Old Girls in Blue were dedicated long-term gatekeepers who had no life outside their wards. Their presence ensured that even the most recalcitrant student nurse came to heel, or departed. Ninety-nine per cent remained and passed their Hospital and ultimately, their State Finals.

One Saturday in March after my eighteenth birthday and near the end of my six months as a Green Girl, my friend Phillip came over to the house with his best mate Bob to take me out for a ride in the car. Freckle-faced Bob had his head out of the car window as I came down the garden path. He was waving an album at me.

"This, Rose, you have gotta hear!"

We listened to the album later on a Dansette. It was a turning point for all us youngsters, The Beatles Please, Please Me album. The group's single Love, Love Me Do was released in early October, just before Damien's death. I hadn't been aware of this or their first hit single Please, Please Me released in January 1963. The album was something else and the vibrancy it stirred in an age group that had a James Dean trying to break out of all of us told me I was getting to grips with things. That evening was almost the first time I was thinking about something other than my training.

My Green Girl training went well and Sister Froggart gave me an excellent report. Sister, Grace and Minnie Mae also presented me with my first nurse's fob-watch with the comment "we're reet glad to be shot of yer ... now go and show 'em 'ow its done the Edgar Allen Ward way!"

Euphoria did not extend to life at home where I was now alone most of the time with my mother. Night after night I would be sitting on her bed talking, talking and talking about anything to distract her. She was afraid to sleep because she would dream Damien was alive. Occasionally she wept enough tears to fill the River Jordan. I felt disoriented at every home-time. I had settled into a nine-to-five routine but was hauled back into the Nether World each evening.

Until perhaps a decade earlier close relatives of the newly-deceased would have mourned for up to a year. House curtains would remain drawn and the family would wear something black. It would have been a bleak, joyless time. We wore black only at Damien's funeral and picked up the pieces of our lives shortly afterwards. Now, six months on, I decided it was time I left home and made arrangements to move into the nearby Tapton Court Nurses' Home in Fulwood to begin my training. This is the posher side of mucky old Sheffield, then one of the most polluted cities in Europe. I was worried about leaving Mother to herself but was also looking forward to the start of my training proper and a new chapter living with other student nurses.

Training commenced in April 1963 at Clark House Training School which was walking distance from the Nursing Home. As long as I can remember I had dreamt of being a nurse to the extent that eleven years of schooling had only got in the way. Notre Dame confirmed I was not academic or sporty. I was one of those girls who would find a quiet place in the woods on cross-country run days and puff on a Woodbine waiting for my red-faced classmates to re-appear.

When motivated I did excel. My best subjects were French, history, English literature and the combined GCE subject, Anatomy and Physiology. Now I was prepared to work hard and enjoyed it from the beginning just as I had done as a committed St. John's nursing cadet.

My ultimate role model, after my medical father, nursing sister Jane and to an extent nursing sister-in-law Nuala, was Mother's ancient older sister, Aunt Agnes. Here was a Scots-born very Old School nurse who in Newcastle at the age of 29 had the distinction of becoming Britain's youngest matron. Plump and bustling with pomegranate cheeks she would utter frequent "och, no, Dear! A good nurse always ..." reprovals whenever I sought her opinion on nursing practices.

Clark House trained entrants from The Royal, the Royal Infirmary general hospitals and from Sheffield's excellent Children's Hospital. All of us attended the first three-month 'in block' period learning bedside nursing theory, practicing the administering of enemas, pass feeding, the insertion of flatus tubes, injecting oranges and so on. There was a litany of nerve-wracking procedures. We were then released onto the wards to practise on largely unsuspecting patients. 'In block' training of a month at a time continued over the three years.

Nowadays, degree-trained nurses spend far less time on bedside nursing and at least two-thirds more time studying the theory of nursing and allied subjects. The late Clare Rayner, ex-nursing sister and Agony Aunt, deplored these changes. She believed a student nurse benefitted far more from her hands-on nursing. It would seem obvious that fundamental things cannot be learned from a manual. This includes interaction with the patient, their family, Ward Sister, physio, doctor and auxiliary hospital staff.

I tutted recently reading an RCN report lamenting the lack of hands-on experience of present-day nurses and the suggestion by some that relatives should be brought in to look after sick family members.

I agree and disagree with Clare Rayner, having been impressed with the degree-trained nurses encountered when visiting patients in hospital. However, I have not been impressed to see agency auxiliaries taking blood pressure, changing intravenous drips and suturing wounds with as little as two days in-house training. Procedures like these require skill and an in-depth knowledge to perform safely, particularly if complications occur.

A general demise can also be seen in the steady erosion over the years in the NHS with regard to a patient's after-care. District Nurses, auxiliaries and Home Helps gave all-round nursing and practical help as required.

Of Royal Hospital and Royal Infirmary girls, the latter were said to be prettier and the former brainier! The five paediatric nurses from The Children's Hospital in our group were different. They were good-natured and great fun to be with, often behaving like kids themselves. They had trained with the renowned Professor Illingworth and wore coloured pinnies over their uniforms. His young patients were encouraged to play. He also instituted open-hours visiting. This was ground-breaking to everyone, including us students who were already steeped in the more rigid Nightingale *diktats* of 'discipline' and 'cleanliness being next to Godliness' being all we needed to know.

In our May 1963 block there were ten of us 'brainier' Royal girls:-

Manic Myrtle the pretty, quixotic Barnsley whippet of whose Twiggy-like frame we were permanently envious; Auburn Anna whose pageboy haircut shone like a cinnamon halo; Ditzy Delia whose Marilyn Monroe tinted blonde tresses and round blue eyes were "boy bait" that we would go on to select or heartlessly reject; Rebel Rose (the author ...) "beat me daddy, eight-to-the-bar ..."; Wise Wendy our wistful, graceful willow confidante; Docile Dorothy dreamy and diligent; Eeny-Weeny Ellie a button-nosed, five-foot-nothing giggler; Just-a-minute Janet who was fleet-footed and "no-messing"; Jolly-Jilly a cute, pint-sized pushover with a Daffy Duck smile; and Tall-and-tame Miriam an all-round good egg.

We were one of four blocks admitted to Clark House each year, all chaste unwed girls, eager to please and as vulnerable as poppies in the wind. All pupil nurses at The Royal were white females at least eighteen years old and hopefully, mature enough to cope with an array of medical situations they would undoubtedly come across.

In truth, we were not mature at all. I doubt whether most teenagers were in the early 1960s. In our case, in the North of England the triumvirate of home, school and Church dictated the tenure of our lives. Parental law ruled absolutely. We also endured punitive school detention and occasional corporal punishment. This was cemented by Confession in the Catholic Church and Sunday sermons in our individual churches. Any fermenting rebellious traits remained but simmering.

We really had no notion of who we were when left to our own devices and were probably equivalent to today's fourteen-year olds. We were obedient pups lacking guile and confidence, or even ability to question. Because our 'elders and betters' dictated our morality and behaviour we did at least know boundaries and limitations. Such naivety was not satisfactory when the safety net was snipped away by those who did not have the same regard for our well-being as our parents did.

Of us ten kindergarten nurselings, five brought serious emotional baggage, principally from traumatic home situations in which they had grown up too quickly. Manic Myrtle, for example had just lost her father a Barnsley miner, whom she idolised. We bonded from the start, both of us knowing how it was to have an untimely death in the family. She could be hyperactive and flippant and make odd statements when she was tense and upset that were puzzling to those who did not understand raw grief. We are still in each other's lives today.

Ditzy Delia by contrast was an innately charming and rather flirty peroxide blonde with bluebell-coloured eyes. She would captivate by tilting her head and fixing her wide-eyed, dizzy-dolly smile on you. She was also a tough cookie, a competent mother-figure to her younger siblings as their real mother dallied from one partner to another.

Auburn Anna was a little older than us and an adopted only child. Alienated from her simple, working-class parents she left home at sixteen to work abroad as an *au pair* in exotic Switzerland. This was a rare adventure for a gal from the North. She was a loner, a serious soul who possibly found the rest of us too prone to giggling and skylarking, happy as we were to enjoy our off-duty time away from punishing viragoes. She played the piano and guitar and introduced us to muesli.

Wistful Wendy was lovely, a quiet, sweet girl. When off-duty she cared for an invalid mum with MS which meant she was unable to join us when we hit parties and the local pubs. It shames me now to think how little was the support we offered her. The rest of our group were also from solid, down-to-earth Sheffield families, unspoilt, straightforward and plain-speaking.

For my part, Ditzy Delia, informed me later, I acted out my grief in those early days by being cynical and sarcastic. I wasn't aware of this and it shows that reactive distress will manifest itself one way or another. However, I loved my new life as a nurse and felt less guilty about enjoying it than some others seemed to. My mother's grief was lessening. She was a willing guinea pig of her GP and family friend for a new pharmacology, the anti-depressant. This was Imipramine and it raised her mood sufficiently for her to take a part-time job for the first time in her life. This was a great help towards her paying off the overdraft incurred by Damien's medical expenses.

After the rigours of Edgar Allen Ward I thought I would cope with just about anything thrown at me during training. I was very soon dismayed at how much of our day was spent coping with a relentless assault from our elders. We were like lambs lined up for verbal slaughter. At break-time in the Nurses' Day Room, the Cig Bin, there was much mimicking of the Bitches in Blue and competitions for who had suffered the worst rollicking of the day. Traumatic training like this lessened in intensity only in our final year by which time, ever-so-grudgingly, we were being looked upon as nurses.

One of the first incidents that shocked us was when Eeny-Weeny Ellie was eviscerated by a junior Night Sister known as Barnsley Bubbles. She strode with menace towards our dining room breakfast table and stood over Ellie who was sitting almost too tired to eat after her first night in charge on a relatively low-key ward.

"Nurse Kane, you're a bloody murderer ..."

The six-foot streak of navy-blue lightning with stick-thin legs and black canal-boat lace-ups actually spat into Ellie's baby-round face. One of Ellie's patients had been discovered dead in bed by the oncoming day-staff.

Alas, such evil verbal assault worked because we became Olympian in our attempts to gain approval from Night Sister Low and her team of Deputy Furies, including Barnsley Bubbles. We simply dared not challenge even the most abusive bullying. It was how it was. If the Staff Nurse had been called away when Night Sister started her dreaded rounds we would try and hide in the sluice for fear of being asked to accompany her around the dimly-lit wards. Even ward ghosts, we joked, were expected to know all the patients' names, ages, diagnoses and treatments. It is under such circumstances a junior nurse is most likely to be struck dumb.

My other room-mate Ditzy Delia did try on Women's Medical, diligently learning her patients' details just in case this should happen. Sister Low duly arrived just after the senior nurse had gone on her midnight break. Unfortunately, Delia failed even before the rounds began because she could not find the ward torch needed for the charts at the foot of the thirty or so beds.

Our daring-for-those-days peroxide blonde apologised breathlessly to Sister Low.

"Well, we'll have to see by the light of your hair, Nurse, won't we?" Sister said tartly.

This *Dame* on the list of awesome *versus* loathsome hospital matriarchs had at least earned our respect. Most of us made bloomer after bloomer on these rounds but the 'awesomes' would suppress a smile and move onto the next bed. On a good night, anyway. On unkind nights the Sister's contempt would cause your ego to seek refuge in a thimble. We knew but did not always appreciate this systemic sadism was there to force every one of us to bow to and integrate with the finely-honed hospital machine.

We had all benefited from leaving home and been able to let off steam, though in a far more innocent way than today. After a tough day at nursing school or on the wards, Myrtle, Delia and I along with some of the Infirmary girls and all five of the Children's Hospital girls in our block became the official party girls. The others were goody-goody students who stayed in mostly and studied.

We saw it as our solemn duty to attend the hops at the nearby university Students' Union, buzz the folk clubs and get ourselves invited to medical student parties. This last was to be done with care! Any of us still 'on the shelf' after weeks or even months without attention had a last resort, the Saturday night Locarno. Here "down't Loccy," a single gaudy glitter ball moved mesmerizingly slowly linked, it seemed, to the movement of the band leader's baton.

It was also a last refuge for creepy guys with Brylcreemed hair and big sweaty hands who needed courage to approach a wilting lass to drop a dire pick-up line and even sadder dancing skills on. It was the pits for a Saturday night, the Last Dance Saloon. If they stepped on your feet it was probably because they were concentrating on their groping. No Salsa here, more likely a slap and the Hands-off Twist.

Being tall did grant me some authority, even protection, as did my thick hair when done up in a Nightingale Bun. Rita herself at *Chez Rita*'s remarked the first time I walked in "ee, we could stoof a set of cushions wi' that mooch 'air wot she's got on 'er 'ed!" In my first year, hospital stodge added unwelcome bulk to my *derrière* and face. So much so, the dishy new houseman whom we'd nicknamed Cedric Casanova, remarked that I resembled Ruth in the Bible. It was a deeply upsetting comment. What we wanted to hear from suitors was how much like Sex Goddess Brigit Bardot we were.

Any crush nurses had on Golden Curls Doctor Cedric evaporated when we heard he had held a pretty third-year nurse captive all night in his room and she had resorted to weeing in his sink. His Warren Beatty-style antics sent most of us into Jane Austen-style paroxysms. This was on top of him reportedly saying he was determined to deflower a nurse a day.

My brother Pascal and his police officer mates would take us out for the evening on police jazz-band nights. Pascal had started the band, thrilled to find a cupboard full of unused instruments at the station at Westbar. He was a gifted clarinettist from his days with Lostwithiel's brass band, the town's star turn at its annual carnival Floral Dance. He had become really good after a couple of years playing at Damien's Jazz Nights at the Old Bodmin Prison.

We weren't averse to pubs either, of course, particularly when a 'Mrs. Mills' was banging away on an old piano. Sometimes we met up with my good friend Phillip and his mates. He would also chauffeur us around to his friends' parties, though many of these would be on bleak council estates across Steel City. The compensation was the warmth of their Royle Family homes with harassed but welcoming mums, dads who were "fair wore out," an inimitable dry wit and a no 'BS' take on life and home-cooking.

On weekdays we had to be back at the Nursing Home by ten o'clock. On Saturday nights it was eleven. For special late nights we had to request a pass from the Home Sister. Any male escorts were permitted into the entrance hall only. Over three years of training we made the most of our weekend playtime, whether during twelve-week study blocks or the forty-four hour week lockdowns to come. All forms of unwinding were welcome.

As soon as we knew the dates of our two weeks' holiday in the Summer of 1963, Delia and I decided we would continue spreading our wings and take the ferry to Ireland. Cousin Connor was in England at the time but his Trinity College uni friends, including Seamus we had met in Sheffield had promised if we could get over they would make sure we had a good time. Half Irish myself and wanting to see the land of my fathers and Nuala's as well, was the deciding factor.

The Holyhead-Dublin ferry crossing we had heard was tediously long and it was unfortunate, on the dirtiest dingiest of ships, the trip turned into eighteen hours when a passenger suffered a suspected heart attack. The Irish way of doing things meant the captain took the tin bucket back to Holyhead even though we were almost in Dublin and we had to do the journey all over again. We were fascinated by the Irish Nursing Sister on the ferry staggering around in a tea-stained apron, fag in mouth. A Mad Madge of the West. It wasn't nursing as we knew it.

The B & B in Temple Bar that opened its doors to us in the middle of the night was just as eccentric. We tucked into the porridge at breakfast, starving after our interminable jaunt on a foodless rust-bucket. We then waited and waited for the rest of the 'full Irish breakfast.' Eventually the landlady explained.

"I sent moi Kevan out an hour ago for more bacon," she said laughing. "Oi expect he's just dropped into O'Malley's for a quick one, you know. Your cooked breakfast will be a wee bit late, girls."

When Seamus and two other lads picked us up for our first treat, a local pub-crawl, we were in for more surprises.

"Grab your drink, girls, we've done this one!" he said at the first and second pubs. "We can't stop too long anyway, 'cos the car's stolen, in your honour, in a manner of speaking!"

"We're stealing the glasses as well?" I asked.

"Ah, sure, everyone takes de glasses wid 'em! Oi expect the pubs'll have the same number at the end of the week as they started wid!"

Off we went in the dusk in the open car, singing one folk song after another without a care in the world heading for a beach picnic apparently, until the *Gardai* flagged us down.

"Ah sure, officer, we'll keep the noise down!" Seamus promised, having the sense to cover the glass of Guinness between his knees with his jacket. "It's on account of us having our English nurse cousins wid us tonight. We're showing them the sights, y'know, officer."

In the Autumn at the end of our first three-month block of anatomy and physiology tutorials, endless bedside nursing procedures, pharmacology study, books, charts, diagrams, procedures and tests we were let loose on the wards with the unspoken words "England and Clark House Nursing School expects ... you do your exemplary duty ... as we have endeavoured to teach you numbskulls and nitwits to do ... and don't let us hear any adverse reports ..."

Kitted out in her crisp new grey nurse's uniform, starched white apron and stiff white cap pinned to her reigned-in curly mop, trying to look like a confident professional while feeling as self-conscious as a nun in a night club, Student Nurse MacFarlane walked tall onto Men's Medical. With thirty pairs of eyes clocking her she was still very much Naked Nurse however much she tried to appear an old hand. Here was a ward where keen observation and attention to detail was vital for the well-being of the patients. Why was it the ward floor was now made of jelly, the same ward I had conquered as a Green Girl only a few months earlier? Stage fright I had not been expecting.

As a pre-nursing Green Girl I hadn't been required to do potentially risky procedures such as catheterisations, putting up drips or inserting a chest drain even when the ward was busy and a more experienced nurse wasn't available. Giving an injection preoccupies new nurses and medical students. It is a form of stabbing after all and is often done in that most sensitive of areas, the backside. Many a strong man turns into a wimp at the hands of an experienced nurse, never mind a junior.

Practising bed-bathing and suchlike on dummy patients in nursing school was plenty of work in itself. On wards it was a different matter, learning how to keep your head with a harridan, or irascible doctor yelling "hurry-up with the dressing trolley ... the IV drip-set, the suture set ... you stupid dolt ... idiot ... bungling moron ... you couldn't be trusted to run for a bus ..." We also had the occasional deranged patient pick up a dressing trolley and throw it at us.

It took a while for us to realise that second and third year nurses would craftily push us forward on the wards to do the bidding of perfectionist Sisters, while they busied themselves with something behind a patient's curtains or in a side-ward. Allowing senior nurses to treat us as doorscrapers was a badge of honour we knew we had to gain if we were to succeed. What was to be avoided was the occasional attempt at serious humiliation, as in being sent around the hospital to find a pair of fallopian tubes or a runaway linen skip.

The days passed and I began to take things in my stride. Meeting up at break times could be fraught with the creation of dreaded scenarios. Here we swapped stories, related minor disasters and warned of things to come. Laying out a corpse was one, as none of us had actually seen one. I hadn't been present at the laying out after my late brother's death and didn't think I could have hacked it anyway.

Most of us Bedside Virgins had never seen a living naked adult male either. It was years later at a dinner with the editor of the Nursing Times and a group of work-injured nurses that an Irish nurse related a story about her strict training, indeed strict upbringing and the first time she was required to lay out a body.

"Ah sure, I remember my first Last Offices with this Staff Nurse who terrified me. Just being with a cold body was pretty freaky as well. We washed the deceased gentleman and hardly spoke a word. I didn't want to screw up as I really wanted to impress her. Well, we were nearly finished when she went to answer the ward phone. She told me to finish off!

"I remembered being told in our first training block we must tie the gentleman's willy in case, you know ... it leaked urine. Well ... having never seen a willy except on our little brothers, you know, I thought to meself ... how am I going to tie a knot in dat ting? I pulled it dis way and dat and thought, Jesus, is he going to wake up and whack me for pulling his thingy about!"

The Irish nurse finished her story by saying how the Staff Nurse had laughed. The incident struck a chord with the nurses around the table but caused the male editor to shift uncomfortably. It wasn't practised now, I reassured him. I didn't explain that the actual procedure was to tie a length of thin cotton bandage in a neat bow around the penis.

As beginners we were only permitted to help wash and feed patients, ask if their bowels had opened and record basic observations such as TPR (temperature, pulse and respiration). These are simple procedures that require skill none-the-less. It also allowed us to observe the patient more closely and note whether they were perspiring, were cold and clammy or restless. We were learning that a pulse can indicate heart arrhythmia, thyroid dysfunction, possible anaemia, even the onset of infection or impending death.

We were also able to chat to patients about any worries they might have because many are less intimidated by younger nurses. Good interaction with patients was crucial if we were to get good reports on each ward. We weren't taught actual people skills. It was more a matter of respect, explaining what we were about to do and seeking permission. Anything other can be an affront to the patient's dignity. This does sound obvious but not all staff treat patients with courtesy at all times. The idea that staff inflict or burden vulnerable and often helpless patients with their own moods or problems is really unacceptable.

For a few in the caring professions like Beverley Allitt, the child-killer, their action is a power issue, psychotic in origin. Abuse of power equals the potential for bullying whether of staff or vulnerable patients. Almost everyone has the propensity to bully if pushed too far or are under stress or tired beyond reason. Traumatised patients can behave erratically. Some patients are simply unpleasant and therefore very provocative. Erratic patients require endless patience, as do those with dementia who won't eat, can be doubly incontinent and who could easily smear faeces everywhere, including over a nurse's uniform.

The bully that enters the caring professions with malicious intent cannot be compared with some of the senior nursing Sisters we had to contend with. They surely believed that such 'firmness' was the best way of ensuring new nurses achieved their own meticulous standards. Along with this came the realisation we had the power to kill or cure. It was uncomfortable also knowing that legal action could be taken against us were we to make a serious mistake. No longer was I five-year old Nurse Twitty Toes, as my Brute Brothers had called me, cleaning tomato ketchup from their legs with them moaning and grinning at the same time.

These misgivings about my being good enough to continue with nursing welled up every three months at each new ward or unit allocation. Before each was apprehension over whether senior nurses or long-serving auxiliary staff would want to show us the ropes or quash any self-esteem we had managed to store. It continued until confidence in my competence got the better of my doubting side towards the end of my second year of training.

It was unfortunate my confidence was badly shaken from the beginning of my training and my first three-month block. When it came to giving my first injection, things could not have been worse. The grim-faced patient yelled and said I was not fit to inject a dead cow and should be reported. It was my worst humiliation as the entire ward witnessed the incident. With any injection into the buttocks there is a risk of paralysis of the leg if the sciatic nerve is touched. I thought this was what I had done because of the patient's reaction.

"Don't fret, Nurse, you weren't that bad!" Sister Frome reassured me. "He is a difficult old so-and-so. We'll let you do the six o'clock injections with Staff Nurse to get you used to it."

Sister Frome was one of the younger breed of married sisters who had a life outside the hospital. I worked very hard over the three months and despite the reputation of these younger Ward Sisters as being a little kinder than their Old School colleagues, I did not get a good report from her. I was devastated and duly summoned to Matron Welburn's office.

Chapter Nine
#Nursing Student ...# (David Martin)

It had been ten months since I had last been required to enter Matron's office. That was when my brother was in the male orthopaedic ward opposite and the feared Ice Queen had shown sympathy over his impending death. Now Matron's tone was glacial. She told me through tightly-pursed lips that my negative ward report was indicative of my following in my big bad sister's footsteps and that this would not be tolerated in the hospital.

Having worked hard and behaved myself to the point of being an exemplary student as I saw it, I was flabbergasted. My sister Jane was at The Royal ten years before me and clearly, her ghost loomed large. Good nurse though she was, she was a maverick, a class act with her anti-authoritarian pranks and wicked sense of humour. I was made aware from the start that a family member with a "naughtiest-ever nurse" tag was not someone to be emulated. Jane's days of tramping the wards were now haunting me.

A shivering Naked Nurse left the chief's office and made her way to the locker room in the basement for a bout of full-blown self-pity. Where was the light, the longed-for break from the re-arisen doom of the last eighteen months, the sadness of her brother's death and family breakdown? To be scoured by Matron, God's Right Hand, was akin to being reviled by Florence Nightingale herself. What did attitude mean, anyway? All in all I was pretty close to the edge and Matron's thin-lipped disdain was too much.

"Oh misery, misereee ..." as the song goes.

My howling in the bowels of the musty-smelling changing room was interrupted by the clanking of a bucket and Nelly coming down the stairs with a view to mopping the floor.

"Ee Nurse, what's oop, Luvvie?"

"Bad report, Nelly ..." I snivelled.

"Never mind, Luv. It can only get worse!"

We both laughed and I thought perhaps my situation was not so bad. Maybe Nelly's smile was the light. I went to find my other block workmates to hear how they had fared. I didn't get much solace here, mine was definitely a negative report.

It wasn't long before I was relating stories about my errant sister that elicited much laughter and some admiration. She had once taken exception to a married doctor having an affair with her friend in theatre, Sigrid and then being unfaithful again with another nurse. She had taken his trousers just before he was off home and steeped them in a solution of red mercurochrome. A Casualty Houseman woke up late one night to find his right leg encased in plaster. He had flirted a little too readily with Sis, was the message!

Junior males had not got away without some character-building on her ward either. One unfortunate young medic walked unsuspectingly into theatre on his first day with a sanitary towel 'mask' across his mouth on the advice of helpful Nurse Jane. She had already expunged the new housemen's bedrooms before their arrival with supposedly necessary evil-smelling sulphur candles.

Perhaps more pertinent to my block mates was the advice I got from my sister about getting patients on-side. If the going gets rough or there is an imminent blistering from On High she said, patients are the best, sometimes the only, allies.

Our three-month allocations came and went at speed, or sometimes not quickly enough. They were challenging, often gruelling episodes that took in medical and surgical wards, geriatrics, orthopaedics, Casualty and ENT. We gained experience in operating theatres in other hospitals as well, at the Sheffield Children's Hospital and Jessop Hospital for Women. Over three years of training we would be spending a year in total on night duty. We would also be studying a year in further school block seminars. Sometimes we were working alongside someone else from our group. At other times we did not see our friends for months.

One thing we had in common was the determination to get out and party. The unspoken rule was never let the sun go down on an ear-bashing. We supported each other as blood sisters, backing each other up through our not-so-finest hours.

The pressure for us to obtain good ward reports and test results throughout our training was relentless. Their shaming us if we stepped out of line was a subliminal whip that worked. A bad ward report meant a roasting and only one session before Miss Welburn's eviscerating stare was usually required for the most recalcitrant nurse to fall back into line. We became obsessed with wanting to please and it was no surprise SRN pass rates at The Royal were high, almost one hundred per cent.

I never received another bad report but even at low points I didn't question my wanting to be a nurse, with its promise of a poorly-remunerated career of hard labour. Choosing to become a doctor's hand-maiden rather than a doctor was of the times. Women were still viewed as chief carers. This began to change in the 1960s and today, nurses study to degree level. The *status quo* of doctor and nurse changed with it.

I am sure today's nurses do not tolerate the contempt and infantile put-downs we endured during our training and early career. My first year was a trial by fire through a scorching forty-four hour week. We must have looked like automatons on the streets of Sheffield traipsing between hospital and Nurses' Home and back, day after day or night after night, week in, week out.

Life would have been all work and no play and made us very dull girls if we had used our free day-and-a-half for study as was expected. It was thanks to my good friend and faithful pal Phillip and medical student cousin Gerry that I didn't go under. They did their share of keeping our group sane with trips out and parties, even cheap cider and barley wine parties. Falling out of bed for early morning duty, post-plonk-party could be a sorry affair but they kept us going.

Phillip would take us around the Derbyshire dales or on killer hikes across the moors around Hathersage and Bakewell in 1963 before falling for my best friend and future flatmate, Manic Myrtle. Mad and generous both, they were made for each other. They are together to this day, still in Sheffield, with three grown-up children and five grandchildren.

Brother Pascal fell for our own Blonde Bombshell, Ditzy Delia. It was thought he might even follow older brother Casanova Billy in marrying a nurse. In the mid-1950s Billy courted sister Jane's nursing friends before marrying her best friend, Nuala. Billy was as much of a hooligan as Jane, tying her to the Nursing Home gate on one occasion, leaving her contemplating a bunch of condoms above her head blown up likes balloons. He nipped around the back for a kiss and a cuddle with Nuala. My guess is she was the lookout, the distraction, whether she liked it or not!

Pascal thought he could go one better than Billy by sneaking into our Nurses' Home after hours. Needless to say this was the equivalent of accessing Fort Knox. It was midnight when I was woken with a start by a man's shoe landing on the floor of my first-floor room and urgent whispering from the garden.

"Sis, let me in, I've come to see Delia!"

Hauling himself up a drainpipe was PC MacFarlane, all six-foot two of him.

"Wake up, someone to see you!" I hissed outside Delia's door.

Her wide blue eyes were a picture when she opened her door a crack and saw my handsome, equally blue-eyed brother. This was a deliciously wicked episode for them, with instant dismissal for the three of us from our chosen professions had PC Pascal been discovered in the house or worse, seen shinning down the drainpipe in uniform at dawn.

Ditzy Delia's eyes shone the next morning after her night spent cuddling and talking with her boyfriend, on her bed, not in it. Our own Teen rules, even as Catholics, permitted petting. Most boyfriends reigned in their passion, most of the time, so unmarried girls still spent much of playtime defending their honour.

"Father, I have let a boy kiss me and touch me impurely," was the term whispered at Confession. Girls and boys had to 'confess' and hope their misdemeanour, even the thinking of 'impure' thoughts, would be categorised as a venial sin. 'Going the whole way' should this have occurred, was a different matter. This was a mortal sin and risky because if the sinner expired before taking Holy Communion, he or she was on the way to Hell.

Purgatory was the promised fate of venial sin. Imagining as I did purgatory as a treadmill of my training regime doubled up for eons with no days off, I was also collecting Brownie points with boyfriends, like Nectar Points or good Karma, in the event I needed to sweet-talk my way out!

This preoccupation with sexual frustration in our teens was being met head on in the mid-1960s everywhere but in our town, it sometimes seemed. Every week we read about the French sex-bomb, Brigitte Bardot and her lovers or the antics of Bad Boy bands such as the Rolling Stones and their drink, drugs and sex lifestyle. Bad Lads loomed large on cinema screens also, with Albert Finney kicking off in 1960 with Saturday Night and Sunday Morning. Here, Doreen (Shirley-Anne Field) is seduced by Alfie but is firmly in control of the situation, unlike Alfie's hapless married lover tied in to the values of an earlier generation.

There was also the burgeoning Hippy movement in the United States advocating sexual freedom escapism ('free love') through recreational drug use, popular music, dropping out of formal education and dabbling in new or oriental religions. The phenomenon of the cult took off with its charismatic leaders who certainly did not look or behave like our parents. This social upheaval was described by the well-entrenched as new Sodom and Gomorrah playgrounds.

With young American men being transported to their death in Vietnam the Hippy Movement was also an anti-war protest, a cry for help even, at the direction in which the unbending social values of their elders was leading them.

Our conservative Yorkshire and Derbyshire towns were not sending young men off to be maimed and traumatised but they were stultifying. The rigid social hierarchy of which our parents were the backbone determined they would not yield from their perception of right and proper values. Nothing was happening here. Everything was played down and was under control.

There were chinks in the armour, however. Mother was agog when Pascal, on duty the day The Beatles played Sheffield City Hall, reported, "Ma, you've never seen anything like it! Those daft girls screamed the place down over four lads playing music. They left their seats in a right state, wet through!"

"Bloody wet theirselves, they did," he scoffed to me later, unable to comprehend it himself. "What the 'eck's goin' on?"

In 1965 and well into our second year, many of us were getting the message about change. To some of us the prospect of treading the same path as our unfulfilled, depressed mothers was not a happy one. Others were kicking out against being treated by the nursing establishment as airheads who would likely marry and drop out of the profession.

We didn't discuss the meaning of life on nights out. Being provocative, unsexy and a threat to the male ego was not cool. "You think too much" was a criticism levelled at me by boys at parties if I tried to start a discussion about politics or, heaven forbid, philosophy. It was a put-down which stung because I didn't want to think of myself as unfanciable. It was not that I was trying to be clever, I

135

wanted to learn.

Paraphrasing Descartes with "I think NOT, therefore, I am NOT. I am NOT, therefore I do NOT exist" was something most males on evenings out could not have coped with. Seeds of doubt were already in my head. If my training was not to lead to the beginning of fulfilment, I would move on to something else.

Even though we were often involved in caring for patients coping with traumatic medical issues, nurses never discussed them in depth. We didn't know how to. We had no training and in most cases did not have the education. Religion, politics and sex were likewise never up for discussion as the nurses I worked with were mostly straightforward and uncomplicated. They were content with the level of communication with patients expected by the hospital and would only chat about it on a superficial level to other nurses.

More surprising in a medical environment was that sexual relationships and contraception were not discussed either. Nurses who had taken the plunge with a relationship would remain tight-lipped. It was something my generation, hopefully the last, had to muddle through on.

An eighteen-year old wanting to take control of her life was not new, of course. My mother was chaperoned when out with an approved gentleman friend. Control factors like these made sure it was her parents' wishes being fulfilled, not hers. She was obliged to finish art school when she married and do the proper thing, support her husband in his career.

She wanted to be a nurse, like her older sister but wasn't allowed because nursing in the 1920s had become a paid profession. Her family believed it to be a voluntary vocation in which the nurse should be of independent means. Remunerated, it was akin to going on the stage.

Along with the unstoppable social changes of the early 1960s was the precedent of my older brothers and sisters escaping Sheffield, the North, for London, ironically known as The Smoke. Listening to them, visiting them and meeting their glamorous cosmopolitan flatmates and friends was a revelation. No-one in Sheffield travelled abroad, remembering this was before the advent of the package holiday. People had one, or if very lucky, two week's Summer holiday a year and would follow an annual pilgrimage to Blackpool, Skeggie or Scarborough. Most had no idea what a passport looked like. If they had sailed on an ocean liner or even more unusually, flown in an aeroplane their parents were probably in the armed forces. We were provincial, docile and trapped.

A big step towards independence came in my persuading three block mates, Ditzy Delia, Manic Myrtle and Auburn Anna in June 1964, early in our second year of training, that we need not suffer continuing imprisonment in the House of Chastity. This strictly-monitored environment was holding back a group of Sleeping Princesses waking to the energy of the nearby university and the '60s in general. Uni students usually spent only their first year in a hall of residence. Why shouldn't we look out for a flat we could share for the rest of our training? The opportunity came when a third-year friend, Jo and her flatmates passed their finals and were vacating their top-floor furnished flat in Harcourt Road that was midway between Sheffield University and The Royal.

The arty attic garret appealed to us immediately and we were considered daring by our more timid colleagues, flying in the face of hospital authority. We were making a grand statement of independence without having thought through the mundane elements of cooking and cleaning and whether we could pay the rent.

The inevitable running out of money before the end of the month was regarded a fair trade for a more liberated life. Free hospital lunch and feasting on days off, courtesy of our concerned mothers, kept us from starving. Our own cupboard was regularly so bare, an evening meal could be a single Jacob's Cream Cracker. If we were lucky there would be a Custard Cream to nibble afterwards. We were all partial to this biscuit and the danger was, being so hungry, a packet would be wolfed in a minute.

The misery of damp and freezing winters with a pitiful two-bar electric heater in our attic sitting room switched on only in the evenings was alleviated by being out as much as possible. Bedtime through Autumn and Winter was a ritual of hot water bottles, damp cotton sheets, hairy grey blankets, a borrowed eiderdown, good book, thick gloves and sometimes a woolly hat to keep Jack Frost at bay.

We were tough post-war kids who didn't know anything different. Youngsters today stare uncomprehendingly when you describe the evil cold of the time before central heating and insulation, of keeping a smoky coal fire alight, or scrambling around for a shilling for the

137

electricity meter, the stink of a paraffin heater or of braving a bath in tepid water in a freezing bathroom. There was generally not even the comfort of a carpet, or television set. I am thankful to have known the before and after.

Clearing up after mad parties with a hangover from cheap cider, barley wine and occasional suspect grog was a labour. Nothing happened apart from thumping heads from a bit too much 'fun.' Times were still innocent and drug-free. Nevertheless, it was exhilarating dancing away evenings to our two scratched Beatles' and one notorious Stones' album. These sounds were what we needed to get the hospital out of our hair!

Some of our colleagues whispered about us as being beyond the pale because of the way we were living it up. We made the most of being admired for holding the best parties in town. Pinned on the wall was a letter from the local police station warning us a neighbour had complained about our noise at weekends. We weren't ruffled since PC Pascal and his pals were the backbone of our shindigs.

Of nurses known to have gone 'the whole way' with boyfriends, one of the more notorious was Grace with her slanting turquoise eyes, *retroussé* nose and black page boy hairstyle. We listened in awe to everything she said about her latest beau and that he had let her iron his shirt! It was an important sign, a rite of passage meaning they were 'doing it' and going steady. Why spoil it for them, we thought. But would he marry her? Would anyone marry her if they split up, were questions we asked each other.

Smooching and petting at a kindergarten level was actually nice since our young men made an effort in their courting. Today's mindless wham-bamming does not compare. It wouldn't surprise me if young guys nowadays thought petting was stroking someone's dog.

On Saturday nights in all weather there would be a line of steaming couples behind the Nurses' Home snogging for Britain, boyfriends desperate to go that little bit further. Here was a parallel to restricted drinking hours and frantic last orders at closing time. There was none of this now we had our own flat. Rare overnight visitors would settle into the sofa. Perhaps, as with drinking, we were pacing ourselves differently.

We were also mindful throughout our training of the little black book allegedly kept up-to-date by medical students in Casualty. You did not want your name in it. It might have become an urban myth but my sister assured me it existed in her day.

I was going out with a post-grad maths teacher named Leo at the time we moved into Harcourt Road. He was still regarded as unusual, a working class lad at university. He was more switched on than me and had benefitted hugely from his educational opportunity. He threw out my trashy romances and gave me proper books to read, like The Gingerbread Man, the Tin Drum, even Descartes' Meditations. With this last he thought it important I learnt that the best philosopher's had tried and failed to prove the existence of God; that religion was not just blind faith.

This was all a huge challenge for the youngest girl in a large family that had little interest in art or literature or changing times, though my father was a well-read cultured man. Leo had an uphill struggle with me, particularly when my influences were work, my strait-laced flatmates and their boyfriends.

I do not recall too many nights in, however and certainly not alone with a male friend. We were lucky to have generous friends who saw it their duty to rescue Damsel Nurses and carry them off to a cosy, if noisy, smoky pub for a warming drink.

Then there was Naughty George!

George was a well-regarded landlord of hapless medical students who also took pity on nurses. In one sense he was every teenage girl's mother's nightmare, a tall good-looking ex-Merchant Navy officer bachelor of about fifty. We adored him but he never took advantage of us young things, sober or drunk. He helped us survive when we were cold, broke and sometimes heartbroken.

It was George who introduced us to foreign friends and foreign food. To us, Chinese food came from a packet and you took to the taste of monosodium glutamate or you didn't. Vesta *chow mein* was the choice if you wanted to appear authentic. Curries were still almost unknown. You had Continental *chic* if you used garlic, or knew how to prepare and eat spaghetti with a meaty tomato sauce, as opposed to the usual slopping it out of a tin. Drinking wine with a meal was still unknown and long before Black Tower, Blue Nun and Piat D'or were being advertised on commercial television as the way it should be done.

George would prepare the real thing for us with huge generosity. At such meals he introduced us to Sikh and Indian medics, our first immigrant medical students from the Commonwealth. We met actor lodgers who had come to the new Crucible Theatre in Sheffield. He broadened our musical horizons with record imports such as River Deep - Mountain High played on a stereo sound system, an extraordinary experience to those of us weaned on the humble Dansette.

He was 'Naughty George' because this was what we called him when about to stagger home well-fed and tipsy, having been unable to resist being plied with the likes of whisky and ginger ale, gin and tonic, liqueurs and good French wine, drinks our penniless boyfriends couldn't afford. He was a star.

Life on the Nursing Coalface for me was not quite so rosy as I started my second year. Matron's daily grand tour and one of her deputies storming around each evening kept us fraught. Should their eagle eyes spot a piece of fluff on a locker or a patient in a messy bed, we were dead, or wished we were. We had long wondered if it was possible to meet their standards and began to think our occasional frantic rushing around trying to make Cross Mummy happy was something aside from good nursing and the efficient running of the ward.

Our collective effort and an inordinate amount of time was spent forestalling or tempering furious outbursts from our seniors. As practicing nurses now, we saw patients uncomfortable with a nurse being dressed down by a sadistic Virago. They knew when a Senior Nurse was about to lose it on a "Hell hath no fury" mission. They witnessed Ward Sisters almost orgasm with fury in unbridled, Gorgon-eyed, lip-spittled verbal attacks of awesome power. No one, nurses and I believe most patients, dared confront this bullying. We were doomed as imbeciles who needed constant disciplining.

Unfortunately for me on a three-month block in ENT I became a target of one of the most merciless Ward Sisters in the hospital. A hospital tyrant's notoriety was reflected in her nickname. Sister G.'s was Aunty Ranty. She closely resembled a blonde Wallace Simpson with her lean, ramrod frame and faded but handsome looks. In all my years of nursing no-one came close to the *hauteur* of this woman from whom one glance could start an Ice Age. Her combined defence and attack armoury included a Miss Whiplash voice that was feared by all nurses who passed through her ward. I felt from the day I started the block that I was being stalked. It was a constant, rather than occasional carping I had to endure in cold, clipped, hypercritical negatives.

"What do you think you are doing ... is one so absolutely stupid that ... take that trolley back to the clinical room and don't ever let me see it set up like that again ... did I, or did I not ask you to ... you'd be lucky to end up with a job as a cloakroom attendant ... get out of my sight ..."

Other nurses were shocked by the vitriol. I was confused since my only other encounter with Sister G. had been when I was in her ward for a tonsillectomy just after my brother had died. She was perfectly fine to this Green Girl as a patient, as were the staff nurses who made sure I had an endless supply of ice-cream. She was all smiles when my father visited. Now the constant undermining of everything I did as "the most incompetent student nurse I have ever encountered" was traumatising. By the end of the first month I was not eating or sleeping properly and had withdrawn to the point where my pals thought I'd had a lobotomy.

I thought, when Sister went on holiday, my situation might improve on her return. It actually worsened when she appointed me her assistant in ENT Theatre. It was interpreted at the time as a huge compliment but the constant upbraiding continued and I saw it as an ever more perverse way of getting at me. Sometimes, in more positive moments and to keep my sanity I thought I might have been selected for grooming as a 'potentially good nurse.'

Theatre duty as a young nurse is daunting enough without the close proximity of a Beast Sister. Sometimes I got a grip on myself in her presence when acknowledging a human side to her, a whispered impossible Katherine Hepburn-Spencer Tracey-style liaison with the safely-married consultant she had been sweet on for years. There was a love-nest it was reported beneath ENT, conveniently remote from the main hospital.

My errant sister's never-forgiven ENT antics might also have had a bearing on my current discomfort. Jane was caught *in flagrante* 'taking off' Aunty Ranty, parading up and down the ward in Sister's actual bespoke uniform, dapper little cape and dainty, highly-polished court shoes.

When Sister was off-duty it fell to me to prepare theatre for the next day's operations of tonsil and adenoid removals and sinus draining. In some cabinet drawers were items removed from patients' throats over many years. Typical was "Fred Braithwaite, fish bone,"

"Minnie Smith (and many others), chicken bone," "Lady Audley, grouse bone ..." Such diversions eased my day but this period turned into a crisis that almost caused me to quit nursing.

All experiences through our three years of training sharpened our skills, as they were carefully designed to do. I could have done without this ordeal by fire. I never employed the same punitive, belittling tactics when tutoring students later in my career. A 'critical parent' response was occasionally necessary where patients were not being treated respectfully and some nursing procedures were lacking. We did not like the Sister Jekyll and Miss Hyde act but did admire our Old-school Sisters' exemplary care of patients and their follow-through.

Another consequence of the training regime was the immaculate cleanliness and efficient running of the wards. Running a ward is not rocket science and it would seem that an easing of discipline and change in nursing standards, or at least hospital procedure today, is responsible for the poor management, abysmal cleanliness and indifferent care in wards we read and hear about with depressing frequency today. We were aware that our matriarchs behaved like they did in the best interest of the patient.

If Naked Nurse became a shadow of her former unsure self over three months of ENT her next block was almost Immaculate by contrast. At last she could see how it was to be a nurse in her own right. This revelation came during our second year school block under the tutelage of our most humane and brilliant teacher to date, Miss T. Here was the first senior that actually talked to us and I would say that all Royal Nurses fortunate enough to have been taught by Miss T. will owe a large part of their professionalism to her. I recall her calm, wise words to this day.

We learnt what constituted a high standard of patient care through communication, politeness, respect and preserving the patient's dignity. Repetition of these mantras was constant. "How would you like to be addressed by staff ... I am Student Nurse ... do tell us if you are concerned about anything at all ... we are just going to take your temperature ... give you a bed bath ... change your dressing, if that is all right with you?"

Soon after being tutored by Miss T. I was chosen by Matron's office to 'special' Miss T.'s father after major surgery. Twenty-four hour, one-to-one nursing was how critically-ill patients were cared for before the introduction of ICUs. I was almost catatonic with nerves at the thought of nursing a laryngectomy patient, especially a relative of senior staff. The larynx, or voice box is removed, usually because of a growth and a permanent tracheotomy (a tracky) is put in place. The actor Jack Hawkins had one. This was a new procedure, the nursing of which we thought was beyond our capability as Second Years. I also dreaded being back in ENT with Sister G.

Sister grabbed my arm when I reported for duty and led me into the side ward set up for Mr. T. She explained procedure and how the equipment worked. There was a large oxygen bottle and mask. A huge kettle with an elongated flattened spout would direct steam into a canopy of draw-sheets over the head-end of the bed. I would be using a suction unit to remove mucus that would otherwise block the patient's airway.

"You can go and fetch your patient from theatre, Nurse," she said finally. "I am told our first laryngectomy procedure has gone to plan *Deo gratias*. Now run along."

I helped the porter bring Mr. T. up to the ward, making sure he was bolt upright all the way. After we had transferred him to the bed I started the kettle. This would provide the constant moist air to help his breathing. A narrow metal breathing tube had been inserted through a hole above his Adam's apple into the trachea and was tied around the back of the neck to prevent it being coughed out. It is permanent when the patient is unable to breathe through his mouth and upper airway because of cancer or an injury or a lung-related illness such as pneumonia.

Tracheotomy care was feared by student nurses. Every successful raw breath is dependent on the breathing tube being kept clear of mucus with the suction catheter. The normal cough reflex is defunct. It is an unpleasant procedure for the patient every fifteen minutes or so because he is unable to breath for a few moments while it is done. A quietly intelligent Mr. T. was calm and co-operative and this helped me put across an air of confidence when I felt as though I was tied to a chair with an open bag of snakes at my feet.

To my awed mates it was as if I'd been asked to nurse The King himself!

"Just imagine, Girls," I preened later, "Matron, Mr. T.'s consultant, Miss T. and Sister G. in and out of that claustrophobic space with

Sister being so pleasant I thought I was losing it!"

As an ex-battered nurse from this ward I was convinced she was being affable only because of the patient and that I would be torn to shreds again later. When I came off-duty that first day the patient was 'doing as well as can be expected.' To my further relief I didn't get a roasting. Nevertheless, I was crackling like thin ice with tension and tiredness and rescued finally by my magnificent mates rushing me across the road to our regular haunt for a cooling lager and lime. The shift had been as challenging as my first night in charge of Pye-Smith Ward with our VIP, the Lord Mayor of Sheffield a few months earlier.

"I would say you've been given a clean bill of health!" Auburn Anna said laughing. Manic Myrtle who was cosied up to my old mate Phillip, now her fiancé, added, "hopefully your sister Jane's reputation has been laid to rest and you'll have an easier ride!"

That following evening I was in the nurses' dining room with Ditzy Delia, filling her in with my "you won't believe ... you'll never guess what ..." news. Delia had been visiting her family in Buxton and wanted to hear all the details. She had also discovered her next three-month work detail was in theatre and was very excited about this. While chatting we couldn't help overhearing two posh charity-shop type auxiliaries on an adjacent table.

"Pussywussy's got fur balls, Dear," said one.

"Oh, my! Poor little Wickums," responded her friend.

Delia and I had never heard of this malaise and nearly blew our hot soup into our laps trying not to giggle at this and the remedies poor Wickums didn't know he was in for. We went into hysterics when they left the dining room, drawing attention to ourselves, of course. It dissipated my tension and I was a lot more relaxed for the rest of the time my VIP patient was in the ward.

He recovered well and I felt I had earned my spurs. Delia agreed it was due in a large measure to Miss T.'s inspiration and encouragement that I had done well. Like me, Delia wasn't convinced about how much help to my nursing career was my period of purgatory with Sister G.

About Delia's theatre block, she loved it so much she went on to make it her career up to her retirement. Sadly she died recently when only in her early Sixties. This was very hard for those of us who shared so many moments of agony and ecstasy in our early years as nurses.

Nurses can be as superstitious as anyone. If we missed lilies brought in by relatives we were usually reminded smartly by an older female patient that flowers associated with resurrection and the Virgin Mary's funeral were not welcome on the ward. Ghosts in dark corners of older hospitals was common, as was the belief that deaths come in threes. Three deaths in one night on different wards at the hands of Naked Nurse when she was a floater was troubling.

I was first called up to Men's Medical to help with the humble but important task of handing out cocoa and Horlicks, one for which no training is given! I had just given a patient his cup of Horlicks after a brief chat and returned to the drinks trolley when the adjacent patient called out "Nurse!" pointing to the patient I had just left. He had slumped and spilt the drink over his bed. I called Staff and turned the patient on to his side to prevent his tongue from choking him. Senior Night Sister Low appeared like a spirit, told Staff to draw the curtains and pulled the patient on to his back again. I stood there mesmerised as the normally unflustered Sister Low began vigorously depressing his sternum area with one flattened hand above the other.

I thought she had lost the plot, bouncing him up and down and with obvious panic asked Staff what Sister was doing to the poor man.

"She's not hurting him, you idiot," came the quiet reply, "she's giving him cardiac resuscitation. She's trying to get his heart started again."

The houseman took over the procedure from Sister to no avail.

"Oh no, he was a coronary thrombosis patient. It was nothing to do with you," Staff said about my concerns as we later laid the patient out. "We haven't had a Horlicks death yet! Thanks for your help this evening. Now you get along to Norfolk Ward."

Norfolk Ward, Ladies Geriatric, was my second floating assignment of the night. I hurried over there and couldn't wait for supper and the girls' reaction to Sister Low's antics.

"Yer what! Wooden Spoon jumping up and down on a corpse ... wey, go t't bottom of stairs! ... let 'em rest in peace, I say!"

I was needed on Norfolk because of the arrival of a gaggle of medical students. Staff was busy and asked if I would demonstrate feeding a comatose patient. The woman, Mrs. P. was in her mid-fifties and had been in a coma for two weeks, a patient who today would have been in Intensive Care. I drew back some bile through the tube coming out of her nose to check it was in her stomach and not her lungs. It turned the blue litmus paper red, indicating it was acid. I injected a little water through the tube using the 20 ml syringe attached, then the feed, then a little more water to clear the tubing. I recorded the quantity of feed on the patient's fluid chart.

I had just finished the procedure when I was instructed to get over to Keeling Ward and relieve the staff nurse there for tea. Here, Staff asked me to sit by a patient who had just been admitted with a stroke. He was unconscious with loud stertorous breathing. I had to check BP and pulse every fifteen minutes and keep his airway clear. It never got to fifteen minutes. When Staff returned from tea I was almost distraught over the patient breathing his last as I was checking his pulse. I helped Staff straighten the man's stiffening body and then set off back to Norfolk where my help was needed again for another laying out.

On my return to the gloomy old ward I really did not want to hear the words "Ah, MacFarlane, can you help with the offices of the dead, bed seven, Missers P. It's gone an hour since she died."

Mrs. P. was the patient I had fed via the feeding tube in front of the medical students. I came over cold and corpse-like myself.

"Don't worry Nurse," the auxiliary I was helping said kindly, "her sweet soul's been released from her suffering body, like a canary from a cage."

"It's not that," I whispered, "she's the third death tonight."

"It always comes in threes, Luv!"

"No, three deaths at my hands tonight ..."

"Well, that's something you're not going to forget!" the auxiliary whispered with a grin. "I've not come across that before!"

I went off-duty in a daze that morning. Manic Myrtle commiserated and said I was hardly Mr. Hitler! To cheer me up she drew a moustache on her upper lip and began marching up and down singing #Hit-ler ... has only got one ...#

I joined in heartily, stepping over our beds and around the floor with the required *heil!* We were in the Tapton Court annexe on the other side of the garden from the main building where our prim Home Sister's office was. She wouldn't hear anything. Wrong! The door opened and Sister stood there speechless for a moment.

"Really, Nurses. Do respect the fact your night duty colleagues are trying to sleep ..."

"Sorry, Sister. MacFarlane had a very tough night and I was just cheering her up!"

Sister withdrew, shaking her head.

My brother Pascal resigned from the Police later in 1964. He was perhaps too sensitive a soul for the police force and knew he was becoming too cynical when dealing with the seamier side of Sheffield where humanity was not at its best. Called to one incident on a rough Council Estate he and his colleague didn't expect to be offered a cup of tea. They weren't prepared for the conditions the family were living in either. On one bedroom wall written in faeces was "our Norah is a cunt."

Disillusionment had built up since the infamous Rhino Whip Case of 1962. He was a junior officer at the time and suffered a year of torment, under pressure he said, to give false evidence. Two hardened criminals accused the police of beating them with a rhino whip during questioning. The story made the national papers. The police denied impropriety.

His farewell do in a barn adjoining a nice Derbyshire pub was a rowdy affair. Leo, brother Simon and I borrowed Mother's brand new van. She thought it more useful than a car and was pleased with it, even if it was mucous green. It was midnight when we set off on a pitch black lane over the moors in the days when the perils of drinking and driving was not something uppermost in people's minds. Pascal and several police officer buddies followed in their car.

It was obvious, merry as we were, my rookie brother would not make the distance. He was taking bends too fast and turned the van on its side. It slid with a sickening sound and stopped only inches from the edge of a steep bank. I was in the back but was first out, impressed with how quickly I could react. Thankfully, Pascal and his mates piled out of their car and were quick in righting the van and making sure we were all okay. Leo and I were shaken, Simon had a deep cut on his backside from a pint beer mug he'd nicked from the pub. I dressed the wound for him and it was very late when I was dropped off at my flat, sworn to secrecy about the accident. Simon would try and pass off the massive dent in the front wing and scraping as having been caused by a lamp post.

I was up a few hours later for work, temporarily upbeat about not receiving a scratch. It caught up with me during the evening and the next morning I could not lift my head from the pillow. My flat-mates

147

reported in for me to ex-army Sister Foggart, Deputy Matron. She would have none of their obfuscation and they had to come clean about the car crash. Deputy Matron immediately informed Mother. Around to the flat she drove, in a panic, in her dented green van and ordered me home for a rest. She said nothing about the dent, no doubt because her favourite had been driving.

Delayed shock was all it was and I was soon fine. Fine enough to put up cousin Connor and a different set of mad Uni chums from Dublin for a weekend. I was on a late shift that Saturday night and Anna looked after them until they decided to take themselves off and do Sheffield Dublin style. As it happened the city was celebrating Ulster Week. Fancy banners were everywhere around the city centre, until a wild bunch of Dubliners decided otherwise.

"Well, hello der, gentlemen!" the boisterous drunken bums muttered as they fell into the hallway early that Sunday morning. They hadn't met our two big Aussie biker neighbours on the ground floor. They did long hours at the Basset's Liquorice Allsorts factory and were keen on early Sunday morning starts for some rough biking across Derbyshire.

I had only just come in when I heard one of the Aussies shout up the stairs.

"Rose ... there's some drunken idiots, eejits, down here say they know you. Do you want us to chuck 'em out!"

Rushing downstairs I was faced with five bleary-eyed Irish lads and a red-faced Connor laden with Ulster Week banners and bunting.

"What's all this?"

"Ah sure, we couldn't walk trough de town wid dese despicable Ulster flag tings! We tought you could decorate your place wid dem!"

"I am sorry about this," began Connor, somewhat contrite about the state in which they had returned.

It wasn't a problem. The Aussies thought it was great and offered to dispose of the evidence. They also gave the likeable 'eejits' a bucket of liquorice allsorts which saved me having to cook breakfast. Anna and I were worried we might get a knock on the door from police later. It didn't happen and we laughed at how uninhibited these Irish lads were compared with the dull guys we had become so used to.

Chapter Ten
#Jesu Joy of Man's Desiring# (Bach/Stokowski)

My next direct experience with saving lives was in Casualty, a unit well-known in the hospital for its humour, tragedy and the macabre. ER or A & E as it is tagged these days, was a nerve-wracking place in which to work because any type of injury could burst through the double-doors at any time.

Casualty was one of the few units at The Royal that treated student nurses as capable young adults, when the student pulled his or her weight. We had to be positive and decisive. We had to be on-hand with the correct instruments, sutures, dressings, fluids and whatever else was demanded by a houseman or woman under serious pressure. If the case was complex the registrar or consultant was called and our level of responsibility rose accordingly.

All newcomers were shown the contents of a huge hamper of life-saving medical equipment on their first day. It was there for use in large-scale emergencies such as a 'plane crash or multiple pile-up.

"Fret not, oh ye of no experience," Sister mocked at those of us concerned about the purpose of each of the items. "We haven't had to unpack it yet, Girls!"

Of course, Voodoo MacFarlane was now in Casualty.

My first few days were uneventful with a sprained ankle, gashes, head bumps, a splinter, vomiting and the like needing attending to. On my third evening, Sister had just tootled off to supper leaving me on my own in the empty ground floor unit when the 'phone rang.

"It's the Sheffield Star here, Nurse. Have they arrived yet?"

"Who are they?" I asked innocently.

"Wey, lass! The train crash, just outside Sheffield!"

I thanked the reporter, heart thumping, for the tip-off.

"You'd best get ready lass, it was a reet big bang we hear!"

Putting the red hot phone down Nurse Dimwit immediately began clearing the area of chairs and tables in the fortunately deserted entrance and dragged the emergency hamper into a prominent position. Telephoning Senior Staff on a break, particularly supper, was vigorously discouraged. However, I felt I had to do it. Sister told me calmly to get things ready and ring again when the first casualties arrived.

Secretly, I hoped she would be slow to return and that I would be photographed with the first casualties and featured across The Star with suitable HEROINE NURSE headlines! Maybe they would even quote our well-worn "saving bleedin' lives" quip.

I was still on my own, holding the empty floor when an ambulance pulled casually into its parking bay, its lights not flashing. I was about to be deluged with accident victims, not. It must have been a full minute before the doors opened and a train driver with blackened face was wheeled in. He had a broken ankle. Behind him was a sooty-faced walking-wounded fireman with his arm in a sling supporting a strained wrist.

That was it! No pictures, no moment of glory, only a cross Sister helping me push the hamper back across the floor and replace the furniture I had moved. It was a goods train that had derailed, no collision and no injured passengers.

It was not always so uneventful, of course. On some days there would be a steady stream of injured people turn up and we would miss breaks and even complete mealtimes. I was never faced with a real trauma, however, in the days before the drunken violence and knife-inflicted injuries that marks weekends at A & E in hospitals across the UK today.

I even had time to chat with patients about their illnesses or those of their relatives they came in with.

"Ee nurse, I 'ad a kerronery when I were on me 'olidays at Clethorpees. I were that poorly I thought me Maker had took me boots off ready to tak' me wi' im!"

I would hear "duodanal" and "arthuritis" and all about "me scrumatics" or "pernoomonia." One woman was returning for a check on her "helicopter pilot" bug. The reading of *heliobactor pylorus* was beyond her.

During our strict training regime we got the 'all work and no play' thing sorted in our favour. We could not have survived those three years of militaristic training without resorting to partying and plonk at least. We were young, with a growing confidence, skills, independence and some money in our pockets with times a-changing all around us.

We did occasionally ally with medical, mostly male, students and were generally happy with the distraction they offered. They suffered similar humiliation and put-downs on the wards. Demolition usually followed their failure to give an instant answer to a question of diagnosis from Doctor God on one of his 'Carry On' rounds. Some students were bold enough to clown around behind the doctor's back and even attempt to make a date with a nearby nurse regardless of what she was doing.

After Sister Low's valiant cardiac resuscitation attempt on Men's Medical, Sister Bubbles let it be known we were to attend the next infarction if possible. It was soon after, at about one in the morning I heard that a patient had suffered a heart attack in the hospital's brand new kidney unit. I was in charge of the adjacent ward and rushed in for a front row view of another live resuscitation. Sister Bubbles had already hauled her patient's uraemic, parchment-skinned body on to the floor. A hard surface was essential, she said. Also on the scene was our play-acting hospital Romeo-if-given-half-a-chance Doctor Cedric who had been passing through the ward.

It was unfortunate that Sister Bubbles put so much effort into thumping, and pressing the patient's sternum with the palms of her hands she broke wind with the might of a thunderclap. I barely contained myself because of some accompanying pantomime from the young doctor. Sister must have been extremely embarrassed but she carried on valiantly pumping. Unfortunately the patient did not survive.

Cardiac resuscitation had arrived. It was developed and improved and now saves countless lives around the world. With it came many a Lazarus tale with consistent accounts of a vision of a brilliantly-lit tunnel. Some 'goners' also beheld a Christ-like figure in the distance instructing them to go back and serve their time on Earth.

Housemen were bad-tempered beasts in the main, ashen-faced and over-wrought, swearing if we didn't set up an intravenous drip up quickly enough. It was possible they had not slept for sixty hours. They were nevertheless, pussycats compared with irate registrars and consultants. Seniors were known to have kicked a nurse's carefully prepared surgical trolley out of temper. Stress showed all the way down the line. At the top, it was anxious-to-please Sisters and senior nurses that could make idiots of themselves on consultants rounds, tripping, dropping things or even forgetting the X-rays or lab reports they had just rushed to and from their office for.

151

We coped because a bad day would end when a ranting sister or doctor went off-duty, or we reached the end of a shift. The exodus could be a heavenly release, like inhaling nitrous oxide and skipping down the ward. Just occasionally the most zealous, like Sister G. went nowhere. Many times I heard of her doing back-to-back shifts.

Discipline and pecking order was not confined to the wards either. The hospital dining room was also wired up, so to speak, with Senior Spies and Sisters' Pets. When we had hoovered as much free stodge as our stomachs could take we had to request permission to leave from the Staff Nurses' table. Sometimes permission was given with a wink and a nod. At other times more aloof Wannabe Sisters would ask us to wait until they had finished their meal.

Ward Sisters had their own dining and sitting rooms, as did housemen, registrars and consultants. Segregation was vigorously enforced. Familiarity was frowned upon even between more senior student nurses and qualified nurses until kinder winds of change began to blow through hospitals and indeed, other institutions.

The Civil Rights Movement in the United States and other parts of the world at that time, 1965, was fighting a heartfelt battle for equal rights. I was shocked by the violence against Black citizens on the rare occasions I watched Ma's grainy black and white television at home. There was a whole stratum of society over there determined to 'keep them in their place.' We were waking up to the fact that this type of class superiority and rigid views was on our doorstep as well.

Our real allies and true saints were the worn out dining-room staff, cleaners and auxiliaries, lovely Rita Faircloughs and Hilda Ogdens who would even wipe away a nurse's tears at mealtimes or in quiet corners of the hospital with their hankies after yet another "it's so unfair" remonstration.

"N'er you mind, Luv. You'll show 'em, one day, 'ee by gum you will!" they would say, teaching us about comfort eating, piling extra treacle pudding or bread and dripping onto childbearing hips.

It wasn't until Angry Young Medical Men, mostly the working class university entrants we thought, began to stand up to and even argue with the Great and the Good that we realized how pathologically obedient we were. Their courage or foolishness could be immense. Any truculence or sign of 'attitude' was efficiently crushed before we started as Green Girls, sometimes even at interviews.

In continuing support for this new empowerment of youth was anarchic popular music including the 'protest song.' People dared to smoke Cannabis openly. Television satire such as That Was The Week That Was, TW3 to the Luvvies, was goose pimple viewing for us on our days off sitting alongside our silent parents. Newspapers could hardly keep up with social changes. The Lady Chatterley trial kicked off things in 1960. The Christine Keeler Affair in 1963, the Scandal of the Century, kept it going and showed clearly, if there was any doubt, that many of our Masters of the Universe had slimy feet of clay.

And not to forget the day in 1962 "the world held its breath" when a young, dynamic President and his cabinet saw off a challenge from what they perceived as entrenched views in the incident known as the Cuban Missile Crisis. We read the newspapers and were getting the idea about politics and the Cold War. It was a serious situation and I shudder now over how close the world came to all-out nuclear war. If I had survived, my nursing skills would probably have been irrelevant in the ensuing apocalypse.

Still, none of us dared answer back at home or at work. We didn't know that some of our violent teacher and angry Ward Sister rages and humiliations were unacceptable behaviour. The word abuse wasn't yet in use for the sexual, physical and psychological assault on children, in domestic and sexual violence and in workplace bullying that had reached the level of criminal act.

We were at risk at all times. When making beds, for example we had to measure the sheet turnovers. If they were not eighteen inches exactly or not to Sister's liking on each of the ward's thirty beds, they would have to be re-made, sometimes again and again. We took this nonsense just like those called up into the armed services.

Patients were only ever abusive or violent because of alcohol or illness. Forty years on from my training, eighty per cent of nurses reported in a 2006 study being abused by patients. This is a shocking and shaming comment on social behaviour today. To think it has come to the point where patients are warned of a £1,000 fine if they are rude or abusive to hospital staff.

Change is ongoing as people's behaviour, need and circumstances evolve. The NHS infantilised patients from the outset. Apart from pockets of excellence, as at The Jessop Hospital, Daddy is doctor, Mummy is nurse and Child is the patient. The hospital hierarchy suffered the same crass mores with doctor/ consultant, matron/ senior staff and junior/ trainee nurse.

It was at The Jessop for the first time I saw patients' emotional needs acknowledged and their worries or concerns not dismissed as hysterical. The Royal was traditional in this respect. Patients were not party to information about their diagnosis, treatment and prognosis, particularly if it was cancer. My brother knew about his because he had read and was able to understand notes left on his bed. Emotional upset in patients was disregarded because repressed seniors did not want to become involved.

At the end of May 1965 over the Whitsun weekend, Ditzy Delia and I went down to London to visit my two brothers Morris and Pascal. Morris was managing the Warner cinema in the West End and we stayed at his tiny flat in Soho. Pascal was working for a travel company developing Cheap Package Holidays.

In those days the cheapest holidays were by coach to the South of France or just over the Pyrenees on very dodgy roads he said, to the 'exotic' wild and unspoilt *Costa Brava*. You could fly to Benidorm or Majorca but we certainly couldn't afford £35 for a 12 to 14-day holiday. As a Green Girl I received three pounds a week. Half I gave to my mother before moving to Tapton Court. After bus fares I was left with about a pound. I wasn't much better off as a student nurse.

Pascal arranged to meet us two travel-weary hitch-hikers from Sheffield at Scott's Bar in Piccadilly. We had just settled into an alcove seat when a barman caught our eye and whispered it was Peter O'Toole sitting alone, smoking in the alcove next to us. Ditzy Delia and I excused ourselves to go to the Ladies to get a better look. This man, one of the great actors of the day after his performance in Lawrence of Arabia in 1962 and Becket in 1964, was unbelievably beautiful. There was no doubt he was appraising us as we passed because, in a state close to knees buckling, we pushed open the door of the Gents.

"Wrong one, girls!" came the silky voice from behind a cloud of cigarette smoke, "unless I am mistaking boys for girls!"

When we emerged he asked, with the most piercing blue eyes if the three of us would like to join him and his friend who had just arrived. Pascal soon ascertained this was Johnny Mercer, the playwright from Wakefield. They gassed for most of the evening while

Ditzy Delia and I passed a couple of hours with a pleasantly sozzled Mr. O'Toole talking rubbish, though he did seem impressed with the fact we were nurses. He was a charmer, a perfect gentleman and it made our first night in London an unforgettable one.

Staying in Soho for the weekend surrounded by neon signs flashing "striptease," "girls, girls, girls," "peep show" and "strip club" with cards and notices advertising models and seedy clubs galore was an eye-opener for us provincial girls. We had a coffee in Old Compton Street at the 2i's Coffee Bar hoping there might be an impromptu session start up. We gaped at the windows of sex shops showing things we had no idea what they were supposed to do. Girls were wearing daringly short skirts, now being measured in inches above the knee.

Pascal loved Soho and lamented having missed the venue in Great Windmill Street where the Trad Jazz movement took off. This was Cy Laurie's Jazz Club, now the Mod Club. He heard that Georgie Fame might be doing the Saturday All-nighter at the Flamingo Club in nearby Wardour Street but wouldn't hear of us being out on our own. There was so much to see anyway during the day we didn't mind. That weekend we wandered around Soho and the West End with our mouths open!

We didn't want to go back North to Hades but it was fortunate the start of my three-month summer stint at The Jessop Hospital was like walking into Mediterranean sunlight. Ward Sister was a kindly, intelligent older mum-type, if I may keep the family analogy going. Now well into my second year and for the first time in my training I began to enjoy learning in a relaxed environment on a ward, no longer on red alert for scathing comments or behavioural meltdown.

Apart from classes with "yes you can!" Miss T., the atmosphere at The Jessop was the most open and friendly so far. It was no surprise it was still running at peak efficiency. It was patient-oriented with the often-exhausted women treated with respect rather than patronised. It was obvious to all of us who did stints here this was the way patients should be treated.

We also liked the pioneering treatment protocol for each type of surgery and the autoclaved packs of dressings for each type of regime. At The Royal we boiled instruments in the steriliser. This doesn't kill spores as autoclaving does. It only kills bacteria. The advanced Jessop packs were a forerunner of the sterilised surgical packs now used in every medical and nursing procedure.

Achieving ninety-nine per cent in my Jessop Hospital ward report was a huge boost to my self-esteem. Gaining such a high mark won me more praise from my flatmates and made me realise I wasn't as dim as I had thought all the way through school. With study, I knew I could do well in my Hospital Finals. These exams we would be taking a few months before the State Finals.

My good ward report was helped partly because I had probably saved a post-hysterectomy patient from bleeding to death. Whilst taking her pulse and blood pressure I noted she was pale, clammy, sighing and restless. I pulled back the sheets and saw the lower half of the bed swamped with fresh blood. I rang her bell, reassured her she would be tended to immediately, grabbed another nurse to stay with her and actually ran down the ward to Sister's office. The patient was whisked back to theatre.

To see a nurse running is rare because it is forbidden except in cases of fire or real emergency. I knew a complication like this after such an operation was a real danger. There is some detective work involved in nursing, listening to a patient or relative and understanding what they are saying. There were many things we needed to be aware of with, for example, post-operative, post-delivery and bed-bound patients. These included adequate pain relief, DVT, pulmonary embolus and inflammation at the needle site of an intravenous infusion. In Miss T.'s words, careful observation "saves lives and relieves distress."

We had dark moments but did manage to laugh. Black humour is sometimes the only way to lighten a serious work load or distressing time. One quiet night on Women's Geriatric at the main hospital, Sister and I were catching up on paperwork. An elderly spinster, a vicar's daughter three beds away from us suddenly sat bolt upright. It made me jump. With hands clasped she enunciated in a well-spoken voice "Oh Lord, send me a motion!"

Staff looked at her watch and said "oops, three o'clock, I forgot to tell you, Nurse. Bedpan, quickly!"

Sister drew the curtain around the woman's bed and I moved swiftly up the hallway. When I returned with the bedpan I was too late even though I had not wasted time warming it under the tap. Sister grimaced and was to say to me later we could set our watches to the event for the rest of the week. I was lucky, two years into nursing that this was my first such cleaning-up operation. Now I knew why my friends occasionally addressed themselves Student Nurse QSS (Queen of the Shit Shovellers ...).

One of my saddest nights at The Jessop with absolutely no humour in it was when another student nurse, Ava, was brought in as an emergency admission. High-spirited elfin Ava was one block behind us. Her room had been next to mine at the Nurses Home and we had shared many laughs. She was admitted because an abortion had gone wrong and she had overdosed deliberately or accidentally. She was saved and the foetus aborted naturally. When she was discharged from the ward she was quietly despatched to the local psychiatric unit.

Even though this was a modern unit in a nice part of town it was, even to us, a place where only 'mad' people were sent. We plucked up the courage to visit her and found her sitting in the Day Room like a Zombie. We were shocked at how the incident had affected her. A houseman's brother whom we knew as a sexual bully and who had tried it on with most of us had impregnated her. It was shameful that she was treated like a pariah by the hospital and expelled from nursing because of the incident. We felt bad but dared not speak out about her despicable treatment and lack of support.

This man had escorted me home one night after a party and out of politeness I asked him if he would like a coffee. His verbal abuse when I resisted his advances was very upsetting. He was so persistent I had to escape into Ditzy Delia's room she was sharing with Loopy Lottie. They woke with a start and were so frightened by this rabid male they hid in the wardrobe. I only got rid of him by threatening to report his behaviour to everyone I could think of on the spur of the moment. I still felt it must have been my fault and that I had led him on when he was clearly a sex maniac.

Ava's illegal termination and attempted suicide was a red light to us at the end of our second year, all still virgins. Birth control was still almost unknown. A pregnancy, a child would have been impossible to carry through. In any case, a condition of our training was that we did not marry, so that we might give our all to the cause of nursing. Even after training, in the days when many women gave up their jobs when they married, young married nurses were treated with some contempt by older nursing sisters. With attitudes and social changes advancing we stood a chance of being married and remaining nurses.

I had broken up with Leo after a year, not because of his Val Doonican cardigans and red hair. More irritating were his habits of dunking biscuits and curling his little finger while drinking tea. I had enjoyed his program "Educating Rose" that had brought me up to speed on jazz and folk music and more sophisticated reading. I was puzzled why I went off the poor guy every three weeks or so. Much as I liked him much of the time, I wasn't madly in love with him and he had to go.

These issues bugged me, I realised only years later, at the same time before my period each month. It was not until the 1980s that PMT, later known as PMS, was recognized and became a syndrome that explained so much about a woman's cyclical behaviour and suffering. Indeed, regular suffering of those around her also. I overheard a discussion in a Health Food and vitamin supplements shop in the 1980s about PMT supplements. One was Evening Primrose Oil under the brand name Effamol. The woman snapped at her probably long-suffering partner about the effectiveness of such things. "Effamol off," he retorted with a wry grin.

My love-life was surely uncomplicated compared with that of a teenager today. Work was our focus and we needed all our energy for it. My emotional life became harder to deal with once I lost my virginity, at almost twenty-two! Much later, my grown-up daughter commented that when a relationship becomes fully intimate is when problems can really start.

How can a girl of twelve or thirteen today deal with such adult issues without the experience of being an adult? I may have been a little old, they are surely too young. Open discussion about a healthy sex life is too soon for young teenagers, though some sort of preparation is essential in learning how to handle what is to come. We had uncomplicated fun because we were just young and daft and not in sexual relationships. There was nothing wrong in innocent dreaming about a fairy-tale romance.

We certainly didn't feel the need to be in constant contact with one another. Telephones were becoming common by the mid-1960s but they were for giving and receiving information and for emergencies. Telephone calls, especially from public boxes were not high on the priority list with the pennies we had to spend. There was no nattering, though I do remember in 1965 it was possible to talk in a call box for up to an hour on four pence, assuming no-one tapped on the glass.

Today's incessant gossiping, texting, e-mailing and preoccupation with social networking would have been considered vulgar and intrusive. People guarded their privacy. It was beyond comprehension forty years ago that it would get to unsolicited advertising, scams, cyber-bullying, sexting, voyeurism, eavesdropping and pornographic images passing backwards and forwards via a gizmo you could hold in the flat of your hand.

Despite the warnings of Ava's demise it was time for a clandestine romance with a junior doctor with whom I had worked on Male Medical. Clandestine because he was married. We had bumped into each other at The Royal. Now he was at the Obstetrics Unit and on my ward at The Jessop and it was time to move things on a pace.

Josh was a Kenyan Asian with a likeable face and exuberant personality. Warm and affectionate he didn't have the repressed reserve of his English counterparts. He won my heart initially by treating me as an intelligent being rather than a Nitwit Nurse, a sub-species to be ordered about and who cleared up after them.

One quiet night on my gynae ward at The Jessop, Josh appeared and asked permission from Sister for me and a fellow student nurse to see a live birth, our first. Below us, in an isolated theatre reminiscent of a 2001: A Space Odyssey set, a young woman was lying on her side in full labour pushing the baby's head out. I was both spellbound and queasy at a scene that reminded me of cows giving birth at Fanshawgate in my childhood.

Dear Reader, this was my Doctor Kildare moment, doubly moved as I was in being present at a live birth and by watching Josh's sensitive treatment of the new mum. I had fallen hook, line and sinker for him despite knowing he was married, albeit unhappily in a marriage arranged by his family. Everything else was to his advantage. Doctors were considered a catch by most nurses and my own father was a doctor whom I admired and respected.

About giving birth, I recall saying to Josh "it won't happen to me!" It did a few years later, of course, with my two Lucky Eggs, Lilly and Kitty.

I was not alone moving into uncharted territory. When Manic

Myrtle decided she would marry Philip, she told no-one about becoming pregnant or their wedding. Her distress at being in-child outside marriage caused her to fail her finals. The shame was deep-rooted and she was unable to bond with her child at the beginning. Phillip had to rush home at lunch-time to feed and care for him.

It was equally sad that we, her closest friends and nurses also, did not have a clue about post-natal depression and most other mental health problems, as with PMT. We were frustrated at not knowing what to do in a situation where a young mother rejects her baby. A judgemental, moralistic culture was still cruel for some and I wonder today how anyone would want to return to these Good Old Days. Myrtle's needless guilt had lessened by the birth of her second child and she was much happier about both children but her angst at the time still upsets me.

It was unfortunate that our training of treating the patient without judgement did not apply to attempted suicide admissions. Nurses and doctors were often sadistic in their treatment of these troubled, usually young people. They were regarded as time-wasters. Some medical staff would even enjoy making their stomach wash-out as unpleasant as possible. You heard comments about it being a pity they didn't succeed in 'topping' themselves. Psychiatric treatment and public awareness seemed to be in the Dark Ages.

There was far more sectioning of patients and confinement in an asylum or mental hospital. There seemed to be no in-between. Women have undoubtedly fared badly through history with emotional dysfunction brought on by hormonal problems or post-natal or menopausal depression could be interpreted as evidence of mental problems. Physical care of patients in hospital was faultless but should patients, or staff, become emotionally fraught they would be given the 'pull yourself together' treatment. It is no surprise we did not know how to handle these problems and why we got short shrift with problems or concerns of our own.

There could hardly have been a family without 'shameful' secrets, much of the shame being Ten Commandments related. They included illegitimacy, homosexuality, bi-sexuality, sexual abuse, domestic violence, bullying, alcoholism, anorexia, bulimia, infidelity, bigamy, incest, paranoia, depression, addiction, rape, abortion, criminality, sexually-transmitted disease, self-harming, substance abuse, embarrassing illnesses, infertility, frigidity, erectile dysfunction, emotional blackmail, job loss, unemployment, debt, bankruptcy, abandonment and desertion.

It was time for us to thank our uptight, obedient families for doing their best during difficult decades and move on in allowing newly-enlightened post-war youth to challenge hypocritical values and repair and restore human dignity.

It wasn't until I was in my second year of training that Mother started getting over Damien's death. Pa was still away at sea much of the time. Simon was at home but Mother was often alone and was welcoming when I turned up with friends. My giddy flatmates brought a breath of fresh air to the house. Pascal and his police pals would call in and entertain us with their hilarious dealings with Jo Public.

Mother liked Leo too. The first time I took him home Val Doonican was crooning away on the television on his fireside rocking chair.

"I can't stand men in cardigans," she said absently.

"Thanks," replied a bemused Leo, sitting by the fireside in his.

Her recovery was in the form of growing confidence from her job in a hidden annexe in Fulwood. It was an eye-opener for me, a home for babies that had been rejected by their parents because of deformities, mostly due to *hydrocephalus* and *spina bifida*. The annexe did not feature in the training of Royal Hospital nurses.

The *spina bifida* element is a see-through hole at the base of the spine of a new-born where backbone and spinal canal has not closed. Sometimes there is a see-through sac on the lower spine that resembles a small jellyfish. Paraplegia and double incontinence were a feature of these children's deformities.

The secret ward had been established by a Professor of Paediatrics, a Catholic who did not believe these children should be left to die after birth. Some of the babies had pioneering shunts inserted in their brains that drained excess fluid into the spinal column. Nevertheless, Mother told me of babies whose heads had grown almost to the width of the cot and who had sores that needed attending to because of this. They had high, shiny foreheads and slanted eyes and as with normal children, Mother assured me, many stood out for their warmth, intelligence and beauty.

She clearly loved working in this place of few visitors. The trauma of rejection many of these babies experienced and the love and care

161

they needed gave her the will to carry on with her own life. I believe she raised the standard of care considerably while she was in the unit. She was a frustrated nurse.

Later in my life when involved in pain management I was privileged to meet a young woman named Melanie who had serious *spina bifida* at the base of her spine. She had suffered greatly from having spent most of her short life in a wheelchair. Few people are tested to such limits. Melanie valued her pain-free time too much to waste it on mean and petty things. She grieved however, for being unable to enjoy a normal life and because of the strain she knew she put on her remarkable family.

She died in her early thirties and was one of three people I have met in my life whose lightness of spirit, humour and lack of guile mark them as special. Her severe disability ennobled her. She dealt with the intolerable with grace, dignity and generosity. Suffering such as this, the deformities of the children in the Fulwood annexe, even the simple joy of Down Syndrome children raise difficult questions about the discarding of 'imperfect' beings at the foetal stage.

I began a three-month placement at the Sheffield Children's Hospital at the time Mother was working with these special babies. There was innovative change in the hospital and it was an exciting environment to be working in. Nursing children was new for all of us in the group. When sick youngsters were admitted to hospital in the Nineteen-fifties they were sometimes put into adult wards where visiting was limited and where there might still have been a harsh regime. In some hospitals, parents were not allowed to visit their bewildered offspring at all.

The five paediatric student nurses with us were a mad bunch. They already had experience on the wards and primed us on which Sisters to watch out for. They had us regular student nurses in fits with some of the escapades, particularly the kids' sayings. Their favourite was a little boy from the run-down Parson's Cross Council Estate who was a frequent admission with a prolapsed rectum.

"Miss, me bum's cum aht again ..." he would inform us.

The formerly harsh regime for children was a different experience for the late author Frank McCourt. In his book Angela's Ashes he writes how heavenly he found it, a desperately poor child in 1950s Ireland, being in a clean hospital bed with regular food. He had contracted typhoid and wasn't fazed by the strict discipline of the nuns nursing him. Being given books to read for the first time in his life was pure joy. This was common with the poorer children.

On my first morning I was taken aback at Freddy and the Dreamers blaring out from one of the airy four-bedded wards. Matron Welburn would have needed smelling salts. I listened to Staff's morning report that half of the ten children and two babies were very ill. One of the paediatric students then took me to a four-bedded ward to meet the children I would be looking after. This was the room from which a Dansette was now belting out I like it, I like it!

"It's for Maureen here. She loves Freddie and The Dreamers, don't you, Luvvie?"

Maureen was a thin, pale child of five or six with damp, thick black hair. She was lying absolutely still with her darkly-lashed eyes closed. A faint smile on her lips was the only way she could respond. Outside the ward, Staff told me Maureen was blind and couldn't move. She was dying from a wasting disease and her family no longer visited.

"Freddie himself came to see her," she said. "He was so sweet to do that. He is her whole life."

The other three little patients were chatty and cheeky and fit enough to be out of bed for washing and dressing. We communicated our intention with Maureen with quiet talk and lightly touching her. She rarely responded but when she did open those blue eyes it was as if this abnormally still little body which had only known increasing disability from birth was on a completely different plane. She cried occasionally, the saddest most affecting weeping. Only Freddie's singing calmed her.

Her death two weeks later seemingly triggered four more, making me feel I was a bad omen on the ward. One boy succumbed to Reyes-Disease, a fatal reaction to aspirin. This is why it should never be given to children under sixteen years of age. The three other children died from cancer.

Witnessing these little children bearing terminal illness with calm dignity was a permanent leveller for me. Cancer survivors Sharon Osborne and jockey Bob Champion said they were able to deal with their illness from knowing children with cancer and seeing how they dealt with it. Some asked, why me? Others asked, why not me?

Within a few years of nursing, the bad omen concern disappeared. I didn't mind it the other way, which is how I was greeted on a regular placing on one cardiac ward. "Patients don't die on you!" the night staff quipped. Even when I was terrified I apparently emitted a quiet calm appreciated by nurses and patients. Staff are occasionally hyperactive and this can provoke anxiety in patients.

After a death on any ward during my training I had to quell thoughts of my own brother's final days. It was an unwelcome coincidence at the end of my second and third years of training that I was assigned to night duty on Arthur Jackson Orthopaedic Ward on the anniversary of his death. This was at 1.40 am on 22 October, 1962. On both occasions it felt as if he had wanted me there.

Reading through the ward reports detailing the last week of his young life was painful. Staff on duty with me said she wept when preparing his Belsenesque body for the mortuary. This was unusual. I have never cried when laying out a patient, though I would have in this instance. This was part of my belief that a nurse must be in control of herself and the situation so she can deal with bereft relatives.

We were taught that it is vital to keep our relationships with patients and their families neutral and professional. I was learning it was sometimes hard not to cross the line. A young life lost is profound. I knew a doctor who visited the grave of one of his patients, a girl who died from leukaemia. It took him a good while to recover from her death.

I was pleased to see Damien's last girlfriend Anne, now a Staff Nurse on a ward for babies with serious congenital problems. Caring for very sick babies is daunting. They are so fragile and have such tiny airways. Anne taught me how to overcome my trepidations before my move to a main ward at the Children's Hospital for the remainder of the three months.

A little boy there began writing me love letters. It was a touching end to a tough assignment. We were on the verge of our third year as students. Time for some serious study for the all-important Hospital and State Finals. Time too for us to be treated as nurses who could be increasingly trusted and respected.

Chapter Eleven
#Yes You Can ...# (DJ Clayvis)

From the outset of our third year we were left in charge of a ward on a day or night shift for an increasing amount of time. This new responsibility was exuberant. Male Medical was my favourite ward. Attempting a diagnosis of a patient with complex symptoms and interesting syndromes before the doctor arrived became a challenge to my awakening brain. Even now, decades after being involved in nursing I try and keep up-to-date with medical matters.

I put this down to Miss T. She encouraged me to think beyond nursing and for a while I considered enrolling as a medical student. This was daunting because we knew the hours and conditions the veterinary and dental students were putting up with. My flat mates were already mocking me for becoming a nursing swot even if it was more a labour of fascination. Three months before the Male Medical block I was on Male Surgical. Though patients were livelier the experience was not as cerebral.

"It's just knives and forks!" one consultant exclaimed. "Pipes, pumps and bellows that need cutting out and replacing if they become diseased or injured."

This drew my attention to how little we know our bodies. Males might know the purpose of switches on a machine or how much oil a car needs to run properly but they struggle when asked how much blood is needed to keep their body working efficiently.

I won't forget Stan on Male Surgical. This thirty-something gentleman wasn't interested in anything practical unless it related to Sheffield Wednesday. He was there because his bowel had failed to heal after an operation. No treatment intervention had been able to close a five-inch cavity and he had to lie over a metal kidney-shaped bowl because the fistula hole leaked. He was also wasting away and was being fed via high calorie intravenous fluids. We were constantly removing the foul-smelling liquid in this bowl and cleaning him.

On his birthday we agreed to a discrete little after-hours party some patients wanted to throw for him and wheeled his bed into the Day Room. Bottles of Guinness and Stout appeared magically and it wasn't long before this midnight gathering could be heard along the corridors, laughter, bottles clinking and music playing quietly on the radio.

"Stan's scored here, Nurse!" said one of the patients, helping a grinning Stan with his glass of Guinness. He didn't know it was passing straight through him.

The patients had placed look-outs and just as I had ascertained the distinct gurgling sound in the ward was Stan's gut the word came that Senior Night Sister Low was in the vicinity. The Ancient Gliding Wooden Spoon as they called her, was about to begin her rounds. We rushed Stan back to his bed station and the walking wounded cleared away the booze and slipped back into their beds. Everything was quiet until Sister shone her torch into Stanley's bowl.

"Nurse MacFarlane," she called under her breath, "call the duty doctor. Stanley is leaking old black blood. It's probably a bleeding ulcer. Take his blood pressure and do hurry up ..."

All of us, including the patient were sucking Polo Mints to put Sister off the scent. It worked. I went to call the doctor and Sister's round was cut mercifully short by her bleeper summoning her elsewhere. The Guinness in Stan's bowl was quickly emptied and on Sister's return it showed the more regular green bile.

We were pleased we had risked a party. The hole eventually healed and Stan went home. He had missed several matches but his 'friends' in Male Surgical were chuffed to hear he was given a free Hillsborough pass for the remainder of the season.

Another frequent patient on the surgical ward was a scruffy little man who would come in to have his testicular *hydrocele* drained. His testicles would swell to the size of rugby balls and keeping him comfortable in this state required inventive nursing.

Young lads were often admitted to the surgical ward with an undescended testicle. The rogue testicle would be pulled down under anaesthetic and tethered with a long black suture to the lad's knee. This was sewn through his inner knee skin to keep the testicle down and prevent it shooting back up. Definitely one occasion I was glad to be female!

One night, a young man was admitted as an emergency appendix. We prepared him for this routine operation and off he went to theatre. Two hours later we wondered what else the surgeons might have found to keep him in theatre so long. When Night Sister appeared on her round she told us the young man had died from an adverse reaction to the anaesthetic. Only after the autopsy and Coroner's report was it learnt his brother had the same congenital problem and had died in similar circumstances. We were saddened by this news. If it hadn't been an emergency the doctors may have picked up on the link and he might have lived.

I had one more run-in with Sister Bubbles, one of our earlier tormentors, after one of my patients with breathing problems swallowed an anal suppository. I left it on her locker and went to fetch a rubber glove. When I returned she was gagging, having 'helped me out' by swallowing the suppository whole, tin foil and all. I went to seek Sister Bubbles' advice.

"Bloody 'ell, MacFarlane, you've done it, now ..."

She started chortling, reassuring me the "daft brush" of a patient would survive.

The final three-month placement of my third year was a depressing stint once again in back-of-beyond Fulwood. A newish ground floor annexe housed neurological medicine wards, male and female plastic surgery wards, a plastic surgery theatre and a burns unit. I was assigned initially to Women's Neuro-medical. This was a tough one, a ward for intractable neurological cases including advanced multiple sclerosis, brain tumours, Motor Neurone and Parkinson's Disease.

One of the patients dying from a rapidly metastasizing brain tumour was an eighteen-year old hairdresser named June. All of us adored this vibrant, freckle-faced girl who resembled the waif-like actress Jane Seberg in her role as Joan of Arc. It was upsetting for June and frustrating for us that she was with older terminal patients in the ward. Knowing she was really missing people of her own age we persuaded her to put a pretty dress on, make-up, a wig to cover her baldness and go home for as many weekends as she could. Her fiancé, her best friend, continued supporting her until her death a few weeks later.

A few years later I was at a party with Phillip and Manic Myrtle and kept saying I knew one of the boys but could not remember from where. Eventually he told me he was June's fiancé and I felt really bad with my insensitivity. He spent the rest of the evening trying to make me feel better. This book is written particularly in memory of all young people I nursed through my career who died far too young, including brother Damien, Melanie, 'orphan' Maureen from the Children's hospital and June.

My sister-in-law Nuala and my sister Jane had staffed the same neuro-med ward. They were colleagues for several months at the time Nuala was courting my handsome brother Billy. Whenever Billy came to visit, these two feisty nurses would put him up to something to liven things up for the patients. Their favourite was to dress him up as a vicar and make him play the role with a touch of comedy.

"The patients loved him," Nuala recalled. "He'd hold their hands and get them all singing hymns. It was sad he was the only visitor many of them had."

My more sombre time on this ward left me with a lifelong awareness of the devastating effects of MS and Motor Neurone Disease. Forty years on there is still no cure for these awful diseases but promising discoveries such as low neurosteroids in people with MS and the use of neuro-implants for some with Parkinson's are proving to be 'life-savers.' Nursing individuals with chronic incurable diseases has become a speciality in its own right with a multi-disciplinary approach. In the mid-1960s we felt rather helpless with these long-suffering, splendid patients.

It was with relief that I moved down the corridor of this bright, modern annexe to the plastic and orthopaedic surgery theatre. The male and female wards were filled with much younger, livelier patients. There were serious cases, including a gentleman who had endured more than a hundred operations to reconstruct his penis. It was torn off in a steel works accident when he was driving some machinery.

The eminent senior plastic surgeon in the unit, Mr. Crawford was building a pancake-roll pedicle penis with grafts from the patient's abdomen. Watching this top man work with his innovative plastic surgery techniques was humbling. This was my first time in a theatre where there was magical transformation before your eyes.

His nose re-shaping, breast reductions and apronectomies was pioneering cosmetic surgery. He worked on burns patients, on tight keloidal skin and on cosmetic improvement, though techniques were not as advanced as they are today and many patients remained seriously disfigured. He would operate on babies with cleft palates and strawberry naevi on their faces and on children with disconcerting congenital or accidental deformities.

Mr. Crawford was President of the College of Plastic Surgeons and we had a huge crush on him because he acknowledged his nurses with warm appreciation as well as being a handsome and modest gentleman. The first breast reduction operations in the unit took place when I was there. The surgeon drew a petal around each nipple with a compass, cut along the outline then peeled it back like an orange. Watching the scalpel cut into the skin I could not believe the patient could not feel it and nearly passed out. It was my first time in theatre since ENT two years earlier. When the surgeon asked me to take the yellow fat removed from each breast to the kitchen and weigh the bowls he had put it in, I thought I was being sent on an idiot's errand. It was, of course, to ascertain he had removed even amounts. Occasionally a surgeon would refer to a textbook with his large-breasted patient anaesthetised and totally naked on the table, her arms fixed in a cruciform position.

Plastic surgery could be much gorier. The breaking of a patient's nose with a silver hammer, for example, so the surgeon could reshape it into a prettier snout was quite unnerving. Hip operations on orthopaedic day were the most gruesome. The cleavers and saws surgeons used to cut through muscle, gristle and bone reminded me of a butcher's shop. All this came back to me when listening to the BBC's World Service after the 2012 Haiti earthquake. A surgeon on the island had to buy saws from a hardware store with which he performed thirty-five emergency amputations in the open with his patients enduring it without anaesthetic.

During our training we found theatre duty the most adult. Liaising with doctors and anaesthetists on a one-to-one in a cocooned unit was quite different from being on the ward. Knowing that eyes were everything when masked and gowned and wearing cute woollen Noddy hats, Auburn Anna and I piled on the eye make-up! Behind my mask, however, I was frequently open-mouthed at the banter.

"Did I tell you chaps about the time I went around the Tampax factory ..."

A senior Theatre Sister can be as skilled as medics in her own field. Unfortunately for us, Plastic Theatre's Sister was a creepy Smiling Spider. Having made this theatre her life we were convinced she resented sharing her knowledge. We were sure she also hid special instruments before going on holiday so that surgeons would be relieved she was back. The medical team had wised up to this and knew where to look, or on panic days, get us to hunt them out. They could be naughty about her and with remarks about our youth and phenomenal beauty unhinging her.

The creepiest aspect of middle-aged Sister Enigmatic was her behaviour as a *femme fatale*. She prowled like a wicked stepmother with a thyroid-eyed smile. This was in complete contrast to other career Sisters who were as innocent as doves. Thankfully, Auburn Anna and I were nearly always together on theatre duty and could laugh about it. The Senior Staff Nurse, an angelic-faced Irish sweetie with a jet black pageboy hair cut was the go-between for Senior Sister and the lower orders. For the two stints of three months we were in this small plastic surgery unit we were instructed by the Senior Nurses. Sister Enigmatic spoke to us twice only.

Our primary task was to prepare the sterile operation trolleys laid out with basic surgical instruments and any others required. Many of these instruments were perfected by Sir Archibald McIndoe at the East Grinstead hospital which did innovative work with Second World War pilots. Those who were burned and disfigured became members of the Guinea Pig Club. McIndoe and Sir Harold Gilles are considered the fathers of plastic surgery.

After preparing trolleys our time was divided between the two theatres. We would be answering the 'phone, tying gowns and wiping brows. On panic days we might be hunting for specific instruments. We would also set up the diathermy, the cauterising instrument that arrests bleeding by sealing blood vessels. The smell of burnt flesh and other theatre odours was hard to get used to. Theatre could be tense, or relaxed and jocular depending on who was operating. We were ever mindful of Sister Enigmatic scrubbed up and ready to assist on main operations. Her glare came across loud and clear if we slipped up, or even if it looked as though we might slip up.

Perhaps they had forgotten how intimidating a theatre setting is to a newcomer. It was a cardinal sin for unscrubbed-up staff to contaminate sterile areas. Worse only was leaving an instrument in a patient or miscounting swabs and the conclusion one of these may have been left inside the patient. If there was contamination during surgery everyone had to scrub-up and gown again and a new surgical trolley be prepared.

One aspect of theatre we did not like was being dogsbodies again. Even though we had practically finished our SRN training we felt like below-stairs maids. As soon as an operation had finished and we had helped bring the patient round from the anaesthetic Anna and I had the chore of clearing away the bloody trolleys, sometimes scrubbing hundreds of used instruments and autoclaving them ready for the following day.

Setting up the sacred trolleys early before each operation day was a major task. We were expected to recognise and know the name of a huge number of instruments. These were usually named after the surgeon who had designed the prototype, or after the operation they had been designed for.

The senior anaesthetist had recently established a recovery unit by the operating rooms. This was soon introduced throughout the NHS. Patients who had complex nose, mouth or throat surgery in particular needed close monitoring to ensure a clear airway was maintained. This was intensive work and Anna and I earned our Brownie points in Theatre and Recovery. There was no room for error here.

When ops' had finished for the day or Sister was off-duty we did get up to pranks with the surgeons, hidden as we were in our cosy theatre far from the annexe's Deputy Matron's office. One morning I dressed up as an Old Dear with buck teeth, camouflage make-up and Anna's red hairpiece as a fringe under a white bobble-hat from theatre. With an old mac, granny shoes and stockings I looked the part, though was perhaps a bit tall. Anna got Mr. Crawford's attention when he came in to the theatre building at 8.30 am for his pre-op' cuppa.

She informed him he had a new private patient, a Mrs. Daniels, who had travelled up from Cornwall as she'd heard wonderful stories about his work with people with her type of disfigurement, a flat chest and goofy teeth! Anna, wearing her mask to stop her going into a fit of giggles, showed him into Sister's office where I sat waiting in my outfit.

"Well, good morning Mrs., er, Daniels. How do you do?" He shook my gloved hand with a bemused look on his face.

"Mornin' to ee, Mister C."

Having spent much of my childhood in Cornwall, I had the accent to a tee.

"What can I do for you?" he asked, his face creased into a smile.

"It's moi goofy toofypegs and me flat chest, Mister C. Oi wants them 'ollywood teef so Oi can kiss proper-loike. And moi titties, I'll have one side done this time and the other one done next time, if Oi like wot you done, 'n' all. You don't look so bad yourself, Oi could go for you if Oi 'ain't got moi noo loverr! Oi doesn't care wot it costs and Oi've got hundreds of pounds in me shoes ..."

When I lifted my foot he blurted out he would be pleased to operate for free since I had come all the way from Cornwall. His eyes twinkled and as I pulled out my teeth all three of us burst into laughter. Anna had just come in with a perfect cuppa. The first lesson we learnt in Plastic Theatre was how His Lordship liked his Tetley's. If there was time for a bit of banter, this was a bonus.

I didn't know any other eminent consultant on whom we could have played such a prank. Mr. Crawford was a sweetie and his complete lack of pomposity was appreciated by us. It was something I didn't come across again until many years later when working with good-humoured Aussie doctors.

I popped in to see Mother at the weekend and my story and using our Cornish neighbour's name cheered her up. It took her mind momentarily off the story in the local newspaper, The Star, captioned "Not Wanted: Dead or Alive." The article and picture was laid open for me. It showed an old piano, our old piano, dumped on the moor, in the middle of nowhere, with a journalist posing before it in a Stevie Wonder suit and dark glasses.

"Oh, the shame of it," Mother wailed. "I asked Simon and his friend if they would get rid of it and this is what he does. What if someone recognises it, or saw Simon? I shall never ask any of you to do anything for me ever again ..."

On the following Monday morning I was on late duty in Plastic

Theatre and my flatmates Myrtle, Delia and Anna were on early shift. Glad of a lie in, I was sound asleep in our attic flat in Harcourt Road when I became aware of a faltering male voice close by me.

"Er, I saw that nurses live here, on the front doorbell and I'm, er, looking for my sister ..."

It was a chilling moment opening my bleary eyes to see a tall, gawky stranger sitting on my bed staring at me. He was jittery. He had the cheekbones of a consumptive and the bulging, darting eyes of a hyperthyroid. I accepted the Senior Service he offered with a shaky hand knowing I had to stall for time. I remained lying down in order to keep my alluring Woolworth's blue nylon nightie from his gaze. He jabbered on for several minutes about his supposed missing sister, a nurse he kept saying and that he'd seen our names by the doorbell. I didn't draw attention to the fact my cigarette was not lit. Though my mind was now in overdrive I was still semi-anaesthetised from a deep sleep and not yet in a state of panic.

This changed when his eyes began roving up and down my shape under the bed covers.

"... you're tall aren't you?"

"I am very tall," I said in as threatening a manner as possible. "Now please go as I have to get up for work."

Unwanted Intruder then stubbed his cigarette out on the floorboards, walked casually to the landing and looked down the stairs. I didn't know how fast I could get out of bed and pull my dressing gown on. When he came back in to my room my mind was now on the concern of being raped and thrown out of a sash window three floors up. There was nothing for it but to scream as he lunged at me. With unknown reserves of strength I prevented him from pushing me onto the bed. He kept telling me to shut up, which I didn't and it was his turn to panic. Almost as suddenly as he appeared, he was gone.

At first I was afraid to leave my room but I plucked up the courage, grabbed the pennies on my dressing table handy for the 'phone box and ran for my life down the stairs. There was someone on the stairs, Una and I nearly sent her, my sweet saviour, into next week. Never was I so glad to see Una. She was a simple Irish girl who had become a regular visitor to the flat since we had befriended her. Ditzy Delia was on duty when Una was admitted to Casualty for taking an overdose.

"Una," I panted, "quickly, go and call the police. Here's four pence.

Tell them a man came and sat on my bed, then attacked me."

Eyes shining, Una took the pennies and disappeared. A few minutes later she rushed back up the stairs.

"Oi dialled 999, Rose," she said gasping in her wonderful Irish brogue. "Here's your money. Doncha know it's a free call?"

She put the kettle on for tea and rooted around for some brandy.

"Did he do dirty tings, wit ye?" not so simple Una asked eventually.

"No, thank Jesus, Mary and Joseph himself."

It was only minutes later Una answered the doorbell and there was the sound of heavy boots on the stairs. It was Pascal's best pal, Big John.

"Wey then!" he said, looking me over. Una told him she thought I hadn't been raped. "What's the matter wi' you, then, that he didn't rape ye?"

For a moment I thought, what was the matter with me, he didn't ... It was not a question whacking six-foot three-inch blue-eyed John, who thought he was Sheffield's answer to every maiden's prayer, should have asked.

"Cum on Lass, get dressed and we'll take a statement down 't Nick and get you to look over some mug shots. We'll take Specimen A with us an all!" he said, picking the cigarette butt off the floor.

The whole morning was taken up with the incident. It was depressing, the number of seedy-looking characters in the Station's rogues' gallery, none of them mine. John even took me out in the Panda Car to see if I could spot the man in the street. Then, kindly, two of them gave me a lift to work. They had phoned Sister Enigmatic from the Station to say I would be late that afternoon. When I arrived she didn't say a word about the incident. My life-and-death ordeal, as it seemed to me, was ignored and the day passed like any other.

I was shaken for a while and was afraid to return to the flat, especially at night and especially if the flat was in darkness. There was nothing fancy at the time like post-traumatic distress. You just got on with your life. It didn't help the next time I saw Big John off-duty in the pub he didn't mention the incident, as if I had just been silly about it.

Chapter Twelve
#It's a Wonderful World# (Louis Armstrong)

Well, not only did I make it to my third year and the February 1966 Royal Hospital Finals, I got the highest mark that year! Of the Sheffield hospital exam results as a whole only our twin with the glass eye, Clare, at the Royal Infirmary pipped me with ninety per cent average against my eighty-nine. State Finals and my long dreamt-of SRN status were only five months away.

I thought we would throw a big party and ride on a high for weeks. There were hugs and congratulations but we were all tired after more than three years of intensive training and pressure and I wasn't surprised there were some slightly sour comments about my mark, almost as if I had let the side down.

At home I was no longer Nurse Twitty-Toes. Ma, Jane and Nuala especially were thrilled. They took me out for an expensive meal at the *Zing Vaa* Chinese restaurant in The Moor in town. Even our fearsome Deputy Matron Sister Foggart softened and the senior staff must have breathed a sigh of relief that Naked Nurse MacFarlane had not gone the way of her sister. Needless to say my confidence was boosted enormously to the extent that if my fledgling career as an NHS nurse at this hospital at least did not come up to my

expectation, I would be leaving, if not quitting nursing.

I may have won grudging praise from Deputy Matron but Matron Welburn would remain as inscrutable as ever up to her retirement in the Spring, cruelly just before State Finals. I wanted the satisfaction of having our own *Grande Dame* of nursing, haughtier than Queen Mary, hand me my Certificate.

After the hospital exams I hoped to staff on Male Medical at The Royal, a challenging environment with endless medical problems. I hadn't seen my friend Dr. Josh either for a while, so that was about dead in the water. Anna was also eager for something new. Instead we were to remain in the Plastic Surgery Open Prison, even after the six months we had already done. There was no let up. Before despatch to Plastic Surgery I was scheduled to work nights on one of the two attached wards to gain experience in pre- and post-op' patient care before the State Finals.

Part of my dissatisfaction was that theatres can feel alien and lacking in human touch. It is said Theatre Staff are there because they prefer unconscious patients. They were also thought of as regarding themselves superior to nurses on ordinary wards. Plastic surgery wards were as bizarre. Here were patients of all ages with skin pedicles growing from a starting point that could be anywhere on their body. The spare skin would hopefully be transplanted on supporting trellises over areas that needed it. Patients often had to remain in one position for weeks and it requires special nursing skills to keep them happy and their new skin uncontaminated. Months of work can easily be destroyed.

I soon befriended a tough, freckle-faced nine-year old named Margaret on the ward. Her nightie had caught fire while she was reaching up to the mantelpiece and she had second and third degree burns over most of her body. Only her long auburn hair and small, defiant face were spared disfigurement.

We changed the little girl's bedding twice a night, first injecting her with an opiate to make the manoeuvre more bearable. Her bandages would stick to her oozing skin. We might as well have given her water because she screamed and cursed while we tried our best to soothe her. This was only one aspect of her suffering. She was backwards and forwards to theatre for postage stamp-size skin grafts. Burns, congenital deformities and accidents are the prime reasons for patients needing pedicles of spare skin. Severe burns may require many skin grafts to repair keloid scarring.

Seeing this gutsy kid in mismanaged pain was seriously draining. I would hear her screams when I was trying to sleep and began dreading coming to work. Fortunately, her spiky personality and sheer determination to survive helped us greatly. It was unfortunate we were unable to confide in senior staff to ease our own emotional pain without fear of being scorned. No one acknowledged, let alone discussed work place stress. As I have suggested, perhaps seniors didn't because it would open their own flood gates of repressed emotion and long-standing punitive attitudes.

Fulwood Annexe was considered to be an outpost for lame ducks, also-rans and 'part-time' married staff. Anna and I felt we had been outlawed to the back of beyond and were losing touch with our pals at the Mother Hospital miles away. We felt like agency nurses. It wasn't long before we heard ourselves grumbling "their loss ... blow them ... out with the old ... forward to new pastures ..." The reality was, at the age of twenty-one we needed a complete change.

Early in the summer Delia and I thought we might go down to London again but were goaded by my brothers into doing something more adventurous. We took up the challenge and dreamt up hitching from Sheffield to London, to Land's End, then up the length of the British Isles to John o'Groats and back halfway down again to Sheffield. It was madness in hindsight when we had only a few days spare and no money, of course. There was a fraction of the traffic on the roads compared with today.

Off we went, stopping over with Pascal in London on our way to Cornwall via Jenny in Lostwithiel. I was very disappointed she was not at home and Ditzy and I had to stay in a Youth Hostel. It was years later I learnt it was Jenny's mother who had not wanted us sleeping on her floor and Jenny, highly embarrassed, had gone away.

We found hitching lifts with lorry drivers easy and they were happy chatting about personal things "seeing as you're nurses, like ..." Cars were faster so we settled on cars by day and lorries after dark for safety. We made Land's End, staying long enough to put post cards in the box before setting off for Scotland.

That next stage to my Notre Dame High School friend Pamela in Edinburgh was a real slog without motorways. This was as far as Anna

177

and I managed because we ran out of time. Our first car ride in Scotland was with a gentleman wearing a tartan tam-o'-shanter. "Did your parents no tell ye not to accept lifts from strangers?" he asked.

Pamela was proud to lay out some plans and drawings for us to look at. An uncle had given her the means to set up a little restaurant on the Golden Mile. She was our age and about to start a business. Fantastic! At least we had achieved what we wanted on that trip in guts if not in miles. It was still a fair way through the Highlands to Britain's most northerly point, actually Dunnet Head, we were told and the chances of a lift would get more and more remote.

In July, Anna and I having passed State Finals and now Staff Nurses, were back in Plastic Theatre. It was crushing, after spending most of the year in the same grinding routine laying out equipment in the morning and cleaning up in the afternoon. My application for my first Staff Nurse's post on Keeling Ward, Men's Medical had been ignored. Wistful Wendy was appointed instead. Happy as I was for Wendy who was still living at home caring for her disabled Mum, I was miffed, wondering why there was no reward for achieving first place in the Hospital Finals. Quiet, hard-working Auburn Anna had requested to staff on the hospital's new Kidney Unit with no joy either. All ten of us from the April '63 block assumed after qualifying

in July 1966 our preference of ward we wished to staff on would be respected.

I went to see the new Matron and was horrified on realising we would only ever be regarded as nurse fodder, staff trained to keep the numbers up. It was black and white to us; if they were not interested in us, why should we be interested in them? Poor management, is how one friend put it decades later. It is only in recent years I have seen a glimmer of modern ideas in the streaming of medical talent for specific units.

The consequence of us feeling unappreciated after giving our all to the Royal was that we applied for and were accepted for Midwifery Training in London to begin in October. We handed in our notice to Matron.

Our confidence bolstered, we were soon consumed with planning our escape to the Bright Lights, the Big City and beyond. We had no idea what we were letting ourselves in for at the Dickensian East End Maternity Hospital on Commercial Road in evil Kray Twins gang territory. With more experience we would have been suspicious of our acceptance coming by post with interviews deemed unnecessary.

Out of our set of ten, only Anna and I had wanderlust. Amazingly, all our other friends wanted to marry and settle down. Manic Myrtle whom I had travelled with in our early training had left the flat and married Phillip. They had no plans to move away from Sheffield. Ditzy Delia was lucky to be staffing in her first choice, theatre and planned to marry soon. She and her new fiancé had decided they would work abroad to raise the cash to buy a house back in Sheffield.

"Why on Earth would anyone want to live in London, or hitch-hike across Europe?" Delia asked as we packed our belongings and tidied the flat we'd shared for two years; Ditzy, Manic Myrtle, Auburn Anna, myself and Jenny who filled in whenever any of us came and went.

Ditzy's sniffy reaction to our quitting Sheffield was no surprise. Once a party girl, flighty and fun-seeking she had become a Northerner again almost overnight after Finals with that dry underwhelming wit that borders on sarcasm. All since meeting her love-at-first-sight 'older vicar' that had us all whispering. She seemed blissfully happy to let her new fiancé change and then control her. Most amazing was how all of them were desperate to settle down in the place they were born in before they reached twenty-one.

179

In the 1960s, girls who didn't go to university had little idea of a life plan or career path. Most would follow their mothers and tread the path of home-making and child-raising. A great fear was being left on the shelf and was the motivation for most girls pitching their energy into finding a husband. Anna and I were determined to get to London but secretly hoped that once we had conquered the world we would be taken up by the Robert Mitchum of our dreams.

We wanted to broaden our horizons forever if we could. With an Irish father, Scottish mother and go-getting brothers, two of whom were already in London, I had no yean to settle down just then. Anna's ambivalence towards her adopting parents meant she was distancing herself ever more from them. She had little in common with her pushy mother and steel-worker dad. For her to be so mature, independent and single-minded was unusual for family-oriented working class Sheffielders.

So keen were we to get away even before we hit London and our midwifery course we decided we would hitch-hike again at the very end of our time at The Royal, this time abroad. We only had four weeks spare. Our plan was to see as much of Europe as possible in two weeks, return to Sheffield for two weeks taking any work we could then leave forever, for London. We didn't know how much we would need and our last pay packet was accounted for, even before it was opened. Undaunted, we scraped together what we could, including my hospital pension fund contributions I cashed in.

Few went to the Continent in 1966 apart from Forces personnel, hippies, musicians, diplomats, politicians, the upper classes and film stars (the "jet-setters.") It was too expensive for most Britons. Paris was too *chic*, the French Riviera was the playground of the rich. Rome was too far and the Italians dodgy. Greece was run by Generals and Spain by a dictator. The *Costa Brava* and *Costa del Sol* as a way of life was in its infancy. This was long before the Internet and travel programmes on television. The first, Wish You Were Here, began in 1974. In any case, most of us didn't have a passport.

Much more the norm was our bracing North Sea resorts. It was to bleak and windswept Bridlington and Filey the good citizens of Sheffield and Barnsley and other quiet towns flocked for the annual week's works' holiday. You got there by train or coach or motorcycle and sidecar or if you were doing really well, in your Ford Cortina.

Anna spoke German from having lived in Switzerland as an *au pair* before training and was considered very sophisticated because of these things. She had travelled by train to Berlin the previous Summer, invited by a friend in the Eastern Sector. She saw her friend in the week her visa permitted but not before being arrested by the Stasi at Checkpoint Charlie and questioned for several hours. They wanted to know how it was she spoke fluent German and who she 'worked' for.

Now we couldn't wait for some *je ne sais quoi* on Mainland Europe! After this we would be in the Metropolis parading on the King's Road and listening to speakers at Hyde Park Corner. We saw ourselves bopping at the Speakeasy Club with the in-crowd. We dreamed of dating a pop star. Most important, I would have my hair straightened at Vidal Sassoon's trendy emporium. Not a Mary Quant or Bob, just straightening. In September 1966 with thirty pounds between us we were ready for the off again, ready for the next stage of our evolution, ready to Rock 'n' Roll and 'do' Europe in fourteen days!

We were lucky in reaching the port of Dover with one ride down the A1 and A2 though it took all day and the lorry driver, a balding, lonely individual was hard to engage in conversation. Anna suggested he could conquer his shyness with a blonde toupée and a Charles Atlas body-building course. He said he would if she waited for him to complete it!

Here we were again with no experience of marital life, or sex, counselling these drivers. "Bein' as ye're nurses an' all, do you mind if I speak to yer personal, like?" was our lorry drivers' usual conversation opener.

After paying our fare as foot passengers to Calais we realised our thirty quid might not get us very far but cheered up on getting our first lift on the *Route Nationale* south within minutes. We got as far as Amiens by nightfall. On our second day we reached Bordeaux and were impressed with the grandeur of the Youth Hostel. Here was the *mêlée* of student travellers we had imagined. We were pretty close to Spain too and it was an exciting feeling we were at last shaking off the dull mantle of our stuffy upbringing.

"It was like being let out of prison," remarked Bob Dylan when he saw Elvis's early gyrations and thrilling vocals. Our liberation was being on the other side of *La Manche*.

Perhaps because our geography was a bit weak we managed to

miss Spain and cross South-West France to Perpignan instead. We didn't mind because waking up to Mediterranean sunlight streaming in the hostel dorm was euphoric. *Vive la difference!* The French drivers who had given us lifts ranged from sales clerk to film-producer friend of Omar Sharif. They were gentlemen who insisted on treating us to a cognac in a bar on dropping us off. We were in awe of their manners and accent when they tried to speak English. The 'ecky thump' Sheffield male was as sexy as a moaning camel in comparison.

The brilliant blue sky became even brighter as we wound our way along the treacherous coast road over the Pyrenees. That section was courtesy of two Italians returning to Barcelona to work. The main road over the mountains was not much better, they said and much busier. The sun and azure Mediterranean, the heat, even in October eclipsed the best days I could remember as a child on Cornish beaches. We felt high knowing the light of the *Côte Vermeille* and bright colours from the brushes of Matisse and many other artist had given birth to Fauvism only half a century before us. We crossed into Spain at a tiny place called Portbou and to our great surprise it was like stepping back a century.

Our Italian hosts, one young and one middle-aged were very kind in giving us an evening tour of Barcelona before taking us to their flat to wash and change before we all went out to eat. This was where our innocence failed us. We had only been in the apartment five minutes when I was fighting for my honour and Anna in the next room was fending off *papa* with her hairbrush. He was chasing her around shouting *"l'amore! l'amore! Ti mangieri ..."*

"What's he on about ..." I said, bursting into the room, pushing him over.

"Whatever it is, he's not having it ..." Anna responded.

We had little choice but to flee and it was around eleven that night after wandering the deserted streets for a while that a hotel night receptionist took pity on us. Not only did he allow two bedraggled hitch hikers in for a pittance of English money, bless his Spanish heart, he showed us to a penthouse suite. *¡Suite nupcial!* he kept saying, grinning. When we saw the huge beds, lace trimmings, frilly curtains and pink and gold cherubs, we got the idea.

Absolutely starving, all we had to 'eat' was water. Nevertheless, we enjoyed a hot bath and caught up on our sleep with a luxurious double bed each. Next morning, bemused hotel staff gave us directions to a youth hostel situated in a grand old hospital near the beach. Here we found the last of the Summer's travellers, those determined to stick it to the end before returning to a much colder Northern Europe. Several of them would be hanging out on the beach later and said it would be great if we joined them.

It had been a testing twenty-four hours. We were half-starved, half-ravished but well-slept. We changed some money into pesetas and had a surreal breakfast in sight of the sea, a thick iced chocolate drink with a shot of something very strong in it that cost the equivalent of pennies. Cornflakes it was not. If they could see us now back at The Royal Torture Chamber, ee, by gum! By mid-morning and slightly unsteady on our feet we found a little shop and bought fresh bread and cheese. Before we had even sat down on the sand our new friends were pouring strong sweet liqueurs.

"Doncha fret about getting drunk as de Devil himself!" Sean, one of two Irish lads said reassuringly. "Drink a lotta water and let the sun sweat it outa youse, then you go for a swim."

It was only then we realised we had forgotten our swimming costumes. Being too shy to swim in our undies, probably because the boys said they didn't mind at all, we spent the afternoon baking in the sun. They were no trouble, happy to be 'pished' all day with drink that was much cheaper than anywhere else in Europe, they said.

By late afternoon our group had grown into one of Australian, South African, German, Dutch and Irish lads and us two English girls We clubbed together for more booze and barbecue bits and pieces and as the sun went down, a fire was lit they said had to be kept going to keep the rats behind the railway line during the night. When we expressed concern about getting back to the hostel they said it closed at ten o'clock and it was alright to sleep on the beach.

I had snuggled up to a blonde, blue-eyed German folk singer named Günther. He was often on television we were told. He certainly was a good guitarist and as he strummed away into the early hours by the light of the fire and the gentle sound of surf we sang songs from our various countries.

It was about two o'clock, after a particularly rousing rendition of Waltzing Matilda when we heard someone shouting from the railway tunnel entrance.

"Oh, oh, trouble!" whispered Günther, slipping his signet ring on my ring finger and turning it to look like a wedding band. "'E thinks we are up to 'anky panky.'"

"Top of the evening to ya, *señor!*" called out death-wish Sean to the caricature of a drunken *Guardia Civil*, overweight, unshaven and wearing a cockeyed tricorn hat staggering in our direction, his rifle pointed at us.

Günther put his arm around my shoulder and apparently assured the Guard I was his new wife. The boys raised their beer bottles and there was much nodding from all of us though we didn't know what about. Sean offered the dullard his brandy bottle and a cigarette. It must have looked odd, just us two girls and several boys.

¡Eh, te quiero ... te amo ... ee lurv you! chortled dozy Pedro with yellow teeth that resembled those of a snorting horse.

He repeated his mumblings about love, took a swig of brandy and sank to his knees, his brass-buttoned greatcoat deflating like a balloon. Two more swigs and he let go of the rifle and slumped in the sand. That was the last we heard from him, apart from his snoring, until dawn when he staggered to his feet, pulled his coat collar around his face and headed back to the railway tunnel he was guarding.

"We should've run off with his shooter ..." mumbled Dublin Mick.

"... and shot him first, the great fat bozo, snoring all night," added jog-along Aussie Benny.

Our next couple of days in Spain were as magical as the first. The town was not as exciting as London but it was lively and the architecture *avant-garde* and *art nouveau*. There were a lot of youngsters about with backpacks shining with optimism and adventure, as though they too had been released from social prisons. It was exactly what we were seeking.

One of the Aussies said we couldn't come all this way and not see the famous cathedral, Gaudí's masterpiece. A small group of us walked into the centre of the city. I asked if it was being repaired because there were cranes around it. Günther explained it was a complicated structure and thirty years on they were still building it. He didn't laugh. He took the trouble to tell me about the building and its famous architect and I liked that.

One of the group, another German guy, invited Anna, Günther and me to stay at his parents' holiday villa nearby. I was now in silly love and felt it must be as good as it gets. Günther was so cool and assured, a dream date. Anna agreed but was wary of what was coming. Actually, Prince von Charming had already told me with characteristic

German positiveness he would make love to me that night at the villa. Anna was shocked when I told her. Being a good Catholic girl herself she brought up everything she could think of we had been subjected to by the Church, parents and teachers. It was the same old 'sin,' 'shame,' 'no-one would marry a non-Virgin,' did I want to be considered 'easy?' She even threw in the trauma of being recorded in the Royal's notorious Black Book of Naughty Nurses!

I didn't bother to argue. I knew also I would never set foot in a confessional again. This was the clincher. Although Günther was very careful and considerate the sex part was a non-event. The greater joy was in having broken the taboo. As my handsome folk singer waved me off next morning on the start of our journey back home, *Guantanamera* ('pretty girl from ...') was playing loudly on someone's radio. It would be an appropriate and poignant reminder of a romantic notion, a passing acquaintance and that silly expression 'losing your virginity.' What was there to lose I was already asking myself?

Günther wrote to me for a while but I was happy for it to be a one-off. Anna remained cross with me longer. I found a new confidence in being an adult and never again attended Mass or went to Confession, or had any wish to. I had called the Catholic Church's bluff, thereby breaking free from its clutches.

Hitch-hiking homeward was a different saga to our swift journey down to Spain. Our first 'lucky' ride out of Barcelona was in the back of a farmer's pick-up truck. When we said we were going to Dover the leather-faced driver nodded and no sooner had we muttered "yippee ..." we were dumped a kilometre down the road at his turning. We felt like *desperadoes* as the morning wore on. Finally, two French boys stopped for us. We should have learnt a lesson from the Italians but we really wanted the lift. We had only gone a few kilometres when the boys pulled off the main road and up a steep and winding dirt road to a vineyard.

Both of them got out and tried to haul me out of the back of the car. Anna was desperately pulling me back in. Then my heroic mate found her fabled hair brush and set upon them yelling "*je karatez vous ...*"

Thankfully, both boys burst out laughing and got back into the car. It was my eye makeup that made them think I was easy game, they said. I promptly cleaned it off.

Unsportingly, they left us on the main road at the bottom of the hill and we had no option but to walk. And walk. The roads were as deserted as the Atacama Desert and we walked in broiling sun for three hours. Nobody motored out on a Saturday it seemed. To make matters worse banks were closed at the weekend and we weren't able to change our last few pounds into Francs. All we had to eat was a very stale stick of bread and a tin of sausages and beans we had brought from England, unfortunately without a tin opener.

Eventually, a lorry took us over the mountains into France as far as Avignon. The youth hostel there was an ancient, low-ceilinged house full to the attic. The combination of being hot-housed with adenoidal snorers, claustrophobic and tormented by our gnawing tums meant we got no sleep. Our fortunes did not improve for the rest of the weekend. On the longest, quietest October Sunday of our lives we stood on the roadside in pouring rain for hour after desultory hour. Eventually we bagged a lift all the way to Paris. Our driver told us it was the worst downfall he could remember in thirty years. It had certainly washed away our Spanish high. Spain, Barcelona was already a distant memory.

By the time we reached Paris we had gone almost three days without food and little to drink. Our gallant chauffeur treated us to a *club sandwich* then dropped us off in front of a police station apologising he was unable to help further. A world-weary *gendarme* in pill-box hat and immaculately pressed blue shirt understood our problem of being unable to change our English money for a bed and breakfast and kindly escorted us to the *Gare du Nord*. A porter ushered us into a waiting room where several other dripping hitch-hikers had collected for the night.

The rain was still teeming down next morning. Anna and I had retained the rock-hard knob-end of our *baguette* and desperately dented tin of beans and sausages as an act of faith. Unbelievably, the porter relieved us of the bread saying he was very hungry.

It was only on the ferry at Calais that our luck changed. A bunch of high-spirited US Army dudes stationed in Germany took a shine to us. They laughed and drank beer while watching us eat everything put in front of us saying how nice we English were and how they could not stand hairy German girls. God Bless America! They restored our happy vibe because they were so easy-going compared with the temperamental Spanish, polite but dour French and over-serious English lads.

One more ride got us from Dover to Derbyshire with light still in the sky that Autumn afternoon. Two dozy Yorkshire lads in their prized Ford Escort picked us up near Matlock for the last few miles to Sheffield. We knew they would be no trouble.

"Where d'you twos cum from, then?" they asked in accents thick as bread and dripping, eyeing our tan.

"Spain!" we chorused like factory girls.

"Oh ... right ... best get in then ..."

Once home we devoured our much-travelled beans and sausages and were rather pleased at being half-a-stone lighter than two weeks earlier. No time to catch up on sleep, however. We were down at the Sheffield Star offices early to place a 'situation wanted' and scour for work on offer. We needed cash for at least six weeks, until our first maternity hospital pay day. We got a reply in the post the following morning that looked like good money and for the rest of the day tramped miles around the city delivering fliers for a new slave master, Brylcreem Bert.

There was no chance of any idling or short cuts. Bert had everything mapped out and met us at the end of whole neighbourhoods, loading us up again and herding us on to fresh letter boxes. It was late when, legless with fatigue I staggered home for dinner as my mother had insisted. She greeted me with the happy news "you've got a night job, Ro. Tonight!"

"What?"

"It's a desperate granny. She needs a maternity nurse to feed a premature baby. The mother is still very ill in hospital."

"But I can't walk ..."

"Tough! I said you would be there at eight o'clock ... tee hee ..."

They were a lovely, well-off family in Lodge Moor who, thankfully, didn't have a clue that I hadn't held a baby since my three months training at the children's hospital. I had looked after babies over the years, particularly my friend Gwynne's in Lostwithiel. My main problem that night would be staying awake.

It didn't get any better as I really needed to keep the day job as well. I had to be ruthless in cosying up to our Brylcreemed Casanova the following morning and mercifully he let me sit in the car with him sorting leaflets whilst his other slaves tramped the streets. Anna was furious. Nevertheless, we finished fourteen days on the trot with the grand sum of sixteen and twenty-three pounds respectively in our pockets. I had more because I had done several nights with the baby as well. However, I was beyond tired and wondered if this was what we should be doing.

It was the end of October 1966 when we left Sheffield finally, eager and excited at the prospect of starting at the East End Maternity Hospital. It still hadn't dawned on us that jumping in two feet first is not the best way of approaching a complete change in employment and lifestyle.

It was goodbye Damien's suffering through a tragically short life; goodbye Notre Dame High, bottle-green uniform, welcoming classmates, Father Keegan and furtive Park Drives in the Convent woods; ta-ra Leo and my trainee comrades; goodbye Naked Nurse and hello Staff Nurse MacFarlane; farewell Tapton Court and Saturday night snogs!; good riddance Matron and her Band of Viragos; *au revoir* my heroic mother, life-saving Sunday roasts, Yorkshire puds and apple pies; 'bye also, weekend hikes across the World's Eighth Wonder the Derbyshire Moors, St. Vincent's Youth Club, Sheffield Uni hops, folk nights, jazz stomps, great pubs and piano dames, Leo and Gerry and all medical students we partied with; the end of my worn out Beatles albums and Dansette Record Player; cheers! West Bar Police Jazz Band and PCs Pascal, John and Chas.

Goodbye to The Royal Hospital, Fulwood Annexe, the Jessop and Children's Hospitals, Sister Bubbles and Miss T.; farewell and thank you all The Royal Hospital patients, cleaners and dining room staff; never again Harcourt Road, nylon sheets, winter fog and ice, smoky steel works, mad parties, cruel hangovers, unwashed pots, bread and dripping, *chow mein,* tinned tomatoes, cheap sausages and Bakewell tart (we couldn't afford the 'Pudding'); *adieu* my first true almost love affair; fond thoughts 'Naughty George' and 'Lawrence' of Arabia; *adiós* our hitch-hike drivers and Barcelona sunshine; ta-ra to my virginity and a fond remembering of our first real taste of freedom.

Chapter Thirteen
#Fings Ain't Wot They Used to Be ...# (Lionel Bart)

The run-down hole-in-the-wall East End Maternity Hospital on Commercial Road dominated a decaying Victorian terrace. It was dirty everywhere. Lorries thundered past incessantly carrying goods to and from the docks. It was a long, unpleasant walk from Aldgate East tube station. The Prospect of Whitby was a few minutes' away on the river bank across Cable Street. Whitechapel, a few streets to the north was Jack the Ripper country. At night you could still be in Dickensian London. The area was Kray Twins territory. It was not a nice place.

If our friends from the North could have seen this milk crate of a maternity hospital they wouldn't have Adam and Eve'd it! It was like a workhouse, an old Derbyshire mill without the scenery. There was no lift for taking women in labour to the first floor. Staff had to haul them up rickety stairs in an ambulance chair. The Premature Babies unit was a tiny over-heated room over-filled with wailing infants. The Sterilising Room looked as though it had last been used by Nurse Sarah Gamps in Martin Chuzzlewit.

Our attic rooms were so hot from the wards below us it was impossible to get a proper sleep. We couldn't open the windows because of noise and pollution from constant traffic and were soon foggy-brained from heat and sleep deprivation. We decided we would rather be hitch-hiking to Timbuktu. This was not the Rock-'n-Roll London we anticipated and certainly not good for our planned 'turn on, tune in' London cool.

From the beginning it was my eldest brother Morris who saved us from utter despondency. One of his jobs was managing a trendy new bed-sit block at One and Two Trebovir Road in Earl's Court. It was on the other side of London and we had to allow travelling time when visiting. We were constantly advised not to be walking about in the East End after dark. It was quite endearing for my brother to be concerned. I was at last being looked upon as a sibling of merit rather than a young nuisance sister.

Pascal was also a lifeline. He now had a basement bed-sit in one of the forty or so rooms at Trebovir Road and was busy working his way towards his goal at the time of travel agent tycoon. Two of their best friends in the block were Christian Iraqi students Iskander and Suhail. Iskander was a tall, skinny only child from a wealthy family. He had a carefree laugh that rang around the flats. He needed it too as smaller, cuddly Suhail from a more modest background baited him at every opportunity.

Arabs cannot resist melodrama and these two did not hold back in argument whether over the quality of Basmati rice from the local shop or global politics. Even when they were all together preparing their much-missed Arab dishes they would be arguing about something, usually politics, into the night. To us they were charming, ideal brothers compared with my own dour siblings. Arab boys are brought up to be protective and kind to their female relatives and friends and are not afraid to show concern and affection. They were very welcoming to Anna and me and to maternity hospital friends we brought along on our days off.

I soon saw Christian and Moslem Arabs were different and that the groups did not mix. Christian Arabs were more Westernized and more liberal but just as passionate about their race. This was especially so after the war in the Middle East in 1967 that shook them all. They became increasingly politicised, particularly with regard to defending the rights of the Palestinians. They referred to the Six-Day War as *an-Naksah*, 'the Setback.'

On our off days, Angela and I would tear over to Earl's Court as if on release from an open-sauna prison. Morris was also a floor manager for the BBC and he put many free tickets our way for live shows. Seeing the likes of Tom Jones and Vince Hill helped anaesthetise us from long shifts at the hospital.

By way of exchange perhaps, Morris took to blonde-haired Sweetie. Bonny and Sweetie were two cutesie American student midwives we had befriended. This helped even more with getting us into the Earl's Court scene as Morris now encouraged us to come along to weekend parties at Trebovir Road when our shifts allowed. A little like Naughty George, he made sure there was a good multi-racial mix drawn from the international students in his bed-sit domain. They were interesting, educated and often entertaining young people in London usually at the behest of wealthy parents. We met many other types at these parties including English actors and models at the start of their careers.

One Saturday night, Bonny and I left Morris's flat with the

prospect of having to walk back to Commercial Road if we couldn't find a night bus. We were mindful of the hospital's advice not to do this but it was in a quiet street in Earl's Court, not the East End, that a man stopped in front of us and exposed himself. The flasher began jumping from side to side so we couldn't pass him.

"You can put that dirty thing away ..." Bonny trilled. He didn't oblige and tall, slender Bonny went for his erect member with the pointed end of her steel comb. We got past him jeering but he wouldn't go away and we decided we should run back to Morris's flat and call the police. They took us on a fruitless search of the streets and eventually and very kindly, drove us all the way to the hospital on the other side of town. One of the PCs was struck with brave Bonny and was pleased she agreed to a date with him.

Day time in the East End was fine. The locals in shops, for example gave us a broad welcome. On winter evenings we had no choice but to brave dark streets to the Prospect of Whitby on the river. A trendy Hawaiian band provided the entertainment at this historic place while clientele quaffed expensive lager. It was on Cable Street when returning to our stuffy prison one evening, Anna and I were confronted by a gang of urchins.

"Gi' us your dosh, gels," the cheeky Jack Sprats demanded. Anna saw them off with a squirt of her lethal hair lacquer.

On another foggy evening we heard shooting in the vicinity of the same pub just after we'd left. Rather than rush back to give first aid we flew, as if we had wings, on to the hospital. It was a gangland killing and we knew then we really needed to watch our backs. This was serious violence and a sorry sign of the times. Sheffield city centre by contrast was a fear-free zone at any time of the day or night.

On another occasion we were waiting for a bus on our way to the West End and a freebie show. A trio of Teddy Boys started pestering us and by the time the bus pulled up they had become a real nuisance.

"Oi, get the .... aht of it or I'll ... get the Old Bill on yer," the conductor said sharply. "These gels are nurses at the 'orspital, ain'tya gels?"

Nodding gratefully, we jumped aboard. We weren't wearing capes or hats and didn't know how he knew. Maybe this was his regular route and he had seen us, or taken our fares. The passengers on the bus commiserated.

"The local Teds would never 'arm you nurses," one said. "We

might get a bashing but you wouldn't!"

Although we were dismayed by the constant tropical temperature in the hospital and by our grim, gothic surroundings our two midwifery tutors were like kindly aunts. Mrs. Small was a pale-faced doppelganger of comedienne Joyce Grenfell. She was married to a Black African poet which gave her exalted status to all nurses in the hospital. She was an evolved metropolitan. Without raising her voice or being intimidating she quietly instructed and supervised our first assisted deliveries. She was as calm and as kind as Miss T. at the Royal. Mrs. G., her co-tutor, was a plumpish mother figure who was also welcoming and encouraging. We had to watch ten births and be familiar with the condition of the mother and possible complications before we were allowed to assist.

Being treated as mature students and not belittled or bellowed at was a welcome surprise. What was vexing was how these dedicated middle-aged Dears could teach us how to be top-notch midwives when the working conditions were so dire. Appallingly so at night.

It was more than once some of us talked about whistle-blowing. Moaning was one thing, reporting serious breaches in standards of hygiene and care in a hospital was unthinkable in the NHS and probably across all other forms of employment in the 1960s. It was a determined, courageous individual who mooted such a thing. A strong union might have helped.

We had suffered intimidation and bullying during our training as nurses as part of a finely-tuned process of depersonalization. We had been trained to obey and to fear. The management at this hospital was likely to be of the same mould as the Royal and we were wary. It would not just be our jobs on the line if we dared speak out. We might never work again in the National Health Service.

Patients are effectively trapped when admitted to a hospital and can do little when they are poorly. All we wanted to do was alert the public to things they should not have to put up with and where standards of care and service were lacking, they should be improved. It was beyond our understanding why some people in management or on medical teams entered this caring profession when they were oblivious or indifferent to the need to act with empathy towards the sick.

Daily chores continued and the countdown to Christmas began.

East End mums and mothers-to-be were almost all tough Cockney women and crossing them could be daunting. Many were worn out from having given birth many times. There were occasional gynaecological emergency admissions. One forty-something woman was brought to us in the early hours needing a vaginal tear suturing.

"Stitch it right up, Doc so 'ee can't get in no more ..." she said without humour to the quiet Chinese doctor we had to call in the middle of the night.

Two Irish nuns also training as midwives had their particular problems in dealing with patients under stress or in pain from vaginal or pregnancy problems. They would frequently get a mouthful about their celibate state along the lines of "wot the 'ell would you know about 'ow I feel ..."

For many of us student midwives, East End Maternity was our first experience of multi-culturalism. Sheffield and Cornwall was mainly white. For Flo and Bo from Nigeria, this was their first experience of working with or nursing people who were not Black.

Flo was exquisite to look at while Bo was a more studious Plain Jane. Their English was correct, clearly articulated and delightfully old-fashioned. Their manners were also exemplary and everyone adored them. They became really homesick as winter in London began to bite and we were shocked when they showed us balls of hair in a drawer. It was falling out, they said, from their misery. They identified with nothing in East London, from its damp cold and complete lack of charm, to food bought in tins and packets. They also found it hard adapting to people who were not friendly in the street or on the bus. They didn't blame them. They could see the run-down environment took its toll on everyone. We agreed. Everyone chats to you on a Sheffield bus as if you are a long-lost pal.

We tried to cheer up the girls from abroad by showing them the London sights that thrilled us. Trafalgar Square, the nearby Tower of London, Oxford Street and the great parks like Hyde Park and Kensington Gardens. Bobbies, bearskin hats and Buckingham Palace too. We also found out where they could buy food familiar to them.

Besides Flo and Bo and the chirpy Americans there was a very serious German girl named Helga. Having a German native speaker around pleased Anna and they conversed at length in German and English, correcting each other as necessary. The remaining students were mainly from Ireland.

One exception was Christine. She was in the year above us at the Royal and the one who had put the idea of midwifery training at the East End Maternity into our heads. She was tall and fair-haired with slanting, searching eyes. She spoke in quiet, serious tones but could be quite sharp in telling us to 'put up and shut up' if we began whingeing about the 'dump.' She wasn't perturbed by the grotty living and working conditions.

On the positive side we were bowled over by watching babies being born, as well as seeing how women of different nationalities coped. This was in the days before routine epidurals and the women might have to endure a long and painful labour. Asian and Italians would invariably break the sound barrier. Chinese mothers-to-be would remain stoically mute throughout the birth process. The warmth and often hilarious bawdy humour of local Cockney women was endearing. We might even have been extra nice to those women whose oily-haired husbands fitted our notion of East End gangsters.

Day Duty was like working in a two-star unit and we had no misgivings. Night Duty was a different matter and like working in the bowels of Hell. The Jessop Hospital in Sheffield where we had done our three-month gynae training had spoilt us with its reputation of being one of the best maternity units in the country. The East End Maternity Hospital was seriously understaffed night after night and conditions at times were utterly disgraceful.

We would frequently work past exhaustion level rushing between pokey labour rooms, cramped wards, the upstairs nursery and tiny Premature Baby room. The worst of the labour rooms was like a cell and down a steep flight of stairs from the first-floor ward. Mothers in labour would often be left on their own while we were setting up life-saving feeds via nasal tubes for premature infants. We would sometimes have to run back to a labour room to 'catch' a birth. Occasionally full-term babies in the nursery would be wailing with hunger if we couldn't steal a spare second to feed them. Cleaning up had to be done quickly.

Hauling screaming women in strong labour up the stairs to the ward nearly killed us too. When eventually we were able to stagger off to our beds in the morning we were unable to sleep because of the oppressive heat and heavy traffic below. Our guilt, stress levels and fatigue after night duty rose steadily.

Anna became the most distressed I'd ever seen her after the

mismanaged birth of a young nurse, like us, in the New Year. Pregnancy in an unwed woman was still heavily stigmatised in 1966, now 1967. This twenty-year old had been sent by her ashamed parents to lodge in an unmarried mothers' home nearby.

We felt great sorrow for her being alone, then even more so when her baby with a microcephalic head was left to die in the equipment room. She did not know how badly deformed it was, as the midwife rushed it away from her after birth. She didn't know either that negligence had caused her to haemorrhage. This was a turning point. Brave Anna was determined to report this particular incident.

It wasn't the fault of our tutors. They were excellent but they also seemed to be in denial about what went on in the hospital at night. It looked to us as if the parent London Hospital Authority considered the local rock solid, jellied-eel and pie-and-mash families, along with the new immigrants, not worthy of a dignified level of care. We understood the cost of building a new hospital in London would be high. We couldn't see it would be so difficult or costly to improve the existing building. It was founded in 1884 as the Mothers' Lying-in Home and there had been almost no modernization done in the eighty years since.

As we were unsure of what to do we ended up consoling ourselves with the thought we had only a few months left of our first year. We would just grit our teeth and give the best care we could when on duty. We also feared for our references and knew if it came to a crunch and we decided to stir things we would have little support. My firebrand sister Jane had threatened to blow the whistle on practices in her hospital in Cornwall ten years earlier. Matron threatened her with dismissal and a negative report. Our parents dissuaded her from appealing directly to the 'News and the Screws.' Though my father was a good medical practitioner and my mother purported always to do the right thing for the underdog, image and reputation was more important in their not-the-done-thing world.

As our working environment became increasingly intolerable we used our days off to escape and explore the great city of London. We usually did this on foot, walking through the City or along the Embankment to Trafalgar Square and often on to Kensington. London is endlessly fascinating and it was a joy doing this while saving our pennies. Our meagre income was a constant worry and being taken out by my brothers and their money-bag friends became increasingly welcome. The situation was soon to become critical.

One weekend, younger brother Simon came to visit from Sheffield. He was with his old schoolmate Mucky Mick, a short Marlon Brando look-alike. We had a good night visiting local pubs and when we returned to the hospital, they said they would sleep in the van behind our hospital flatlet. We had just moved to the block at the back of the hospital and were benefitting from better sleep.

Two middle-aged Irish nuns shared the room next to us and we got on well. After we bade Simon and Mick good night I began to worry whether they would be safe in the alley and called them in to sleep on the floor. The next morning we were summoned to Matron's office. The nuns had reported that we had entertained men in our room that night and on one other occasion. This was true. Anna and I had two other male friends from Sheffield stay over because they were too hard up to afford a B & B. There was, of course, no hanky-panky. The fact it was my brother and his friend the night before made no difference to the situation.

Matron was fair and understanding and quite different to Matron Welburn but told us firmly the privilege of having a room in the block was withdrawn and we would have to move back into the attic dorm. I couldn't bear the thought of returning to it and said I was not prepared to do this, or allow two nuns to be the cause of our having to move. It was war ...

Our tutors tried desperately to persuade Anna and I to acquiesce to Matron's bidding. My dutiful elder brother made doomy proclamations about us becoming nursing outcasts should we not complete our Part One Midwifery. I reminded him he had conveniently forgotten he had been a rebel in refusing to go back to school at the age of twelve on his return from Ireland.

We were steadfast. We had certainly had enough of the hospital and of being treated like errant schoolgirls. Now we were being judged morally once again by the Catholic Church and with great bravado packed our bags. With only a few pounds between us we decamped to Earl's Court on a chilly January morning. My disapproving brother said there was no room for us in Trebovir Road and we had no option that day but to spend our last few quid on a freezing double bedsit in Coleherne Road a few streets away.

It was a small comfort that the glamour we had been missing came to us in the form of folk singer Julie Felix living upstairs. We had been lucky enough to hear her at a recording session of one of the BBC's The Frost Report programmes on which she was the resident singer. We heard she was David Frost's girlfriend but was about to get married to someone else. We were nervous about what we had done to our nursing careers but at the same time knew there was a big glamorous world beyond hospital walls. We were now ever more determined to be part of the Swinging 'Sixties.

Refusing to ask for financial help from anyone, I began working in a burger bar and Anna in a cake shop. Our pay was dire and our liberation wobbly. We were having to think for ourselves for the first time, knowing we were only a hair's breadth away from being on the street. Our resolve soon strengthened again and we decided it would be many more miles before we threw in the towel.

While my brothers were determined to give me a hard time, Suhail and Iskander were not. They declared they would look after us. They called in regularly to make sure we were surviving and insisted we come around to their digs when we could, to warm up and have something to eat with them. In between time we got to know all the places in West London that were making London Town such a vibrant place. The world was beginning to know this great capital city in a new and colourful form far-removed from the sepia and silver tint of Empire.

On our doorstep was Carnaby Street, Biba, elegant Chelsea, the King's Road with its Saturday fashion parade of mini-skirts, vinyl clothes, the see-through look, boots above the knee, coloured hair and big plastic jewellery. It was so strange to see clothes of black and white check or solid bright colour or worked into a Mondrian design. Kensington Market was Hippy Land, reeking of joss sticks, spliff smoke and with a tangible two-fingers attitude to the establishment.

Mingling now with black cabs and London buses were E-Type Jaguars, Italian sports cars that came up to your waist and cars with art, even fur, all over them. They were the marque of the pop star. The one we really wanted to see was John Lennon's psychedelic Rolls-Royce, the car with a bed, television and fridge in it they usually used to get around town in.

We were also blessed with fantastic museums, cinemas, galleries, theatres and clubs, though we could not afford this last. We frequently ducked into the V & A, the Science Museum and the National Gallery.

Coming to investigate Swinging London and contribute to its energy was a mass of other youngsters from around the world. Earl's Court was becoming known as Kangaroo Valley. Two vivacious Aussie females lived in the crummy bed-sit next to ours and would laugh the day and night long. They were freckle-faced Jill and her friend Denise, an actress who would have made a perfect Moll Flanders. Their determination to experience everything London had to offer was amazing.

We all felt we were coming up for air for the first time. These Down Under girls' lightness of being was new to Anna and I and helped us shed our strait-jackets and start feeling good about having fun. We didn't quite know what to make of the picture of her boyfriend Denise kept by her bed, actually a close-up of his erect penis!

It was good that Anna was like Prince Charles, level and sensible while I was impatient to be loved and in love, often choosing unsuitable dates because I still had little notion of my own currency. She hadn't been infantilised by religious claptrap and had outgrown her adopted parents so was able to pull me up by my bootlaces when necessary. She became my anchor and it was just as well she disapproved of the other aspects of the Swinging 'Sixties in full throttle everywhere we went, Free Love and drug-taking.

In quieter moments from the burger bar and when not caught up in a social whirl I was reading more than ever. R. D. Laing's anti-family ideas in psychiatry were discussed everywhere. I had long ago read Self and Others and The Divided Self and was now labouring through Interpersonal Perception. I was inspired by Fromm's The Art of Loving, about our needing love objects and about damaged souls associating love with struggle. Soul-searching was an 'in thing' and I ploughed through many unsatisfactory New Age books in my own quest.

Herman Hesse's Siddhartha was a good introduction to Buddhism and a balance to the over-emphasis on Christianity I had endured. Other books on Eastern mysticism went some way to explaining the pop world courting dope and gentle religions. I loved Kahlil Gibran's parables and poems, so beautifully written. I had The Wanderer by my bed and was always looking for other work by him when scouring bookshops on Charing Cross Road. The suspicious Sheffield lot would have found my new reading incomprehensible.

It was an exciting and sometimes confusing time when the rules and regimentation of our parents' generation were changing as fast as you could say *Amen*. Meeting bright young people from a wide social background rejecting the notion of the infallibility of elders and their often aggressive demand for obedience, was its own revelation. I was gratified to be viewing religion more from without than within. My resolve to shake off once and for all the double hook of Confession and Mass was applauded by my non-Catholic friends who pointed out it was extremely creepy, even salacious, for child and adult alike to be blackmailed into admitting so-called guilt in their intimate secrets to a supposedly celibate male in a darkened corner.

Even now, thinking of my seven to twenty-one-year old self entering the confessional booth brainwashed into divulging the most personal aspects of my life to such a stranger or risk going to Hell, makes me cringe. I see Confession now as a form of sexual abuse.

"I have kissed a boy and allowed him to touch me impurely, Father," once led to a heavy-breathing priest asking to see me afterwards. Abused by a priest when I was eleven as I have said, I can imagine the salacious joy a homosexual priest might experience with similarly intimate 'admissions' from boys. Despite what the Church might promote, priests and nuns are not divine or necessarily good, moral, asexual or abstinent. They are human. All Catholics know this even if they do not want to admit it. Is allowing their children to be abused in any of its many forms, as well as be brainwashed, really part of their faith?

Once only I was told at Confession that God really loved me. This was a shock, as I now had to take on board the new notion that God might love or not love me, or even like or not like me personally. I neither needed nor wanted the imaginary friend Dawkins wrote about later in The God Delusion. He was being forced on me.

Taking a rest from growing up in our more immediate circumstance we carried on our own music scene in Earl's Court 'doing our thing.' Anna had a lovely folky voice and would sing for hours accompanying herself on guitar, often as a homage to Joan Baez and her protégé Bob Dylan. When flush we would spend the evening in the Troubadour Club on Brompton Road at the end of our road. It was a pilgrimage for folk fans. We always hoped Dylan would drop in again for a set but like the Second Coming, it was not going to happen.

We liked Baez's Black is the Colour and her renditions of traditional folk song, including Barbara Allen. As a quiet romantic herself, Anna frequently sang Farewell Angelina. She was a bit shy when asked by our Iraqi friends to play and would oblige but from their little kitchen with the door ajar. I both admired and envied my long-time flatmate's talent and it was many, many years later before I got around to learning to play and sing a bit myself.

We started our sing-songs when students in Harcourt Road. Wherever we went around Sheffield on social evenings in the early '60s someone had a guitar. A sing-song would often draw the night, or morning, to a close. It was the same in London. Maybe we had drunk a little too much or would have to shush the guys still battling politics but it was a perfect end to an evening and perfect way to feel loved-up. It didn't matter after this if we got soaked in driving rain or chilled to the bone in thick, swirling fog while walking home.

Chapter Fourteen
#Help Me Make it Through the Night ...# (Baez/ Kristofferson)

A couple of months after we had moved to Earl's Court, Anna and I received a call from my brother that two German acquaintances had turned up in London. We had met them in the Autumn on a local Spanish train, those with wooden seats, on our way to the French border. They were heating water on a Primus stove and asked if we would like a coffee. The tall fair one Albert, fancied Anna like mad. He admired her beautiful red hair and the fact she spoke his language fluently. I was left with Axel, dark-haired, hunky but arrogant. Axel was not suited to his friend's choice.

"Vye he like her? She is not a beauty enough for 'im!"

Their manners had not improved in the six months since we had seen them. Their criticism of London and Brits was non-stop. They didn't like the noisy Aussie-hijacked pub in Earl's Court Road and were certainly not impressed with our tatty bed-sit where they grudgingly asked if they could stay the night. Gorgeous Albert began to kiss and cuddle Anna. As before, Axel sat next to me in disgust. He eventually remembered I was there and thought he was going to kiss me.

I knew what was coming but was not quick enough to get off the bed in time. I didn't know what was worse, having beer puked over me or my bed. The pompous prats sloped off with their backpacks never to be seen again. We howled laughing, chanting "we won the war, yeah, yeah, yeah!"

Finding it hard to make ends meet on burger bar salaries became critical and we began scouring ads' in the paper. I spotted a wanted placement for a discrete private nurse and asked Anna what she thought. She didn't like the sound of it but said she wasn't in the mood to talk about nursing for a while yet.

It was Nurse Innocent then, that arrived in uniform the following evening for an interview with a very plummy gentleman in unbelievably posh Eton Square. I rang his bell gawping at the "Lord This" and "Lady That" plates above and below his.

"Dooo sit down, Nurse ..." he began in the most intimidating of accents. "I would like to ask you a few questions about your credentials, if I may?"

He was appraising my uniform as I spoke and I knew he was not really listening when he asked suddenly,

"So, my Dear, are enemas more common in France than in England, would you think?"

"Er ... I don't really know, Sir."

The penny still hadn't dropped.

"But you do give enemas ..."

"Yes Sir, many an enema, with olive oil, Prednisolone, very slow phosphate, caffeine ..."

"Oh, gosh! Jolly good!" he said, a faint smile now across his lips. "Well, follow me, would you? I would like you to attend to me now, if you have the time ..."

Nurse Innocent followed her patient to a very grand bathroom where his equipment was hanging on the wall. This was an old hot water bottle with a modified stopper and rubber tubing leading to a thick rectal catheter. There was a clip rather than tap and no syringe, funnel, feeder or thermometer. Fortunately I had brought my own surgical gloves. None of it was as clean as I would have wanted. He showed me the room where he would make himself ready and asked that the liquid be warm rather than hot.

My patient was ready, lying naked on his front on a spotless white towel and rubber sheet on Wilton carpeting. There was no IV stand and it then dawned on Nitwit Nursie what he was after. I inserted the lubricated catheter into his rectum, held the hot-water bottle filled with warm soapy water at waist height, higher than normal and released the clip. The bottle quivered, his Nibs began to moan.

"Harder, push it in harder, Nurse, please! Squeeze, please ..."

Despite having no training in this particular technique I refrained from shoving the catheter up to his tonsils, lifted the bag to shoulder height briefly to some loud gasping then shut off the supply of liquid. That was enough.

"Now you just lie there quietly while I take these things back to the bathroom ..."

I left him moaning gently, cleaned everything in double quick time and then, looking at the toilet, decided I would teach him a little lesson. Locking the door, I waited.

His tapping on the door a minute later was at first polite.

"Nurse, excuse me, Nurse. May I use the l-a-v-a-t-o-r-y? It is rather urgent, my Dear ..."

"Won't be a minute ..." came Nurse Not-so-Innocent's reply.

"I really DO NEED to go, Nurse ..."

He eventually returned to the living room where I was waiting. Dressed impeccably once again and with his composure regained he gave me the ten pounds agreed. When he asked if I might come back the following week I was surprised to hear myself say, politely, I wasn't able to and even more surprised that he began begging me to.

It was only out in the street I felt ashamed and actually ran, in uniform, out of the square. I may have proved my skills as the Enema Queen and the tenner had got me out of trouble considering it was a week's wages for one hour's work but I was ashamed. I needed to talk it through with my equally innocent confidante, duped also by an elderly homosexual's harmless penchant for a bit of rubber tubing.

Was it the beginning of a downward spiral to attain financial stability in my so-far impeccable nursing reputation? It was straight ethics *versus* much-needed easy-peasy bum-titillating cash. We reminded ourselves of the single private floor at The Royal the union had agreed to. All of us in those days were profoundly opposed to any form of private nursing. Even those nurses that succumbed to its better pay and glamorous décor still found it hard to get used to the anathema of appeasing demanding patients in private rooms.

The ethics won. Fearing we could be sucked into the Sin Bin we agreed it would be *bona fide* agency work only and "nowt' kinky!"

Three months after throwing our nursing careers to the wind we were in no hurry to go grasping it back. I found a full-time job as Nanny to a boutique owner's children. The boutique, named Mata Hari was *à la mode* and opposite Earl's Court tube station. My main task was nannying two sweet kids in an expensive flat in Nevern Square while their parents zoomed about multi-tasking around this, their first business venture.

Part of the deal was a day or two a week on my own in the new, double-bed sized shop surrounded by the latest fashionable clothes. The kiddiewinks, Pip aged five and cutie Chelsea aged eighteen months were delightful, as were their parents. Pay was ten pounds a week, when my rent was five. "Jammy" was the thrust of Anna's comments.

Action at last, I thought, excited to be right where it was at! My employers were savvy *fashionistas* with gorgeous kids. Their hyperactive mum was a stick-thin Mary Quant look-alike who was clearly the driving force. Hefty five-foot nine Naked Nanny Rose on the other hand was hardly the Twiggy-type you'd expect in a hot-shot fashion boutique of the day. This was the era of short, straight hair and the wispy female with legs up to her armpits. I probably had the thickest Pre-Raphaelite mop on Brompton Road. However, they felt lucky having a trained nurse on the cheap and I went with that.

Entering the small bathroom in their trendy apartment on my first day, I was taken aback to see the bath half-full of 'bloody' paint. Hubby was the first to get home, thrilled with the way their new venture was going. He was sheepish about the paint, there since opening day. He had gone out at four in the morning with the idea of dipping the soles of his boots in red paint and making bold footprints leading from all directions to the shop. A policeman, unfortunately had come around the corner, leaving hubby hopping in and out of doorways making his escape. Bucketing the paint out of the bath had slipped down the list of priorities.

The shop was decorated in *art nouveau* style in purple with crystal trinkets and silver framed posters with early 20th-century themes. All day long, girl-child customers with bouffant hair and eyelashes like copulating spiders tottered in and out, flicking at speed through the micro-mini dresses and skirts in sizes eight to ten, about the only sizes the shop stocked (yes, times have changed). What they were desperately searching for, I do not know because they were unable to communicate this with me. Unfortunately close enough to hear every word of their conversations with friends all I wanted to do by the end of each day was advise these empty-headed fillies to get a life.

After two weeks I was almost brain-dead myself from being fashioned-out and having suffered but two LPs on the record player. The Rolling Stones, the group's first album and Herb Alpert's Tijuana Brass were the signature sounds of the shop and had to be played over and over at full volume. I Can't Get No-o Satisfact-i-o-n and Ta, ta, ta, tum, tah, ta-taah, taah ... still hurt on recall.

The amazing shop front featured a six-foot high black and white painting of a doleful Mata Hari, *femme fatale*, dancer and spy shot by the French in 1917. Many customers thought it was me, with my puppy-fat face and Dusty Springfield eyes.

"Ee, 'ow long did it take yer to trowel that on, then?" my old mates chorused, jaws dropping at my panda eyes and *derrière* just about covered by a bright purple mini-dress. This was my first visit to Sheffield in months for Ditzy Delia's Registry Office wedding. I shrivelled more at the prospect of an alcohol-free reception. Ex-party girl's in-laws were teetotal.

Meeting up with my student nurse friends again in Sheffield was to experience a time warp. They had surely stopped still in their sensible shoes, whereas Anna and I were still busy travelling Planet Playpen. I loved them all and my old home town but knew I could never go back to live there.

A greater surprise was Phillip and Manic Myrtle's meteoric rise into money. Old friend Philip's carpet and fashion shops were making a fortune and he and Myrtle were happy and settled with two young sons. Myrtle's initial *post-partum* depression with her first-born had been guilt-triggered by many factors they had now overcome. Tough Barnsley Girl and sensitive Catholic Council Estate Boy would always be an ebullient, generous couple.

I didn't get the same sense of well-being with Delia. She was clearly over the moon marrying someone older and quietly controlling. Presumably she would make good with the stability of a father-figure husband as an antidote to her own disrupted upbringing.

Which left me, with whom the whole notion of domestic bliss could lead to paroxysms of panic. It wasn't just about wanting to have fun - and penury in London certainly was not this - it was much more about seeking a wider, richer experience. London had beckoned as its own land of opportunity and challenges, a place where one could experiment with different lifestyles and learn from people of all persuasions, orientations and ethnicity. My consciousness lit up on hearing J. G. Ballard remark that a multi-ethnic country makes for a vibrant and broadminded culture and that the United Kingdom had improved immeasurably from having a multi-cultural society.

Back at base again I enjoyed looking after the boutique owners' children over the weeks. The business of fashion accompanying it, the bit of the shop floor I was on, was not so fulfilling. My bosses were naturally passionate about their frocks and were fraught as frogs in a drought before each Saturday's fashion parade on the King's Road. I would be sitting in the shop with as much *joie de vivre* about the business as the dummy next to me wearing 'the latest.' While they were desperate to beat with the very pulse of fashion, I could only think of reviving my own elsewhere.

With so many foreigners around making life and contemplation so much more interesting, my next escape could only be in one form, working abroad. Once again it was just a matter of how I was to fund this next step in my evolution.

One April evening in 1967 in the boutique, I was poring over the Evening Standard's jobs pages looking for anything more exciting than my current penance. My eye fixed on "a unique up-and-coming new venture." It was the imminent launching of a refurbished paddle steamer, the Queen of the South. It had been acquired by the St. James Hotel which was in the smart end of Victoria. I rang immediately and was given an interview time the following morning.

Secretly, I had also done some research and applied to the United Nations Association (UNA) hoping to be chosen to work in Jordan in the Autumn as a nurse volunteer. A second choice was required. Mine was the Amazon and I could only hope with the warped luck I was having, I really would not be punted up these tropical backwaters.

My first choice of sponsored work was supported by three positive reasons. My Notre Dame school friend Elaine was teaching in Jordan as a UNA volunteer and had written how much she was enjoying her life in the Middle East. Having spent time with my brother's Iraqi friends in London I was very interested in learning more about Arabic culture and lands, the cradle of two great religions of the world and even of modern man. Iskander and Suhail and their warm Iraqi friends were so easy and friendly. They were obsessively hospitable, if pathologically argumentative and had from the beginning been very caring to me.

The third reason was both the strongest and weakest. The UNA would pay my return flight, board and accommodation in the chosen hospital and pay pocket money of three pounds a week. Salary it was not, experience it would be. All I could do was wait, hope someone's eyes on the UNA selection board would alight on my 'trained at The Royal, Sheffield' and find something in the interim to prevent me from going under with boredom, or penury.

I would miss being Nanny Rose to my two young charges but two nights earlier a pint-sized, middle-aged male had charged into the boutique in a state, demanding to try on some dresses. Because there were only two flimsy screens to change behind in the tiny shop and nervous of his intentions, I began to worry about girls coming in, a transvestite in the changing area and the safety of all of us.

The man was a sad specimen. He lived with two Aussie girls, he said, who had threatened to beat him up if he didn't return home in a dress. He was becoming increasingly agitated so I gave in, shoved him behind a screen with a couple of dresses and rang owner hubby. He sprinted down from Nevern Square and turfed the weirdo out. That night, someone fired several airgun pellets at the glass door of the boutique. Some were embedded in the frame. This was not the sort of excitement I needed.

Hubby gave me the following morning off I requested and feeling like I was jumping ship, I hurried to the paddle steamer interviews at the St. James Hotel. There was already a buzzing crowd of mainly young students, some actors and art and design post-grads in their early twenties. Everyone was chatting nineteen-to-the-dozen waiting for the low-down on the "unique adventure."

The paddle steamer would sail daily from Tower Bridge to Herne Bay to Southend and back, stopping at both piers. This was before the main part of Herne Bay Pier collapsed in a storm in 1978 and before Southend Pier was dogged by fire and closed permanently in 1982. Staff were required for the steamer's café, restaurant, shop and bar as well as for stewarding. Hours were ten until six, three days a week and from ten in the morning until midnight on the other two days. On those two days we would remain on board after the day trip to welcome guests for the evening dinner cruise down the Thames Estuary and back to Tower Bridge.

Beside me at the interview was fine arts graduate Celia. She was super-bright, like Jenny my Lostwithiel friend. We clicked straight away and were to become firm buddies. I liked her intelligent eyes that reminded me of bluebells in a breeze. She was so cool. She wasn't fazed by anything and I found myself laughing non-stop with her about the Carry on Steaming being presented that morning that we really couldn't think of as work.

As was the way in those days, most of us were hired on the spot. I gave two week's notice at the boutique, got fitted up with a Jack Tar sailor costume and began work as a waitress on the venerable old Queen of the South at the beginning of May. Celia ran the cigarette and sweet kiosk. I served snacks and lunches and waited at *cordon bleu* dinners on the evening run. Younger brother Simon had managed to slip in as a bar man. He had recently applied to be a trainee chef at the St. James Hotel and this was part of his experience. All the crew hit it off, chosen well by the company, I would say. All of us were seizing the moment. At last, London life was becoming real.

My weary table-waiting mate Sandra carried on burning the candle at both ends. She would stagger on to the boat on many a morning having partied the night at the Bag O' Nails or Speak Easy Club. She would tell us stories of musicians that had jammed there and the pop stars, including Beatles she had rubbed shoulders with. For a time she hung about with one of the Monkeys and listening to her we felt vicariously closer to the glamorous notoriety of the Pop world.

"Wait 'til the girls back home hear this!" was a frequent exclamation in our bed-sit.

Even at the launch party the day before the steamer cast off, one of the journalists, a Peter Pan-faced trombonist said he'd heard a rumour that Radio Caroline would soon be operating from the steamer. This 'pirate radio station' the hippest on the air and one that all youngsters listened to had been banned from operating from those leggy, Second World War Maunsell Forts in the Thames Estuary and from a ship off the English coast in a classic People *vs* Establishment battle.

The tide was turning with the government promising more entertainment and local radio throughout the United Kingdom. The days of the three BBC radio stations we had listened to since the War, the Home Service, Light Programme and magnificently named Third Programme of classical music, were numbered.

On yet another seminal occasion in our London experience, this one in July 1967, the paddle steamer remained at Tower Bridge to acknowledge the Gypsy Moth IV. Francis Chichester had just completed the first single-handed circumnavigation of the globe and was to be knighted that day by the Queen at Greenwich. There were hundreds of boats around us and tens of thousands of people cheering as this rather frail-looking gentlemen sailed right under our noses in the tiniest of craft. We were in awe of this sailor alone 226 days at sea, leaving port in one direction and returning from the other. It was an astonishing achievement. Not far behind his little yacht and presumably part of his escort was the Greek tycoon Niarchos in his luxury number.

The crew were aware I was a nurse and I was often called to give first aid to passengers who became unwell or injured, especially when the estuary was a bit choppy. My most worrying call out was to the captain himself. This elderly Sea Dog was suffering a bad reaction to eating strawberries. The company insisted he complete the evening run as he was the only officer with a Master's Ticket. I had to remain on board to keep an eye on him. I became worried as his temperature climbed and insisted on speaking to his doctor.

"Don't fret, miss," the captain croaked. "I had a coronary last year and I'm still here ..."

Once again I was running, this time to the telephone box on Tower Bridge. The doctor who was somewhere in Sussex could hardly hear me and thinking I was probably a crank was somewhat dismissive. I returned to the waiting boat and informed the only other senior officer it was on his head, the captain remaining on board. I said he had to remain in bed and we had better pray. The senior officer took the boat out and back that evening with its dinner guests blissfully ignorant of this little bit of Upstairs, Downstairs. I was much more aware of potential peril at sea after this and would wince every time the rather rusty old vessel bumped into the flimsiest of Victorian piers when berthing.

We were occasionally a bit naughty about a crafty drink. None of us knew how to open wine bottles, especially Champagne and it was supposed to be done by those with catering experience. We had to do it occasionally and if it was rejected as being 'corked,' a term many people still use incorrectly, it was put to one side for later disposal. How we served dinner slewing around half-cut with disposed-of wine, especially on choppy nights, I will never know.

When the two whippet-thin Irish boys who were the regular chefs on dinner nights got to join us we would end of crying with laughter. They were a funnier double act than Morecambe and Wise. These were the occasions when, young and carefree, we loved our open-air nautical job.

It wasn't long after I started the job that Anna began a relationship with my brother Morris's best buddy, Kenny. She later married him and they eventually had three children. This was my second match-making triumph after Myrtle and Phillip's union in Sheffield! My new best friend Celia came to the rescue, inviting me to share her tiny top-floor flat in nearby Pimlico. It was lovely and I enjoyed the change of

scene from Earls Court.

It was not long before I became aware of a drama in the making. Celia was quiet one night but desperately wanted to talk. She told me she thought she was a lesbian. I didn't have the words or experience to comment on a pronouncement like this but could see she was looking to me to lead. She might even have been testing me. I was flummoxed. In the days when homosexuals suffered serious victimisation, demonization and often blackmail here was arty, intelligent, kind and brighter-than-most, lovely Celia. She was not a deviant, butch, a dyke or mentally ill. She was just Celia.

My mind went back to the previous week when I had flu-like symptoms and felt really awful. Celia had run a bath for me with candles around it and helped me in it. I asked her cautiously about this and how did she feel that I was most definitely heterosexual.

"You have the most beautiful *mons veneris*," she said quietly, "but if you are not a lesbian there is really nothing I can do about it."

"But you said you had a boyfriend some time ago?"

She bit her lip.

"I've had two male lovers. There are nice boys about. And, well, boys lead and as I'm 'fem' that sort of suited me."

The head girl at school had initiated her, maybe even confused her, she said. This was at the classy Lady Margaret School in Parsons Green. Celia was there at about the same time as journalist Janet Street-Porter.

My only experience of homosexuality up to then was saying hello to Queenie at the embroidery shop in my childhood days in Lostwithiel. Also accepted by that sexually broad-minded community were two eccentric lesbians whose cottage was more the talking point. They kept an open house for feral pigeons and it would have made an authentic guano-plastered set for Hitchcock's The Birds.

My first concern was what would I do if Celia tried to kiss me? This was silly since I knew what I would do. Girls learn this early on with boys they are not keen on. Celia was a grown-up and circumspect about her private and social life. It was me who needed to get a life.

Needless to say I didn't flee from the flat in disgust or in fear. She had already made me realise I had been immersed in medicine for too long. In introducing me to art, poetry and classical music, even the lives of the composers in their historical context, she was carrying on from my first Sheffield boyfriend Leo who had initiated the Educating Rose programme. It would have been daft for me to leave the flat and both of us stopped fretting.

My programme of education continued and began to include *avant-garde* films. We saw *Jules et Jim*, 2001: A Space Odyssey, Blow-Up, Fellini's 8½ and many other late-night art house films at the Paris Pullman in South Kensington. Not that I understood half of them but I was trying. Rather harder was the comprehension of Celia's abstract painting. She would trot me around galleries shouting at me to open my eyes! This to a girl whose only exposure to art was to sentimental pictures of Saint Francis or cowering under harrowing images of blood, thorns and halos. Seeing truly magnificent Renaissance paintings of Christian stories as art, with emphasis on the piece's place in the history of art was a real revelation.

A friend from Notre Dame High School remarked recently that attending a grammar school, particularly one affiliated to a religious order, doesn't mean you get an education. I came to it later, in the late 'Seventies with the Open University. I learnt more in the OU's one-year foundation course than in twelve years at school. I was up to speed with my twin passions of music and reading. It took a while longer to begin an appreciation of art and the history of art.

I was lucky to be sharing a flat with Celia at this stage in my life. Her friends too were of the time and not to be missed. Artists introvert and extrovert trailed up to the Pimlico flat, strung-out in flower-power skirts, long scarves and floppy hats, embroidered loons and blue smocks with deep front pockets, sometimes with French berets. There were tantrums and tears, or glazed eyes and laughter, sometimes a bottle of something strong or a bit of weed.

Celia told me years later that many came to stare at me, a vision of Northern loveliness. She wouldn't have touted me like this! I felt a lump with pink lipstick who sat around in my non-fashion statement blue nylon Woolies' nightie and pink fluffy slippers from Sheffield. Mata Hari I was not, more Georgy Girl.

Life in the 1960s was transient and full of hope and high ideals. London moved at a pace and if you were special you pushed the boundaries. The rest of us endeavoured to keep up and were able to move easily from one job to another. It was unfortunate our spell keeping up as seafarers came to an end within weeks of it starting. The Queen of the South was diagnosed with terminal engine trouble and would be retired but I was already sorted for the next stage.

Approaching Tower Bridge for the last time we were heartbroken that Radio Caroline had not happened on our watch. I had worked with a great bunch of young hopefuls. We would miss the steamer crumping Southend Pier and holding our breath as we passed the buoy marking the huge quantity of explosives festering since 1944 in the SS Richard Montgomery on a sandbank off Sheerness. Very disconcerting it was being able to see the mast of this wartime cargo ship that will one day, according to experts go up with a boom that will be felt in Belgium.

For the moment I was still waiting for word from the UNA. Biting the bullet, I returned to a more sombre working mode in starched uniform as an agency nurse, on nights mostly, around London in private homes, private clinics and NHS hospitals.

Chapter Fifteen
#How Many Roads Must a Man Walk Down ...# (Bob Dylan)

It felt good getting back to doing what I knew best even though I had reservations about nursing private patients. This would have been a red rag to a bull to the girls, to most people, back home. A break of more than half a year from nursing had given me time to reflect.

It was inevitable my first private patient would fit the perception of spoilt aristocrat. He was an elderly French Count whose initials HRH were embroidered in gold on the doormat outside his room. He had the same doctor as the Queen, Lord Moran, the one who advised a whisky as the best nightcap. This aristocrat required minimum care and on some evenings I had warm conversations with his friend, a well-known writer and nephew of Somerset Maugham, after he had seen me penning away quietly. I was at Janet and John level by comparison and appreciated the advice that I should continue reading as widely and write every day to keep my mind practised.

The London Clinic near Harley Street was more exciting. This street was the Mecca of Medical Hakims where the great, the good and the greedy practised their specialities. In the 'Sixties the clinic was one of only two private medical and surgical units in London. It was patronised and therefore funded, I suppose, by the rich and famous from all over the world. This included Arab royalty who were known for being demanding, if not outright obnoxious.

My charges were, in the main, courteous and easy to care for except for one adolescent playboy named Ibrahim. He rang his bell repeatedly one evening in his room. London Clinic nurses were allocated a maximum of five patients so they were usually able to answer calls quickly. The bell pests knew this. Responding to the call, I came in on a grinning Ibrahim pointing to his puny erection and a box of whisky on top of the wardrobe. There is only one thing a nurse does in such a situation. Smiling brightly, I walked to the sink, soaked a face cloth in cold water and dropped it like a wet parachute on his member. That did the trick.

On another night I was tending an American lady in her private room coming round from a hysterectomy. It was fortunate she was still only partly conscious and the lights were low when the door burst

213

open. An Arab lady in a black *burqa* with be-jewelled head scarf and dark glasses over her shrouded head floated into the room in a wheelchair. The gormless porter pushing her had got the wrong room. My patient screamed, the Arab lady shrieked. I told the porter to take a walk.

My patient chuckled, thankfully. "The Grim Reaper I did not want to see!" she said. She could have made a fuss. She could even have had a heart attack.

We soon got to know the clinic's Who's Who, the in-patient crowd. Barbara Cartland would request all her covers, even that hiding toilet rolls, be changed three times a day. Everything had to be co-ordinated in one of the lurid pastel colours she was renowned for. Elizabeth Taylor became a favourite from when she was admitted seriously ill with double pneumonia. She almost died and a tracheotomy scar was added to her medical accoutrements. Both the Duke and Duchess of Windsor were patients, the Duchess (Wallace Simpson) in 1964 for "facial surgery." It was King Hussein of Jordan's hospital of choice in London. He carried a gold-plated revolver for protection and would entrust it to Matron before an operation.

One regular nurse at the clinic had looked after the Queen Mother at Clarence House at the time the Press rumoured she had a colostomy. She had been telling and re-telling the story from Land's End to John o'Groats in order to cheer-up new colostomy patients. The nurse said she was a sweetie and that she and her family could be wicked in their humour towards the ingratiating and to some less pleasant aspects of life. They were not that precious.

Successful high-powered people impressed me with their energy and charisma whether I liked them or not. They exude a powerful aura even when ill or recovering from surgery. Brits tend to understate their ability and power. American and Jewish entrepreneurs are the other way, super-charged with a ferocious certainty.

Some patients had obviously been pampered or expected to be so for the money they had elected to pay out and could be a nightmare to look after. They were typically neurotic and paranoid about every treatment and medicine given. One old chap, a jute millionaire with multiple phobias would put on surgical gloves and a rain cape before going to the bathroom to keep germs off him. He was not the normal bell pest, he was just getting his money's worth while being rude and ungracious about everything we did for him.

He did take the time to explain to me that the *goy*, those of us who are not Jews, are here to be exploited. He didn't use the word screwed but this is what came across. He was quite open about it, without any niceties or morals. All his life he had only been interested in making money, from anyone, preferably the *goy*. Once he referred to me as *shiksa*. A Jewish boy explained its meaning and apologised on the man's behalf.

Years later I grimaced on overhearing some thinly-disguised sarcasm from a mature nurse to a hospice patient who would endlessly ring and apologise, ring and apologise.

"... we are here to serve you ..." she said tightly, when it seemed to me the patient was only after a little reassurance. I understood the nurse's frustration but the patient was terminal and received no visitors. She died three days later.

Another patient who nearly did cause me to walk out on the job was a retired director of a Swiss pharmaceutical company. He growled and snarled like a wolf hound throughout his stay, not bearing me to touch him in case my germs contaminated him. The quantity of water he drank through the night had to be metered precisely with a sterile spoon and cooled to a temperature measured by a thermometer. He would sip half from a green baby beaker on his right side and the other half from a yellow baby beaker on his left side. His soap, flannel and nailbrush had to be placed to the millimetre where he wanted them or he would erupt in a fury. His slippers were to be brushed before he wore them and so on and so on. He slapped my hand if I grasped his arm incorrectly. Always I was referred to as "it."

On his departure he reverted to charming director to whoever it was collecting him, as if butter wouldn't melt in his foul mouth. This sort of man becomes as big a monster as his wealth will allow. I told the agency I would not nurse the likes of him again. They suggested I laugh such things off. You can only rise above such people if you are prepared to be more demonic than they are and this is no laughing matter. I had one life and no intention of moving in such a direction. There is often deep-seated chauvinism, even misogyny in such people and I haven't got time for these things either.

The mark of the truly great is that they belittle no one. The best always have a self-deprecating modesty and gentle humour with it. My first VIP, the Lord Mayor of Sheffield was such a person. Champions, whether brilliant, ambitious actors, musicians, sports

215

people or CEOs, tend to be obsessive perfectionists. Some I nursed were a hair's breadth from being sectionable psychiatric patients.

A twice-decorated bomb-disposal expert was such a patient. The precise and exacting qualities required for him to be the best at his job took over his later life. He became an irrational obsessive about the minutiae of his health. He drew strikes on his toilet wall so he could report bowel movement accurately to his long-suffering doctor. Visiting his GP daily if he could, he would be armed with a ream of notes about his health issues. On top of this he would refuse almost all medication advised because of possible side-effects.

His loyal wife was at her wits' end, forced to sit for hours as he detailed research on his daily health worries. Should her concentration lapse he would begin again, and again if necessary.

As mere nurses in clinics treating private patients in those days, we also had to endure smarmy consultants changing dressings and removing sutures from their *milch cow* patients, sweet-talking them to yucky levels. At least they were doing their own dirty work. Many of this type of doctor barely acknowledged their NHS patients, or nurses.

To keep the work coming in that Summer of 1967 and have some variety I registered with an agency in Earls Court that placed nurses in Nursing Homes throughout West London. They asked if I could start a week of nights in Fulham that night with a short shift by way of induction. The resident Aussie Staff Nurse showed me around a large run-down house. She had to take a week off and said the week should be quiet and uneventful. Then she asked me if I had a reputation for patients dying, or not dying under my care!

Assuming she was being jocular I told her I was a good omen. It was remarked during my training that I was good news in this respect.

"I cob them all," she said. "They just peg out on me and I'm thinking, it's not good for my reputation."

"Or the patients!" I added.

I wanted to tell her to cheer up a bit as she had a rather sad, pinched face in half-light that might have frightened residents. She did have a reason for asking. A lady who had just taken up residence, a cookery writer for a national broadsheet was strong on premonition, including one of her own death even though she was relatively fit and active around the Home. I got the idea when Staff introduced me to her in the kitchen where she was preparing a cup of cocoa.

"Will you be with me?" she asked quietly taking my hand.

I was a bit spooked but replied I would, of course. At about three that morning when I was putting my coat on for the walk home, Doom-laden Staff came running down the stairs to our little office.

"Come quickly, the Cookery Lady is asking for you. She's in some sort of fit, or trance."

We ran back upstairs and I took the distressed lady's hand. She calmed, smiled at me then slipped away. How she knew she was going to die when she was apparently fine a few hours earlier I will never know. A spiritualist nodded sagely when I told the story some time later and said the lady's spirit-guide had picked me.

On laying her out I felt resistance when trying to insert cotton wool into her vagina with tweezers. We did her the honour of not packing her with cotton wool to prevent leakage.

"No way are we going to deflower her," Staff muttered.

One of the residents was a serene Russian aristocrat, from coiffured silver hair and crystal blue eyes to Cinderella-size feet. She was a diminutive figure with skin as fine as a Fabergé egg who lay motionless on her bed for most of the day and night, hands cupped as though embalmed. She had all her faculties but preferred living in her past. I had time to chat to her, usually late in the evening or early in the morning. She readily recalled the circumstances under which her family were forced to leave Russia in 1917 and told me in detail how she was related to Czar Nicholas. Her description of her daily life as a young woman in Saint Petersburg at the turn of the Nineteenth Century was spell-binding.

I enjoyed all my jobs that Summer. Nursing Homes were generally quieter and because we had fewer patients to care for at the London Clinic and doctors did some of the routine work, nights and days could be slow there also. I began to plead with my agencies for hospital work again, nursing at the coal face.

Because of my lengthy period in Plastic Surgery as a student I was booked several times for the Roehampton Burns Unit at Queen Mary's Hospital in Wandsworth. As at Fulwood, I could not get used to the environment. Room after overheated room housing patients suffering at every level, mental, emotional, physical and physiological was overwhelming. Shocked by the sight and smell of patients so badly mutilated by flesh and tissue-melting flames, with lungs also scoured by corrosive smoke, I couldn't distance myself sufficiently and declined further placings. I had learnt a limitation. A nurse must be able to control her feelings. Patients quickly sense recoil, pity and dislike.

The NHS part of the private St. John and St. Elizabeth Hospital in St. John's Wood needed extra night staff for a week. Day Staff showed me around at the start of my shift and said it should be a quiet night. "Be prepared for anything!" Night Sister countered.

It was midnight when I realised Night Sister was agitated about something. She asked if I minded delaying my break. I offered to cover for her if she needed to go off and do something. She said it was kind of me but she was actually worried about one of our patients.

"Have you ever had a post-op' patient lose it and become difficult?"

"No Sister, only through hearsay."

"The danger sign is the eyes taking on a vacant or angry look. Dialogue with any sense to it stops ..."

As she was speaking there was an almighty crash from Mr. Clarke in bed thirteen leaping out of bed in front of our eyes and pulling his IV stand over.

"Call the houseman ... porters ... anyone from the next ward ..."

As I was on the telephone I saw Mr. Clarke pull out his catheter and drips and Sister try to stop him clawing at his gown and the dressings around his abdomen. Fortunately the houseman and two porters were there within minutes. Sister was on the floor by then, restraining the patient in an arm lock helped only by the sudden Olympian strength of this man being fettered by his gown over his head. There was blood and broken glass everywhere.

Two patients had gone to Sister's aid but as the porters took over I got them back into bed. The houseman managed to inject paraldehyde, without ceremony, in the patient's flailing buttocks. The smell of the solution was unmistakeable. The patient was out cold within seconds.

Sister went to change her uniform and tidy herself up. I apologised for not helping her physically and not being quick enough in getting help from the adjacent ward. She assured me I did well and she wouldn't have wanted me to join the fray.

"Two nurses wrestling a patient on the floor is not the image we need to portray!" she said sportingly.

Although the rest of the week went without incident and I quite enjoyed the action, shall I say, Celia picked up on my general pallor of dissatisfaction. She announced it was time we spaced out with a bit of wacky baccy. Neither of us smoked or drank much and she had a small stash of cannabis that had been tucked away for ages. We had experienced secondary inhalation of the stuff on many occasions but never actually smoked it. We were curious generally about psychedelic and mind-bending experiences that people were talking about to the point of it being old hat at London parties. A spliff would do for the moment, Celia said.

"They told me this is Mid not Mex and anything better would be a waste!"

"What does that mean?"

"Haven't a clue ..." she grinned.

She heated up a rather large lump of cannabis resin on a spoon, picked little bits off it and mixed it with some Golden Virginia. She then rolled an oversize cigarette very badly compared with how we had seen it done at parties, lit up, inhaled and started coughing. I was watching water bubbling around some eggs in a Pyrex saucepan on the gas stove as I took my first 'toke.'

Sharing our scant knowledge of the drugs scene we agreed to stop each other leaping out of the third floor window if either of us lost the plot. People had done this taking acid, LSD, along with roasting babies in the oven, we had heard. We inhaled and coughed, coughed and inhaled and continued to stare at the bubbling water.

"Celia?"

"Yeah?"

"I don't feel any different. Do you?"

"Nah!"

We giggled on deciding the cannabis must have passed its sell-by date. We were actually giggling rather a lot!

Whilst agency work was a well-paid doddle my missionary conscience kept prodding me about millions of people around the world with no access to medical care. Anna and I had applied to the Red Cross to be sent out to the epicentre of a crisis. There were major earthquakes in 1966 in Turkey and China. In the Xingtai disaster, 8,000 people perished and more than 38,000 were injured. Flooding and typhoons had killed tens of thousands in Bangladesh. Famine in India had killed a million-and-a-half people only two years earlier. A full-scale civil war was going on in Nigeria with tens of thousands maimed or starving. Quite rightly we were told we needed more experience. The UNA did seem a more appropriate way to start.

The last letter I received from Elaine who had been out in Jordan for almost a year was at Christmas. She loved the teaching but was deeply disappointed at the way Midnight Mass in Bethlehem was conducted. As a good Catholic girl she thought it would be the most thrilling moment of her life.

"Everything we learned about is there and more," she wrote. "The candles in Manger Square were so moving. Then we had to descend some narrow stone stairs and duck through the Door of Humility into the Church of the Nativity. The door was altered centuries ago, lowered to keep horse riders out. It was awful, hot, claustrophobic and local guys kept pinching our bums. Then someone stole my purse ..."

Bethlehem had been tapestried into my tiny brain from my first Away in a Manger and I wanted to discover the Middle East and biblical lands, for slightly different reasons now. I liked my surrogate Christian Iraqi brothers Suhail and Iskander because they were comfortable in their own skins in the same way that Americans and Aussies are less inhibited than Brits. Could it be that Jews and Arabs in that part of the world are the same people? If they are, why were they psyching themselves for all-out conflict? Why was biblical Armageddon being touted?

I had tried to talk to the boys about this but was overwhelmed, if not overpowered by their argumentative stance. In anticipation of a UNA interview I had begun swotting up on Middle East events. This was mostly through newspaper items and keeping an ear to the radio. Having Christian Arabs in our midst brought it alive.

My first interview with the UNA was tough. Of course, they jumped on my having given up midwifery training in the East End Maternity Hospital halfway through the Part One course. A midwifery qualification was a pre-requisite for their nursing volunteers, they said. I kept my cool and talked a bit about our Iraqi friends and how they compared London with their homeland. They seemed satisfied eventually and I was over the moon to receive an acceptance letter the following day.

In the 'Sixties few young people went that far abroad. Some went as *kibbutz* volunteers, or trod a Hippy Trail to India and Morocco. Almost none of my school friends and none of their parents had travelled, except in the Services during the War. My ship's surgeon father was unusual in having been cruising the oceans blue for years. Mass travel was on its way, Pascal said. He had just been commissioned by a travel company to open up a sleepy fishing village called Torremolinos for the first *Costa del Sol* package holidays. He was also looking at other back-of-beyond fishing communities near Valencia earmarked for development. An all-in-one holiday like the ones he was putting together was still exotic at the time.

After receiving my UNA papers I attended an induction day with dozens of other chosen volunteers to prepare me for my year abroad. I would be leaving at the end of September and was the only one going to Jordan, to a local hospital in its capital Amman. We were strongly advised not to get involved with the local boys or girls or become politically active. That was about the sum of their advice.

Mother wasn't happy about my going alone to the Middle East but that was as far as her concern went. There was no stopping me anyway, I thought. The Iraqi boys were ecstatic and said they would make sure their Jordanian cousins saw I was safe. They were worried about me going out because political tension in the region had been growing for months.

It was near the end of May when Suhail came rushing into our flat.

"Rose, Rose, trouble ... Nasser has blockaded the Israeli port of Eilat on the Red Sea!"

"That won't affect things in Jordan, surely?"

"No, no, it is very serious," Suhail insisted, "this is war. But Egypt cannot do such a thing on its own. There must be a bigger plan. Our Jewish cousins will know what is going on, they are very clever people. They must respond or be over-run. That means there will be big problems through the region, including Jordan ..."

He was correct. Fighting broke out a week later, on June 5th, between Egypt, Syria, Jordan and Israel. It lasted six days and was soon being referred to as the Six-Day War. The map of the Middle East was redrawn as the boys said, in blood.

221

Crowds of us in the Earl's Court enclave collected nightly in the Iraqi guys' large double room in Trebovir Road. It became a Conflict HQ with elements of watching a Soccer World Cup Final. The other sixty or so student tenants of all nationalities traipsed in and out to soak up the excitement. Sporadic news items from the World Service and very occasionally on television were seized upon. Newspapers were devoured during the day and reports reported on in the evening.

It was my introduction to *realpolitik*. Remembering there was no tweeting, texting, blogging, mobile phone clips, Internet, video or mass television coverage. BBC radio went off air after the shipping forecast and National Anthem; television shut down after the Epilogue, also before midnight. If you wanted to make a telephone call to the Middle East you had to ring the operator and book it for next day. News was only as instant as the next morning's newspaper.

The Cuban Missile Crisis of 1963, only four years before, was not forgotten. Russian and American communication was via Radio Moscow and Voice of America broadcasts beamed on through BBC transmitters in London. Kruschev backed down because of the several hours it took to communicate with his commanders in the field. Unknown to the Americans the Russians would have met an invasion of Cuba with tactical nuclear weapons that would probably have decimated American forces. Kruschev realized he was not in control of these weapons and the consequences of their use.

Understandably, our Middle East contingent was cock-a-hoop at news of an Arab victory, with Egypt claiming the destruction of the

Israeli Air Force. It was actually the other way around. The entire Jordanian and Syrian air forces were destroyed on the ground. Russian air force jets also joined the affray and six of them were shot down for their trouble. Apparently, many Arab soldiers just gave up and went home. Part of Earl's Court plumbed the deepest depths. We felt very sorry for Suhail and Iskander. I was glad real casualty figures, 30,000 Arabs soldiers killed, were not known for some time.

The Jordanian King's fourth wife Queen Noor writes in her memoirs that her husband wept at losing the Holy City. She also believed the level of stress he endured at the time led to his premature death at the age of sixty-three. Hussein's grandfather, King Abdullah, fought with the British to take Jerusalem back from centuries of Turkish control. To lose it to Jews was Hussein's nadir. Being a Hashemite descendent of Mohammed he had custodianship of the Holy shrine in Jerusalem, the second most important after Mecca.

The Occupied Territories were now a no-go area to Jordanians. Jerusalem and Bethlehem would be out of bounds for me also, soon to be residing in Jordan. That wasn't so bad, I thought. The Holy Land would be around for a while. I was disappointed I wouldn't be able to meet Elaine out there.

Not everyone saw the conflict in such a profound racial, tribal or biblical way. Morris, for example fixed a banner across the boys' bed-sit balcony exhorting *"Viva Israel!"* Plebeian in its language and sentiment it did not endear himself to his good friends.

The UNA wrote to me within days of the war and at a hastily-organised meeting announced they would have to postpone my placing. They wanted me to consider my second choice, that of sailing up the Amazon to give health care to the Indians.

Despondent, I mulled over the new offer, envisioning Amazonian mosquitoes nibbling me alive and Anacondas waiting to take me in as one lump. I declined on the spot and stuck my neck out by saying Jordan was surely the place where volunteers were needed most. They gave in once again. It freaked my parents and older sister. Elaine was sent home from Jordan but the fighting didn't worry me. I reasoned there were a lot of people out there for whom life had to carry on and remained steadfast in wanting to develop my nursing skills.

At seven in the morning on September 30th, 1967, Intrepid Nurse MacFarlane set off on her mission to patch up the Middle East. I was accompanied to the airport by surrogate brother Suhail, nursing buddy Anna and paddle steamer Celia, my best mates. My family did their usual and stayed away. Their approach to caring for their daughter/sister was consistent, you've made your bed *et cetera, et cetera.* Although I was twenty-two years old I probably had the emotional age of a girl of sixteen. We weren't worldly-wise and our relationships had been lightweight and adolescent, when adolescents were innocent about sexual matters. The 'everything goes' mantra may have bubbled around us in London and we tried to be sussed and cool like Germaine Greer but inwardly my girlfriends and I were still gauche sixth-formers.

Waving a forlorn farewell to my bleary-eyed friends I felt like a cloistered nun off to do missionary work. Having never been to an airport, never mind up in an aircraft I took fright as the engine pitch rose. The bemused male steward ushered me hastily up the aisle of the half-empty 'plane.

"Everything is humpty-dumpty," he said, "and you might like to sit near the galley with us."

Calming down, I was pleased to see my back-up had raced to the top of the Departures building and were waving like mad. I was off.

Goodbye for the moment my stalwart, sensible Auburn Anna, great Cockney mums and The Prospect of Whitby but good riddance to the East End Maternity Hospital dump; bye-bye Mata Hari Boutique, Queen of the South, mad mid-'Sixties London, Biba, Minis, Mini Mokes, *mini-jupes*, the maxi, Kensington Hippy Market, Earl's Court bed-sit land, brother Morris, Suhail and Iskander, mad parties and late-night debates and arguments; bye-bye Cobbers Denise and Jill, my nursing agencies and to London Town in general; good riddance to my lousy cash flow.

Not forgetting a big hug to you guys who were always uplifting, always an inspiration, always there in times of need - Dylan, The Beach Boys, The Mamas and Papas, The Kinks, The Beatles, The Monkees, Pink Floyd, The Who, The Stones, The Bee Gees, Joni Mitchell, Joan Baez, Melanie, Janis Joplin, Dusty Springfield and many more including lovely Cilla of course, who, as I am revising this manuscript in August 2015 has just died too young ...

Chapter Sixteen
#Learning to Fly ...# (Pink Floyd)

The elation of cruising over the Alps and Mont Blanc, lulled me to sleep. I was woken on our descent to Beirut where I was changing aircraft for Amman. We were late, our connexion had gone and we were being transferred to the Hotel St. George for the night, the cabin crew told me. They were curious about my journeying to Amman alone and for the first time I felt vulnerable. All I knew of my destination was its name, Hospital Oasis and its director Dr. Jibril S.

The ground steward escorting me off the aircraft into the Arrivals building at Beirut International Airport looked like Suhail and was just as friendly. He even waited with me for my cases. There was no need to pay for the hotel, he said. I could sleep over at his flat in the city.

Fortunately, someone was watching over me.

"No ... certainly not ..." a voice behind us boomed. The frightfully English lady stepped between me and the steward. "You come with me, My Dear. The steward has work to do elsewhere ..."

The kindly lady, a diplomat, ushered me into a cab. Airlines didn't charge for accommodation under such circumstances, she said and under no circumstances should I go off into a strange city with a strange man. I got the message and as promised, locked my hotel door. Now I had a thumping headache from jet engines, airport bustle and traffic. It was also warm in Beirut, much, much warmer than London. That evening, feeling cooped up, unable to rest and homesick just to add to my misery I rang the desk for two aspirin. The manager brought them up on a little plate with a white napkin.

"I hope these cure your headache ..." he said grinning.

I grimaced when he had gone, my aspirin were Mint Imperials. I had arrived in the Middle East.

Fragile from a very early start next morning, I didn't like the turbulence the smaller aircraft hit on the way to Amman. For most of the flight I peered over a sun-soaked, caramel-coloured landscape of desert and hills with touches of green as far as my tired eyes could see. The light was sacramental, waking up a dormant area of my brain under-stimulated by our temperate climate. Endorphins soared as we skimmed over white shoebox dwellings. I had only seen pictures of people on donkeys in my Bible books. When I saw my first elderly Arab gentleman in full garb and stick riding one I nearly wept.

"*Ahlan wa sahlan, yanny!* Welcome, Nurse Rose!" a vivacious, giggly girl called out excitedly. "I'm Nadia, a belly-dancing SRN come to meet you!"

Nadia, petite and busty with mischievous nutmeg-brown eyes gave a cheeky little shimmy in front of a line of strangers outside the Arrivals Hall. She had hot-footed it back to Jordan, she said, just after the war panicking about her family. I complimented her English, interjected as it was with "bloody," "damn" and "bugger."

"I trained at the Frenchay Hospital in Bristol! My good English is due entirely to my wonderful friends there ..."

Nattering away as if she had known me for years, she guided me to an old Chevrolet pick-up where my new boss Dr. Jibril, a portly forty-something Jordanian gynaecologist, obstetrician and director of Amman's brand-new Oasis Hospital was waiting. After a warm, welcoming handshake and dismissal of my apology for my delayed arrival, I gave an inner sigh of relief that these two people spoke good English and that we seemed to be on the same wavelength.

The charismatic duo took me to the Hilton Hotel first for coffee and an amazing array of little cakes. They told me of The Oasis, a baby itself on the edge of town on the road to Salt. My heart sank when I realised they were talking about a maternity hospital. What had I done in persuading the UNA to dispatch Midwife Mugwumps to teach a maternity hospital's staff how to deliver babies?

"Yes, *yanny*, Rose," said chatterbox Nadia, "it is a very bloody busy fifteen-bed maternity hospital with plans for expansion. Isn't it *Hakim?*"

Dr. Jibril said it was early days. There would eventually be an outpatient's unit, a pharmacy and more. He apologised the temporary kitchen was in the ground floor nurse's dorm opposite the room Nadia and that I would be sharing. The two cooks had to make do with a bedroom sink for washing pots and pans in. The front entrance too, they laughed conspiratorially, was still without plate-glass doors. A village lad was paid a pittance to lie across the entrance at night to keep them all safe.

I got a taste of the building site when Nadia and my meagre

luggage were dropped off. Doctor and I then sped off for an appointment with his elderly parents, the hospital's benefactors, in Jebal Amman nearby.

Abou (father of) and *Um* (mother of) Jibril lived in a large stone-clad house that was cool to the point of being cold in that late summer heat. From the moment Naked Nurse walked up the polished marble steps to be introduced to the doctor's elegant parents she felt bedraggled and uncomfortable. She was greeted warmly by father in traditional head dress, a long white *gelabiya* and Western-style jacket and diminutive mother wearing a floral summer dress. With them was the doctor's beautiful younger sister Sarah, a modern maths student at Beirut University, also dressed in Western clothes.

I wanted to laugh at my serious discomfort. Here was I, penniless and barely-educated coming out to Amman to advise highly-educated, well-off and impeccably-mannered 'natives.' *Abou* Jibril may have been illiterate and in insecure times carried his wealth around his waist in the form of gold bars but his construction business had funded most of his sons and daughters through top European and Lebanese universities and paid for the hospital.

'Bye, 'bye those arrogant myths and stereotypes born of Empire, shattered within an hour of my arrival.

My UNA induction had advised it was impolite to decline Arab hospitality. It didn't mention how much alcohol was included. It was ten in the morning when I accepted a large tumbler of Scotch Whisky and iced water. By the third, knowing I was taking in alcohol while dehydrated, I was worried about making my second big event of the day, lunch with the head of the British Council who was also Consul.

Dr. Jibril dropped his new volunteer off at the Consul's bungalow, laughing perhaps a little unkindly at my trying to look and sound sober. The bespectacled Old School diplomat in his linen suit and his jolly wife seemed oblivious to, or were being polite about, my inebriation. An aperitif was followed by a salad and wine topped up by a hovering Jordanian Jeeves. Being the Consul, with a large portrait of Her Majesty gazing upon us I could hardly refuse this hospitality either. This was one occasion I was thankful for my father's insistence on good table manners and our acquiring a taste for alcohol from the age of thirteen so we would not disgrace ourselves.

My appointments continued in the afternoon with Dr. Jibril introducing me to his Scottish wife Marie, their two teenage sons and two younger children in his flat attached to the hospital. I really wanted to sleep but once again food and alcoholic drink were laid out for me. I was now really struggling and only partly paying attention when we eventually began the tour of the main building.

It was a maternity hospital that would be accepting gynaecological and general patients, which was not how it was described by the UNA. By the way the doctor was talking, my responsibilities were stacking up at every corner. I did like the open aspect of the buildings, all new, clean and white. Sun streamed in everywhere. Parts were still bare and there was wooden scaffolding up but it was a functioning hospital with several auxiliaries and other staff beavering away.

Not so reassuring was a large camp or compound on one side of the hospital and army barracks and an ammunition store on the other. Most unnerving was an anti-aircraft gun surrounded by sand bags on the waste ground behind. Doctor Jibril saw my concern and retrieved a piece of paper stuck to some barbed wire. On it was a crude drawing of an Israeli Mirage fighter jet with big blue star and the words 'Next Time These Will be Bombs' in Arabic.

"Air forces call this a leaflet drop," he said. "They have done two or three since the June War. The soldiers manned the gun for a while. Now they don't bother!"

The room I was sharing with Nadia had its own bathroom and toilet and he hoped it was satisfactory. I was too embarrassed to say I came from an area in the North of England where many still had no bathroom or toilet of their own. He had to deal with delivery of building material and a family arriving at the hospital's main door and I really appreciated that half hour on my own.

My tour was cut mercifully short again. I had done my best to make acute clinical observations while trying to walk in a straight line. I wasn't sure whether to laugh weeks later when the good doctor said he was thankful I was a bit tipsy that first afternoon. He was very worried I would notice he had put a patient with a wound infection in a two-bedded ward with a patient recovering from a caesarean.

It was almost in a trance I sat with the family at the end of the day with an unbelievably tasty hot garlic chicken with leavened bread, fresh salad and *hummus* ordered in from a nearby restaurant. I was feeling more at home. It was impossible to feel awkward or tense in the company of these people. Unlike so many British men, Arabs encourage small talk and light humour. They made me feel good without being in the least bit sleazy. Only my Sheffield mate Phillip, cousin Connor and brother Pascal were like this, along with Suhail and Iskander who were great ambassadors for Arab culture.

As the evening wore on with Jibril and Nadia continuing to jabber away I was too far gone to participate after my fifth bout of eating. I did hear the doctor say he thought he was being sent a middle-aged missionary nurse volunteer. And how his flirty heart had lifted when he saw young me descending the aircraft steps. Thankfully in the Middle East, a plump behind, as mine, was celebrated in this part of the world. Twiggy-types were associated with poverty and not considered attractive.

At last in bed I drifted off somewhere in sweetly-perfumed Arabia. The trouble was I didn't feel too good.

"Nadia has been a great help," Dr Jibril remarked on my first round with him the following morning, early and not so bright. "I think you would rather just look today! From tomorrow night you will be on call for deliveries, if this is okay? I'll detail your other duties this afternoon. Nadia was our only trained nurse and she has agreed to continue as Nurse-in-charge while you get to know our routine. She hasn't done midwifery, unlike you!"

A chill came over me again as we went up the cream-tiled staircase to several one-, two- and three-bedded wards on the first floor.

"Of course," he went on, "we must continue to exercise great care with deliveries. If we lose a male child, the family could, well, I won't surmise ..."

"I'm whacked," he said, "having been on call, night and day since we opened in the Summer. It is pure luck I haven't buggered up a delivery, doing it when sometimes I have been half asleep."

Our first jolly ward round was a lot to take in. I did comment on an untidy office desk in what should have been a pin-clean operating theatre. Filing cabinets and piles of correspondence and memos all over the sterilisation room floor next to the theatre added to the mayhem.

"Oh, the theatre is my secretary's office, when we aren't operating," he chuckled reading my face.

I was concerned about how long it would take to clear up and scrub clean for an emergency but this was only the first of many mini-shocks that morning. The Royal Hospital in me screeched again at the piles of intravenous drip bottles, tubing and other patient paraphernalia two young care assistants had piled up inside the empty Baby Nursery. It was attracting flies. The doctor dismissed it. Coming from very poor homes, he explained, the auxiliaries didn't throw anything away. It disappeared for recycling.

More a problem he went on, was them not washing their hands between attending their tiny swaddled charges. Their experience of water shortage outweighed this strict rule.

I soon learned it was not just water in short supply. Everything a busy hospital needs including blood and oxygen was a problem. Operating sometimes on a wing and a prayer hoping the gas in the bottle lasted out was a major stress. The frequent shortage of blood, essential medication and dressings and sometimes hostile family members just outside the theatre door contributed to what could be very trying days.

Doctor Jibril next showed me the pride of the hospital, a fifteen-bed ward, labour suite, nursery and examining room. My office was here also. It put the dingy Victorian hospitals I was used to in the UK to shame. Because the project included new medical technology it was inevitable the recruitment and training of suitable staff would not be easy. Not one trained nurse could be found in Jordan for the hospital's opening, the doctor said. Newly-trained Nadia walking into his office in June asking if he needed help was a godsend. Until then the entire staff was made up of auxiliaries with no medical experience, a Jordanian anaesthetist and himself. This was mostly due he admitted, to his budget being unable to pay more at the moment.

I was amazed at how diligent his 'peasant girls,' his auxiliaries, were. The more mature gems instructed the younger less literate or illiterate girls on changing drips and dressings, suturing wounds, doing straightforward deliveries, recording observations as best they could and monitoring premature babies in the Nursery. All this continued smoothly when the doctor was off-duty. Not once did I hear a complaint from these extraordinary girls about their hours or the pittance they earned. Board and meals was included and I suspect some of their food was taken home.

On the ground floor was a reception area and switchboard and empty rooms that would eventually be a pharmacy and X-Ray area. The laboratory was run by an American, Jan whose husband was

Jordanian. Doctor Jibril's offices, outpatients and consulting room opposite the door-less entrance were here also. Half-way up the marble staircase was a huge panoramic window overlooking the Amman-Salt road that disappeared in the direction of the now sealed off West Bank and Jerusalem.

The unfinished kitchen in the basement was the domain of a charming middle-aged woman Um Samira and her butch assistant, six-foot Fatima. She was always dressed in a long embroidered Bedouin dress with a white head scarf covering most of her face. She had a deep voice and slightly menacing presence. Um Mohammed, a tough, tiny woman occupied the laundry next to the kitchen. Here was a washing machine and large floor area on which she sorted the mountain of dirty laundry. She slept on this at night.

At the end of my first working day Dr. Jibril tapped on our door and came in with a bottle of whisky saying he would like to offer luck and happiness to both Nadia and I for the coming year at the Oasis. I put my notepad away, my head spinning from what had been thrown at me during the day.

"A tiny amount," I said. "Alcohol almost finished me off before I started!"

At the end of my first week Nadia who lived nearby, managed to get home for a day and night and was happy to cover for me on her return. I wanted to sleep but the doctor insisted I have a day off away from the hospital. His assistant anaesthetist Rania and senior auxiliary Nina were given the responsibility of my safety.

The girls first advised me not to wear a short dress or skirt, especially in a service taxi which several strangers might take at the same time. We were taking a taxi into town to have a coffee and look around the *souk* and market stalls. The girls were very respectful with their advice. They had begun by addressing me as *sitt*, 'Miss' Rose. Now, at the end of the week I was *sitt Malaki* which Nadia translated as 'Miss Queen.' This was because I was tall, fair-skinned and to them, highly-qualified. She said it was their way of respecting my authority.

Amman, on the Damascus-Jerusalem road has taken in refugees through history. The city expanded greatly with the influx of Palestinians in 1949 and 1963. They were coming in again that Autumn of 1967 displaced from territory occupied by the Israelis after the June War. I was thrilled to see signs in Arabic and English to places I knew of from my earliest religious instruction, Jerash, Jericho, Bethlehem, Galilee, Damascus ... Almost anywhere in the countryside could have been a film set for a biblical blockbuster. It was hot, dusty and dirty and just as a pair of romantic Western eyes envisaged. The taxi ride into Amman showed distinct areas. The poor districts had baked mud houses and animals in yards. The wealthier areas of an educated Middle Class had elegant modern houses, shops and hotels and people in Western dress. The *souk*, an ancient bazaar, was in a poor downtown area. Old men everywhere rode donkeys, carts were piled high and pulled by an emaciated donkey or horse or wiry young man. Modern traffic weaved between them beeping.

I was relieved the local girls were with me in the *souk*. The slightest interest in anything on view triggered huge pressure to barter, then buy and I was too polite to walk away. Every stallholder offered a small cup of thick, sweet coffee. Even the girls who were used to the patter said it could take time to buy one small item. I was learning there was a distinct *cullshee bukra* ('everything tomorrow,' or *manyana*) attitude to everything, except politics and barter.

"Please Miss, we have what you are looking ..." shopkeepers would insist in well-spoken, ear-caressing English. "... let me first show you zees and zees ... very cheap and what you want ... more coffee ..."

After the market the girls took me to a coffee house they liked. It was cool and dark and smelt divine. Another amazing array of little cakes was laid out on the engraved brass table around which we sat on cushions. I told them I would like to pay and they thanked me.

Rania was Dr. Jibril's assistant anaesthetist when Dr. Malik and his wife were not available. In reality she was a semi-literate auxiliary. She had been taught dot-to-dot anaesthetising techniques without knowing any anatomy, physiology or theory. She was, however, a natural and was trusted even in major surgery. The exquisite Bambi-eyed Nina was similarly street-wise and loyal and well-deserving of her title of senior auxiliary. She had delivered triplets on her own during a couple of nights earlier when Dr. Jibril was away and I was out for the count from exhaustion.

"Miss *Malaki*," she said excitedly after waking me, "not one baby, Miss. Not two baby but three baby I deliver!"

I stumbled into the premature baby room to see all three asleep in a wooden incubators heated by six electric light bulbs. The nurses had named them after Dr. Jibril, his wife and me. They were strong

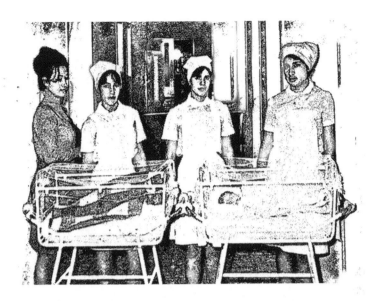

enough to go home the following week. I was amazed in the year I was there that no babies or theatre patients were lost. These girls' monthly pay was about five pounds and they often put in a sixty-hour week. It was far less than my twelve pounds and they worked as hard. It was the going rate, the good doctor said. He paid their board also.

They asked me if my first week at the Oasis had put me off the rest of the year. I had found it uphill, I said and hoped it would not turn into walking up Mount Everest in high heels.

There was a silence before Rania asked "is that same as walking up a sand dune all day and not to see the top?"

"Yes, yes!" I responded and we all burst out laughing.

They asked me if I liked Dr. Jibril. He was very kind and a very positive person to work for I replied. Their English was not up to my thoughts about people with date-brown eyes. They are like ancient archives of wisdom and rage and great experience. They can be deeply affecting and puzzling at the same time. He was a Christian secular Arab who had spent time in England and founded the Arab Student Union. He was very proud to be an acquaintance of Anthony Wedgwood-Benn MP and Middle East journalist Michael Adams. As a Christian Arab and committed *Ba'athist*, I knew from my Iraqi friends his political views would be challenging.

Rania was a little younger than me and I was curious if she was allowed to have a boyfriend. She had a boyfriend, she said and to my

233

surprise described him as an Arab Teddy Boy. He even had an old American car. Not only that, she stayed over with him in the city when she had the chance. I expressed surprise as this was modern even in England. Her family were not so strict, she said. They talked about her in the village, that was all.

Nina was a year or two older than me and I asked her if she wanted to marry.

"I like boy but my family will not permit marry. I am betrothed to older cousin for a long time. He is nice man, farmer who works hard. I hope it a good marriage. But I make excuses," she added laughing.

That evening I was led to the basement. I had heard music from there without knowing that many males and most of the female staff, including Armenian-Jordanian Nadia met there to chat, drink coffee or *chai*, dance and laugh the evening away. Nadia was belly-dancing as I walked in, gyrating hypnotically, not to that oboe-like finger-hole instrument with bulbous end but to drumming, hand-clapping and the sound of little bells being shaken.

"She very good!" came the response when I asked about her talent.

Our hilarious anaesthetist Dr. Malik, who reminded me of Groucho Marx, was not about. I had noticed he had the hots for Nadia. Over the months, the crises would be over the younger auxiliaries and husbands chosen for them. Many times it was tears because it was an older, sometimes very old, male relative whom they didn't even like. These basement evenings were occasions on which they could forget these family obligations, a destiny of servitude, even misery through their married life.

"Girl normal needs chaperone, aunt or brother or male," one said giggling. "Possible look at boys but careful because chaperone look very careful at us also! We like hospital because no chaperone here!"

This was the first of many evenings in the cool basement with the hard-working assistants and end of a superb first day out in Amman.

My immediate concern on my grand tour of the Oasis Hospital was hygiene. As a newly-trained nurse a high standard of cleanliness and good sterility practices in the theatre and delivery suite were things I could pass on with confidence. This is fundamental to good nursing. The girls in the hospital were receptive, most of them speaking some broken English. All were keen to learn English and nursing practice.

The hospital was already commendably clean and tidy thanks to Dr. Jibril's wife dragooning the young cleaning boys with a verbal bullwhip. I soon found they would scuttle off if not instructed and checked upon. Asking them nicely to do things didn't work. They were scallywags and expected to be yelled at.

"Yes *sitt*, me sorry *sitt*. You give me nice smile, I work very hard!" These boys had nothing. They lived on their wits and slept and ate as they could. At the hospital they slept on the roof on old matting. Even the poor wouldn't talk about them. You couldn't engage anyone in conversation about the refugees in the camp by the hospital either. A single contemptuous remark suggested the occupants were part of the latest influx of Palestinians from across the border.

I got through my first night on call with no problems and managed to sleep. On my second night I was just dozing off when an auxiliary came in to say one of the women was ready to give birth. This would be my first delivery as a midwife. I felt perilously under-qualified having only fulfilled a quarter of a maternity course but I was more concerned about my lack of Arabic. I needed to know the woman's medical history, a vital safeguard for an impending birth.

Hurrying along to the labour suite with my white coat over my nightie clutching Margaret Miles' midwifery textbook like worry beads, I introduced myself to the Bedouin woman. The wonderful Salome-eyed auxiliary translated my questions and relayed the woman's answers in Pidgin. The birth went without problem and I conveyed my silent thanks to my favourite tutor at The Royal, Miss T. for her reassuring "babies deliver themselves ..."

Her advice had not included what to do in tragic circumstances in a culture like this where a patient's family were honour-bound to avenge a death by dispatching the nurse or doctor deemed guilty of causing the death.

Naked Nurse breathed easily for the rest of the night but wondered what she was doing half-way around the world on three pounds a week with pressure like this. Nadia was very supportive. She said my not having full midwifery qualification would soon be a thing of the past. I would learn much from Dr. Jibril, as seen in the excellent care the senior auxiliaries were demonstrating under his training.

At the end of the week Dr. Jibril called me into his office and asked with a big smile if I was ready to put on a matron's cap! As there were only two of us trained nurses, I thanked him but couldn't take the promotion too seriously. My additional areas of responsibility were a different matter. From the following Monday morning I would be overseeing nurse training and hospital hygiene. I would be in charge of all wards, the labour suite, theatre, out-patients and pharmacy. I was twenty-two and had beaten Aunt Aggie's record of being the youngest matron in Britain at the age of twenty-nine! I might even have been the youngest 'Matron' anywhere.

Gawd help us ...

I qualified only a year before Nadia but she was fine about my promotion. Was it a pat on the back or desperation, I wondered, or was the doctor being crafty? Highly susceptible to praise, of course and being a people-pleaser, I would no doubt work myself to a masochistic level of fatigue. He had the measure of me already and I was shoved in the deep end.

Assisting in theatre the following week was my next big challenge. I had only staffed in plastic surgery and orthopaedic theatre. Being first assistant and scrub nurse for caesareans, gynaecological operations and general surgery was as nerve-wracking as delivering babies. Not wishing to usurp Nadia's status as first on site, I happily let her induct me in this unfamiliar environment.

"Don't fret, you'll soon see it's only knives and forks!" Dr. Jibril reassured me.

It was the second time I had heard this in my career. The trouble was I had the distinct feeling I was being primed on how I would be using them on a patient.

Every day over the coming weeks brought surprises, some emergencies and many laughs. The biggest shock for this Sheffield girl in the Middle East was learning that the young girl in the doctor's family was not youngest daughter but a slave. They had bought her from a desperately poor family for the equivalent of £40 when she was a toddler.

She was then seven or eight, an invisible mite whose job was to clean the children's bedrooms and assist with their meals. She was a pathetic sight, barefoot, pathologically shy and dressed in one of the doctor's wife's old frocks that reached the ground. She slept like a dog on the floor of their room. I didn't mince my words in telling the doctor how I felt about this. His reply was that slave children were normal in Jordan. All long-time resident wives had them.

In later years I regret not having pressed much harder for a better deal for this girl and children under similar circumstances. I might just have had enough clout to set up a regime where the girl would at least learn to read and write. Unfortunately I was running close to empty most of the time and already pushing things by speaking, sometimes arguing about it more than once. The Jibril family were kind enough to the girl but she was just a slave. I tried talking to her but she would shy away. She had no communication skills whatsoever.

Slave children were not my only discomfort. I could not get along with total male chauvinism evident all around. All the nursing staff were very upset witnessing a husband divorce his wife in the labour ward after she had given birth to another 'unwanted' girl.

"I divorce thee, I divorce thee, I divorce thee ..."

It was as easy as that. The woman, not yet recovered from birthing was now a social pariah, destitute, without rights. On broaching this I was reminded smartly that in the United Kingdom pregnant single women, along with spinster-status women still endured restrictive, demeaning and often discriminatory treatment.

There were other instances of a brutal disparity between male and female. Another husband went into a serious sulk about his wife producing a clearly unwanted *binti*. He didn't divorce her but he refused to help us when we were fully stretched and his wife began haemorrhaging. Dr. Jibril physically kicked his backside and told him to get downstairs and fetch blood or see his wife die.

There were also occasions of celebration, as when a mother of thirteen girls finally gave her faithful husband a boy. The father did love his girls and couldn't be faulted for desiring a boy child, as most men and women would in this situation. The tall, balding man and several older daughters peeked anxiously through the theatre doors during the caesarean.

"It's balls, *yanny!*" Dr. Jibril shouted to the father, who immediately began weeping.

We were rewarded with ten bottles of champagne demolished that night by eight of us, including our anaesthetist.

It was actually bad timing because the following day we had a visiting American professor from Beirut. He would be performing a rare operation on a woman with a double womb. My hangover was so incapacitating I had to ring Nadia on her day off to come in and take over as Theatre Nurse. Fortunately the visiting professor's surgical registrar was assisting him in theatre. The professor was a tall, brash, jocular John Wayne. His sidekick was a monosyllabic, unsmiling but handsome Gary Cooper.

I was very proud of our smart theatre once the doctor's sulky secretary and her desk had been ousted. John Wayne and his deputy scrubbed up at the sinks and I sprinkled surgical spirit copiously over their hands. Our Hired Guns then strode towards theatre in their white wellies, hands high, to the theatre table where I tied their gowns and assisted with gloving.

Our rescuing angel, running late and more than a little nervous about such an illustrious presence in Theatre came rushing up behind us, also with her hands in the air after scrubbing up. Unfortunately she didn't see the surgical spirit on the stone-tiled floor and slipped. She zipped gracefully past the professor and to stop herself being wedged beneath the operating table and patient she grabbed "Gary Cooper's" white theatre pants. They went down to his ankles.

In a pure Carry On moment, I pulled the Registrar's trousers up for him. Dr. Jibril helped an acutely embarrassed Nadia off the floor. She thought the Registrar rather dishy and this was not how she had wanted to be introduced

"Say, little girl, are you alright ..." the professor asked chuckling.

The operation to separate the patient's double uterus went well and Dr. Jibril took all of us to an expensive eating house afterwards. The next day he said he was pleased our esteemed guests had enjoyed themselves despite a moment of farce that could have turned into a disaster. Nadia and I showed our own flirty doctor our knees, bruised from the professor having groped them throughout the evening. He was lost for words.

Chapter Seventeen
#Sirat el Hob ...# (Umm Kalthoum)

Nadia's Armenian parents were kindness itself to me. Her mother, father, brother and both sets of grandparents lived in a modest house in the centre of Amman. Looking after them all took its toll on her mother, Nadia told me.

Not long after I arrived, the senior ladies prepared a welcoming feast for me. It took them three days and the most exquisite dishes covered several tables in the two large ground floor rooms of the house. These people did not know me and I was very touched. None of my nearest and dearest back home would have put themselves out to this extent for family, let alone a stranger.

Our steep learning curve on how to cope with local custom and accept such hospitality included being careful not to admire anyone's clothes or jewellery. After remarking how pretty I thought the necklace our secretary Grumpy Una was wearing she took it off and handed it to me.

"*Foddal, sitt,* please," she insisted. I had no alternative but to accept it as a gift.

When several pin-ups of Rubenesque Arab beauties appeared on my bed head I knew it was Yusef, my cleaning boy and didn't have the heart to take them down immediately. He slept on the hospital roof, the domain of this clique of adolescent boys. Unfortunately, our chummy relationship changed after about three months. My mother gave me her beautiful Victorian amethyst and pearl engagement ring when I left home to go to London. The ring, my Sheffield Royal Hospital badge and sister Jane's precious nurse's buckle she had given to me I stored in my locker. They were missing one December morning after my room had been cleaned. All the staff were questioned but the items were never found.

To this day I feel a pang from the loss of these cherished belongings while remaining aware that these cleaning boys worked long hours for a pittance. Being a Robin Hood theft made it easier to accept. The boys would never have bought anything for themselves. They seemed happy, uncomplicated in the main with no possessions except a well-worn T-shirt and shorts. If they stole it would be to help feed a large family or pay some other vital debt within the household.

If it was Yusef then it was best if I looked at it as reciprocating on a long tradition of offering hospitality to a stranger in the desert who might have been in difficult circumstances. It was not impossible I might find myself in need of similar generosity.

An occasional melancholy in my first months in the Middle East was not helped in my missing basic English things. No one escaped the *mu'addin* at local mosques intoning the call to prayer through tinny speakers at dawn, midday, mid-afternoon, sunset and late evening. The sound of the Egyptian diva Umm Kulthum, the 'Star of the East,' was everywhere. Her singing was a form of therapy for Jordanians articulating a deep sadness over the most recent war. To me her wailing and glottal stops was maudlin listening, as was Fairuz, the 'Jewel of Lebanon' bemoaning the Arab world's tragic loss of Jerusalem.

On good days these alien sounds were very affecting but my ears tuned to a breezy Love, Love me do, wistful Michelle, *ma belle* and the Stones' reflective Ruby Tuesday found Arab pain expressed through music hard to bear. It was bizarre when the weather was so blissfully blue-skied, to walk down to the *souk* and think I was wandering through a rainforest weeping tears.

I began to crave upbeat pop music and the ordinary sounds I was brought up with. Birdsong, laughter, the burble of running water and of spoken English that was a planet away from harsh, guttural Arabic. I even missed gentle moaning about everyday life in dear old Blighty. There were no cassette or CD players, no record player to hand, few portable radios and therefore no Western music. My contact with England was an occasional letter and World Service broadcast on an ancient crackling radio.

Fortunately, pop music I could relate to was blasted out at parties given by Nadia's more risqué Christian friends, particularly those who had formed an acting group. One of them Nadeem Sawalha they told me proudly had recently left to seek acting work in London. He became a well-known actor, as did his talented younger daughter who played Saffy in the British television series Absolutely Fabulous. His other daughter once acted in EastEnders and is now a feature writer and promoter of healthy eating.

Whatever their tribal or regional background Arabs feel their Arabness to a depth Westerners find hard to comprehend. There was resentment that occasionally boiled over against cultures, the infidel, that tried to impose its will. Despite this, immaculate manners among Arabs prevailed and was admirable, as was their self-deprecating humour.

Our tall, gawky bespectacled switchboard operator, receptionist and theatre porter was Abbid whose home was the area beneath his desk. He provided occasional entertainment for Nadia and me. On quiet evenings when the speakers on nearby minarets started up he would sidle upstairs with a little mat and with great pantomime take off a Moslem at prayer. He wouldn't get away with such antics today.

When portering in theatre he might slip on a white doctor's coat and hang a stethoscope around his neck. He would stand behind Dr. Jibril mimicking and instructing until the doctor got wind and shouted "Abbid, you bugger, *imshi, yella!*"

One morning he called in to my office looking troubled.

"*Sitt ...*"

"Yes, Abbid ..."

"Patient in number five room, Um Sarah, she ring me on switchboard and ask me to stroke bosoms. She very pretty but I say no but she keep ringing."

"Good boy, Abbid. This is very good that you tell me."

Um Sarah was one of my first patients and I got to know her well. She was also my first theatre case when I had assisted in a vaginal repair operation. She was back in theatre the following day, my day off and I couldn't make sense of the ward report and why she had returned. I asked the doctor about it on our ward round.

"Erm, well ..." he began cautiously, "you should know ..."

I stared at him impassively.

"You may have noticed I was stitching her vagina a little tighter than is natural ..."

I continued staring at him.

"Well, her husband told me she has a lover in Beirut ... who has a bigger penis than his ..."

"Yes ..."

"... he wanted me to make her tight so that only his penis would fit. He 'tried her out for size' that evening after her surgery and said she was still ... erm ... not tight enough ... I had to take her back to make it smaller ..."

I felt my face flushing with anger.

"Please bear in mind, Nurse ... Matron, I am called upon frequently for a hymen repair for young women who aren't intact, for whatever reason. It may be innocent, using a home-made tampon or strenuous games or horse riding or ... well ... you know. They come to me secretly before their wedding, or at the request of their family, or their husband-to-be or his family. The incident with Um Sarah was unfortunate. Her husband would have divorced her had I not agreed to carry out the surgery and as you are learning, she would then be classed as badly-damaged goods."

I was unable to comment then but had some questions that evening. The doctor reiterated how women, married or not, were closely watched with regard to men outside the family group. The only males they might see without restriction, even unsupervised, were their doctor, dentist and hairdresser. He was frequently propositioned, he said. The woman might be desperately lonely in an arranged marriage, or desperately sexually frustrated.

The doctor also told me he ran a clinic within the hospital for frigid women. This explained the moaning behind closed doors on Tuesday afternoons. He had learnt clitoral stimulation techniques at St. Vincent's Hospital in Dublin, he said and would stimulate the women to show them what an orgasm was. A typical case would be a woman married at fourteen to an insensitive, selfish older husband. I was quite taken aback by this enlightenment in a culture, far ahead and in a sense, so far back in time from our own Swinging 'Sixties and Free Love times.

The doctor's interest in sex didn't stop with the frigidity sessions. I was invited into a gynaecological examination of a girl who the doctor said was his favourite young patient. She was an innocent flaxen-haired Bedouin girl of nineteen, probably a descendent of Christian Crusaders. The girl's mother, a toothless woman dressed completely in black sat unconcerned that this man asked her incredibly beautiful daughter to lift her embroidered *djalaba* to her waist and sit on the edge of the couch. He lifted the dress above her bare breasts and asked her to hold it up. These are what he wanted me to see.

"Here," he said gently squeezing each breast in turn, "are perfect breasts."

I was getting the idea this doctor loved women, their femaleness and that he, we, were certainly not working within the rule book of an NHS hospital. I had no idea, until later, how far he was going beyond the call of medical duty in his care of his female patients.

"You should see my patients' notes!" he went on in English in front of an uncomprehending mother and daughter. "God help me if the husbands or parents could read them ..."

My first call-out with Dr. Jibril did not sound so innocent a celebration of female sexuality. He woke me around midnight and told me to grab an emergency medical kit. We had to attend a girl at a hotel who had been assaulted by her husband. This was the terrified girl's wedding night. Her arranged-marriage groom had penetrated her and decided she wasn't intact. Becoming sexually violent, perhaps to make her bleed and satisfy the waiting relatives that his bride was a virgin, he caused a vaginal trauma.

Jibril shooed the gathered peasant families away and sutured the deeply shocked young woman. We made her as comfortable as we could. I have never forgotten the fear in her eyes at being brutalised in this way with an audience and felt deeply for her starting married life traumatised, in shame and probably shunned by some of the family.

Returning to the hospital Dr. Jibril said he had signed a certificate to say the injury had occurred because she was a virgin.

"I always do this, whatever the circumstances," he chuckled.

Nothing seemed to bring the doctor down. He was a compassionate, non-judgemental man from whom I was learning a lot. This incident made me feel sick.

Back in my room I could have done without gormless Abbid sitting on the edge of my bed bawling fake tears with Nadia shouting at him.

"*Yarrabee* Abbid, you are a donkey!"

She started to laugh as she showed me Abbid's expensive mohair jumper, one that must have cost him several month's wages. He had been creeping down at night to where our no-messing washerwoman Um Mohammed slept amidst her laundry. Her response to being pestered for her favours was poetic. She boiled his beautiful jumper until it shrank to a size about right for a two-year old.

We told Abbid to go and apologise for offending her and say he had learnt his lesson. We pinned his tiny jumper on our wall as a future warning about such behaviour and next morning congratulated Um Mohammed on this particular treatment of fine knitwear. I was glad of the comic relief but still needed to talk about the hotel bride incident with Nadia before I could sleep.

In many ways the hospital staff were like innocent children with no malice or understanding of cynicism. When it snowed across Amman early in January 1968, young and old were out at dawn in their pyjamas throwing snowballs at each other with utter abandon. Whenever my patience was strained the assistant cook, deep-voiced Fatimah was delegated to bring me a fresh young carrot on a plate as a peace offering. We English revere them apparently.

I had put Fatimah in the small room adjoining the ten-bunk dormitory the young nurse auxiliaries slept in. She spoke a few words of English and understood her extra duty was to keep them chaste and out of trouble. She was an imposing figure with an authority the juniors took notice of. I only saw her occasionally, always in a long black embroidered Bedouin dress and white headscarf wrapped carefully around her hair and chin.

Needless to say I was very embarrassed to learn that broad-shouldered 'Fatimah' had a sex-change operation soon after I left Jordan. I don't know what he called himself after this. To have a group of unsuspecting virginal nurses buzzing around him in their dorm and washroom must have been like telling a child to look after a candy store with his hands tied.

The way Jordanian families came together to support each other, whatever the financial burden was impressive. My first Arab male friend in Jordan, Michel, looked like the French singer Sacha Distel and was kind and attentive. He told me he sent half his wages to England to help keep his brother in college there. He would get a good job on his return and in turn be able to help the family as a whole out of poverty.

We were both circumspect with each other in our relationship. The British Council had advised female volunteers not to date local lads. His family had advised him to be careful with Western girls in case they tried to lead him astray.

One Saturday, Michel was very pleased to be able to take me to a widow's party he had been invited to. We drove to a small village nearby and the first thing I saw was a group of elderly women in a circle outside the church dancing in a slow and measured step. There was a crowd of men around the church entrance, many of them with scimitars. Michel parked and just as I got out of the car a volley of pistol shots made me jump. The women began whooping and hollering, scimitars were thrust into the air. Michel was beaming.

I caught site of a bride, a very young girl coming down the hill on the arm of her proud father.

"Michel," I shouted over the commotion, "it's a wedding party, not widow's party!"

After the ceremony in the village's modest Greek Orthodox church Michel escorted me back up the hill to two small houses, one on either side of the road. The women filed into one and the men into the other. Because I knew no one, he bravely led me in to the house with the men. I was not comfortable at first because the attention was now on me, rather than the bride who was in the road with her young husband accepting congratulations from all sides.

"You are not an Arab woman, clearly," Michel said smiling, "so you will be treated as an honoured 'male' guest!"

Sure enough, after the initial surprise at my presence, I was soon being offered small balls of roast lamb, rice and pine nuts in a delicious dried yoghurt sauce. Each was rolled for me by a different man and I was expected to accept and eat them all. With these came one measure after another of *arak*, a barely-watered aniseed drink like Pernod served in a tumbler full of ice. Glasses of the stuff kept coming and I didn't want a repeat of almost being floored on my first day in Jordan. I had the sense to ask Michel to watch me and please take me away when he could see I had drunk enough.

To his credit he did this, probably within the hour, with his firm hold on me helping disguise my wobbly walk back to the car.

On another occasion he took me to a typical Middle Eastern restaurant to meet his amateur acting friends. One of them, a trendy hairdresser in leather trousers, was Nabil Sawalha, brother of Nadim who had gone to London to try his chances as an actor. In this liberal company I faced my biggest challenge thus far. A large *hookah*, a hubble-bubble with several rubber pipes with silver mouthpieces coming from it was being moved around the floor. Jordan was a relatively liberal Islamic culture regarding hashish and alcohol. I had even seen hookahs enjoyed by people sat in the street playing Backgammon. It was perfectly acceptable, harmless and sociable to share this method of inhaling hashish with friends, it was affirmed. I was implored to try it.

Unlike Mr. Clinton, I did inhale and it did have an effect on me. I couldn't believe how good I felt! In an instant I was about to start my rule of the world on an imaginary Turkish carpet with my subjects giggling at my feet.

On this occasion, being on call that night, I moderated myself. With alcohol it is not too difficult to regain a sense of responsibility and slow down. Pleasant though the effect of the hashish was, what almost sent me into a panic was having no idea how to 'sober up.' For a short while my high prevented proper communication. Fortunately this feeling passed quickly and I was relieved at not being called that night to deliver someone's baby. I did have a great sleep but it will remain my only experience of a *hookah*, no matter how congenial the gathering and persuasive the friends.

It isn't my intention to criticise the country I was a guest in but I have to say other occasions and company were far from pleasant. In general I felt privileged to be welcomed by the Jordanian people and thoroughly enjoyed my stay. Being up-beat, happily complimentary and generous to a fault they made me feel the best I'd ever felt in my young life.

The people who did not welcome me to the fold were the pretentious Western or westernised Jordanian wives of people who had some connexion with the Civil Service. Marked by their mannered behaviour, expensive suits, ostentatious jewellery, loud voices and fake smiles they would cut me as soon as they saw my C & A evening wear or Biba lunchtime couture. Anyway, Biba's darker colours suited my skin and hair colour.

At one evening gathering I attended with other UNA volunteers I overheard one of these wives say I must be a prostitute for my parents to allow me to come to Jordan alone. I began to wonder what their game was. I met many of their spoilt daughters who, my age or younger would attempt to chat. They soon fretted about boredom, their restricted existence and social life 'back home.' With some sympathy, I wondered if they might not benefit from volunteer work on real issues, such as slave children. I had escaped my stifling social background and was free to make mistakes and learn. Clearly, they were not.

The closest this particular diplomatic wife could come in her reference to prostitution was an emergency delivery I was called to in the middle of the night. I had pulled my white coat on over my knee-length nightie and wasn't wearing knickers. The husband complained next day. Dr. Jibril backed me up and was furious with the man for making the complaint. Neither garments were see-through so the husband must have been guessing. With this kind of comment and behaviour I began to think harder about such things. I didn't believe I was in the wrong.

Arabs were as bemused about the liberal 'Sixties in Britain as were my parents' generation. This occasionally translated into us Brits being available for 'free love.' One afternoon, a sprat of a visiting pharmacist began telling me how much he liked The Beatles and Free Love. Getting fresh over a coffee in the isolated theatre suite office turned into him chasing me around the table proclaiming his desire for me. It was one occasion I was pleased to see Grumpy Una clomping into the office with some papers.

Two positive things were emerging from my growing up in the 'Sixties and a now unpleasant and pervasive chauvinism all around me. One was the realization there is no reason why women should be the underdog, second-class citizens without status when they are clearly as capable and as bright. The second was unacceptable behaviour towards people of a different class, culture or racial group.

In Jordan this last unacceptable behaviour was only as far away as a Civil Service party. Not across the board, of course. It was still a joy to watch top diplomats in action. Beneath them, status was clearly in use keeping people in rank and file. Observing first-hand the dying days of full-blown class snobbery was not edifying.

It didn't work with Americans and Australians, however, as was confirmed over the years working with doctors and specialists. They had thrown off the shackles of social class distinction and didn't put up with it. Americans were slightly different in that they had their own class, those with money and/or employment status and those without. There was an uncomfortable co-habitation of these various echelons of 'upper class.'

At some gatherings volunteers were obliged to attend, Ammanites were regarded as a sub-species. There was no precedent from the Boss, whose portrait hung everywhere in official buildings. As a role model in a distinguished life-long career as *diplomate extraordinaire* Her Majesty was occasionally eclipsed.

"How do you get on with these frightful A-rabs?" I was asked by one ex-Pat with a gently-smiling HM looking over her from the wall.

"I like them very much ... it's you I find frightful ..." I wanted to reply.

I was still too much firmly in my rank to speak out like this. Anyway, isolated in a Middle East hospital I really needed to hear my own language and keep in touch.

The UN should have gone into greater depth about matters that constitute culture shock. I first saw this in Alvin Toffler's book of the same name. It was new thinking and prescient when it came to this *ingénue* roving far from home paying homage to my valiant Victorian lady nurse forbear. I would have appreciated being made much more aware of how depersonalising culture shock can be. Nadia was my saviour initially. Having experienced a much freer British lifestyle she had her own struggles, risking being labelled as unmarriageable if she continued being seen out in such a small town partying with abandon. There were no easy answers.

Left largely on my own to make sense of a totally foreign environment, things came to a head at Christmas, a bleak time for the depressed, lonely or hard up. It felt odd not wishing patients, staff, friends and family a Happy Christmas. In British hospitals carols were sung around the wards on Christmas Eve. A side ward would be transformed into a party room to which all staff would drop in. Christmas Day was imbued with a tranquil *bonhomie*.

After many years in Jordan Dr.

Jibril's wife didn't feel the need to decorate their apartment with seasonal baubles and gaudy Christmas tree. Christian Arabs naturally celebrated Christ's birth but did so discretely so they didn't cause offence in a predominantly Moslem culture.

A welcome bit of news was the return of Violet, Elaine's volunteer companion and friend from Notre Dame High. She wanted to be with her boyfriend Simon Regan, a cocky reporter for the News of the World who later founded VIZ magazine. I occasionally took a taxi down town to see Violet and the other UNA teacher volunteers. They lived in a house on the second *jebbel* down the *souk* road.

Their work load was a doddle compared with mine. It was not as ideal as it sounds because it probably contributed to some of them getting into an emotional mess and not necessarily with local boys. There were some wild parties run by our embassy and British Council elders and betters with the time between Christmas and New Year being a good excuse to let go. A few of these men, after a few drinks, could be disgusting old *roués*.

New Year was marked by a sacrifice. A woman was admitted in a state of agitation about giving birth. I got the gist that a sheep was to be killed at the time of her baby's birth at the behest of the local shaman because she had lost seven previous babies. We had to allow the husband to do the shaman's bidding. Jibril reminded us if the baby died we would be for it. At least he got his way with the sheep being slaughtered on the hospital steps rather than in the Delivery Room.

At six in the morning on New Year's Day the woman gave birth and the message was hollered downstairs. The bleating sheep had its throat cut and fresh blood was rushed upstairs in a dirty tin can. The husband poured it all over his wife's vagina while we were cleaning up the afterbirth. I had already winced at seeing the dirty 'good luck' metal hoop the woman had probably endured around her middle through her entire pregnancy.

The baby did well in hospital over the next few days. It died at home a month later from malnutrition.

From my first day in Amman I heard Dr. Jibril and his friends and many others I'm sure, cracking jokes about the Arabs losing the Six-Day War. The Egyptian air force, they quipped, was wiped out because the pilots were more concerned about finishing their cornflakes. The doctor was a Christian Arab, as were Nadia and my

Iraqi friends in London. These families tended to be more Westernised, had close ties and were viewed as liberal progressives. Dr. Jibril was a *Ba'athist* with left-wing political tendencies and it was a badge of honour to have spent time in prison for his beliefs and actions. He said openly he hired Communists whenever he could. He was also proud of having taken part in the July 14th Revolution in Iraq in 1958 which saw the overthrow of the last Hashemite King, Faisal.

Dr. Jibril seemed to be serious about marrying me to his best friend, Kamal Nasser, a well-known Arab poet. He was expelled from the West Bank by the Israelis in 1967 and released from Jordanian custody early in 1968. He became a frequent visitor to the hospital chatting with the doctor. He had a pale skin, a noble nose and talked with great eloquence to the point of bluster, making up for lost time perhaps. We would also listen to him reading his own poetry on the radio in beautiful classical Arabic. He was a highly cultured man from a very wealthy family who told me he was a personal friend of many writers and philosophers including Sartre and Genet.

I didn't know at the time what a political animal he was. Within two or three years he became spokesman for the Palestine Liberation Organisation, a member of its executive committee and editor of the PLO newspaper *Filastin al-Thawra*. I was fond of him, a forty-ish man with a mission but despite continuing hints had no wish to be his wife.

These welcoming people, the Jordanians I had met, could surely never become the brainwashed insurgent violent fundamentalists of today. Even though a political innocent, I had picked up on how the consequences of the Six-Day War would affect others around the region. At least six refugee camps had been set up inside Jordan in recent months for Palestinian refugees, making ten in all. The original camps had been festering twenty years. There were dozens of others in Syria, Lebanon, in Gaza and the West Bank. It was no surprise when the soon-to-be *Al Fatah* party held one of its first meetings in Dr. Jibril's apartment at the hospital early in 1968. Kamal and other senior figures including Yasser Arafat were there.

As pretty young 'Matron' my role in this not-to-be-talked-of meeting was serving coffee and little cakes and chit-chatting in English to these gentlemen. As a United Nations volunteer I should not really have been there. Having been caught in the cross-fire of many a passionate discussion among my London Iraqi friends about beleaguered Palestinians I enjoyed the intrigue around the meeting but didn't ask any questions.

The reality of the politics hit hard one April morning in 1973 when I was back in London. To open The Guardian and see a picture of Kamal with his jaw shot away by Israelis in West Beirut was deeply traumatic. The symbolism, of him being PLO spokesman, would not have been lost on anyone in the Middle East. He might have been a verbal terrorist but he was not a killer, as far as I knew, though he described himself as a freedom fighter. *Al Fatah* were fighting for their identity, perhaps even their survival, as the Israeli underground movement had in the 1940s. Palestinian land and homes were slowly being taken away from them.

A great body of them evicted from Jordan were now under direct attack in Lebanon from the Israeli army in what they were calling Operation Spring of Youth. It was part of their revenge on Palestinian militants for the murder of Israeli athletes at the Munich Olympic Games the previous year.

"We grew up side-by-side, without rancour before the Six-Day War. The Middle East never had an issue with the Jewish people," a student in Trebovir Road told me. Israelis and Palestinians had bumped along together reasonably peacefully for twenty years. The Saudi king, Feisal went further back in his interpretation of the problem. He put his view of a Jewish homeland succinctly to a US envoy.

"Why should Palestinians have to pay for the Holocaust? Let them be given land in Germany as reparation ..."

Like the well-regarded Jewish actress Miriam Margolyes who bravely voices her opinion on Palestinian human rights issues, I too have always spoken out against the wretched apartheid situation in Israel/Palestine since my time in Jordan. My call is one for a peace accord with local and international law respected. I am surely joined by all the heroic nurses and doctors who have worked in war-torn areas. To take away land, livelihood and life and torture, humiliate and degrade human beings is against everything we stand for.

I was puzzled by a seemingly light-hearted reaction from Dr. Jibril and his friends to the humiliating defeat of the Six-Day War. It wasn't how Suhail and Iskander had taken it and they weren't even Palestinian. Nadia said it was both bravado and resignation that there would never again be a Palestine they could call their homeland. There was a lot going on behind the genial front of many Jordanians I would never understand.

One night towards the end of March 1968 I heard far-away rumbling when it was usually pin-drop quiet. In the midst of several other things on this particular night duty I was caring for a fourteen-ounce premature baby the staff referred to as *habibti*, 'darling,' trailing her everywhere with me in our one specialist incubator heated by six light bulbs. This was the only way I could monitor the tiny tot's body temperature and prevent cooing staff, patients and visitors alike lifting the glass lid and handling this tiny being swaddled in cotton wool and tin foil suit.

It was about two in the morning on her first precious night on Earth when I realised the rumbling was getting louder. There had been leaflet drops by the Israeli Air Force and the barracks next to the hospital had moved up a gear in both the number of soldiers and its activity. There had also been distant air raid warnings and aircraft attacks along the new border between Jordan and Israel, notably a couple of weeks earlier in al-Karameh less than thirty kilometres away where there was a large camp of Palestinian refugees and fighters. A chill came over me as tanks rumbled past us westwards on the Salt road, a long line of them. Surely it was not another war so soon I fretted. What should I do about keeping the hospital safe? I went to call Dr. Jibril.

"*Balash baradi*," was his dismissive response over the entry phone, who cares. He was going back to sleep.

It was, he advised next day, the Jordanian army on its way to another confrontation with restless young Palestinian men.

"They have nowhere to go and nothing to lose. They are now the *diaspora* and will become a big problem here, in Lebanon, maybe Syria. But we have a hospital to run."

Habibti lived for a week, an achievement that would have been a record even in a proper UK premature baby unit at the time. Jordanians would normally have been voluble at such a death. We felt very sorry for these parents as they left the hospital after a week sobbing quietly.

Chapter Eighteen
#Love is All Around Us ...# (Troggs)

It was inevitable Naked Nurse would be seduced in Jordan. With hindsight I don't believe any twenty-two year old would have stood a chance in the circumstances. Dr. Jibril and I were not often out of each other's sight day and night. We came through medical dramas and tender moments together. I was a young idealist become almost as passionate about the hospital. He was a womaniser, I was vulnerable and so on and so on.

On the positive side, with Jibril's encouragement and coaching more appropriate for a junior doctor than a nurse I had begun to exude confidence. His "you can do this" attitude and thinking outside the sterile packaging was a million miles from the tyranny of NHS training where every step of the lonely road was marked by fear and bullying. Making me Matron in my first week at the Oasis Hospital was an immense boost to my fragile ego and a clever move on his part.

It was fairly obvious after the umpteenth night of being wined and dined there was much grooming by my employer, also a positive, attractive and very talented man. In our favourite restaurant down the road, the evening meal was served in low lighting with cushions on the floor around a large engraved brass table. An iced *arak* would be followed by olives and delicious dips of *hummus*, *taramasalata* and *tabbouleh* with hot *pitta* bread. Several dishes would be laid out including exquisitely

flavoured meats such as garlic-coated chicken with subtly-flavoured vegetable dishes, salads, rice with *leben* (dried yoghurt sauce) and pine nuts. We might be there for hours, three or four of us or more, or just the doctor and I.

It was on warm evenings like this with musicians playing quietly in the background my thoughts drifted occasionally to packed pubs, spittle and spilt beer, eyes smouldering from pipe and cigarette smoke and having to shout to be heard. You might be lucky with the occasional 'Albert Finney.' More likely you would be regarded as a rag doll with breasts. If it was a local dance or, if desperate, the Sheffield Loccy you could also be in for large sweaty hands, an erection pressed hard against you and BO. Old Spice was the standard 'come on' and 'cover up.'

Our young boyfriends up North and to a lesser extent in London in the early 'Sixties had little idea of personal hygiene. Weekly baths were the norm even for manual labourers because of freezing bathrooms, inefficient coal fires and back boilers. For those without bathrooms it was a tin bath in front of the parlour fire. Clothes weren't particularly clean either. Wash day was Monday and you wore the same set of clothes, the same underwear, all week.

It was noticeable on arriving in Jordan that Arabs did not smell anything other than pleasant. Cleanliness is an Islamic requirement for prayer and because of the heat. We also found Arabs affable and much easier to converse with. With people who were also positive and complimentary my endorphins must have moved into overload.

Demanding though work was at the hospital or out on call in Amman and nearby villages I loved what I was doing. It made my three pounds a week less of a problem. It also made me forget the good doctor was married. Years later and occasionally during those first months of our affair in Jordan, I wondered what I was doing and why I hadn't put up a better fight. There can only be one outcome in single girl *vs* married man with status, four children and a very nice wife, especially when he tells you it is but an affair.

He admitted early on he was a womaniser. He loved and adored his family and gave the excuse that each extra-marital liaison had been pursued with a sense of anger and need to prove his virility in the face of racial belittlement from European women, including his wife on first meeting. With a little more emotional maturity and more experience I might have laughed in his face, so to speak and told him to get lost. The situation, however, must also have suited me.

Little comfort came from Naughty Nadia confiding she had started an affair with Groucho, our married anaesthetist. Many of the UNA volunteer teachers had also been drawn into webs of older ex-Pat spider males through boredom and insecurity. White Mischief was alive, kicking and weeping and was not the kind of moral support we should have been getting from the UNA or British Council. One girl my age was openly carrying on with a senior married member of the British Council staff and couldn't handle it. In my worst moments incarcerated in the hospital I felt like a hostage, isolated and succumbed to Stockholm Syndrome.

Within our self-serving bubble of dangerous liaisons, Nadia and I justified our snatched carnalities as a reward for the crazy hours we worked. When we were able to take time off from the hospital as the bit on the side, we would be taken to more discreet nightclubs with free-flowing booze and excellent Arabic food. Our intractable fatigue kept us in a state of surreality. This is how it is when your life is about mental, emotional and physical survival. None of this twilight activity, I am pleased say, interfered with the goal of bringing nurse training and hospital practice in line with the NHS model we knew.

We were on more dangerous ground in taking the occasional amphetamine than incurring the wrath of the wives. Neither Nadia nor I coped well with down-sides when extremely tired and pill-popping was easy and effective. Easy because Nadia and I had the key to the pharmacy and effective because they really did give us more staying power on long, arduous night shifts.

I knew about these little marvels from my mother. She was of a generation in the post-war period that were prescribed them, the original "Mother's little helpers," as if they were Smarties. It wasn't just depressed mothers with dilated pupils. They were the cause of Elvis's lifelong drug dependency and ultimate demise. They have been prescribed, or purloined in vast quantities for decades by all sorts of "others" from military personnel to pop musicians.

It is likely, had I not given in to this older man's charms, I might have had a more extensive social life with people of my own age. You don't see it as a problem at the time. It might even have prompted the reaction of "boys of my own age are boring."

I didn't become fully aware of this until two decades later when a friend confided that her seventeen-year old daughter had been seduced by an older man who ran a youth charity. His partner was a child protection officer. Reading a letter written by the girl to no one in particular was heartbreaking. She was in the couple's flat, or on their boat on the pretext of baby-sitting. She was in a bedroom next to theirs and was desperate to talk about the situation. She went through college in a flat paid for by her lover who also made sure she made no real friends of her own age. She was effectively robbed of her youth.

He only gave her leeway to escape when he realised his bid to become an MP was in jeopardy with her around. If he had been elected I would have exposed him. Perhaps I still should. She was groomed for her virginity at sixteen and is now an emotional wreck in her early thirties. This story made me realise as an adult how much I was exploited in Jordan in my year of voluntary work.

Three months after starting at the Oasis Hospital, Dr. Jibril's wife had to return to her homeland because of a family tragedy. She asked me if I would look after her family. The silly infatuation stage moved to one where I hoped she would not return. When she did, several weeks later she had to suffer hearing her two youngest say they wanted me to be Mummy. I saw then I could not break up this marriage, or take her place. She loved her life in Amman. She was well-liked and must have endured many difficulties living with her workaholic womanising husband. A reality check was fast approaching.

On the night of my twenty-third birthday in March 1968, Marie challenged Jibril and I for the first time. We stumbled up the steps, arms around each other on our return from a celebratory night out. She was waiting in the deserted hospital foyer, though Abbid may have been there asleep under the reception desk. Within seconds, pink mists of delusion and denial turned to a red mist of shame and despair. We looked sordid and cheap, rather than a couple in love-to-die-for that I had so carefully been promoting to myself.

We went to my room first where Jibril was very nasty indeed in telling his wife she was to go and he was marrying me. They then disappeared into their apartment. Dr. Jekyll's sudden change in his belittling of and sneering at his blameless wife was a shock. I hadn't seen this side of him and was repulsed. Nadia had warned me.

My brain went into overdrive and I covered my head with a pillow. A million taunts were coming at once, half of them "I told you so ..." I was on my own, without friends and a long way from home. My head spinning from too much to drink that night was the least of my problems.

Deliriously happy when out celebrating, Naked Nurse had flipped. She was showing herself no mercy, she had trashed her good work as a volunteer, let every side she could think of down and was now to be seriously punished. A righteous zeal was now hissing in her ear that she had become a moral mess because she had rejected the Church. She should have attended Confession, Mass, services, lit candles and prayed ... The sneering got worse. It was a revenge Naked Nurse did not want to be around for and she decided she wanted to die.

I retrieved my set of pharmacy keys and marched grimly down the corridor. No one was about, not even Night Sister Nadia who usually saw me coming in. She could not have missed our entrance that evening and was probably hiding, stunned by the thought it could have been her. As I unlocked the door I could hear Jibril and Marie through a distant wall, voices raised and the younger children crying, all because of me. In full *hara-kiri* mode I went methodically along the shelves of the "Eat Me," "Take Me" bottles and packets.

My mother had occasionally given me one of her barbiturates to help me sleep on changeover days at The Royal. Picking up the pretty little red capsules of Seconal, I strode back to my room. Pouring a large whisky and pushing the wardrobe against my door I got ready for the Big Sleep. I repaired my make-up, changed into my Woollies best pale-blue nightie, wrote a silly farewell note and swallowed the pills with the Scotch. I lit a Camel, coughed a little as I didn't really smoke and stared at the ceiling. It wasn't long before the mind chatter at last began to diminish and a blissful amnesia was caressing me into a deep, deep sleep.

When my bleary eyes opened some time later to shadows and bright lights it was not to a figure at the end of a tunnel encouraging me to come forward, or go back. It was Groucho standing over me on one side and Nadia on the other. Groucho wasn't tickling the back of my knees as he usually did in theatre. He and Nadia were giggling, trying to insert a catheter into me. I wanted to tell them to sod off so I could get some sleep but passed out.

When I woke again it was night outside and my bedside table lamp was on. I spat out the hard rubber airway tube and saw I was also rigged up to an intravenous drip-feed and catheter bag. The hasty mini-theatre around my bed included suction equipment, a tray of instruments, empty IV bottles, syringes and paper towels all over the floor. A couple of half-empty bottles of whisky and glasses were on the table.

Nadia peeked around the doorway then came in, hands on hips.

"Oh, you are awake, you bloody bugger! We had to put a catheter in and a wee bag 'cos you bloody well weed on me when I got in beside you as I was so bloody tired on our first night's watch."

Speaking too fast and sounding too shrill, she told me how our sweet new, ancient Palestinian staff nurse had come up to my room because I was late for my lunch-time start. She and Abbid pushed the door open. I had a cigarette burn on my shoulder and they couldn't wake me. Visions of my being found looking like a Pre-Raphaelite heroine were dashed when Nadia said,

"You looked bloody beautiful with your make-up on and like a damn snoring corpse when we cleaned it off. A right bloody tragi-comedy!"

Dr. Jibril came in to do a bit of yelling but Nadia told him to shut up and bugger off.

A little later, sitting up in bed gulping water feeling very sorry for myself and my pounding head, Nadia returned to tell me about the rest of the drama. She held my hand and said she, Groucho, Jibril and Marie had taken it in turns to watch me around the clock in my room so keeping it secret from the rest of the staff. Abbid wouldn't have been able to read my note even if he had opened it.

The night turned into a party, she said, with some drinking and making merry. Jibril and his wife sat with me until dawn arguing across my unconscious body about the little affair. They were either argued-out or had come to a compromise somewhere because they were all smiles when they visited later.

When fully awake I felt wonderful with my over-taxed brain having benefitted from my best sleep ever. Jibril said I was totally exhausted from endless eighty-hour weeks and the upset over being involved with 'senior management.' He said we should talk about it when I was ready.

I felt so much better but if I thought I had paid the price with my cry for help and that everything was now hunky-dory I was seriously mistaken. I was absolutely clueless about the payback to come.

Some days later I was walking down the King's Road in rain without a coat and loving it. I was still glowing from the rather different Spring of the Middle East. People in Chelsea in coats, scarves and hats looked at me. I was taken aback by the traffic and had to be very careful when crossing the road. I had two weeks off in England and was on a mission to bring back some new surgical instruments and, at my request, at least two trained nursing staff to join me in Jordan as volunteers.

There was an extra incentive in finding nurses. Nadia took me to the airport at Amman and blurted out she wouldn't be at the Oasis when I got back. She had found another job in another private hospital run by nuns and been lured by better pay. One of my first calls in looking for suitable candidates would be the East End Maternity Hospital and I was going to walk in there as large as life.

My arrival in London was a complete surprise to those who had waved me off six months earlier. I stayed in my brother's bed-sit house in Earl's Court. He was as underwhelming as ever, greeting me as if I had only popped out for some chips. Iskander and Suhail whooped when I rang their doorbell. They were just the same, warm and affectionate, now on the verge of joining the real world on finishing their degrees.

Returning to London was like going back to the future. Long skirts with Pucci psychedelic prints were new, as were peace symbols, head bands and large raggedy shoulder bags. Unisex was the buzz, with long hair, Afghan coats and tie-dyed T-shirts. I heard mid-Atlantic drawl from DJs on the radio, cool American lingo in the streets and Flower Power poets talking about Peace, Man. Some of my brother's student and actor tenants were now taking pramfulls of uppers and downers. There was more stoned clap-trap at parties than before. My conservative brothers though, remained steadfastly outside the loop.

I squeezed in a weekend trip to Sheffield on expenses and smiled on the train journey back at the lack of change up there. Mother reacted with predictability when I told her of my attempted suicide.

"Oh Rose, how could you, when I've had so much to bear ... blah, blah ... I am fond of you all but I only ever really loved Damien ... blah, blah, blah ..."

That was it. Same old Sheffield, same old Mother. Same old.

My escape to London and experience of work abroad had toughened me up against her facility for emotional blackmail. I was shaking my head now, no longer controlled by the guilt it was intended to elicit. Too many years had been spent on the thankless task of trying to make her happy. It was a pity, as masochism and martyrdom are a lousy way to live. As she saw it, we had all cocked-up one way or another and proved her right about the misery of motherhood.

She did have her good moments, of course. We could giggle for hours when mimicking the "po-faced norms" she called them. Most of my friend's mothers did appear to be either mad or miserable and their husbands resigned and dour. It was also good to have a laugh about happier moments, when we were a family. That ended when I was five years old, now a long time ago.

After my two-week working sojourn, with my bag packed and a taxi waiting to take me to Heathrow, I sat agonising over whether I was making a colossal mistake in going back to Jordan. Almost the only reason for going back, with Nadia no longer there, was honouring my contracted year with the UNA, though I wasn't impressed with their disinterest in their young charges. I hadn't missed anyone, not even Jibril since he had shown his true colours. It would be a return to the same daily routine, the same dog-tiredness. I had benefitted greatly from being dropped in the deep end of hospital administration and was learning something new every day about nursing but was not convinced this was enough.

Some cheery news came with a response from Auburn Anna in Germany, just two days before my flight. She was in Germany staying with her friend Sigrid, also a trained nurse and they were looking for something to do. Yes, they would love to come out to Jordan! They were already packing and would leave from Berlin and catch up with me in Amman a few days after my arrival.

The second reason a taxi was outside was because of the large suitcase I had bought in John Lewis. Jibril had given me £100 for surgical instruments and expenses, more than two months of an average working salary amongst my friends in London. About half went on instruments from a shop near Harley Street. I bought some clothes and things with the rest, fed up with living in a nurse's uniform. Una told me they were holding about £50 of wages for me so if Jibril kicked up a fuss they could have that.

For my journey I put on a very nice designer suit. My hair had been straightened and the hairdresser had shown me how to wear a good quality hair extension. Even straightened, my hair was too thick for a hat but I looked pretty okay as I got on the 'plane.

I was still looking for stronger reasons why I shouldn't return. Marie had used her trump card in saying she would leave Jordan if Jibril divorced her. She wasn't bluffing but was gambling on whether she would be taking her children with her. The Jordanian court would take her husband's side. I had no intention of carrying on as before. I didn't know how truthful he was saying he loved me and would divorce Marie. In any case I could not have stepped into her shoes.

It was time to right the wrong at least, I naively presumed. Jibril would slip quietly into the background, Marie would be grateful to have her fallible husband back and life would return to normal. I was still under his spell but could not erase the memory of how vile he had been to his wife, in front of me, when she didn't deserve it. My little brain should have realised I would eventually receive the same attention.

My New Look was a hit from the moment I boarded. Before take-off I was propositioned by the Egyptian gentleman next to me. I changed my seat and started chuckling when a handsome, grey-haired Italian tried his luck also. By the time we landed at Rome he was begging me to get off with him so he could show me his villa. The attention was good for my ego and I could see how easily girls can be persuaded to do, well, anything.

I didn't want to get off the aircraft in Italy anyway because it was raining and my new hair would frizz. The airline staff began to insist, for security reasons, because they were taking a break. I had two more hours to keep it straight before arriving in bone-dry Amman where Nabil would then keep it under control.

As the stewardess's smile was beginning to slip, a tall 'Tony Curtis' with golden curls, a deep tan and lapis lazuli eyes got up from a seat several rows behind me in an otherwise empty aircraft. I had noticed him earlier walking up and down. His short-sleeved shirt had two pockets and two gold stripes on epaulettes on his shoulders. I thought he was a steward but he introduced himself to me as the co-pilot.

"Is there a problem here?" asked Blue Eyes with a big smile.

The female steward repeated the security regulations.

"I'll stay on board with Miss ..."

"... Nurse MacFarlane."

With a big smile, he asked if he might sit next to me. Wow! Phew! Adonis had spoken up for me and now wanted to sit next to me! His name was Alex and he was Jordanian-Armenian, like Nadia. He was the co-pilot but was sitting out the flight because a trainee pilot was on the flight deck. We chatted non-stop until the rest of the passengers returned from the transit lounge and he asked how long I would be in Amman. He wanted to see me again. When I said I lived in Amman he replied this was perfect because he did too. This was a date Nurse Happy-Head could hardly refuse.

Three potential suitors on a four-hour flight culminating in a Tony Curtis-cross-James Dean pilot asking me out was an elation. Bingo! Out with the Old, in with the New, Alex. After passport control at Amman we crossed paths again. He was in full uniform and cap. He said he looked forward to meeting up very soon just as Jibril and his wife waved to me, smiling. They had come to pick me up and were polite and friendly on the drive back to the hospital.

The staff were as enthusiastic as ever and said they were pleased to see me and I began to feel okay about being back. I was glad to have made up my mind to see the year out and really hoped it would be as an effective nurse without emotional hassles. I didn't put too much into a date with Adonis Alex materialising. He was too good to be true, a playboy figure who would surely have a girl in every airport.

I had just sat down that afternoon to rest from the journey when my phone rang.

"*Sitt Malaki, marhaba!* A call for you."

"Hello Abbid, good to talk to you. Who's on the line?"

"A Mister Alex, *shukran, sitt* ..."

"Hi there, Rose. Can I come over this evening to take you out for dinner?"

"Er, yes, Alex. Erm ..."

"... at eight o'clock?"

At eight exactly I was on my way down the stairs pleased with new shoes, slinky dress and shoulder bag, looking like Chelsea Girl. My ears picked up a growling, then a whine coming down the road at speed and I thought for a moment the ack-ack gun was being primed for firing. I was nearly right!

"*Sitt Malaki,* come, see car!"

Abbid was hopping about as the bright red E-Type squealed to a halt and its engine was revved before being switched off.

"He King Man, with Mister Bond car!"

"Yes, Abbid, 'bye Abbid!"

My lithe, long-legged heart-stopper ran up the steps into the entrance foyer. I extended my arm, limp-wristed, perhaps a little too theatrically. Alex kissed my hand and followed up with a little bow.

That night he drove me back to the hospital in a more discreet Opal he parked beneath his parents' house where he lived. It was too late to meet them on that occasion. I couldn't have been happier and couldn't wait to tell Nadia when we met up at her new hospital for a much-needed gossip. She and Groucho were still an item she said over the 'phone that afternoon. She also warned me about thinking I could dump the doc and everyone would behave like grown-ups.

Doc tapped on my door within minute of my return that night.

"Can we talk ?"

"Sure, come in."

He came in and sat down.

"Did you miss me in England?"

"Yes, of course but it has to end, Jibril."

"I see it didn't take you long to forget me."

"You're talking about my date?'

"He's a playboy. Good luck," he sneered.

Jibril's eyes were cold and unsettling. He was still in charge of the hospital and of everyone there, including me. I realised only then, here was a man who would not have been all smiles and joviality when called to arms in his early days as a Ba'athist, a freedom fighter. There was but a flimsy door without a lock between us and I was scared.

My routine at the hospital quickly resumed but with two major differences. Jibril barely talked to me. Countering this was an explosion in my social life with Alex my life-saver. For my first two weeks back in Amman he drove up to the hospital almost daily. We drove out in the country or swam in the pool at the Intercontinental Hotel. He treated me to lunch and afternoon snacks in some beautiful little restaurants. It was usually *meze,* dozens of little dishes of everything from mashed aubergines to artichoke salad to *stifado,* seasoned beef stew. On evenings when we could co-ordinate our free time he would take me to dinner and perhaps a club.

The weekend before he was due in Karachi for training on a new aircraft he flew me to Beirut in a friend's private plane. I was terrified when taking off down a very large runway in a very small aircraft but he was in control. Off the ground it was amazing, if a little noisy, with a real close-up of the desert and rural life away from towns and villages.

Wearing a strapless, gold silk mini-dress, with a deep tan, slimmer frame of late and beautiful sandals he had bought me, people looked at the pair of us as we walked into Beirut Casino.

"Nothing too it," he whispered, with me clutching his arm, "when you're Tony Curtis and Maureen O'Hara!"

It was years before I realised I was not bad looking. Many of us don't know it. Vanity and even care in personal appearance had no place in a society of brothers and workers who jibed at a bit of lipstick and laughed if you asked if the dress was pretty. I tell my two daughters they are full of beauty because I want them always to feel good about themselves. Glamour magazines don't do this. They are more likely to ping your self-confidence.

The sun was strong that weekend in Beirut and my face became as red as a fire blanket. Back in Amman and bidding Alex farewell for a whole month while he was training in Karachi, I could not tell him I was dreading my return to the Oasis because I had no idea who would be skulking there, Dr. Jekyll or Mr. Hyde.

When I got back on Sunday evening I found Anna and Sigrid in their new room in the basement and was thrilled to see Anna after so many months. My friend whom I'd trained with in Sheffield, travelled with and worked with in London. Sigrid was a tall, bosomy girl with a freckled face that resembled a friendly pig. She was rather serious, with a troubled bleakness about her and I wanted to hug her. She had suffered as a young child in Germany towards the end of War Anna confirmed. On top of this she felt despised simply because she was German.

We hadn't been chatting long when Dr. Jibril called me upstairs to the theatre. I had to listen to him for two hours, until after midnight, berating me for anything he could think of, it seemed. He taunted me about Alex again. Finally, a new line, he said I was making him so ill with jealousy his old kidney trouble had returned. He showed me his swollen ankles. I was shattered from my weekend in Beirut and really too tired to argue. When I was on the point of screaming at him to get out of my face he dropped in the line that even his wife thought I was callous dropping him and going out with Alex.

Immediately I feared for Anna and Sigrid. He had picked them up from the airport and when I asked what they thought of him, they said he hadn't been either friendly or welcoming. He should have been deeply grateful for the girls coming out to Amman to help his cause for little in exchange. This was deplorable.

The many women he'd had affairs with he treated as he wished but because I dared to opt out of our relationship, for the sake of his family, I would pay in meeting his chauvinism head on. His rapid downward spiral in the two weeks I was back was mesmerising. Rejection does hurt but silly me was naively looking for him to act like a good Brit, to be fair, even understanding about our split when his simmering Semitic nature was not going to allow it.

However much I chuntered on that I still loved him but that I'd pulled back because of his family commitments and so on, he would trash my response, calling me a whore, a nymphomaniac, a cheap hussy who flirted with every man in the hospital.

This went on all week. He wouldn't let me sleep. He would time it perfectly after a day or night shift, knocking on my door when I was thinking about going to bed. The tragedy of the dying days of such a man with a young woman is that they both begin to believe everything said. To make it worse Anna and Sigrid were cool towards me because he was being a pig to them also. I couldn't blame them and felt awful. The whole hospital was suffering from the fall-out.

It came to a head three weeks later when I heard a commotion above my room with an emergency theatre admission. I would normally have been called to scrub up for theatre but this time I was apparently not required. Running upstairs I saw the stupid man through the theatre doors about to operate on a patient with two untrained staff assisting. I scrubbed up, gave a grateful-looking girl some instructions, checked that the anaesthetic was being administered correctly and fetched more instruments I knew would be needed for this exploratory operation on a patient with ovary pain. We worked on in silence and the operation went satisfactorily. Afterwards Jibril came to my room.

"I want to apologise."

"Okay."

"You British put us to shame. I was being a typical arrogant Arab, putting my problems with you before the patient's interest. You didn't and I feel ashamed."

"Thanks for coming in. Can you please keep this stuff outside work? It doesn't make it any easier."

"I'll try."

"Thank you."

"I bet Alex is screwing around in Karachi ..."

"... Goodnight Jibril."

He didn't leave it there and wanted to start a major row. I sat tight, put up with as much abuse as I was going to that night, then told him I pitied him. Big Mistake. He gave me a look that could have incinerated the Gods and left my room in silence.

The next day at lunchtime he was waiting outside my room. He knew exactly when I would leave my room for my afternoon shift. Without uttering a word he hauled me down the corridor and into his empty flat, empty because the rest of his family invariably spent the weekends with his parents. He locked the door behind him and dragged me into his bedroom. He threw me onto the bed put his hands around my neck and began to squeeze hard. I struggled and went into shock when I realised he was determined to harm me and I could do nothing. He was simply too strong. He eased the pressure when I went limp and while I was gasping for air he ripped my uniform from top to bottom, raped and bit me.

Clutching my clothes to me, I rushed out of his apartment into my room and bathroom. The person I saw in the mirror was not me. I will never forget the terror on that young woman's face. My clothes were in tatters, I had bite marks over my upper body and severe bruising on my upper arms.

I told no one, not Anna, or Nadia when she rang the next afternoon. I had to accept this was how many men behaved towards women in this country, especially if the woman had dared criticise the man's masculinity. It was my fault it had come to this. Everything he was saying about me must be true.

Alex was due back from Karachi a few days after the attack and I was frantic about covering up the visible damage. He knew nothing of my past liaison with Jibril, as I had hoped it would fade away. Even though Alex was a Christian Arab who must have had many Western girlfriends I was afraid he would turn like Jibril, condemning me as a loose woman for having an affair with a married man.

On the night of his return I arranged to meet him at a party at the bungalow in town where the UNA teachers lived. With Nabil's expertise my hair was the best it had ever looked. I was a stone lighter since we were in Beirut and had a tan even deeper than before now the Summer sun was really beginning to scorch. I put on a pretty dress and forgetting my trauma of the last week concentrated on looking forward to welcoming my boyfriend home.

He arrived at about ten and with his generous smile told me how much he had missed me. God, he was a good-looking boy and greeting him could not have been a greater contrast with the ugly events of the weeks he had been away. He didn't leave it at saying he missed me. He said his mother approved of us being a couple. When I said gently I would have appreciated more news than his one post card from Karachi, he apologised profusely for the oversight. I didn't need to tell him I had been worried about how he felt about me. He took the words out of my mouth. He didn't know my fear was compounded by the pain of Dr. Jibril harping on that I would soon be dumped in turn.

He took me to the Hilton the next afternoon for tea. It was too hot for long sleeves and the bruises on my arms were still visible. I was partly telling the truth in telling Alex the doctor was not suited to my spending so much time out of the hospital and that he had grabbed me when I had been rude to him. The smile slipped from Alex's face.

"I think I need to have words with this doctor."

I pleaded with him not to cause a fuss and that I was fine about it. I actually felt sick with concern over Anna and Sigrid, as there seemed to be no limits to what Jibril was capable of. I had been to the British Council offices and asked about my contract. Naturally they wanted to know why and so I couched my story in terms of 'another of the volunteers' having trouble in her workplace. She needn't put up with it, was the response. They would interview the parties, intervene in police or legal matters if necessary and would afford all assistance, providing emergency funds and accommodation if required.

I felt better knowing these things and even better in my young guy's arms. I insisted lights were kept low on the nights we were able to stay together so he did not notice the bite marks. They healed and nothing more was said about the bruising. He was now almost the only reason I had not packed my bags and returned to London.

Despite reassurances of support from the British Council I would not have dared report the rape to the police in Jordan. At twenty-three, I dealt with it as best I could. This included accepting that at least the man had retained some masculinity in assaulting me in the way he did. It was totally unacceptable but I had no choice but to put up with it.

Forty years on in Jordan, the lover of a man accused of adultery can still be jailed as it could be deemed her fault the married man was led astray. In September 2012 the first ever case brought by a Tunisian women against two police officers for raping her was, a week later, facing charges of public indecency and possible six months in jail. Here was vindictiveness and complicit behaviour from other males, as well as sexual violence. Cultural change in that and in many parts of the world continues to be a long and painful process. In 1968 I stood no chance of redress.

Rape is frightening, degrading and depressing. About the after-effects of being raped, I tend to agree with Germaine Greer about the importance of evaluating this and surviving. It took me years to recover from the depersonalising and helpless terror I felt from this man's unrelenting mental torture, a habitual, traditional use of power against women. This was worse than the sexual violence.

I decided that June with less than four months before my volunteer work ended, I would put up with it no more and stand up to the good doctor. If necessary I would threaten him and could only hope if it came to this, something would emanate from my mouth that would indeed cause him to stop and think.

Chapter Nineteen
#How to Save a Life ...# (Fray)

The atmosphere at the hospital improved. I put up with Jibril's moods because I had come out to the Oasis Hospital as a commitment to the UNA and the project in hand. He and his family had built the hospital to offer decent health care to poor women. Making money from it was not the priority. The doctor's progressive thinking as a Ba'athist socialist and dedication to a wide range of women's medical and sexual problems were no doubt of great benefit to the local community.

Harassment didn't stop through my final months in Jordan but I dealt with it and continued to enjoy the work aspect. The workload eased now we were four trained staff including our lovely ancient Palestinian Juliette. We managed to have fun on the wards while establishing a training programme based on our combined experience and teaching materials. My colloquial Arabic was coming on, with the occasional *faux pas*.

One day, the sewing girl was going down to the *souk* for material and things and I asked *"bide zip kabir, yanny,"* 'I want a big zip.' I showed her the measurement, twenty-six centimetres, on a tape measure and didn't notice her put her hand to her mouth. Nina overheard.

"No, Miss, very bad!" she exclaimed.

She couldn't continue because she and the sewing girl started giggling. Marie happened to walk into the sewing room and I asked if she could explain why the girls were laughing. She had a brief exchange with Nina in Arabic and laughed out loud herself.

"You want a penis this big from the *souk* apparently, *yanny!*" she said spacing her hands like a fisherman might about the one that got away.

Marie had come looking for me to ask if I could drop in during the evening and say goodbye to their friends who headed a major newswire office in the capital. They were a refined, cultured family I had met earlier in the year. At their wits' end they asked if the hospital could help with advice and care of their American daughter-in-law. She was a beautiful willowy self-harming dancer who spent her days walking around the hospital corridors with us like a transfixed gazelle. All of us talked to her and listened but she sweetly and patiently out-manoeuvred every argument or line of persuasion. She was rational, coherent and absolutely single-minded about wanting to die.

"Hi, Rose, I've swallowed some pills I found in your clinical room," she said in greeting, one morning in the middle of my rounds. Jibril and Groucho rushed her to theatre and pumped the contents of her stomach out.

"Why did you do that?" she asked in surprise as we took her back to her room for observation. "I'm going to kill myself, one way or another."

After this drama and a distressing week of twenty-four hour observation from us trained nurses mostly, Jibril advised his friends they must take her back to America where sophisticated psychiatric help would be available.

Her husband, a tall gentle giant was in despair that evening he came to say goodbye. He could not grasp the situation when they were a liberated family, his wife had everything and they adored her. He took her back to the United States the following week. I never did hear the outcome of treatment I assume his young wife underwent.

Anna and Sigrid had another bad week when Dr. Jibril told us he had agreed to carry out an abortion on a young woman who had flown in from London especially for the operation. The Abortion Act 1967 was being hotly debated in the UK. It was passed in October and become law in April 1968. The girl was the English girlfriend of a Jordanian friend's son. We were all in theatre when the tiny foetus of five months was terminated. Anna was sure it was breathing when she took it to the scrub room and practically accused Jibril of leaving it to die.

He swore it wasn't alive but we all felt very bad about having a moral dilemma thrust on us. I agreed with Anna on this one. We refused to assist with any more terminations unless they were discussed by us all. The doctor agreed.

Rania, sensing the unhappy atmosphere offered to take us all out the following day. Boyfriend T. was a natty dresser and really enjoyed his Yankee car. A careful grooming of his hair with a Kookie comb when getting in and out of it was part of the ritual. He almost made the jive with his few words of English in a strong Arabic accent. "Cool, Daddy ... you catch my drift ... flying solo tonight ..."

We set off on the Madaba road south-west out of Amman with him driving like a maniac and Rania, Sigrid, Anna and I hanging on to each other singing Elvis hits. We couldn't get to the East Bank of the Dead Sea because of an Israeli military presence and so turned towards the hills overlooking it. We left rolling green fields behind and began kicking up dirt up a steep, narrow, winding road through barren, rock-strewn hills with occasional scrub and thorn bushes.

At the top we were rewarded with a spectacular view across the deep blue water to the West Bank. We were in a pink and grey wilderness, bleached and salt-encrusted. With pines and scattered rocks dipping away to the north-western shore of the Dead Sea and hazy mountains beyond, it looked exactly like the line-drawings and lithographs in books I knew from my schooling. There was nothing else up there except the ruins of a monastery and a cooling breeze.

"Very special here to Christian," Rania began. "*Jabal Nibu.* Moses see here Promised Land! He write Ten Commandments."

She waved her hand towards the Salt Sea and Israel beyond.

"Of course, Mount Nebo ..." I was awed for a moment but could not think of anything profound to say. Rania said it for me.

"Big trouble now, Promised Land ..."

We took several bags of stuff we had grabbed from the hospital kitchen out of the trunk of the car and set up a picnic on the huge stone slab on rocky legs at the summit. Maybe it was the very table on which Moses' carved the Commandments. Anna remembered from Sunday School that Moses spent his last days on this mountain.

271

She was not sure we should be eating off it until Sigrid pointed out the remains of the picnics of others.

It didn't take long before all of us were quite merry on beer and warm, watered *arak*. T. was scanning the distant shore line where he had seen flashing of the sun against mirrors and windscreens. He was almost sure it was the Israeli military, perhaps engaging with the new Arab guerrillas. We strained our eyes for ages but heard no sound and saw no movement except for the sea and mountains crinkling in the midday heat.

T. courageously let me drive his hallowed automobile a good part of the way back to Amman after I said Alex was giving me driving lessons on a race track in his snazzy E-Type. T. was impressed I could handle a Jag - his interpretation of what I said - and because its previous owner was King Hussein's brother, Prince Mohammed. The girls cheered as, gingerly, I moved the American monster off down the dusty road. Easy really, when automatic!

Incredibly, Alex trusted me with both his cars, letting me drive the Opel back to the hospital some nights on my own and park it. You didn't need a licence in Jordan in those days. Driving was fraught with danger in the countryside with children playing and donkeys motionless in the road. At night in Amman it was surreal. Drivers treated the newly-installed traffic lights as decoration. Families sat outside watching them change magically with little sense of what they were there for and they were soon removed. If you were unlucky enough to have an accident or injure someone the family came knocking on your door. Someone said to me years later I started as I should have carried on! The E-Type was the first and last car but one I ever drove.

The girls at the hospital loved my romance with Alex. The closest many of them got to the kind of love they could dream happily about was through 'Bollywood' musicals. They would form a little group in a corner in the hospital watching, or hang out of the window giggling when Alex pulled up in his car and opened the door for me dolled up for dinner or a club.

Most of our outings were to restaurants or bars and the occasional party. Alex was light-hearted and fun and wasn't it every daft girl's dream to go out with a looker in an E-Type? He lived at home with his fair-haired, good-looking Armenian mother, his father who was in the oil business and often in Basra, Iraq and his ten-year old sister who had curly auburn hair. He had paid his way in America when training as a pilot and loved flying and the high-life that came with it. It was just what I needed at the time.

When he was not in town I went out on social occasions with Crimper Nabil. He was a platonic friend as he had a neat French girlfriend who was away in France. He did expect a kiss and a cuddle but I didn't allow anything more, even if he did have the first circular bed in the Middle East, he said. Warren Beatty could have based his character in Shampoo on Nabil Suwalha! Guys had begun to notice me since my change from blob to swan.

When Alex and I became engaged towards the end of my year in Jordan, it was more to stop people whispering and protect both our reputations. He did say the months he had been dating me was the longest time he had ever been faithful.

Anna was not having such a smooth ride with her love-life. She had decided to travel to Germany and on to Jordan because Kenny, her boyfriend in London, was reluctant to commit himself to a permanent relationship. She was desperate for the situation to right itself because she loved him.

She did get out and about in Amman soon after arriving in April and was treated royally, as I had been. She was touched to be invited to visit the family of the cleaning boy allocated to her in the new basement flat. She was not so ebullient on her return from the village that evening because she had suffered eating a whole chicken and other dishes by herself with the family of ten watching. She got the impression there was little food for them at the best of times. Nadia consoled her by saying the family would have got a real lift from her visit and had probably stolen the chicken anyway.

On another occasion a local elderly Sheik took a shine to her from a distance while she was walking about in the nearby biblical town of Jerash. He took the trouble to find out who she was. A telephone call was made to the hospital asking if the Sheik could pay a courtesy visit to Nurse Anna. We couldn't wait to meet Sheik 'Omar Sharif' as we pictured him. Anna was commendably polite and pleasant when her admirer, a frail chap of about seventy got out of a jalopy and tottered up the steps.

Leaving the Shaky Sheik and Anna to develop their friendship,

Sigrid and I positioned ourselves at a reassuring distance with Abbid at Reception. A few minutes later Anna came running towards us squealing and hid behind Abbid. Her admirer had brought her a snake in a jam jar as a present and was insisting she take it out and hold it.

Grateful families and patients had been very generous to me considering we cared for some very poor people. I was presented with a bale of pink satin ribbon by one husband for bringing his child into the world. Another family came up to the hospital several days after the wife had recovered from an operation and with great ceremony insisted I receive a donkey from them. It went to a good home, to the family of one of the cleaning boys who were in greater need of one of these endearing beasts of burden than I was. Dr. Jibril joked it was fortunate it was not a camel. He laughed heartily at mixing his metaphors after saying they were a different kettle of fish.

There was another severe jolt with the reality of the politics of the region at the end of the Summer. Alex and I were sunbathing by the pool at the Hilton hotel where he usually stayed between flights. When the sirens started up no-one moved. I was really frightened but there was only laughter and some rude finger gestures to the empty blue skies. It was a false alarm, *inshalla*, 'as God wills.'

Not so the following night when I was back at the hospital and was chatting with Anna and Sigrid in the basement flat. Dr. Jibril rang the moment the sirens started wailing again to say he hoped we would be okay in a real air raid because the cleaning boys had just finished painting a large red cross on the roof. We were immediately concerned there was no shelter for us to retreat to. The basement at the rear of the hospital was level with the now manned ack-ack gun.

"There is an arms depot in the barracks next door," he added cheerily.

Moments later one or more jets thundered overhead screaming like Dervishes. There was a sickening silence until the ack-ack gun started its thumping noise wildly into the night sky, a little late.

Dr. Jibril rang again and said calmly "a bomb hit us and bounced off the roof, the boys say. Mercifully it didn't go off but it can't be far away and is live."

He told us to get into uniform and pile as much first aid and intravenous equipment as we could in the back of the pickup. We didn't need any more prompting. Twenty minutes later we were on our way to Salt which lies about halfway between Amman and the Dead Sea. The doctor's family lived there and said it had been badly hit.

When we arrived at a small clinic in the darkened town we weren't prepared for our first casualties of war. The three of us through our training and nursing experience thought we had seen everything in the way of injury, suffering and pain. Here was a long line of partly-clothed young teenage boys lying across the floors of two rooms. Some of them had crude rubber tracheotomy tubes poked into slits in their throats, some were without arms and some without legs. Bright red blood oozing from hasty bandaging contrasted sharply with the charred skin and patches of smoking tar stuck to their bodies. The Israelis had dropped napalm on this bunch of kids.

There was a cold silence in the make-shift operating area in one of the rooms except for brisk commands from the doctors and nurses operating on the boys by the pitiful light of little oil lamps. Only just before their turn were they administered anaesthetic or morphine for an amputation or removal of the napalm. We did what preliminary work we could for them on the floor. Most were in agony but still had the grace to thank us politely. Several boys died while we were holding their hands. It was heart-breaking.

Dr. Jibril told us on the way back to the Oasis late that night they were kids from one of the older refugee camps. Six of these, established for displaced Palestinians after the creation of the State of Israel in 1948 had been kept going as political propaganda, he said. The new Palestinian guerrilla groups had been using and abusing the younger boys for their own political purposes. Now it seemed they had been lined up as cannon fodder in the knowledge that no one other than medical personnel would give a damn.

We weren't interested in whether they were terrorists, or being rowdy, or whatever the reason was for the area they had been in to be subjected to this. It was unforgivable.

Anna and Sigrid were deeply traumatised by our experience in Salt. Sigrid wept all week because it reminded her of the end of the war in Germany, when as a little girl, she and her family had lived in the woods without proper shelter and survived on grass and berries. She said her bad teeth were a consequence of this period of malnutrition. I recovered more quickly as I had been in Jordan for several months before them and was in a small way primed for such an event.

We got no sympathy from anywhere in the hospital. At the beginning of the year when the weather was surprisingly chilly even for me coming from Derbyshire in the North of England, I had taken blankets and tinned food to the refugees in one of these older camps by the hospital. I had seen inmates jumping up and down in the freezing cold flapping their arms. It was a dry biting cold I didn't get used to despite the hospital's central heating. My charity to these poor people, I was told cynically would end up at the *souk* next day.

Anna and Sigrid were spared another traumatic episode when I was on duty alone with Rania one Saturday afternoon. An older woman was brought in from the refugee camp. She looked sixty from what I could see of her face but was probably forty. We could find no records of ante-natal care or any previous visit to the hospital yet she was about to give birth. It seemed from what she was saying she did not know she was pregnant. Worse, she seemed to be saying she could not have a child in the normal way. Rania confirmed these things. I pulled her clothes above her distended abdomen and knew she had to have an immediate caesarean. Doctor Jibril was out that afternoon and it looked as though I would be performing my first surgery without supervision.

We scrubbed up as best we could with the woman screaming in the background. Rania anaesthetised her with great calm saying she sincerely hoped the woman had not recently eaten. I quickly laid out some instruments.

Gritting my teeth in far from ideal circumstances and with the doctor's words "it's only knives and forks" going through my head I made an incision across her abdomen. Subcutaneous tissue was splitting with an imprisoned baby desperate to get out. Although I had seen the operation several times I was deeply concerned about cutting an artery or nerve or damaging a vital organ with only Rania and myself on hand. I couldn't have been more grateful to see Jibril come in to the theatre, pull on a gown and rubber gloves and help lift the baby out of its mother's splitting womb.

"Well done, my nurses," he said quietly when he had checked everything, "that was very well done."

In September, not long after this emergency caesarean we were very glad to have the expertise of a senior paediatrician, Dr. M. T., from Westminster Hospital. It was a prestigious moment for Dr. Jibril and the Oasis to have another senior doctor on staff. He was a tall, thin serious man with an Inspector Clouseau moustache. As with our own Groucho it made it difficult to take him seriously. No matter, he made an immediate difference to the standard of care and working practices and once again we were learning much.

A couple of weeks later he was regretting having left a cosy hospital in London. The fraught fellow came running up the steps into the Oasis and into my office looking as though a mob was after him. He had knocked over a child on his way in from his flat in the centre of town. The boy had run straight in front of the car.

"I'm sure he'll be okay," Dr. M. said, shaking his head. "He was concussed and has a bone fracture in his arm but I don't believe there is any internal bleeding or damage. He was taken to another hospital but the family somehow found out I worked here. They swear they will kill me if the boy dies ..."

The poor man was white as a sheet and I reassured him as best I could. We found him a safe place in the hospital where he could sleep and arranged for some of his things to be brought up from his flat. He didn't leave the building until two weeks later when we received word the boy had recovered and gone home.

There is no middle way in the Middle East. If angry, Arabs shout. If upset they yell or cry. They are spontaneous open people. On the one occasion during the year when a female patient died, a coterie of friends and family came to keen, howling their heads off when the deceased was being prepared for her funeral. Once they had done their duty they left, chatting away. Because the woman was Moslem she had to be buried within twenty-four hours. Her funeral was attended by males only.

Lighter moments became rarer for us three. In the ten months I had been in the country as a UNA volunteer Dr. Mad Dog had become so irrational I returned in desperation to the British Council offices. His almost nightly tirades had exhausted me. I had tried to stand up to him but was now beginning to fear returning to the hospital after being out with Alex. It was putting a strain on my relationship with Alex.

The middle-aged deputy chief interviewing me didn't say much. I fell short of telling him about the affair but from what I said about Jibril's behaviour and what he had probably heard he realised how intractable the situation was. There was no high moral tone directed at me. He probably knew that I knew he was having an affair with one of the young UNA teachers. The best course of action regarding my situation, he concluded, was to move me into the teachers' bungalow as the girls were still away on vacation.

I felt very low in, as I saw it, letting the UNA down. In addition I might have been pregnant with Alex's baby, with his being adamant about not wanting children ever. I had used the cap but knew it was not one hundred per cent reliable. It had not been a concern with Jibril because of his vasectomy.

The UNA teachers' Raj-style bungalow in town was plain and utility and devoid of distractions like a telephone, radio, television or DVD player with which I might console myself. I was left alone for several days with nothing but my own misery for company, until Jibril turned up at the door to take me back to the hospital. He had been interviewed, he said and promised he would behave.

Whatever threat the British Council issued worked. He was full of apologies and almost his old self. My delayed period must have been playing on my mind because I told him and was relieved he behaved like a grown-up for the first time in months. He said I should be examined so I knew one way or the other and that it would be kept from the hospital staff. I talked to Anna about letting Jibril examine me in view of his recent behaviour. She said she would assist him in the closed theatre. She would give me Pentothal and a little gas and air and reassured me she would be with me at all times.

After the examination Anna and Jibril left me on the theatre table to sleep off the anaesthetic. When I came to, rather groggy, my immediate thought was no one should find me there. I tried getting off the table and landed in a heap on the floor. It was fortunate no one saw Matron *Malaki* crawling on all fours to the nearby office. I found my way behind the desk and passed out. Anna and Jibril went into a panic on seeing the empty theatre table.

I wasn't pregnant and was relieved but it was deeply upsetting hearing I would need corrective surgery to my womb to become pregnant. This was difficult to grasp in view of my mother's eight births and Grandmother enduring thirteen pregnancies. I couldn't react to Anna telling me that evening that Jibril had wept in theatre after examining me. She turned her back while tidying up and turned again to catch him kissing my vagina. He really had been such a bastard I had no feelings for him anymore.

The diagnosis gave me an ambivalent attitude to contraception as well as knocking my ego over the ability to have children. This was, after all, what was expected of all young women in those days. At times like this it could even be viewed as an occupational hazard. My infantile womb must have corrected itself, my GP told me much later in the UK because I did get pregnant, without surgery.

Alex decided we should wear rings, plain gold bands. He said people talked about couples being out together a lot. Once engaged and especially seen wearing rings, you are apparently treated as a wedded couple. Everyone who knew Alex showed astonishment at this commitment from a confirmed Romeo and sworn bachelor.

My time in Jordan with this tall, blue-eyed Jude Law was good for me when a Shallow Sheila. To this day he is about the most handsome man I have met. Anna was not impressed. Good-looking, she conceded but lightweight and a man who would not be faithful for long. She didn't mince her words in telling me I was jumping from frying pan into fire. It was a raw moment, losing Anna's confidence. There was actually little competition with the doctor's bright, sparky intellect.

Alex sealed our fate one evening uttering the magic turn-off "you think too much."

The UNA was annoyed I would not be staying a second year. I used the excuse I was marrying Alex who did not want me to work. I should have told them the truth about Jibril's appalling behaviour, if not about my own indiscretion with a married doctor. It was just relief that very soon all this would be behind me. I wasn't abandoning Anna and Sigrid. They were not official volunteers and had agreed with Jibril they would support me and the hospital until September. Nadia remained a rock through thick and thin.

The UNA was quick in sending a replacement midwife. Her name was Ruth. She was a strange, squat, smug individual with a sickly smile, impervious to how uncivil Jibril now was with his trained staff. In the few days we knew her we saw her eyes light up only when she was picking up bits of gossip or tittle-tattle, as though she was storing it like nuggets for goodness-knows-what. No one warmed to her. It didn't matter to me. I was only glad there would be a smoother transition.

Before leaving my post at the Oasis Hospital the British Council thought I might like to join the UNA teachers on an expedition to the oasis at Waddi Rum. It was a beautiful place in the desert and I was pleased I made the effort. It was while quenching our thirst under the palm trees that an elderly gentleman invited a group of us into his tiny house. It was empty except for a bed, chair and table, above which was a signed photograph of T. E. Lawrence. He was still immensely proud thirty-five years on that Lawrence himself had given him the picture.

At Waddi Rum we slept in a large hut there for desert trekkers, botanists and ornithologists who came to marvel at the surprisingly abundant bird life. The scene was timeless. Serene Bedouin women washed clothes in the water, scrubbing them on stones. It was not surprising this place has been regarded as the biblical Eden. Travelling back in a jeep past a Crusader castle and forts manned by Jordanian soldiers was tedious apart from seeing the soldiers on their backs smoking, hands behind heads, their rifles leaning against a wall.

Missing visiting other historical places in Jordan and throughout the Holy Lands was a big disappointment. It was not the sort of thing Alex was interested in, though we did spend one afternoon on a dusty hillside in searing heat looking for Jordan's national flower, the black Iris. I had no money when I arrived in Jordan and none when I left. Jibril said early on he would fund a trip to Syria if I was prepared to deliver some confidential letters to people in Damascus. He then decided it was too risky. Not that I would have agreed to do it anyway.

Eerily, while touring Dorset in the Spring of 2012, I had just written about Waddi Rum and told my husband. My laptop was on my knees, some car seats being almost the only type I can sit in for any length of time. He stopped the car because he wanted to photograph a Wedgwood-style portico we had come across at a country graveyard in the middle of nowhere, actually Moreton. Here we discovered T. E. Lawrence's grave.

It was a Proustian moment linking the old man at Waddi Rum with my meeting Peter O'Toole in a Soho pub and marvelling at the actor's likeness with Lawrence, then seeing the headstone with his name on it in a peaceful place in South-West England.

As ever on leaving a chunk of your life behind somewhere, you wish you had done more. I was pleased to see in London in 1969 in a trendy shop in Brompton Road, Violet had worked hard on her dream of sourcing and importing Bedouin dresses, local furniture,

Arabic jewellery and artefacts. She was able to visit Israel where many Jordanian gold and silver craftsmen relocated over the decades. I learnt more about local crafts from her shop than I did when I was there. A salary of three pounds a week did not permit shopping trips. Her boyfriend Simon died in 2008, I read. I have no idea how far their relationship went.

Alex did indeed say he would not want me to work if we married. Being a wife that lunches, turning a blind eye to child slavery, female misery, infidelity and the prevailing chauvinistic tyranny bubbling below the surface of Jordanian culture was a no-brainer. I have no doubt that from my thirties onwards, had I remained, I would have risked being stoned in the market place for a sustained onslaught on the intransigent gentlemen of Jordan's omnipotent *Ulema* regarding their miserable view of women and women's rights.

What would also not have worked was having children. Alex would have been granted parental rights had we separated. As a Pilot Officer he had met and was proud to have flown King Hussein around Europe and it would not have been fair to compromise him with the possible revelation that his wife had once consorted with a *Ba'athist Al Fatah* sympathiser.

Jibril drove me to the airport at the end of September 1968. This emotionally complex, highly intelligent man had car-crashed through my life. He was charming, even mesmerising. His tutoring showed me I could easily become a doctor if I wished. This was more valuable than everything else I learnt in that toughest of years as a nurse. In one of his rare rational moments of the previous six months he apologised for his demonic side having come to the fore. He said again he loved me.

As we sat as we had begun, over a Turkish coffee, we were both depleted and shell-shocked. Nothing could turn back the clock. There would be no kiss and make up, no forgiveness, no tearful reunion or running away together. It was our Brief Encounter finale.

Goodbye for now to ancient Amman, the Dead Sea, the West Bank, celestial light and sunshine, ack-ack guns and sad refugees, my proudly-delivered Jordanian babies, the best bedside carers-cum-belly-dancers, cleaning boys, Mr. Fatimah and my very own crimper; take care gormless Abbid and all little slave *bintis*; bye-bye to the best cafés, clubs, wonderful strong coffee, sweet *chai*, stellar Arab cuisine, beautiful embroidered Bedouin robes and bartering in the *souk*; farewell Zany Nadia and to my own Armenian 'Crusader'; *Ma'salami!* Doctor Mad Dog's angelic side for teaching me to be a braveheart, to lose my timidity and go for it; *haram* to Israeli planes dropping leaflets and napalm on young boys ...

Chapter Twenty
#Song for Bernadette ...# (Leonard Cohen)

On landing at Heathrow I was already missing warm, friendly Jordanians. Alex flew the aircraft into London and I was staying with him at the Royal Garden Hotel in Kensington for a couple of days. There were envious looks from the hotel receptionists at deeply tanned me with my modern Greek God with his twinkling azure eyes but I felt like shouting out I had no intention of returning to Jordan as a desperate housewife. I didn't love Alex but was grateful to his lightweight, loving and generous self. He kept me sane when Dr. Mad Dog was doing his best to demonise and dehumanise me. I also enjoyed the glamour breaks from living on a pittance and working silly hours.

My brothers and friends in Earls Court liked Alex. It was not difficult as he was good-looking, smiled a lot and was just very pleasant, like an airline pilot. Being older than me he did look out of place among a welter of cosmopolitan youngsters wearing smelly Afghan coats made worse with patchouli oil and wacky baccy smoke infusion. Zapata moustaches and shoulder-length hair was now the look for males under thirty. They also looked grimy and pale.

Morris kindly fixed me up in a vacated bed-sit in Trebovir Road and Alex invited us all to dinner at the Royal Garden Hotel. My brothers were pleased. The last time they saw me was post-suicide-attempt and they would be concerned I might be turning into another anorexic, reclusive Sulky Sis. I might occasionally go out on a limb but was soon hauled back by the voice of reason. I was still New Age and my London friends were still tree-hugging, pot-smoking Love and Peace, Lennon and Harrison followers, according to my brothers. So what was wrong with a bit of idealism?

A great help on my return was the UNA's £40 resettlement grant but I had to get back into the mainstream. Despite working at junior doctor level for a year, the patriarchal NHS would not allow Naked Nurse to do half the medical tasks that had become routine including setting up drips, assisting the surgeon and prescribing medicines. Another stint with the nursing agency that had given me great jobs before I went abroad seemed my best avenue.

My nurse friend Mary in the Mayfair agency office still had a bed-sit in Trebovir Road. She met Alex when we were dropping off my things and invited us in for a real Irish coffee, one in layers, with the cream floating on top. Alex was in uniform ready to return to Amman.

"Just look at the two of you! Jeez, you look like film stars!" she raved in her soft Dublin accent. "You went out to Jordan as a missionary and found Hollywood. And that tan. You make me sick!"

Pascal passed the door.

"Will you look at this! Do you recognise your baby sister!"

Pascal grinned and said I had lost my puppy fat. He asked if we would like to come along to a George Melly gig that evening. Alex couldn't. I declined because my room needed sorting. Mary said I should call in at the agency in the morning. They were dying to hear what I had been up to in Jordan.

"Ah, Nurse MacFarlane," the office manager began in a crisp NHS tone that I loved and hated, "I'd like you to start at Sloane Square tomorrow morning. Your patient is Mrs. de B. Come in and have a cup of tea with me and tell me what you've been up to in Jordan, what with that nasty war. And you have a handsome fiancé, we hear! And do you still have your uniform ..."

It felt as though I had never been away.

Mrs. de B. was a warm-hearted 'Queen Mum' in bearing and breeding. The family were part of the royal 'in' crowd, her elderly cook Lila informed me. She had several homes she moved between during the year according to the season, whether fishing, hunting or racing. It was on her son's estate that Prince Charles supposedly proposed to Lady Diana Spencer on a bale of hay. The luxurious Belgravia residence hardly brought me back into the real world.

While Mrs. de B. was recovering from an operation, I supervised her medication and helped her bathe and dress. Soon the work was nothing more irksome than selecting her favourite crooners to play on the gramophone while she attended to her correspondence. Several times a week her chauffeur would arrive at eleven and I would accompany her to Fortnum's or Harrods or her *corsetiers* Rigby & Pellar.

"Do choose something for yourself, Rosie Dear," she would say in Harrods. I thanked her each time saying I wasn't allowed to accept gifts.

Once, in the lift, she exchanged greetings loudly with Lady Spencer-Churchill who was then in her eighties, a very striking woman and somewhat deaf. Several times a week my charge's handsome Harley Street doctor would call causing Mrs. de B. to go "all-of-a-flutter." Lila was most concerned and looked at me for confirmation. I suggested she did go a little girly but did it matter?

"Well, yes," Lila whispered, "she's talking of leaving him some of her precious paintings and her chandelier, for goodness sake! She's never been like this before."

Her son and daughter-in-law called every Monday for luncheon and insisted I join them. It was a slightly uncomfortable experience but kind of them. They would ask if I had a good weekend. I had, I always said, without mentioning Kensington Hippy Market and its pungent smells and stoned youngsters, or noisy parties in Earls Court where people were as repressed as ever despite Free Love and Enlightenment, or were experimenting with alcohol and Mandies and other prescription drug searching for the ultimate high.

Their stock reply to my polite return was they had lunched with the Kents, or the like.

Like Cook, they too were concerned about Mama's flight of fancy and asked me to keep an eye on the situation. As if I could! I actually loved the idea of her having a teenage flight of fancy at her ripe age. I showed her a photograph of Alex, so handsome in his uniform.

"Oh no, My Dear ..."

That told me.

I caught up with my reading in my first week with underground magazines, the dailies, Nova, Rave, Fabulous, the iconic International Times. They showed our role models were spearheading separate fronts. One was led by the high-IQ Germaine Greer clones, the other by a simpering sweet Marianne Faithful, Twiggy, Sandy Shaw clique. I interpreted some looks in the street as admiration for my thick curly hair. Back in damp London Town it was close to an Afro and a huge contrast with the straightest hair I had ever seen girls parade with. Celia was ever the same, telling me to stick with the Sarah Miles look and scolding me for wasting time on 'Sixties throwaway consumerism. One hand agreed, the other still wanted Biba's latest earth colour cotton cardigans and tops.

My next patient was the antithesis of Mrs. de B. She was the snooty mother-in-law of a recent high-profile Cabinet Minister. I was ostracized on sight and not acknowledged thereafter except by her pointing or tapping her finger when she wanted something. Her long-suffering housekeeper told me she went into a major sulk when her last nurse left. I did everything I could to help the lady feel at ease to no avail. Her family were equally disdainful except for the tall, handsome, chatty daughter.

"You mustn't let it worry you. I have long been the Black Sheep so it doesn't bother me now!"

Little needed doing for the hostile old duck and I would sit in the study for most of the day. Her kind housekeeper Millicent crocheted beautifully and taught me to be proficient at it. I was there long enough to crochet a dress as a surprise present for my mother for that Christmas 1968. Being paid handsomely for making a dress was quite a contrast to my three-pound, eighty-hour week in Jordan.

Auburn Anna left the Oasis Hospital a month after I did and was similarly pleased to be back in the civilization we knew. Sigrid returned to Germany. Anna said little about Jordan and there was no message for me except from the girls, who missed Miss *Malaki*. She warned me my replacement Ruth was stirring things, jealous it seems I had been so young a matron. Anna said she had never met anyone with so many chips on her shoulder.

Things were at last going well with Anna, as commitment-dithering Kenny had clearly missed her. They began living together again in Trebovir Road and Kenny became our Mr. Stability. While we were being fashion and New Age chameleons he was off every morning to the Ministry of Defence, returning to Trebovir Road in the evening to play chess with Morris.

Iskander and Suhail were at the end of their studies and now sharing bed-sits with girlfriends. Iskander was with Nona whom I'd met in Amman. Her family left Palestine after losing their large house in Jerusalem to the Israelis without restitution. She envied the freedom us single ex-Pat females apparently enjoyed and in a supreme moment of liberation took a plane to London to see what it was all about. I was so pleased it was Iskander she took up with. It took great courage on both their parts and I particularly admired Nona's resolve. She was also one of the most hospitable people I have ever met.

Towards the end of the year Ruthless Ruth in Jordan topped the vile behaviour list by inviting Alex to dinner with the express aim of telling him everything she had been able to piece together about my relationship with Jibril. I found out by way of a Dear Joan letter from Alex ending our engagement which I suppose was Ruth's miserable intention. I didn't like the thought Jibril was implicit. Alex didn't ask me about my side of the story and after I was over the shock of Ruthless Ruth's unwarranted bitchiness I was relieved not to be wearing his ring. He said he threw his out of his plane's window.

At one of Iskander and Nona's lively dinner parties in December I sat next to a distant cousin of hers, Farid. Unlike most Arab boys I'd met he was quiet and wasn't joining in the political fray with all the yelling and passion involved in getting a point across.

"He's a Christian Arab, almost English," I told Anna. "He's not rowdy and always arguing politics."

Most of the Arabs I met in London and the Middle East were Christian rather than Muslim. They were polite to each other but there was a segregation I saw clearly when an Egyptian Muslim graduate came to Trebovir Road. He was an Air Force pilot at the time of the Six-Day War. When Iskander asked him if he'd shot down any Israelis the Egyptian laughed, admitting they were too busy eating their cornflakes to scramble in response to the sirens. All of their aircraft were destroyed on the ground.

"Ya haram!" 'what a pity!' was his comment.

Farid was from a well-to-do Palestinian family in Bethlehem, many of whom had moved to other parts of the world. His mother died while he was at Catholic boarding school in England. He cried for a bit, he said and that was it. Now he was in his last year of a Bachelor of Law degree. I thought it was so cool being born in Bethlehem. There is a romance here for all Christians, naturally and I had been thwarted from visiting it by the Jordanian stamps in my passport.

He invited me to an evening meal with him and his flatmates in nearby Eardley Crescent. It was a *donor kebab* takeaway and sickly-sweet *chai* in small glasses. This was a supreme effort for these pampered boys and I was touched. Farid's flatmates were elegant George, a fair-haired, fair-skinned Sudanese Arab and Esau, a small and very funny Palestinian Christian Arab. Esau came from Nablus on the West Bank, another biblical town I wanted to visit. Both boys were welcoming, easy going and chatty and the opposite of shy, mumbling English lads. Esau talked eloquently about life in Nablus and how Israeli occupation had affected it.

The most attractive feature of Arab boys beside their relaxed friendliness is their deep 'pools of gravy' eyes that emote in a way other colours do not. I must be an 'eye woman' I thought, since Jibril and Farid had this beguiling feature. The name Farid translated as 'exceptional' or 'unequalled.' At least he kept me in order Celia eventually remarked, though I was not sure what she meant.

Nona told me he was twenty-one and a motherless innocent. Naked Nurse's mothering instinct was tripped into taking care of such an individual, just enough to guarantee the boys liked me coming around to fuss over them. The flat was invariably a forlorn mess. Like Italian boys, Arabs are waited on by women so much it's a wonder they can breathe on their own. Celia mocked me for pandering to this type of chauvinism and teased me that I needed to wise up and have a good think about what I was doing.

Early in 1969 Anna decided she didn't want to nurse for a while and started part-time at a suntan and sauna salon that had just opened in Knightsbridge. It was the first in the UK to have suntan beds. There was also a sauna, dipping pool, a masseuse and a part-time hairdresser. The local authority stipulated an SRN had to be on the premises to supervise the tanning tables. It was a cushy number with good pay. She insisted I come down and she would arrange some pampering.

She liked Farid on first meeting and said he was more my type. From the beginning we didn't go out much as he took his studies seriously. "Swinging" though London was, it needed energy and money to be a part of it. Most Sundays I would help him with his revision of the interminable number of cases that set precedent in law.

Out of the blue, like the Dear Joan letter, was Alex's phone call asking if I could meet him at the Royal Garden Hotel for a drink. He had just met my first Jordanian 'boyfriend,' Widow's Party Michel, who told him I was as pure as any Jordanian girl *et cetera*. He wanted to apologise for spurning me and for listening to Ruthless Ruth's stories spun about me at a time when she wasn't even in Jordan.

He wanted us to try again. A warning flashed up with him saying "I don't know what it is about you but I'm not normally the faithful type ..." I knew he had been unfaithful. Nadia and Nona, whose judgement I trusted implicitly, had warned me and I declined his invitation. We never communicated again.

At a party at Farid's place in the Spring to which Anna, Kenny, Nona, Iskander and Celia came, I wore a red dress I had crocheted myself keeping going skills taught me by housekeeper Millicent. A red bikini underneath it rather than a lining or slip was very daring. Silver finger nails and toe nails completed the look.

"Wow!" Anna and several other admirers, including Celia commented. Farid engineered me onto a balcony, little more than a ledge above the street and told me he thought he was falling in love with me. Such things are music to young ears, if they are receptive to it.

"Is this declaration *prima facie, de facto* or *ad litem* ..." I asked, having picked up some of the Latin from his law books and dictionaries. I wanted to add something about lust but could only think of 'crime of passion.' Farid expanded readily on my points 'self-evident,' 'existing in fact' and 'for the duration.' I wouldn't get one over on him!

Soon after visiting Anna at the salon I began covering for her on the occasional session. It was usually when I should have been catching up on my sleep from night shifts at various Nursing Homes and with private clients around Kensington. Many well-known actors and celebrities dropped in to use the sauna perhaps because the Celebrity Telegraph told that a sauna, new in Britain at the time, was good for de-toxing the liver. Others just liked the deep cleansing of the skin. John Mills and Eileen Atkins, well-known for her stage performances in the Killing of Sister George, became regulars.

The hairdresser at the salon was Gianni who assisted Elizabeth Taylor's Parisian hairdresser on the set of 1963's block-busting Cleopatra, the film that went on to feature her relationship with Richard Burton as a modern-day Antony and Cleopatra. He still attended to Taylor's hair and travelled around the world with her and Burton. Their chauffeur would pick him up when he was needed.

Gianni was a sweetie and between clients would natter away about "Eleezabet." For a reason he never explained he usually had one of her untrained pooches with him. Shots of Burton in a candid documentary picking up poo in an obvious 'love me, love my dogs' affair made me smile years later. Gianni had to do the same with the one he was looking after.

We were all ears, of course, on Burton and Taylor at home, or more usually when they were in London, at the Savoy.

"I luv 'er," he said frequently, "but 'ee is a peeg, I 'ate him. 'Ee drink and treat 'er bad."

He also said she had no vanity, "she use any ol' cream on 'er face!" Once he spoke about Taylor's son, Christopher I believe, her second who would have been thirteen years old. She was worried "becoze 'er leetle boy, 'ee luv to dress up in 'er dresses and shoes .."

We did experience enquiries from people who thought the Kensington salon might be an upmarket extension of Soho services. Auburn Anna, who was as innocent as the day is long, took a call one evening in reception.

"Do you do relief massage?" a man asked brusquely.

"Oh, yes, Sir! Joan here does a first-class job."

"... so how much is a relief ..."

When Anna twigged she told him to take a hike and put the phone down. Soon I was covering for Anna on day-time shifts if she wanted extra time off or an interesting agency job came in she didn't want to miss. It was a convenient arrangement and easy money and we carried on with it through the Summer.

As the decade wound down there was a tangible sense that a never-to-be-repeated era triggered by Beatle mania was losing its 'we can do anything' ebullience. The vitality of the music of the 1960s, its challenging films and colourful, edgy fashions had empowered and inspired a generation. Everyone we knew felt alienated from their parents and their seemingly dull and dutiful way of life. We now had to work out where we wanted our future to go.

The Beatles' gradual demise reflected my apprehension. Most of us had aligned ourselves with their energy and talent from their first singles and LP in 1963. They gave their last public performance on the roof of Apple Records at Savile Row at the end of January 1969. I happened to be walking past in uniform that crisp sunny afternoon but just missed it. The crowd in the street was still buzzing, along with several bemused policemen.

The personal lives of some of the group were soon wide open. In March John and Yoko did a 'bed-in' at the Hilton Hotel in Amsterdam with a loose message of peace that was of greater concern to our generation in America. Paul married Linda and the police chose that day to raid the Harrison's house for drugs. The story of the bust was all over the papers when I started the first of three nights at the Chelsea Hospital for Women in March 1969. I knew Pattie Harrison was in a private room somewhere in the hospital and came across her and her husband by chance while I was removing flowers.

"Oh, don't take the flowers away," George drawled, "they're l-o-o-vely!"

I stood there for a moment smiling inanely. If I had managed to speak it would probably have been banal anyway. The buzz in the canteen that night was, of course, about Beatle George being in the building. The whisper was that his wife was in because of fertility problems. It was suggested the smoking of dope might have something to do with it.

Just after I came on duty the following evening the couple were leaving and walked past the women's six-bedded ward in which I was taking observations. To my embarrassment there was some hissing and cat-calling from the patients. The recreational use of drugs through the late 'Sixties did not impress everyone.

After a decade of a dissolute lifestyle of many in the entertainment business whose lives were propelled by or lost to drugs, sex and alcohol, a Day of Reckoning loomed, as with Brian Jones over-dosing and dying in his swimming pool. There were many other casualties, including Marianne Faithfull who disappeared into the streets of Soho as a junkie, saying later it all became too much to handle. Martin Amis wrote years later about his vulnerable sister losing out on endless relationships, coping by becoming an addict then dying early as a consequence of the liberal 'Sixties.

'Doing your own thing' was being interpreted by some as having the right to live off the DSS. People did walk around town with half-finished canvases under their arm, didn't wash and smoked dope openly in the street. Many were drop-outs from art college or university. Why not, some argued? Sons and daughters of many a wealthy family received an allowance. The fact theirs was being paid for by a public who may not have wanted their taxes used in this way escaped them.

There were also many high spots, such as two astronauts landing on the moon on Saturday night July 20th, 1969 during a 'Looney' party we were bopping to at Trebovir Road. We crowded into Suhail's room in the early hours of Sunday. He was the only person in the block with a television set and was so excited about the event, along with an astonishing 600 million people around planet Earth. This was almost one fifth of humanity. The picture was grainy but we knew the achievement would be unparalleled in our lifetime.

I was still reading voraciously, with Celia my guru for what was hot and what was not. Doris Lessing became a favourite author but I found her feminist-leaning book The Golden Notebook hard to fathom and thought I must be dumb as everyone was raving about it. We tackled R. D. Laing's The Divided Self in which he wrote about how the dysfunctional family can cause the most sensitive member to become schizophrenic.

We thought The Graduate in 1967 was hot. Film hotted up more exploring a stream of sexual themes including full nudity in If ..., exploitation in Rosemary's Baby, orgasm in Barbarella, homosexuality in The Detective and a lesbian love scene in the Killing of Sister George. Celia and I went to the Paris Pullman regularly up to my leaving for Jordan. We enjoyed them all including our own season of French films, Je t'aime, je t'aime, of course and Marianne Faithful strutting her stuff as the Girl on a Motor Cycle, though we thought this a bit cheesy.

Sylvia Plath's The Bell Jar was provocative with regard to confronting suicide and emotional issues. She had as tough a time in New York as many did in London and committed suicide in 1963 in the year her book was published. Fritz Perls' Gestalt Therapy struck a chord. "I am me and you are you. And if together we like each other, that's fine. And if we don't like each other, that's fine too. Because I am me and you are you ..."

Eric Fromm's The Art of Loving made a deep impression as the first proper book about love I read. It is an elusive and difficult subject he approached with compassion and perceptive analysis. Pat phrases like "know thyself" and "be true to yourself" tripped from many a mouth. It was only in later life I began to glimpse what "know thyself" meant.

It was sometimes a relief to move away from narcissistic navel-gazing and pitch in with Iskander and Suhail on the ramifications of the Six-Day War. They were wary of returning to Iraq under secular Ba'athist Saddam Hussein and were sceptical about the intentions of a colonel named Gaddafi who overthrew the monarchy in Libya in September 1969. What would be the consequences of Yasser Arafat being elected leader of the PLO? The Palestinian problem, the statelessness and homelessness of many of them was growing and my sympathy for their cause moved with it despite my rough ride in Amman.

Pascal's basement room was the meeting place where discussion into the night was at its rowdiest, lubricated by beer in tins. To be taken seriously by my dude brothers I had to read the broadsheets. Everyone was well informed but they did listen to my recent experiences in the camps, watching tanks passing and Israeli planes dropping leaflets about the *Al-Fatah* 'threat.' My experience nursing youngsters hit with napalm prompted a grim silence.

Issues in the Middle East were not confined to bed-sit land debates. There were marches to Hyde Park Corner and Trafalgar Square. Many of the Arab student were convinced they were being watched. It was whispered it could only be MI5 or Special Branch, or Israeli intelligence. No one had any idea how to be clandestine in the face of brute politics like this so life carried on normally. My tacit support for displaced peoples in the Middle East was of no consequence although it raised awareness with people we talked about it with. Tragic to me was a generation of children across the Middle East who would grow up brutalised, with only one goal, revenge.

The Arabs were zealots compared with the torpor British people exhibit over issues that deserve more discussion. University students were actively campaigning over nuclear disarmament and Vietnam, certainly with more fervour than they do about anything today. Enoch Powell's Rivers of Blood speech in April 1968 had opened a can of worms over immigration in the West Midlands that British people were uncomfortable debating. Apartheid was a similarly unrewarding topic of conversation at parties or in the greengrocer when debating whether to buy Cape grapes or indeed, Jaffa oranges.

Palestine was not the only hot-spot around the world, of course. Nineteen Sixty-eight was a year in which students around the world questioned their elders in earnest. In May, French students and workers kicked off. In August the USSR was on its own campaign of keeping an old order in place with the crushing of the Prague Spring.

In Mexico City days before the Olympic Games were to open in October at least forty-four student protesters were shot dead by the army. The Games were also marked by a Black Power salute on the rostrum that athlete Tommie Smith later wrote was a salute for human rights. There was another massacre in the city after the close of the Games.

As Autumn 1969 advanced, the mumsy agency boss thought I would appreciate a longer posting at Quince House Nursing Home close to my flat. I wasn't disappointed on ringing the bell of yet another Nursing Home run on sawdust when a rake-thin woman in slippers, with cigarette in bony hand opened the door. The agency didn't say Quince House was the Fawlty Towers of nursing homes with its Art Deco entrance the single redeeming feature of the building.

"Is it yourself? Come in, Oi am Matron. Follow me."

Matron's office was the basement kitchen with a table by the window so she could see people approaching her front door. Her ancillary staff were kin from Southern Ireland. One of them, Maisie was a tiny forty-something with white hair who kept quart bottles of Guinness in the dottiest resident, Lady N.'s room knowing Matron never set foot there. These she would start opening early if Matron went off-duty early.

Maisie had long ago broken all the taboos of her strict Catholic upbringing by living with her Arab lover and resigning herself to her fate in Purgatory. She was then jilted by him and never recovered. I sympathised with her utterly and my own Thousand-and-One Arabian Nights of dastardly deeds, which she wanted to hear again and again, ratcheted up her misery hugely.

The other full-timers were the Ugly Sisters from Carlow who bullied and cowed the residents, taunting them about being abandoned by their hoity-toity relatives. Even Maisie would mutter "dey tink dey're the bleedin' Raj," when the Guinness spoke for her. Trained staff at the Home, us agency nurses, did our best for the mainly aristocratic residents. It did seem most had been dumped. Few received visitors and they had regressed to grander times.

The residents were the rock of the establishment, some of them having been there a very long time. There were five bedrooms on the second floor and no lift and I was soon losing weight. In one of the singles was Dora, an artist who had been trained by the doctor and Great War artist Henry Tonks. He was known for his paintings of shattered soldiers, often depicted without noses. Mad as a hatter and blissfully happy, Dora would rest on her bed feeding biscuit crumbs to mice. We were encouraged to order what we liked on her account at the local chemist. The Ugly Sisters did and sneered at us for declining.

Next door to the Mice Lady's room were two sweet and gnarled octogenarian sisters Bertha and Harriet, said to be aunts of the Queen Mother. Bertha had Alzheimer's and would lie in her cot most of the day quietly gibbering. Harriet was relatively coherent. Their rooms were like the others, dingy with brown lino and cheap rugs and some bits and pieces of their own. When we asked Harriet about the Queen Mother she drifted off into days of yore remembering her niece seeking the advice of their father, an envoy to China, about marrying 'Bertie' who was to become George VI. Her father had recommended this course for the young Elizabeth, she said.

The Queen Mother visited these two ladies once at the Nursing Home, apparently. Only their old gardener Bert called, cap in hand, salt of the earth when I was there.

"He likes me the best ..." Bertha would spit after he had gone.

"No, he does not, he likes me! And he kissed me, so there!" Harriet would retort. We left them to it.

One morning in Harriet's room when my colleague June and I had just finished assisting Harriet with her ablutions, June thought she could get away with a quick smoke. She had just lit up when we heard Matron's footsteps dangerously close, though she almost never bothered to look in on the inmates. To our horror, she knocked and walked in, handbag in the crook of her arm. June instinctively handed the cigarette to Harriet who put it straight to her lips.

"Ah sure, Harriet, I didn't know you smoked?"

Sweet and gracious Harriet, who was becoming increasingly vague, rose to the occasion.

"Oh, one doesn't mind the odd cigarette, does one?" she said, puffing away.

No one had ever seen her smoke though I suspect she was blowing rather than sucking. Matron tripped off down to the basement for her own tea and fag marathon of the day after promising Harriet she would get some smokes in for her.

Matron was pleasant enough to work for and happy to leave us to our routines. She had for years been feeding her family on groceries ordered through the Nursing Home. That was all she seemed to do, fill in requisition slips while puffing fag after fag with cuppa after cuppa. Her top floor apartment was sumptuously furnished. All her children went to private school, she told me. She bought a house in Hampton Court for her retirement.

Laziness and canniness were art forms she had mastered. Not once did any of us receive or were asked to write a nursing report on individual patients unless we did it to cover our backs on something we didn't like. The resident's food was so bad that over a couple of weeks Cook and Matron would be away, I told Matron my trainee chef brother could cover and that he would be cheap. I didn't mention he had finished his catering course and was, by all accounts, rather good.

We plotted giving the residents a superb menu instead of their usual niggardly portions of fish fingers or tinned spaghetti or beans on toast for supper. It was actually too late for the change to Simon's *nouvelle cuisine*. The residents wouldn't touch it, the rot had well and truly set in. Staff enjoyed his meals, however and we indulged for the two weeks we had the Nursing Home to ourselves.

On the whole, I loved looking after the last of the Gertrude and Martha, Bertha and Harriet brigade despite being treated as a sub-species.

Over the months I was concerned about Maisie sinking into alcoholic dependence. She was only kept on because the residents loved her. All we could do was try and minimise her self-harm. We knew this was not working when she staggered in one wet October morning with a black eye and torn stockings saying she had woken up in the street outside her bed-sit without her keys. She had no idea what had happened during the night. Rehabilitation didn't exist in those days and it was very upsetting watching a slow suicide.

Matron was not in the least sympathetic. Her interest in her staff went as far as enthralling newcomers by name-dropping the great and the good who had graced Quince House with their presence.

One such was Joan Sutherland's secretary's mother being in the Home for a while. The bragging was about the great diva herself popping in to see the woman when in London. It reminded me of the stultifying time we endured as kids with Pa's obsession with opera and cocktails, thimblefuls of which he would pour for us.

I had seen more of him in recent months, since his retirement as a ship's surgeon. Still restless, he was a locum at a local GP's practice and on call to the shipping line. He was impressed with my tid-bit about his favourite *coloratura* soprano.

A distinguished Egyptian gentleman who insisted I call him Shaucut was admitted one evening and I helped him settle into his room. He was a banker, until his bank was nationalised by Nasser in the late 'Fifties. He became chief financial advisor to King Saud who abdicated in 1964 and was obliged to retire because of Parkinson's Disease. I wondered many years later if the strain of trying to reign in a king who spent money on himself and his family to the extent of almost bankrupting his country had triggered his illness.

I enjoyed nattering with Shaucut in colloquial Arabic. His English was perfect but my Arabic made him smile. Here was someone else I was comfortable with that would lead to a lifelong appreciation of older folk. They don't have the insecurity of younger people and don't feel the need to upstage or compete. Long lives are far more likely to hold interesting tales. Very little seems to perturb them, except bowel movement perhaps.

He was awaiting a bed at King's College Hospital where he would be trialling a pioneering drug, L-Dopa, for his deteriorating condition. His doctors had high hopes for the drug he had brought over from Switzerland, so new it was still in powder form. Parkinson's strips people of their dignity, their ability to communicate. Shaucut whispered that if his deterioration was not at least arrested by the drug he would consider his life at an end. The least I could do in the ten days he was at the Nursing Home was to spend time in cheerful conversation when I was not pressured by other things.

One of his close friends, the actor Omar Sharif phoned regularly and I had to relay my patient's response during their conversation as his speech was desperate and fragmented. Another friend was Mohammed Heykal the widely respected editor through the 'Fifties and 'Sixties of *Al-Ahram*, Egypt's biggest-selling newspaper, who sent good wishes via a visit from his brother-in-law. He was very kind in taking me out to dinner in order to be fully briefed.

Joan, another resident in a three-bedder on the ground floor of the Home also suffered from advanced Parkinson's. Her miracle cure, a 1950s lobotomy had left her as in *rigor mortis* with an expressionless face and body as stiff as a shop dummy. She also had early Alzheimer's but there was still evidence of her sweet self beneath these afflictions.

Shaucut was given an admission date to the hospital in October and I promised I would visit when off-duty. I managed this at the end

297

of his first week at the hospital. He walked towards me, shook my hand firmly and bade me a good evening. The drug was miraculous.

On subsequent visits I realised his son Moswen, a likeable but irresponsible playboy, could not understand my altruistic motives towards his father's well-being. It reminded me of the wealthy Jordanian wives who were ultra-suspicious of why I would want to volunteer for hard work for three pounds a week.

Three weeks into Shaucut's treatment I arrived at the ward to discover he had been discharged. The nurse on the desk had clearly been instructed not to pass on contact information. I was puzzled and upset until it dawned on me it must be Moswen. I thought we had become chums and he understood his father had asked me to visit and I liked him enough to do this in my own time.

Just as the winter cold was biting I heard that both Anna and Souhail's bride-to-be were pregnant. Anna and Kenny had arranged a Registry Office wedding as she had no family to speak of and Kenny's would have been miffed at their bun-in-the-oven nuptials. The revolution had started after thousands of years of "thou shalt not." Many of the Commandments were being rewritten also by the New Order in London.

In November I thought of moving in temporarily with long-suffering Mother in her one-bed basement flat in Bayswater. She had moved to London from Sheffield to be near a seriously anorexic Sulky Sis. The nuns at the Tyburn Convent at Marble Arch had contacted her about Sis whom they knew from her charity work. Ma started working for them, cleaning the chapel and doing light shopping in exchange for grace-and-favour accommodation. I was pleased the agency asked me to take a break from Quince House to do a month of nights at the prestigious Moorfields Eye Hospital.

Moorfields was a research unit and hospital with patients from around the world admitted for pioneering operations and procedures. It was an NHS hospital but it reminded me of the London Clinic with its two- and three-bed side rooms. Calm, unhurried care was required as I was to learn on all ophthalmic wards I worked on subsequently. Many of the patients could not see us because of blindness or bandaging after surgery.

The nights were so quiet at Moorfields, I couldn't help brooding over Jibril and Vile Ruth. When I began writing about my year in

Jordan, as many people had asked me to do, I kept focussing on toxic events. Vexation, sorrow, hurt and anger poured onto paper which was promptly torn up. It went on like this for a couple of weeks. Night Sister kept asking when my 'story about Jordan' would be finished.

After a month and just about out of excuses I felt cleansed enough and settled down to write the piece, as requested. The brain usually finds a way of dealing with distressing events with varying degrees of success. To this day writing is my way of freeing up emotional log jams.

I was walking down Earl's Court Road towards Quince House the week before Christmas and heard my name called from a taxi. I was taken aback to see Shaucut looking so sad and ill. His Parkinson's was back with vengeance. His treacherous son was with him.

"Why haven't you been to see me since I left hospital?" he asked. I looked at Moswen who was extremely uncomfortable.

"Because the nurses wouldn't give me your address or telephone number. Of course I would have come."

Moswen tried to change the subject. His father ignored him.

"Please come and see me," he insisted with great hurt in his voice.

He gave me his card, I kissed him on the cheek and told him he looked wonderful. It was all I could offer the poor man since I had been compromised by his son.

On Christmas Eve, Celia and I felt sorry that Farid and his flat-mates would not be having a real English Christmas dinner, especially being Christian and decided we would cook them one. Most of the local shops closed early on the 24th and we didn't have much money anyway so it had to be a watery chicken casserole.

We prepared it in my tiny kitchen in Trebovir Road on Christmas afternoon and took it wrapped in towels through the deserted streets. We had some wine and a laugh with the boys until about midnight when the doorbell rang. Sister Jane had found out where I was and began haranguing me over missing the sacred MacFarlane Merry Christmas dinner at Pascal's flat.

"Mother is very upset ... we're very disappointed in you not coming ... if that's what you think of us ..." and so on. She was a little tipsy and rather aggressive. Wearing a fur coat she looked her usual elegant self except for the purple Christmas cracker crown.

"We could take you more seriously if you took your crown off!" Farid said laughing.

Jane left, a little more mellow but I was glad I had made a stand against the tyranny of a family Christmas, a little late at the age of twenty-four. Rows and general manoeuvring were a trademark of the clan's annual gathering.

I went to a do a few days later, invited by bit-part actress Gloria with a noble nose and long bleached hair who reigned over the adjoining house in Trebovir Road. She hustled me in and said she couldn't talk because Frank was about to 'phone.

"Frank ..."

"... Sinatra!" she responded airily. "I'm doing a film with him in the Spring ... Sheriff and the Dirty Scrubber ..."

I'd learnt not to take much notice, though we did keep a look out for her when it was released as Dirty Dingus Magee. The crowded flat reeked of cannabis and there was a baby in a cot in the middle of it, seriously stoned. No one seemed bothered about this child abuse in their midst so I took the mite outside walking about for some time in the freezing night air trying to normalise her.

There were a couple of flurries of snow in Bayswater. I moved to Ma's flat probably through guilt and because she liked to see the New Year in. Pa had been summoned to cover for a colleague on a winter cruise. On that last New Year's Eve of the 1960s I was told wearily I would wear out an already well-played Kinks record if it was played one more time.

#Thank you for the days,
Those endless days, those sacred days you gave me.
I'm thinking of the days,
I won't forget a single day, believe me ...#

... of the decade in which I moved back to Sheffield from Cornwall, enjoyed the *bonhomie* of Notre Dame High School, watched Damien's traumatic illness and death, passed my SRN, went hitch-hiking in Europe, made the unwise move to the East End Maternity Hospital, did odd jobs in London, volunteered in Jordan and returned to London with inner turmoil and disquiet.

What would the 'Seventies bring?

Chapter Twenty-one
#The Long and Winding Road ...# (Lennon/McCartney)

In February 1970 I didn't realise how tired I had become working five and sometimes six shifts a week. At Quince House I occasionally went straight from a run of days to a run of nights, sometimes with a day shift at the sauna salon in the interim. Falling asleep on duty had never happened to me before, not even with the ludicrously long hours at the Oasis Hospital.

Taking tablets to help me stay awake must have contributed to my general malaise. I sometimes took pills under the informal supervision of my father when he was in Bayswater, or after 'prescribing' them to myself from his ever-increasing samples of medicines. I always looked them up in Mims manual. It got to the point where I also looked a wreck. Pa warned me that well-being would return with changes in lifestyle, not quick fixes.

My twenty-fifth birthday passed in March and marked the fact I was without aspiration or direction and now a quarter of a century old. It was not a welcome marker. At Quince House I didn't blame Matron for threatening to tell my agency I was moonlighting and that I was not being efficient. She simply told them she didn't need me any longer. Suddenly I was without regular work. I wasn't too bothered about having to move on. I needed a break from caring for elderly people, much as I loved them. Perhaps I just needed a break.

The word depression was not taken very seriously in those days. I didn't know about it but knew something was wrong when I found myself unable even to enjoy the sunshine. I wrote to brother Billy about it because of his experience. He wrote back that Winston Churchill called it the 'black dog.' I made an appointment to see a local GP but the bugger shouted at me about everyone coming to him for 'happy pills.' It was no consolation that others in Earls Court were having problems.

Within a couple of weeks I could not afford my rent, such is the reality, the grind of the Big City. I asked my mother if she could lend me £100 to keep me going while I sorted myself out. She obliged but a few days later I was summoned back to her basement flat for a "meeting." The loan turned into a confrontation between my mother, two older brothers and me pathetically justifying my existence. I fell between embarrassment and laughter at this caring of sorts for a younger sibling. The meeting was a wake-up call and I was soon working again through my Mayfair agency, swapping with the ever-busy Kensington salon. At least I caught up with my sleep.

Gianni breezed in and out still entertaining us with Burton and Taylor stories. One day he brought in six of this great star's gowns she generously thought the 'girls at the salon' would like. I was too cool and hippy chic to consider wearing creations like these, Dior or not. Same for Anna. They were beautifully made, the first *haute couture* we had run our hands over but shocking pink and lime green net creations we could not wear. A tall Australian nurse, another part-timer at the salon certainly couldn't either, as 'Eleezabet' was tiny. It didn't stop her taking the gowns away, her eyes shining with good fortune. We must have been mad not finding somewhere to store them.

After the loan incident I began to think about the extent of Mother's general detachment from the family. They were still there, a generation of women frustrated and unfulfilled in their role as wife and nanny. Most of my female friends seemed to have a problem in even liking their mother. I was quite close to mine. We shared an emotional history and a sense of the absurd. Our relationship was stable as long as I accepted she would never love me as I had seen other mothers love their daughters.

It was many years later she said I was the best-looking girl in our extended family. She had made sketches of me from photos, an honour we thought had been reserved for Damien and her brother Bill. Sulky Sis also said she had been ticked off because Mother wouldn't hear a word said against me because of the way I helped nurse Damien in his last months.

She was good in making a home for us wherever she lived. Most of the MacFarlane clan were in London now, though Pa was largely absent because of endless locum duty or cruising. The little Bayswater flat was cosy and we did laugh there. Once we peeked into the grounds of the Tyburn Convent and giggled at the nuns playing football. They had a passion for it that elicited laughter among them, if no comment. These Carmelite nuns were a Silent Order. Mother was waiting for one of them to boob.

For a change from nursing and to add another feather to my

nursing cap I applied to train with the Family Planning Association in Mortimer Street. Since 1930 the FPA had been open-minded and non-judgemental to all seeking advice from them, including now, single people. The organisation's medical staff were treated as practitioners in their own right. They were trusted to think for themselves and there was no punitive, restrictive atmosphere as in many NHS hospitals. It was a return to the positive side of my nursing experience in Jordan.

Training went on through April and May at Pike House and was a mixture of evening sessions and day-time lectures. It certainly broadened my outlook, as all aspects of nursing had done so far. A jolly American doctor was one of my favourites. She suggested the Queen of England would surely not be taking the Pill. Her method of birth control would, therefore, be the Dutch cap. She really did wonder if female members of the royal family had the cap brought to them on a velvet cushion! Her eventual point was that all women would need advice and instruction on birth control methods.

She told us stories that would be passed on gently to women seeking advice. One was about a woman being so impressed with the Pill she cut it in half every day to share with the neighbour and could not understand why both of them fell pregnant. Another was the wife who insisted her husband also take a Pill each evening, just to be safe.

The most bizarre tale of recent months, the doctor said, was about the vicar's wife coming in to the clinic for her first six-monthly check. Staff ascertained she had been inserting the oral Pill in her vagina. They were naturally curious about what she said was a normal sex life and why she had not become pregnant. Normality, it was discovered was her husband ejaculating in her navel. Birth control was a new subject to most women, even after half a century. It had not caught up with this innocent couple.

Farid, George and Esau continued swatting in earnest in Eardley Crescent with Farid now doing a Master's Degree. I didn't think law studies would have suited most Arabs because they tend to be over-emotional. He was not an emotional person and there were signs the intensity of studying law and plain over-work were taking a toll.

Celia referred to him as Mr. Black and White because of his cold logic. I called him Harold Macmillan because he had an old head. He was typically public school in his cocksureness while being likeable and interesting. I loved him nevertheless and we seemed to have a good relationship but I wondered how much I was putting up with. As a party animal it made me uncomfortable being asked at social gatherings "where's the boyfriend?'

There were lighter moments, as when his cousin William visited. He reminded me of Billy Bunter except he would lounge around in a smoking jacket smoking cigars he bought in Burlington Arcade. I found a posh Arab telling dashing stories good fun. His cousin thought he was a braggart and should be brought down a peg. They saw their chance one Friday night and put a Mandrax tablet into his glass knowing he would not be able to detect it over the metallic taste of the beer he was slowly drinking.

Like his compatriots he did not really drink and regretted being persuaded to buy a Watneys Party Seven for the weekend, because they were the 'thing.' He went into hyper drive, turned up the music and beginning a striptease. He eventually staggered off half-naked and we found him asleep on the toilet, his velvet jacket pulled over his head. It was fortunate this was in the days before mobile 'phones and video clips that can be viewed around the world in minutes.

London was moving on apace, stopping for no one. Perhaps it was the Baby Boomers a couple of years younger than me now powering things along. I saw the dismissal of some fashion as being "so 1960s." We heard the criticism "pseud" levelled at people who were not convincing in their chosen path or purported beliefs. "Get real" and "wise up" were levelled at others for a variety of reasons. Bread, meaning money, was common.

We also heard and used cat, fat cat, chick, cool, dig, fab, far out, flip, freak out, fuzz (for police), go all the way, going steady, hacked, hairy (for risky or dangerous), hang loose, hip, hunk, mind-blowing ... It was mostly imported Californian cant from the music scene and didn't integrate entirely, as Disney versions of European fairy tale and folklore did not either.

Our protesting about every aspect of our former lives was easy to sustain in London. I happily swanned around with the notion that rigid parents were out of touch. We were the new grown-ups whose elders were Neanderthal, joyless warmongers. My older brothers remained solid and traditional. Moving to London might as well have been pitching a *yurt* in Mongolia for what they cared of impassioned debate about nuclear disarmament, Peace, Love, Understanding and a reappraisal of consumerism and materialism. They were still mocking my passionate, politically-tortured friends.

They and Mother were dismissive of us having become self-indulgent and barmy, if relatively harmless. My father considered pop music "a painful cacophony" but grudgingly agreed that my favourite folk singers Joan Baez and Anna, had voices. The harder-edged counter-culture of drugs, rock 'n' roll and widespread violent protest in America was beyond their comprehension.

We were like fish out of water back in the provinces. Relatives and friends were clearly threatened by what they saw and read about London life. Skirts had shortened up North but it must have been a hysterical sight to my old school and nursing friends when I visited, stumbling along the Ecclesall Road in my clunky boots and psychedelic gear with my face painted up with Twiggy-style eyelashes.

My female friends and I were feeling the kickback of our liberated times as the opposite sex made up for lost time. The Pill had made a huge difference to the way New Man approached his relationships to the extent of becoming a self-centred commitment-phobe. In London anyway. We had hot-footed it to the capital to escape the provincial pressures of marrying early and bearing children. Those of us hankering after relationships beyond casual sex might soon be moving back, as some of us were longing to be cared for in the good old traditional way.

So where were we to find stable, reliable, kind and humorous men, we might ask after another night of giving a little too much, if this was the case? Some young women were definitely losing the plot with promiscuity causing them to slip into bouts of self-loathing. Guys did what guys do and moved on. It was understandable that many males had moved to the Metropolis to escape the prospect of taking over the treadmills their fathers had spent their lives on. Smoking dope in darkened corners, hiding behind loud music and expounding on this and that was no alternative.

The Hippy Movement was fading. Dropping out wasn't so hip and drug 'use' was for losers. References to the more positive New Age, Gaia, the notion of World Government and end to war, hunger, poverty, disease and discrimination were everywhere. More wholesome things our American Brothers and Sisters had led the way in were being absorbed. These included the back-to-the-land movement, organic farming, co-operatives and greater respect for the environment. We did get sneered at over health foods and a vegetarian inclination. Some of Celia's friends said health foods were a saviour after the cheap, unappetising, highly refined and largely non-nutritious bulk they were served up at college.

People were also searching for something to feed a spiritual need that mainstream religion had failed to provide. More accurately perhaps, they had been able to break away from the straitjacket of what our parents or community directed. People brought up in a Christian tradition now dabbled in Buddhism, Hinduism, Taoism and Neo-Paganism. Zen Buddhism was much debated. Being without a central god figure and with the emphasis on personal enlightenment suited many. Dope, magic mushrooms, LSD and easy meditation were latched on to by those on the path to *satori*.

We were scared of LSD after what had happened to Peter Green of Fleetwood Mac and Syd Barrett of Pink Floyd. Horror stories of babies cooked in the oven and people happily pirouetting out of upstairs windows were urban legends we were wary of.

The Beatles became involved with Hare Krishna in 1969 and with Harrison's single My Sweet Lord later in 1970, some interest came of this movement. The group's brief period of study under the Maharishi Mahesh Yogi in 1967 and 1968 also injected Indian culture, more than religion into dour Christians and sombre Catholics.

I had a passing interest and noted Private Eye's more shrewd reference to the Maharishi as 'Loadsamoney' Yogi Bear. Ascetic cults, divine Rolls-Royces, multinationalism, tax avoidance and private helicopters did not convince me, or the Beatles, either. It didn't suit them that this 'divinity' made a pass at one of their party, Mia Farrow.

Becoming an agnostic or atheist was not easy after the religion thrust on me. It is not as simple as simply ignoring indoctrination from childhood. Part of my protesting, now I was wising up, was religion being a bastion of male control.

Into this heady mix was also tossed crystals, Tarot cards, *I Ching*, divination, meditation, holistic medicine, ufology, spiritualism, Vegan vegetarianism, animal cruelty, the occult and therapy. One of Celia's clique, a guitarist with Pink Floyd kept us up-to-date on therapies. He was really hip, if a bit LA of five years earlier with beads, chamois leather shirt and headband. He smashed his guitar up in front of his parents when they laughed at him for going to therapy.

Anna and I had a secret envy of people who were able to indulge in a hippy lifestyle with the collective intent being to change what they perceived as a loveless world, even if they were doing it on the dole. They cared little that society judged them as parasites. Cults were mostly hearsay in Britain, especially the type where angels fear to tread. The 1969 Tate-LaBianca murders shocked and sickened us.

Celia and I dabbled in the *I Ching* and at one stage divined on every aspect of our lives, sometimes before leaving the flat in the morning. It is exquisite prose and much more uplifting than the "verily I say unto thee" stoning and smoting of the Bible, though I still had favourite passages from the King James. Other friends were barmy Ouija board enthusiasts, rolled dice, or were addicted to an upturned glass and lexicon cards around a table.

I couldn't relate to astrology and it was tedious being asked on first meeting what Star Sign I was. It was hard enough getting rid of the make-believe of the Star of Bethlehem and Three Wise Men. At the salon I found *masseuse* Joan's declared Piscean intuitive abilities intriguing despite being a science-oriented sceptic. During one massage she pressed sore trigger points between my shoulder blades and asked if I'd had some serious stress at about eleven o'clock the previous night. When I told her it was possible, after a telephone call, she advised me to drink proper unsweetened barley water.

With such people you do wonder how much attention you should pay to things you are not aware of, especially when you are trying to drop ghosts, God, spirits and past lives.

It was disconcerting discovering that being a Piscean was exactly me, so to speak, "poet and dreamer who can be a martyr or saviour; unworldly but cannot bear to see others in pain; caring, compassionate, sympathetic, loving, susceptible to addiction" and so on. I was less keen on the "wet, drip and slop" description from another newspaper. I held back from huffing about it after matching appropriate astrological character traits to several friends.

Lennon and Yoko Ono were busy with their potent Make Love Not War messages. With such a strong anti-war movement all around particularly over Vietnam and nuclear disarmament there were times I felt uncomfortable as a 'peacenik' with a family war hero. He was Uncle Bill, a twice-decorated DFC and Bar pilot from his days in Bomber Command. I never knew him as he was shot down in occupied France early in 1944 on an incredibly dangerous mission dropping equipment for the Resistance in the Ardennes and possibly a female SOE agent near Le Mans the same night. He flew undetected around Paris with dawn in the sky but was doomed with the mission having been compromised. Thank goodness I refrained from rubbishing Uncle Bill to my mother who idolised him.

Only as I got older did I appreciate the heartbreaking commitment of young men and woman through the two World Wars in series such as the World at War narrated by Laurence Olivier with a musical score by Carl Sagan. How could I not be proud of Uncle Bill and his young crew shot out of the sky by a waiting Messerschmitt fighter?

Around the time of my birthday in March 1970, Celia was teaching in an art college in South London and took the bold step of taking out a mortgage on a basement flat in Fulham. It was a revelation seeing someone savvy enough to buy a flat. To her it was obvious. If she was to part with money each week for digs, it should be towards a place of her own. This was a rare thing for someone young and single to achieve at the time.

She needed financial support in the form of a tenant and asked me if I would like to share with her. The newly-modernised two-bedroom flat was at the junction of Finborough Road and Ifield Road, between Earl's Court and Fulham. A tiny garden backing onto the Brompton Cemetery made it 'des res' for us. A bad-tempered prostitute who hoovered between clients the night long lived in the flat above. Above her were two of Celia's art school friends, Hannah who had schizophrenia and Sarah who was refreshingly normal and uncomplicated like me and my Northern friends, supposedly.

It was another change I welcomed, this time from the York Stone paving and painted white Regency of Trebovir Road to the Yellow Stocks and green shabby of Brompton.

Two doors away resided Johnny and Gracie, Kensington and Chelsea's self-appointed Pearly King and Queen. They were a real laugh. Celia met them in their junk shop and they became firm friends. They loved to talk about their celebrity status and that The Beatles had once invited them to something or other. Plump, toothless, six-foot Gracie was a timeless outdoor Londoner. Johnny too, with a face like a left-over Covent Garden tomato.

They proudly showed us their smother and skeleton suits. The smother suit weighed a ton with thousands of mother-of-pearl buttons stitched on it in horseshoe, heart, anchor and cross motifs.

Also trimmed with buttons were Johnny's rakish cap and Gracie's 'titfer,' a plumed creation of Music Hall proportions fit for a Cockney Empress.

Celia had a brilliant idea one grey afternoon just before half-term. She had found more part-time work teaching at an East End school she said definitely needed livening up and persuaded the school to invite the Pearlies to open the school's annual sports day a few days away. Back at the flat that Friday afternoon after the event she poured herself a large glass of wine. I could see the occasion had not given her the kudos she hoped for.

"As I speak," she began in answer to my inevitable question, "I expect my dismissal is being arranged."

"But everyone loves Pearlies!"

"Yeah, except that Gracie turned up all glam, popping out of a tiny little sports car in more ways than one. She had a friend with her, the 'Bishop of Medway.' Johnny had to mind the shop and a Pearly Queen couldn't make an appearance in costume on her tod."

She gulped some wine.

"Well, when the mums and grans saw her there was whispering at first, then the cat-calling started. She's none other than Gracie D., one mum told me, very well-known locally since before the War. Our Gracie's an old-time Pro. And the 'Bishop' was long ago exposed in the News of the World as a charlatan!"

"A Vicars and Tarts Sports Day ..."

"... and my name's mud."

As expected, Celia was not invited to resume teaching at that school in the Autumn. Our Pearlies admitted some of the snooty Pearly families had long been making things difficult for them but they were genuinely engaged in charity work in Kensington and Chelsea "when needed around this Borough!" Gracie added with a smile. As if to prove the point it was not long afterwards they were invited to Fulham Hospital to open a fête and said we must come along to see them in action.

Moswen, my Egyptian Parkinson patient's playboy son found out where Celia and I were and rang out of the blue in April. He asked cheekily if he could bring his stuff and stay a few days because he was between flats.

"You've got a nerve, Moswen," I ranted. "*J'accuse!* After cutting me off from seeing your dad, thinking I was only after his money."

"Whoa, sister Ro!" he laughed. "Tell you what, you and your lesbian flatmate can punish me. I'll bring the S and M gear!"

He was incorrigible.

We expected him at eight that evening for supper. His eight o' clock was midnight and I refused to let him in, until he started banging on the door. He got a mouthful about courtesy and good manners and that some of us had to go to work in the morning.

Shaucut told me of his exasperation at his son's dissolute lifestyle. Swarthy attractive Moswen revelled in introducing me to rich Saudis who had flown First Class into London for a day or two just to buy silk ties or be seen at a party. They were rich and bored.

On an invite to a nice restaurant in Kensington I was appalled at the rudeness of one of these young men to a waitress. I told him he couldn't speak to people in England in this way. Moswen whispered I couldn't speak to a Saudi prince like this. Prince So-and-So himself said "you can't speak to me like that ..."

"Oh yes I can," I said firmly. "She didn't deserve such an attack, you're just throwing your weight around ..."

There was a deathly silence, so I went on,

"I've just been a year in the Middle East volunteering for almost no pay and seen how you treat your poor and your women. Then you come over here and try and do the same. You are a sad group of people ..."

A princely sulk is something to behold and I nearly started laughing. In a sense they were children and it was not their fault they were empty-headed and superficial. But they were an advantaged social elite with enormous financial power that could have done so much more. I also knew I was on dangerous ground and that my abrasive stand would make no difference.

Moswen told me next day his friends were very upset. Perhaps they will think a bit on the concept of treating people with respect I suggested. He ignored me and said I might get a death threat.

"Huh!" I started contemptuously, "they haven't got the bottle ..."

No more friendly months later I asked him, casting an eye around the stuff he was bringing into the flat what he was reading apart from Playboy. Intelligent though he was, his interest of the moment was specific. One of his bags was full of sex toys. Celia and I had never seen such things and were mesmerised, clit ticklers, dildos, nipple clips, coloured condoms. Here was all the fun of the fair! We were clearly behind in *boudoir* titillation techniques.

"It's surprising ..." he began.

"... spare us the details, Moswen," Celia interrupted. She put her hand on a Japanese cine camera and asked suspiciously what he used that for.

"That's a different recreation," he admitted cheerily. "I point it up mini-skirts on the escalator, for my friends back home! Swinging chicks and all that. My friends love it as girls don't wear mini-skirts out there!"

"You behave while you're here, Mister 'M for Moron,'" she warned.

He didn't. A couple of mornings later he was in his dressing gown sitting on Celia's pride and joy blow-up armchair. His dressing gown was open and she shrieked because he was sitting there large as life with an erection. She went at it with gusto with the biro she was holding. Moswen dodged her frontal attack and Celia succeeded only in puncturing the vinyl. Chair and erection deflated. We started hitting him, telling him he was a bad boy. You couldn't take him seriously.

It was a surprise to see among his belongings several carefully packed gramophone records. They were BBC sound effects and were part of his grand plan to become a radio DJ and presenter, something I learned in YouTube clips in 2013 he had aspired to in a Cairo radio station.

As the Summer term started, Celia, a strange mixture of impressive self-confidence and crippling insecurities, was worried about getting enough part-time work. She had given up competitive athletics to go to art college, hated teaching and stayed sane only by painting. I insisted she come to a party Pascal was throwing to try and relax. By the Saturday of the party she was behaving very oddly and as Pascal welcomed us in, she rushed past him into his bedroom wardrobe. She was calmer during the evening after taking one of the low dose Valium tablets she kept in her bag.

I mixed grape and grain that night and crashed out in Iskander and Nona's room. They generously camped elsewhere, as people sometimes did on party nights if their flats were taken over. At least the thirty or so bed-sits in the adjoining houses were clean, Habitat furnished and filled with luckier students, graduates, actors and dancers. Most other digs we visited around London were ghettoes with mildewed bathrooms and toilets, orange-box furniture from junk shops and mice.

It was a great surprise when Celia knocked on the door at about midday in the same clothes she had been wearing during the evening. She had not left Trebovir Road, she said and my brother was amazing. He had charmed her into his bed. My thumping head was forgotten suddenly.

"My regular, died-in-the-wool, Tory businessman, Trad Jazz brother?"

"Uh, huh!" she grinned. "I have been so fed up with the neurotic young guys that hang around me, it was a great night for a change. Your brother too!"

Did she have any new plans regarding boyfriends *versus* girlfriends, I asked? No, she said, it was a one-off but she thanked me for insisting I went to the party. It wasn't what I had in mind but it had lifted her out of the doldrums.

I was not pleased when the following Saturday morning I arrived at Farid's place after a very tiring night shift to find Celia in the kitchen. Spending the weekend in Eardley Crescent had become the norm for me. With no party the night before a beaming Celia should not have been there. She had slept with a friend of mine, she blurted, Farid. "I don't know what came over me ... I wanted you to hear it from me first ..." She then added, smirking, she'd had not one but two orgasms with him.

Farid was still in bed. I was aghast and humiliated and too tired to have a row but when I raised my voice he went from smug to aggressive. He had done nothing wrong, he said and why was I so upset? It was only sex and we were always going on about experimenting, after the films we had seen. Weaknesses in his character I did not want to know about had surfaced that morning.

Celia's behaviour was also unforgivably unkind and I wanted her to disappear forever. Farid became sexually excited by two women, two conquests, in his presence and his mind was along one track. I was not receptive to this kind of a male reassurance when Celia had gone but I was tired and vulnerable and put up with it when I should have walked out, just as I should have with Jibril.

Not too long afterwards I became pregnant. Working in Family

Planning and now expecting a child in as un-ideal a situation as I had been warning other young women against annoyed me. How could I be pregnant with a womb that would need corrective surgery? In a moment of humour I wondered if this was a 'miraculous birth' with my Bethlehem-born partner. My attending GP said it was possible my womb had corrected itself.

Two of Farid's Singaporean Chinese law student friends also announced a surprise baby. He was a brilliant Buddhist on a scholarship and she was Catholic and fretting about being punished for her sinning. Each of us, including Anna and Souhail's fiancée could take comfort in having around us other mums-to-be supported by their partners, except for Georgy Girl.

Farid was worried his father would cut his funding if we married. For my part even if I braved it and moved back to the Middle East I risked being tarnished as an immoral woman for becoming pregnant before marriage. Living in the Palestinian community in Israeli-occupied territory would have been even more difficult than living in Jordan. Forty years on, Palestinian children have only ever known growing up and survival in a war zone.

We talked of termination, safer now with the advent of the Pregnancy Advisory Service but the Catholic in me wouldn't let me follow this through. Farid was brazen in uttering the words "now I won't go to Hell ..." He only just saved his bacon by saying if it was a boy we should name him Sacha.

Anna said when she told Kenny about my situation he was sick in the bathroom. Doctor Josh too was physically sick when he read my letter on coming out of surgery. He drove from Kidderminster to London to see me. I hadn't seen him for a while though we kept in touch after I left Sheffield. Celia's Catalonian ex-boyfriend Isidrè was staying with us and he was a great comfort. These three men saw me as a victim.

One of the benefits of the '60s was being able to have male friends without connotation, expectation or coercion. Josh remained a good friend for years with him lamenting his shotgun wedding. As Asians in Sheffield in the early '60s he and his girlfriend had been obliged to marry. Despite a big crush on him when I was a student I knew a relationship would not have worked because of cultural differences and because he was already married, of course.

Isidrè was our tall Che Guevara, rock solid and a grown-up

compared with some of our Flower Power friends. He educated us to the horrors of the Spanish Civil War and how the Catalonians had made a stand against Franco. Celia and I had both been to Spain and had an idea how fear ruled there. She tended to treat this gorgeous guy with indifference, while I wished I'd met him before meeting Farid.

He remained supportive and kind through my pregnancy as Farid became more and more detached. I didn't pursue anything more intimate and would have appreciated reciprocation on my males from Celia. I was still in love with Farid and for a long time found the double-whammy of being pregnant and rejected, alienating and upsetting.

Celia insisted I stay in the flat as long as I wanted because she knew she would never have children. Her friends were wonderful, though some came to peer at me, a Miraculous Conception in their midst. My family were not in the loop as I was doing just fine with my mates. I had embarked on the ultimate example of the joy, or the occupational hazard, of being a young woman and it looked as though I would be going it alone. It was a bizarre time with us all making it up as we went along.

Between Nursing Home shifts I was looking after private patients for a well-known London doctor, Lucy Hampson. Mary at my agency gave me first option on these 'soft' home nursing jobs because Dr. Hampson asked her to. This really helped restore my ego. I did the occasional stint in NHS hospitals at busy times and didn't feel sidelined as I had after my first private work. As long as us agency nurses showed ourselves capable, hospital nurses generally left us alone.

Agency nursing around London seriously tested our standards of ethics and care, particularly regarding elderly people. The Sheffield Royal had done a good job on me and I never lost it with any patient however taxing they were. Nursing Old Devils, as Kingsley Amis termed them can require extreme patience, especially at the end of a shift when feet long to walk off the ward. "Bed pan, Nurse," shouted for the umpteenth time can test and test again. Marker One for night duty exhaustion, especially after ten or more consecutive nights was whether you had the will to warm a metal bedpan under hot water for your most demanding patient.

In recent years reports of appalling standards of care, especially of the terminally ill and elderly indicate staff are running on empty without feeling able to say so. A good Ward Sister will pick up on exhaustion and low morale and strategies should be in place to work out what can be done to help staff regain their initial enthusiasm for wanting to nurse. Disinterested, cruel and careless staffing is toxic to the system. Surely it is kindness and understanding that is required, not punitive action?

In the mid- to late-Sixties, monitoring of standards in non-NHS Nursing and Rest Home care was lacking. Trained agency nurses would attempt to improve matters for residents who never went anywhere and who were fed a miniscule, barely nourishing diet. Residents cannot be happy as under-stimulated institutionalised zombies. Those at Quince House were a generation of obedient, clean-living ladies to whom anarchy and rebellion were unknown. Poor sods.

As upset as we were by the Ugly Sisters' freedom to bully, our young obedient selves had been unable to do anything to counter it, not least because we had no idea what channels this could be done through. It also introduced the sickening notion of the ostracizing of the whistle-blower in a continuing effort to hide unacceptable care and inadequate management. This poor state of affairs is still with us forty years on.

Through the winter of 1970 my advance reading for parenting was Winnicott's The Child and the Family and The Child and the Outside World. I felt the pressure easing even before starting out, with his writing about being a "good enough" mother. A. S. Neill's child-centred policy at Summerhill school was also a guiding light. Like Anna, I wanted a new way of doing things where my children would be seen and heard and not unduly punished or shouted at.

Our generation had been reared according to Dr. Truby King's ethos of discipline, discipline and discipline from our very first breath. We were treated as objects to discipline rather than feeling, reacting bundles of innocence. We were fed four-hourly, never on demand. We weren't to be picked up when we cried lest it 'spoilt' us and we were outside in the pram in all weathers because the fresh air was best. My mother was triumphant about having her brood of eight, potty-trained within three months. She sat us on a potty after and sometimes during feeds.

Anna and I met regularly to compare each other's experience of pregnancy and for her to pass on tips. She had only ever been intent on creating a wholesome family unit of her own. This was a consequence of her family background and time spent in Germany and Switzerland. She introduced me to Swiss Müesli and fresh juice. She and Kenny were quietly absorbing the new thinking on child-raising by aiming for these things to be standard for their kids. They were determined their daughter would have a loving upbringing without corporal punishment. With awareness of environmental issues growing, Anna also realised polluted cities were not ideal places in which to bring up children.

When Anna gave birth, her widowed father coming down from Sheffield ostensibly to do the right and proper thing with his daughter having produced a granddaughter. He was proud to show her £500 he had stashed in his boots. It wasn't for her, of course. He also told her the circumstances of her adoption. Her mother had miscarried and was in the women's ward recuperating.

"There were a prostitute in the bed next to 'er wi' a baby she didn't want. It had red hair. After a bit o' negotiation and a blind eye turned by the maternity staff your mammy left wi' baby. That were you!"

When Anna rang Kenny blubbing he said "aw shut up, you're not the only one!"

With Mary's kindness I was able to work right up to a week before delivery in February 1971. My last patient was an elderly lady in Putney who had suffered a stroke. She was a sweetie and it was a pleasure helping her with her recovery. After lunch I would gently walk her around her flat before her nap.

"Now you rest on the settee as well, Rose and I'll wake you up with a cup of tea."

It left Rotund Rose wondering who was the patient.

Moswen rang before Christmas and said he would like to take me out. We greeted each other politely. He knew the episode with his father still ran through my mind.

"Er ... Dad ..." he began, without being prompted, "the L-Dopa treatment was abandoned after several months. He did what he threatened ... back home ... he jumped out of a second-floor window ..."

Chapter Twenty-two
#God Must Hate Me ...# (Simple Plan)

I was in Gracie and Johnny's flat in February 1971 during a knees-up with Gracie playing the accordion when I felt the first twinges of labour with my child. My mind yo-yoed between the primitive and the radical. Some days I wanted my brothers to show some macho care and force the cad, the father, to face up to his responsibilities. At other times I looked forward to the challenge of bringing up my child on my own.

Because Celia and I and a couple of other friends had spent a second Christmas away from our families I hadn't seen my mother in months. As far as I knew she didn't know I was pregnant. Then Jane turned up one day, her usual sweet self and said very little, as if her young unmarried sister being pregnant was nothing to get animated about. There was nothing she could say really, though the MacFarlane Bush Telegraph would shortly be buzzing.

The day before the most amazing day of my life I had a sudden burst of nidification compelling me to get my hair done, lay out baby things and make sure everything was good and ready for my Prince or Princess's arrival.

Not wanting to be a nuisance during the night I took one of Celia's Valium tablets in the early hours and didn't 'phone the birthing unit until nine o'clock. The midwife who had been with me from the beginning arrived in a taxi. By now I was in agony. It was business as usual for her and the driver who moaned the whole journey about the price of everything.

I was the only client at the pioneering GP-led unit at St. Mary Abbot's, Kensington that morning and was guaranteed full attention. Nevertheless, midwives were benign brutes, I decided. To add to my beginner's distress and feeling like a heifer about to calf I was subjected to an enema. At least that trial took my mind momentarily off birthing pain. Lilly was born in the afternoon and I was encouraged to sit up and bring my daughter up for her first cuddle.

Farid, chivvied by his Singaporean Chinese friend who had just given birth, arrived in time to cut the umbilical cord. He had a large lump on his forehead, because of stress the midwife suggested. I told her he was from Bethlehem and my middle name was Mary. She laughed and said it was an old story!

To this day I have not felt such a creative high. I thought I'd given birth to the universe. I did feel sadness for Manic Myrtle being seriously depressed after her first-born a few years earlier, punishing herself for becoming pregnant outside wedlock. That was in Sheffield. Thankfully, attitudes in London were more grown-up.

I was still having trouble about our inter-relationship now we were three and I could have done with the comfort of being loved at that time. My record to-date had not been a good one. As I saw it, I was fighting a losing battle having been most of my life at my parents' beck and call, bending over backwards with them openly preferring other siblings.

Did I care? Yes and no. Celia had sorted her thinking regarding her parents. She knew she had been a provocative brat being very bright and an only child. She decreed I was lucky not to have pushy or over-protective parents twitching over my every move. As for "scumbag" Farid she also proclaimed, I was free to bring up my child my way, hopefully with liberal values rather than with the ways of the Middle East hovering over us.

Placid Pascal was my first visitor. My little girl had large hazel eyes, a heart-shaped face and mass of thick, dark hair like her mother's at birth and he agreed she was an exquisite child. He took the cue from me of course, as he was male and until only recently, Brute Brother. He informed me semi-detached Ma who lived only a hop, skip and jump away, would visit me at home in ten days or so.

I was up and about almost immediately as Mama Nurse on the ward, put in charge when staff went off for a cuppa or fag break. My weight returned to just under nine stone within a week because of this and because I was too excited to eat. I was perhaps a touch manic! The nurses hoovered up my abandoned meals and told me my milk supply would be fine as long as I drank plenty of milky drinks and water.

Farid did become a serious and responsible dad, if part-time. He loved Lilly until the end of his studies when she was two years old. He said his goodbyes and returned to the Middle East. He knew he had almost no chance of making a successful career as an Arab lawyer in London. The Old Boy network would have seen to it even though he was an Old Boy himself from a top Catholic school. Overriding everything was the fact he did not love me. And that was almost that.

It was later in that year, in October 1973, that the Yom Kippur War blew up. It had been Sadat's secret intention for at least a year to invade Israel again. This Egypt did, with Syria, Jordan and Iraq and material support from the Soviet Union. Sadat declared he would sacrifice a million Egyptian soldiers if necessary to take back lost territory. It could so easily have become a confrontation between the Western powers.

Once again I thanked my lucky stars I was not out there, a second-class citizen in a war zone with a small child. I might also have been sidelined by Farid's family in Bethlehem even though they were highly-educated and westernised, unless I was assertive from the start and spent time manoeuvring.

There was compensation in the Pearlies becoming instant surrogate grandparents, spoiling Lilly with presents and being really kind to me and to Celia. They helped enormously with the furnishing of the flat, charging little or nothing for two Victorian grandfather chairs, a writing desk and magnificent *chaise longue*. This became the *pièce de resistance* covered in white and black fur scraps, real concept art by 'Celia!'

Huge abstract art canvases, her best pieces, hung on each wall. We made a big effort from early in my pregnancy to make the flat respectable and not too hippy. We all knew the stories of babies being taken away from unwed girls by Social Services.

When Gracie asked me if I could attend yet another hospital fête as moral support, I could not refuse. The trouble was, with Celia teaching, I didn't have a babysitter.

"Don't worry abaht that, Rose," said Gracie. "Johnny's not feelin' too good and is stayin' home. He'll baby-sit though, woncha, Darlin'?"

The afternoon arrived and they called with a newly-painted Victorian high chair from their junk shop as yet another gift. I showed Johnny how to warm her feeding bottle and Gracie said we would only be a couple of hours.

At St. Stephen's Hospital on the Fulham Road we were shown to seats for honoured guests and given a cup of tea. Gracie, fully decked out this time in her costume and hat with long coloured feathers had been swigging steadily from a half-bottle of whisky and didn't touch the tea. She woke with a jolt as it spilt across her lap. I made the excuse

319

to the administrator that The Queen was a little under the weather.

"It's me nerves, Rose," Gracie whispered. "It's just a bit of medicine for me nerves."

I insisted we walk home that afternoon after the event and Gracie soon perked up, especially after the admiration of passers-by on the way. My baby-sitter also looked as pleased as Punch when we got in. Four-month old daughter was on her back sleeping blissfully looking like a stuffed cushion.

"See, Rose, sleeping like an angel, 'int she!"

"Was she good?"

"Yeah, little Darlin'. She woke up an' I gived 'er the bottle, like and anyways, she seemed a bit 'ungry still, so I gived 'er anuvver two bottles wot I made up me self. Sort of guessed the amounts, you know. She bloody loved it!"

"'Ow bleedin' much 'ave you given her, for gawd's sake, Johnny?" Gracie asked, looking with alarm at an empty tin of baby milk powder. Lilly slept for ten hours after her triple feed.

Later in 1971 when Lilly was six months old, I returned to Quince House on a part-time basis. My 'maternity leave' had only been possible with savings and money Farid got to me regularly, though the amount varied. Matron welcomed my bringing Lilly along and

even spent some time playing with her. Lilly would sit happily in her new, beautifully-decorated high chair in the kitchen being entertained by Cook and staff.

The Home was still in a time warp and as dilapidated as ever. My two favourites, the Queen Mother's ancient aunts had died and left their large house and assets to the gardener Bert. Sweet-faced Maisie was still emaciated but looked happy. Her fortunes had changed. She had a 'toy boy' who she believed really cared for her. They were living together and it was clear over the next few weeks he was being good to her. She was off the Guinness and it was wonderful to see this turn for the better.

Lady N., the glorious aunt of Three Men in a Boat actor Peter Bull who visited her regularly was still on the first floor. Whenever anyone talked to her she would trill back with a semi-detached stream of "does one? ... one does, doesn't one? ..." clarification. Her hook nose floated from her face like a sail seeking a breeze, a dew drop hanging perilously from its noble tip.

Next to her was now Mr. C., father of a celebrated Scottish television doctor who was as dour and charmless as he was on screen. The old boy would get drunk every other Wednesday night after his dutiful and likeable daughter had visited with a half-bottle of whisky. After the inevitable banging and crashing we would rush upstairs to Mrs. Forsley-Carr shouting "get oot of meh room you ghastly man!" and Mr. C. on his fortnightly attempt at climbing into her bed.

Mrs. Forsley-Carr was a Scottish peer's daughter with a pert, nicotine-stained nose-tip. To add to her delightfully shabby appearance she invariably had faeces under her fingernails. She would smear Velouty de Dixor face-slap on every morning and dress up ready for going out. With a smouldering fag dangerously close to setting fire to a hat and veil fit for a royal wedding she would sneak out of the front door and spend the morning being led back and forth across the busy road by a league of gullible gentlemen. We would eventually spoil her game, lead her back inside under protest and triple lock the door.

"Be off with you, Nurse, blooming skivvies! You're only jealous I can attract these lovely gentlemen ..." she would say. Her vexation would escalate into a full-blown tantrum if she didn't get a large Sherry.

Next to Mrs. Forsley-Carr was a delightfully frail, gently-mannered sparrow, Mrs. de G. Among items showing her provenance was a family tree in a leather-bound volume dating from the Norman Conquest. One morning I took in her tea to find her standing in two inches of water.

"Is that my tea, Dear? My feet are rather cold, you know."

"It's because you are ankle deep in water Mrs. de G!"

I bellowed down the stairs for a member of staff to turn the electricity off before sploshing into her room.

Also new was ex-headmistress Barbara who had the distinction of being the only ordinary resident. We didn't have to go into La-la Speak with her. It is important not to patronise people who are on the edge of dementia or whose mind is elsewhere, but being bawled 'at one' by most of the residents took some getting used to. It was like being spoken to as though 'one' was a horse.

A delightful surprise one morning was the appearance of buxom, rosy-cheeked Denise, my Aussie Moll Flanders friend who had taken a job as cleaner. She and Jill were in the same flat in Earls Court, still discovering London. Denise's favourite penis picture was no longer by her bed. She hadn't seen her married theatre director boyfriend in Oz for a while and wasn't sure if she missed dressing up in just a pinny and red high-heeled shoes while cooking for him. Like a lot of us in London early in the 'Seventies she was trying to work out what being exploited actually was.

She was now angsting over her latest man friend and his suggested living arrangements as Jill was about to return to Australia. I met him briefly, a sleazy, older individual. He wanted Denise to move in with him and his wife and she could not get her head around being in a *ménage à trois*. How could a decent girl be sucked into a situation like this, I asked myself? I didn't have the answer. Telling her to walk away from it would probably only have added to the emotional confusion.

Of the two second-floor rooms reserved for detoxing alcoholics that had included Brendan Behan before his death in 1964, one had a lady who had become allergic to herself. She was the second most horrible individual I nursed in my career. Every word she uttered was spiteful and twisted, making it easy for me to imagine why her own body had revolted against her.

Her doctor was the Queen's homeopath Dr. Marjorie Blackie. Dr. Blackie's treatment protocol with regard to her patient's skin peeling off her body was a strict one. I had to put Hymosa tissue salt lotion on her face, Calendula cream on her body and serrated cabbage leaves on her buttocks. Several other homeopathic substances were administered at other times, along with Mogadon at night. The inclusion of a benzodiazepine, a chemical cosh was a surprise.

Matron had asked me to 'special' her which meant I was shut in with the devil almost eight hours a day. She did not, or could not stop her vituperative attacks on my personal appearance, my character, how bad a nurse I was and so on. Under such circumstances and still thinking at the age of twenty-six it was my duty to put up with such diatribes, I began dreading coming in to work. It was as though I had learnt nothing while passing through the NHS mill, Jordan and caring for people who had been grateful for far simpler treatment. I was not impressed with myself for not knowing how to deal with the trial of nursing this patient.

Fortunately, the woman soon had new baby skin on her face. Within two weeks the skin was renewed over her whole body. I have not seen an improvement like this with any other technique. Having my bubbly, innocent daughter down in the kitchen helped a lot in getting me through those two weeks.

When the harridan departed, a Jewish woman who had lost all her family in the gas chambers at Auschwitz took her room. There could not have been a greater contrast in personality, though this lovely lady would buzz us from the top floor constantly. I had long since returned to my pre-pregnancy weight by being busy and was now concerned I was getting too thin from climbing four flights of stairs often just to offer reassurance.

I found many older Jewish patients during the 'Sixties nervous and insecure. This was hardly surprising with a traumatic recent history and the shadow of the Holocaust still over them and what remained of their families. This woman was the only one in the Nursing Home to have a non-stop stream of visitors. It shows that if you are nice to people, people are nice to you. It's simple, really. As with Arabs, I was impressed with how close Jews are as a community when most of the other residents, aristocratic or not, had been abandoned.

One night when looking at my bills and thinking I needed more part-time work Dr. Hampson rang to ask if I was able to return to nursing some of her patients. She had one particular young mother in mind. I could oblige on my afternoons off from the Nursing Home providing I was able to bring Lilly with me. The client agreed.

Her name was Janey and she lived in a well-appointed house in South Kensington. She was a pale Jane Asher look-alike and a gentle, kind soul. Her baby girl was the same age as Lilly but was born with *hydrocephalus*. The excess fluid on the baby's brain was being drained via a permanent shunt into the spinal canal. Katie, the baby, also had strange red 'rubber-band' rings around her wrists and knees for an unknown reason. She made a non-stop nittering sound.

She was a sad little bundle compared with my bright and beautiful baby. It was an incongruous situation with me, a penniless single mum with a perfect little human being and this top-drawer couple who had gone through hell and high water to have a child, one to whom they could offer everything but who had serious physical and probably mental health problems.

Our meet-and-greet session was fine but on my second visit to baby-sit, Janey was in a terrible state. She confided her brother Tim was a schizophrenic. He had taken a taxi to Baker Street but couldn't pay the fare. The taxi driver became angry so Tim knocked on a nearby door and marched in ordering the bewildered house-holder to pay the fare. Her brother then believed he really lived in the house and was eventually taken into police custody. Janey's Godfather was an eminent judge and her husband was a City high-flier. There would be considerable embarrassment if the story came out.

I offered to have Katie at the weekend to give Janey and her husband a break. It was a heroic act on my part as I would have the tiny mite and Lilly in my small room. She kept us awake from Saturday night to Monday morning with her loud nittering. She wasn't uncomfortable or in pain, it was a neurological malfunction.

I did this twice more. The couple moved a year later and I hope their little girl made progress with the help available at the time. Janey made a great impression coping with grace under serious pressure. There was no self-pity or blaming of anyone. It is sometimes assumed that people who enjoy wealth show disdain or repugnance for something they don't like. Some do because they don't have to hold back or put on a false face. Janey was a good person.

Some of my private aristocratic patients were truly horrible, treating me and their servants like a lower species. I have never nursed a royal patient but understand they have their moments of rudeness with staff also. I used to think such people were a dying breed who would eventually come to terms with their rarefied world of privilege being on its last legs. If they did not change and begin treating staff with dignity and respect they would end up fending for themselves. Unfortunately, this sort of privilege will be around for a while. Even television soap celebrities will try and get away with poor behaviour until reminded tartly, perhaps by the popular Press, who they are or where they came from.

Some I nursed were so arrogant you could but laugh. One idiot thought I should leave the room backwards with my head bowed, as was customary with the monarch. I advised him if I walked backwards with his full commode and stumbled, its contents could end up over him. He didn't think it was funny, just that I was being impertinent.

Though not short of work now that Autumn, extra pennies were welcome. My health visitor happened to be an ex-prefect from my old school in Sheffield. I was grateful she began referring parents to me who needed evening child-minders.

The first baby I looked after was six-month old Harry. His parents were pleasant young hippies but the husband had a brief affair while his wife was pregnant. He contracted syphilis from the liaison and passed it unwittingly to his wife and unborn child. They were working hard in dealing with their problems. It was yet more evidence that the liberated lifestyle London offered could have unpleasant consequences.

Anna and I continued seeing each regularly. She and Kenny had moved to a greener, more relaxed Barnes and Lilly and I would take the bus down there. The way in which Anna reasoned gently with her cute little daughter was impressive. Both of us were aware of the loud threats and negative commands emanating from the mouths of many a young mother around us.

When I was working and even when not, Celia loved looking after Lilly. She had been kindness itself in encouraging us to stay in the flat, thereby absolving herself of the original trauma. She made Lilly a little oil cloth pinny and a mobile of glass beads on fine copper rods. Lilly was sitting on my knee in her cute brown cotton cardie and leggings and the pinny when Celia hung it on the mantelpiece. As the glass beads tinkled in a rose-scented breeze wafting in from the garden it was a magical moment for us both to hear my daughter's first peal of laughter.

In the six years I had known Celia she was still agonising over which side of the fence to jump. Bi-sexuality she could not handle. She had been serious with two boys at college. Rupert specialised in photography and was dressed as a Dandy at a party when I met him. Isidrè was visiting Cornwall in the Summer she worked in an ice-cream parlour on the sea front near where her parents lived. They had put on an exhibition of their daughter's work in the village.

Isidrè lived with us a short while in the Pimlico flat when I was pregnant and her relationship with him was more enduring. She had been to Barcelona and met 'fat Mama.' One of her biggest traumas was breaking off her relationship with him, when she realised her destiny was to love someone of her own sex.

He and I comforted each other over this and my own bombshell of becoming pregnant. She must have loved him because she appreciated he and I remaining platonic friends only. The last I heard, he had married and opened a language school in Terrassa in Spain.

Once Celia had got to grips with her sexuality it wasn't long before she fell in love with a colleague at one of the East End schools she taught in. This was Jan, an enormous Aussie English teacher who was cheery and strident and drank for Australia. She had a handsome face and thick shoulder-length hair. Soon Jan was marching into the flat in Fulham after school invariably devouring a yard-long *baguette* pasted with Vegemite. In her other hand would be a bottle of scrumpy. She looked like a bag lady in a long dark woollen skirt and dandruff-specked polo-neck jumper. Washing was not her thing.

Celia and Jan enjoyed a honeymoon night at the Hilton after which they made up one of the twin beds to shock whoever it was bringing them breakfast. Once the honeymoon was over Celia had to insist Jan bathe regularly and often had to push her into the bathroom.

"Oh, my God, Rose! You have to see this!" she shrieked one day.

Jan was squashed in our small bath. Boobs floated like two bald heads. In one hand was a whisky and in the other a cigar. Ash had fallen on her voluminous grey knickers and bra she had decided could be dealt with at the same time.

"G'dday Cobbers," she cackled, "care to join me?"

Non-smoker Celia drained the bath and showered the cigar and her friend clean.

These two ladies were soon planning to move to Australia but not before we had marched off to every film in a season of Jan's male film idol Humphrey Bogart. Bright and scathing, we did not contradict Jan too much as she could render most people stutteringly inept. When we were instructed to accompany her to a live appearance of her all-time heroine Marlene Dietrich we acquiesced.

This legend of stage and screen was amazing. At seventy-something, Dietrich tottered onto the stage in her famously tight pearl-coloured sheath dress looking like a thirty-year old. Prior to donning this priceless gown, she wriggled, it is said, into an even more punishing corset. It is also known she would pull tight sutured thread from either side of her head above her hair line to emphasise her high cheek-bones and make her skin taut. A long white mink coat over her shoulders and trailing behind her ensured a stunning entrance that evening, until she fell over backwards.

She was immediately lifted upright as if nothing had happened and proceeded to give one of the best stage performances I have ever seen. "Falling Off Stage Again ..." was supposedly the quip of the stage hands at this star's appearances when worse the wear from alcohol.

After the show Ms. Dietrich was driven slowly away from the stage door in a Rolls-Royce through a great crowd that broke into applause. As she passed with the window down she made eye contact, reached out and patted the back of my right hand. I had been graced with 'the look' and touched by a probably bi-sexual Goddess of the Twentieth Century! Jan was consumed with jealousy, the more because I was not even a committed fan. It was the only time I managed to stand my ground with her.

Lilly was the first baby in our clique and was spoiled a bit. To outsiders of an older generation it may have seemed the antithesis of good upbringing. I was also a captive audience to friends dropping in. Girlfriends with boyfriend troubles would trot around knowing they'd find a sympathetic ear. One of them, Michelle was a lonely friend of Celia's, a tiny French girl with a perfect figure who had guys galore after her. Some girls never find true love however gorgeous they are. Michelle was one of them.

There was one friend, Sarah in the top flat above us, who was perceived as being free of problems. In this respect she and my nursing *amigo* Anna were the two sanest girls of us all. Sarah would come down in the evenings to chat or baby-sit after returning from working on the restoration of George Harrison's pile, Friar Park at Henley-on-Thames. She reported that George was easy going and kind and very involved in the restoration of the Neo-Gothic folly he had saved from demolition. Sarah's mother was one of the few parents her daughter and us 'renegades' respected. She too was working on the restoration of Friar Park and this was cool.

It was something of a shock on return visits to Derbyshire seeing how comparatively complex our London friends were. From the late 1960s to the present my nursing friends in Sheffield remain reassuringly normal. Those of us who needed to escape did so for many reasons; the glamour and excitement of the big city, the creative or financial opportunities, the determination not to fall into the rut of peers and parents. It was always going to need courage since moving down to London did not guarantee a good job or place to live or happy-ever-after romance or even a caring-sharing partnership. The actual move was just the first part of the battle.

My grown-up daughters confirm today that tables turn. Many of their female friends around the world are now the careerists or bread-winners with their male partner remaining at home. One of Lilly's friends in Berlin in the late 1990s (both girls were high-fliers at the time) had to ask her husband how to change their child's nappy when she had a rare turn on domestic duties.

Life was not so straightforward for me at the end of 1972. I knew I would make myself ill again if I continued working full-time at night and looking after my toddler during the day. I had to quit the Nursing Home and after sitting in my agency for two hours with no work offered, fretting that my baby-sitter needed to be relieved, I went to the local DHSS office and signed on as unemployed. There was nothing on offer there either.

It was only in hindsight I saw that complications over the dollar and other currencies coming off the Gold Standard, the huge rise in the price of oil and ramifications of the Yom Kippur War would change forever the ease with which I could get work. The days of any of us being able to quit a job we didn't like on a Friday and start somewhere else on a Monday were over. This followed on from a real and ongoing hike in prices from the time of Lilly's birth in February 1971 with what many were calling the Great Decimalisation Scam. Just biting, from January 1973, was the sharp rise in the cost of food particularly, with Britain having joined the Common Market.

If I did catch up with sleep and was able to spend more time with my child, the slide towards serious money difficulties began. I would soon be unable to pay my rent and realised that my pay at the Nursing Home over a year had only enabled me to keep my head above water. I had a few pounds saved and Farid was still sending me a regular, small amount of money each week. In the days before charity shops, most of us collected Green Shield Stamps. It took a long time to fill a book but the occasional redemption for a useful 'gift' was welcome. I had a friend who worked nights in a petrol station. He sometimes gave me full books with pages of stamps from the same roll. "Don't ask," he would say.

I also had time to help my two older brothers with their business venture in double-glazed doors and windows. This was a new idea at the time and orders and enquiries were coming in steadily. They couldn't afford a receptionist at the site at Putney and asked if I could come each morning to man the 'phone. They offered a fiver travel money for the week. It was the least I could do as they had helped me many times since my arrival in London.

It also got me out of the flat. There was an Indian shop next to the yard and the owners' daughter was Lilly's age. At lunchtime when I finished I would take the girls to play in nearby Bishops Park at Putney Bridge, a lovely stretch of green by the river.

After several weeks of this, I got back to the flat one afternoon to find a DHSS inspector waiting outside for me. It had been noted I had been leaving the flat at the same time early each morning for weeks and he was aggressive in demanding my Benefit Book. When just on the edge of vagrancy it was too much and I burst into tears. When I explained I was helping my brothers and none of us considered it to be employment he handed the book back to me with a warning about taking cash work. He was surprised I knew nothing of the Family Income Supplement.

I don't know if his act was kindness or sympathy. He admitted it was the woman upstairs who had reported me. Angry though I was, I didn't inflame the situation by telling him her employment status as a prostitute should perhaps be checked. She could not have known I was receiving benefits unless she was in the system also.

It was an ugly example of the stress and indignity people on low income endure and it stayed with me through many of my subsequent campaigns from the 1980s for people having to live on various forms of benefit. It was ever clearer something radical was needed, even a move away from inner London as Anna and Kenny had managed for their child. I needed to find adequate work while having time to be a good mother, an acceptable mother.

Before Celia and Jan departed for Melbourne in Autumn 1972,

329

Celia and her friend Jo often took Lilly out for a drive in Jo's bright red 1940's sports car. He was a keen photographer and enjoyed photographing Lilly. One Friday evening I came in from work worn out after a week in a private clinic and frustrated that payment would not be in my bank until early the following week. I was about to drop onto the sofa when I noticed Celia glowering.

"You take the biscuit!" she rebuked. "Look ... just open your eyes, Rose ... how many years have I been training you?"

She pointed to the far wall to a poster of Lilly photographed in her pushchair on Hampstead Heath. It was a really nice picture and I was embarrassed.

"It's been there for days, girl. Jo and I hatched a surprise and you didn't even notice!"

As much as Celia had tried to make me see things with an artist's eye I remained myopic. I am an aural person, loving music, poetry and radio above all. It was a touching thing for them to do and I started to take care of the growing portfolio of pictures of Lilly.

There was more to this kindness. Celia had known Jo from school and I had known him for almost five years. He liked me, he confided to his art school friend, to the extent he wanted to marry me. He first spoke to Celia about this when I was heavily pregnant. He was so-named by his school pals after the tall, gentle blacksmith, Jo Gargery in Great Expectations. Kids have a knack of being spot-on in such things. Jo had the calmest and kindest nature of any man I had met. He was also very shy and this was his problem with me.

Lilly was now nearing two and needed a father, a kind and patient father figure. On our first formal date Jo took me to a swish restaurant on Brompton Road. In essence, he was a vintage car enthusiast, country boy, accountant and amateur photographer. High-living was not his thing and I was concerned how he would handle an evening in a classy eatery.

"Would *Monsieur* like a drink to start with?" Pierre asked.

"I'll have a cup of cocoa!" Jo responded at the late hour, looking at his watch.

His sweet nature and understated humour was an attractive trait. However, I was not in love with him. He knew this but was undaunted. He must have assessed his situation and the direction his life was moving in as earnestly as I did mine. It was highly unsatisfactory bringing up a child in a poky basement flat in a traffic-choked area where our only greenery for a constitutional was a cemetery. Having a child also made me realise London was a singles' town. I was now determined to set off on a path whereby my daughter could enjoy childhood in open spaces and sea breezes as I had in Cornwall and Derbyshire.

Lilly remained somewhat clingy to her main parent but did take to Jo. We set a wedding date for the day before her second birthday. Buying a house in Jo's home town of Gillingham in Kent, still plenty green in those days, was the next challenge. The situation for first-time buyers was as hard then as it has ever been.

Farid was predictably relieved with the news of my impending marriage and with Jo taking over his role. He was shortly returning to Bethlehem to marry his first cousin and to practise law. I knew he loved Madeleine. His Singaporean friend told him to go home for the last Summer of his studies and sort himself out regarding his relationships. He must have come to an agreement with his cousin then because he mentioned her frequently after this. We would never see him again, though there were dramas to come.

My other urban neighbours and eccentric friends, particularly the Pearlies, were ecstatic about the wedding. They had been invited to open a Gay restaurant in Brompton Road around the corner from our flat and Gracie, who insisted on organising my Hen Night, thought this would be a perfect reception venue.

"Special rates 'n all," she said, chuffed, "free! 'Ows that!"

How could a girl say no? I loved gays for their quick repartee and wicked humour.

Dressing up for the grand do in my Nicky Clark top and Biba skirt, I waited for Johnny and Gracie to pick me up from the flat. They had taken the trouble to don their full regalia, plumes and all that Gracie had to guide through doorways. Behind them was a slip of a girl who looked instantly familiar.

"This is Monica Rose from off the Hughie Green telly show, Rose. She's coming wiv us, tonight, int' ya Darlin'? We thought you two would like to chat!"

It was cute-faced Monica, a celebrity in the days when there were only three television channels and only one in colour. Millions tuned in to every programme on offer. She had come to fame on Hughie Green's Opportunity Knocks talent show as his Cockney sparrow 'sidekick.' The public took to her after she'd appeared on his show in a talent spot. He kept her on because her cheeky banter caused the programme's rating to soar.

My Hen Night is a surreal memory. The gay guys were euphoric and crazy, placing us at the top table in this *bijou* of a folk club and restaurant on the Old Brompton Road, The Troubadour. Pushy guests recognising Monica insisted on impromptu auditioning with corny renderings of I'll Walk with God, The Old Wooden Cross and anthemic Shirley Bassey numbers. As they sang their drunken hearts out, Johnny was stashing bottles of champagne around the £2 full-length fur coat I'd purchased from a Fulham Road junk shop for my wedding. The champagne was freebies but the kindness was there.

Returning home tipsy I found my new flat mate Julie in bed with my younger brother. When I passed through her room again later in the morning an even younger Jude Law look-alike with golden curls was in her bed. He was a sixth-form pupil of hers, my brother having been ejected in the early hours. Iskander's wife Nona had already referred to the rapacious Julie as a 'slot machine.' Julie however, saw herself as living the Free Love lifestyle.

She was the most sexually adventurous of our friends as well as being clearly irresistible. She had taken over Celia's place in our flat. Being a couple of years younger seems to have made a big difference in lack of inhibition and repression. She was bright company and easily likeable but a bit of a narcissist and not as thoughtful as Celia. She would often leave the flat in a chaotic state with the sink full of unwashed pots and pans for me to deal with.

I was now really warming up to leaving the Metropolis for a more regular life with my young daughter and sound-as-a-bell husband-to-be.

Chapter Twenty-three
#Into the Mystic ...# (Van Morrison)

Moving away from West London after six mind-detonating years became a statement of intent, a mission almost. Re-acquainting myself with my former Sheffield self was a pre-requisite for my adjusting to being a conventional housewife and mama my husband could be proud of. The £80 that management accountant Jo gave me to buy furnishings for our new house in Gillingham paid for a double mattress and linen. The remainder was wickedly spent on clothes for Lilly and me. Having survived on a low income for so long I couldn't resist splashing the cash on different priorities. Okay, so I had lessons to learn about budgeting. At least I had given Jo a wedding gift from my last pennies, a silk tie from a gentlemen's outfitter in Bond Street.

Our marriage ceremony commenced at the ghastly hour of ten o'clock on a February morning in 1973 at the Kensington and Chelsea Register Office. Considered to be the hippest joint in town in which to plight one's troth, many a celebrity and pop star had paused on the steps in a weird and wonderful outfit for photographs. In keeping with infamy this bride wore an intricately embroidered, ankle-length black Bedouin dress with red platform boots with the £2 fur coat resting on her tense shoulders.

Up to my marriage, every significant event from gaining Brownie, Guide and St. John badges, my first Confession and Holy Communion, passing the Eleven plus and six GCEs, to giving my first injection and passing Nursing Finals, selection as a UNA volunteer, delivering a new-born for the first time, to having lovely Lilly and finally going legal by getting married (even if after the event, so to speak) was my growing up. Suddenly I no longer felt a fraud or wondered when the Stasi would be requesting an interview.

My favourite older sister and two bleary-eyed brothers heroically turned up as the family. That was a good turnout for us. Our semi-detached parents maintained their tradition of not attending any of their offspring's weddings, even though they only lived a mile away from this one. Nona and Iskander came along with Nadia from Jordan now married to an Englishman. All arrived bright and early along with other London-based friends. Lastly, new flat mate Julie arrived with not one but three current lovers, my younger brother, her sixth-form pupil and her long-term boyfriend.

As the Registrar began, bewildered Lilly burst into tears howling "M-u-m-m-u-m-my." Nona took her outside so we could get the deed done. Afterwards, as it was still morning we'd arranged the wedding breakfast of bangers and mash and champagne back at the flat. Yet more bubbly was a gift from Naughty George whose brother ran an off-licence in Cheyne Walk and claimed to be Mick Jagger's chief supplier of booze.

Breakfast set up the crowd for the move to elder brother Morris's Bayswater flat for the afternoon reception and evening party. Before leaving I did a deft Elizabeth Hurley costume change into a more appropriate cream crepe dress. My ultra-smart sister Jane's expression on seeing my unconventional wedding attire was priceless. It was a last homage to London fashion wackiness. Rebellion must now give way to respectability.

Hubby Jo's redoubtable widowed and disabled mother Dora came up on her own by train from Gillingham where we would begin married life. Arriving in time for the afternoon do, his devoted mum put my parents to shame. It just wasn't the done thing for them to be openly demonstrative to, or about "one's encumbrances" as we often felt ourselves to be. I had long called it the Queen Mary Effect.

"Is one ready for one's tea, does one think?" Mrs. de G. at Quince House would enquire. Her father was a professional diplomat in India. Her generation of well-bred young things was brought up to serve Queen, Country and Empire. There was no place for "I." That was vulgar and inappropriate.

My Middle Class parents weren't far behind. They did their duty with not an inkling we might need to be made a fuss of occasionally, to prove we mattered. I did sometimes feel like an anorexic, though not over food, when I witnessed affection from other parents towards their offspring. It is pointless trying to reverse matters as I learned later as a flawed parent myself.

No one says it better I believe, than Phillip Larkin:

They fuck you up your mum and dad.
They may not mean to, but they do.
They fill you with the thoughts they had.
And add some extra just for you.

But they were fucked up in their turn,
It widens like a coastal shelf.
So get out while you can.
And don't have any kids yourself.

Thanks to my older siblings this day of celebration would be remembered. Jo wasn't at all fazed with meeting my eccentric family and cosmopolitan friends all at once. Nadia and her husband drove Jo and I back to the flat in Earl's Court in the early hours in their Mini. Memories of our erratic course down the Bayswater Road as if avoiding giant wine bottles and of me going cold knowing I was responsible for a small child makes me shudder today. The afterglow from being the centre of attention and receiver of good wishes and presents lingered for days. Weddings cost an average £20,000 in 2012. Ours was closer to twenty quid and I am happier with that.

Next morning I kissed goodbye to my home of almost three years, artist Celia's flat, with its many memories borne by genuine London 'Sixties and already slipping into nostalgia. We zoomed down to suburbia *en famille* in the red sports car with our presents, baggage, left-over booze and hangovers. Our half-empty Victorian house in Windmill Road, opposite the Medway Maritime Hospital was now, charmingly, home.

Dora lived around the corner. The wise woman was welcoming even though I had to be, with a child in tow, a loose woman. She won a scholarship to grammar school but her parents couldn't afford the uniform. Becoming a parlour maid in the 1930s and then a married woman was her lot in life. I could have received short shrift with this woman whose little artisan house was so clean I felt a slut every time she called around to mine.

The over-the-top 'cleanliness is next to Godliness' of her generation began stalking me immediately and still occasionally guilt-trips me today. It is a female neurosis. Even Germaine Greer reports she loves "a good clean-up" as stress therapy. My mother didn't have hang-ups about immaculate homemaking, even after having to get down-and-dirty when she lost her five servants to war service. She wasn't imbued with the 'spotless gene' as was Jo's mum along with many of the harassed mothers of my childhood friends. Their lives were defined by the extent of domestic prowess because they weren't allowed to go to work. My mother's ilk felt little need to do more than utilitarian dirt-busting. My generation, well ...

This was one occasion where being a nurse let me down. It placed extra expectations, that me and my immediate environment would be germ-free and spotless. I took some comfort in the knowledge that true aristocrats, many of whom I had nursed, were the least concerned. Cleaning was for servants and anything shiny was just frightfully *kitsch*. They were absolutely comfortable surrounded by faded grandeur, piles of it.

A consequence of this stalking was that when my defences were occasionally overwhelmed, poor Jo would come home to his fraught wife surrounded by the contents of the kitchen cupboards and drawers desperately emulating a Five-star Clean. The front room would be a temporary repository to be straightened as the place for unexpected visitors that must be kept pristine at all times. At the best of times gleaming mugs, pristine nets and sparkling windows were on an impressive 'to do' list.

"Did Mother pop in, by any chance?" he would ask politely grimacing, stepping through the fallout.

I also suffered twitches when visiting Jane who must have had my share of the clean gene. She was a Hyacinth Bouquet with knobs on. Equally trying was popping next door to see 'Lady,' as Lilly had nicknamed her.

Jo pitched in helpfully by buying a twin-tub washing machine, the "boon to women everywhere." The complexity of this boon almost defeated me in what to wash first at what temperature and so on. However much I steamed over this New Age cauldron, risking feeding my red hands into the lethal electric wringer, I could never match Lady's brilliant washing line of clothes pegged out with stunning precision. My husband today no longer remarks on tissues or lippy left in pockets (on the occasions I put stuff in the machine) but did break his silence when he found both his mobile phones rendered useless by a 60-degree wash.

To help with the little time New Man Jo and I spent together, bless his grey underpants, he would do the ironing on a Sunday night to be sure he had a pressed shirt for work. Off he would go First Class with City gents in their bowlers and pin-striped suits. He worked in London Transport's accounts and we enjoyed seriously good travel perks; free journeys to Kent's finest beaches in the summer, London's museums in the autumn, theatres over the winter and visits to family and friends in-between.

Mum-in-law was sweet enough never to comment on my eccentric home-making and became a good nanna to her step-granddaughter. Attitudes towards single mothers and couples living together changed rapidly from the end of the 1960s. We were there, paving the way.

Even when I had Lilly there were still euphemistically-named Care Homes for single mother in big cities. Magdalene Laundries were still going strong in Ireland. In these Catholic institutions run by Sisters of Mercy and other orders, single mothers were effectively enslaved, often for life. I believe their babies were taken away. Now there are centres where twelve- to sixteen-year olds, gymslip mothers, learn how to cope with their babies while continuing their education. They seem to be tougher but their "wotchoo lookin' at?" confidence is defensive not positive.

There wasn't much I was sure of on the domestic front but I muddled along, caring most of all about being an emotionally-bonding mother. Despite occasionally feeling confined, even trapped sometimes, I mostly enjoyed playing house. I am pleased to say that, despite all these pressures and lack of sleep, I survived my first year as a genetically hopeless housewife, determining that playing with the kids was preferable to having to pop Valium from failing to live up to a mother-in-law's spotless regime.

If I had conquered the tyranny of housework, that second *bête noir* of youthful married life, cooking and baking for my family, would be harder. Dora being a throwback to the time of Cora Cavewoman did all her own. Like the pinny-fronted mums all around she made proper gravy from pan juices, greens water and gravy browning. She could hold her own against those bastions of the WI who could bake a steak-and-kidney pie and perfect lemon meringue while potting jam and knitting toilet roll covers in their stride.

The pressure from 'Lady' was more subtle. Our sixty-something gem of a neighbour was, like Dora, a domestic paragon. She also daily fed kids angel cake and biscuits over her garden wall. It was only a matter of time before my kid asked why I didn't have nice biscuits and cakes like Lady.

Buying meat from plump butchers with five-o-clock shadow was daunting. Supermarkets and pre-packed meats didn't exist then. Their arrival has made the complexity of meat-buying a doddle and perhaps as a consequence its taste tasteless. The old-hand homemakers in the shop knew the lingo and weren't perturbed by the blood-splattered aprons and cleavers, sawdust and handling of meat and money together.

"A bit o' lean prime and piece of silverside, Sid ... two hearts, lights and a crown of lamb ... some faggots today, Ducks ..."

Too embarrassed to ask in front of a shop full of ladies about the various cuts, never mind how they should be cooked, I was the equivalent of the young guy coming out of the chemist with aspirin instead of condoms. Sausages, lamb's liver and chicken I recognised but even these staples occasionally became burnt offerings. Where was my mother when I needed her?

Once I had settled into a domestic routine I was able to take stock of my surroundings that make up the Medway towns, Gillingham, Chatham and Rochester. Whole streets around us were constructed for naval officers of all ranks when nearby Chatham Dockyard was a hub of military and naval activity, when Britain was a great maritime power. I took Lilly out every day and found it all very interesting. We were close to the Great Lines, the ridge overlooking Chatham and Gillingham along which are the remains of many forts constructed to protect the naval facilities at various times from the Spanish, Dutch and French.

At the top of the road is Chatham Hill. The most prominent building there, long derelict, was Jezreel's Tower. This was to be the headquarters of the New and Latter Day House of Israel, until James Jershom Jezreel perished after bursting a blood vessel in 1885. The sect and its many local businesses waned under the mismanagement of his widow known locally as Queen Esther. Esther rode around Gillingham in a fine coach while her flock who had given all their possessions to the church were expected to live in humility and poverty. Nothing new here regarding religious sects and charismatic leaders then. The incomplete castle with its eight towers was demolished in 1961. A Jubilee Clips works, weedy and padlocked occupies the site today. A mosque, two Sikh temples, a Temple of Light and Mormon church in the area keep the alternative religious theme going.

I liked living close by this piece of potty history. Jezreel planned a hydraulic rotunda within his headquarters which would slowly revolve and take him 30 feet up and down while he preached. A glass dome and electric lantern meant the message of the Flying Roll could be beamed to Essex. Long live Holy Rock-'n'-Roll and its rebel rousers!

Jo was kind in telling me to relax about trying to be an accredited *hausfrau*. He was thankful not to have married his mum, he said. As a boy he was not allowed to lie in bed beyond six am, for he was not going to be a slothful boy. Healthy, wealthy and wise perhaps but I was to observe over the years he and others brought up in this tradition were, strangely, ready for bed rather than partying by nine in the evening.

There is another beast young women battle constantly, hormone fluctuation. Our oestrogen/ progesterone ratios are difficult to measure and notoriously difficult to control. This has always left females open to misunderstanding, adverse judgement and violence, even execution as witches, I believe. This is a monthly battle I frequently lost, feeling wretched as a witch.

Men are fortunate in their testosterone level remaining constant into their later years. This is probably why they can find it very difficult to fathom and sympathise with a woman's more unpredictable emotional reactions, particularly to seemingly trivial issues. The PMT syndrome wasn't defined and explained until the 'Eighties thanks to the pioneering work of Dr. Katrina Dalton. Before then mood swings were judged as psychiatric in origin and a sign of mental instability. It can never have helped that lunar cycles are of approximately the same duration. I don't believe an actual link has ever been proven between women's periods and lunacy.

It isn't helpful for women with PMT issues to be demeaned. Adverse comment on a person's hormonal state shows lack of judgement. Only very occasionally will a man understand the circumstances and be kind and loving even if it keeps him on his toes. In the early '90s when a BSE (Bovine Spongiform Encephalopathy) and CJD (Creutzfeldt-Jakob Disease) link was of real concern to health officials I was sad to overhear a lorry driver refer to his wife as suffering regularly from "that there Mad Cow Disease."

Is it a female thing I often wondered, regular weepiness and flying off the handle (no link intended to witches)? In some cultures males emote or weep as freely as the 'weaker sex' do and it is not regarded as a weakness. I would say it is preferable to the repression the stiff upper lip approach can harbour. Men are uncomfortable in the company of a woman or women who are clearly upset. They don't know how to handle it and the woman will often only be waiting for him to get a grip on the situation, to show some understanding, even tenderness.

I wish I had known about these things. It would have given me an insight into how my monthly cycles were affecting my behaviour. I would have endeavoured to be less self-critical and more patient with myself and others even if my own invisible demons were giving me hell. It was fortunate Jo and I were good friends and his dry wit was a tonic.

"If you don't stop arguing," he mused at one of my PMT rantings early in our marriage, "I'll throw myself off the back step!"

It was inevitable by the summer of 1973, with a hospital opposite the house, I would be planning a return to work, even though eight-hour shifts can be tough. Being a wife and mother is already hard, twenty-four hours, seven days a week. Discipline, resignation and devotion to the task in hand may have helped mothers and grandmothers before us when they were coping with multiple children without gizmos and disposable nappies. It may be we are more able to talk about difficulties, there is more support from women of our own age and more professional help. We also have many more 'boons' than our forebears could have dreamt of.

Jo was working hard too, out of the house from six in the morning to seven in the evening, five days a week commuting from Medway to London Victoria. With Celia in Australia, Auburn Anna on the far side of London and Nadia in Brighton I didn't have friends to call on. We did ring each other but girls didn't spend hours on the 'phone then as we might do today because it was expensive.

The solution to this, to Lilly needing playmates and to a bit more money coming in lay across the road. The hospital had a new well-equipped, well-staffed nursery. I could also see lovely grounds and a staff swimming pool from our front bedroom. The problem was I had been out of the NHS loop since 1967 apart from occasional agency postings. I longed to get back to bedside nursing, basic, simple nursing making sure patients in my care felt their well-being mattered to the best of the Health Service's ability.

Three months into married life I went for an interview. The gap was not considered to be a problem and I was employed to start three nights a week with Lilly attending the nursery during the day.

Discovering that I was pregnant around this time was great news for us both, though timing could have been better. The week before I was due to commence work Jo, Lilly and I went up to London to look after my mother's flat in Bayswater so she could have a little holiday.

On our first night in London we enjoyed a pleasant dinner with my brothers Morris and Pascal and cousin Connor and his Chilean fiancée. They drank a toast to our happy news but I woke in agony in the middle of the night and passed a tiny foetus. I wrapped the miniscule twelve-week form in tissue paper and rang the local A & E at St. Mary's, Paddington. They advised me to come in. I told Jo what had happened and that a cab would take me to the hospital. Although I was now bleeding heavily, I assured him I would be fine and he must stay with Lilly.

Whilst lying in A & E with excruciating uterine cramps I could have done without the houseman giving me the third degree about the reasons for my miscarrying. It was upsetting, until I remembered there were many prostitutes in the area and it was probably a routine event for him. Once vetted, I was admitted for a D and C (dilation and curettage) later that morning to clear away retained placenta.

I wasn't devastated to have miscarried because the month before I had been in contact with a neighbour's child who was blind and deaf from her mother having contracted rubella. This, German Measles, is a highly contagious viral disease that can have terrible consequences if contracted during pregnancy. I gave the child a cuddle not knowing I was pregnant and she had rubella. My new GP took a blood test. Ironically this came back as negative the day before I aborted. Perhaps nature knew best, nevertheless.

What I hadn't anticipated on returning to Mother's flat the next day was how weak I would be. It was a worrying situation because Jo had an important audit job at work and couldn't take time off. I rang Auburn Anna to ask if Lilly and I could stay with her in Barnes for a couple of days.

Normally, I am stoic about such things. This time it was a real struggle getting me, my child and a bag across London. I don't know if it was my hormones going into shock, or the anaesthetic. I had managed to postpone my night duty and was grateful for the help from Anna and Kenny. Within days I had regained my strength and was ready for my return to Gillingham and night duty.

Deputy Senior Night Sister Ward was a small, handsome woman with a kind face and Malteser-brown eyes. Medway Hospital's uniform was a deep crimson woollen dress with a white ruff-collar.

"There'll be no problems with you, my Dear!" she said glowing. "I trained at The Royal myself!"

Sister Ward's kind words about my *alma mater* were touching. So much had transpired since my commencing nursing proper I was beginning to remember my training as a cakewalk compared with what nursing had thrown at me since. The battle-axes had done me proud by making me a 'good enough' nurse. Deputy Night Sister took me on a grand tour and introduced me to the staff nurse I would be seconded to that night. Starting in D1, the orthopaedic side, the following night would "ease me in."

Sister Ward didn't tell me my second night would be with the boss, Senior Night Sister Dodd. She was a stiff-backed automaton with a dry humour. "Never receive blood other than your own, my Dear. You don't know where it's been!" was a typical piece of advice. She generally spoke in imperatives and could be highly critical of her bosses. Here was a senior nurse who was a law unto herself and difficult to connect with and a twinge of the discomfort of my early days advised me I needed to concentrate on what I was doing.

Unfortunately, on my second night I boobed.

D1 ward was a modern T-shaped block with a ten-bedded men's ward at the top of the 'T.' There were smaller rooms off the longer corridor. When I arrived that evening, before meeting Senior Night Sister, Day Staff rushed me around the ward introducing me to the patients. When we had finished with the patients in the single rooms the staff nurse said in a hushed voice that the last was a prisoner who was scheduled to return to his Open Prison the next morning.

I have always preferred nursing male patients. They behave well, they don't beat themselves up with anxiety or worry as female patients can do. That night most of them in D1 were very up-beat as well. It felt good being back in the NHS with the thought that times were changing, that things were definitely more relaxed than when I was a Green Girl a decade earlier.

As I took the medicines around, the guys in the ten-bedder were very cheerful indeed and showed me bottles of booze they were hiding from "Dragon Dodd." They asked if I minded them having a quiet 'party' later for the 'con' as he was leaving in the morning. How much more chilled the NHS had become since my training days I thought, grinning. They saw Nurse Greenhorn coming.

I was soon busy on my rounds and it was not until my supper break in the early hours when all had gone quiet on D1 that I began ticking off my list of patients. My heart sank when I reached the single rooms. On my very first night in charge a patient, the convict, had done a runner.

Within minutes my auxiliary and I had scoured the wards, staircases and windows. We got the porters looking around outside. I had only just missed him because the fire escape door was open. Sister Dodd was up in the lash of a whip and I braced myself for her tongue.

"Serves them right, Staff!" she said affably. "The Prison Service refused to supply a twenty-four hour guard. What did they think a nurse would be able to do if he wanted to abscond? They will be here in a minute and if they throw a tantrum, have none of it. I understand he was in an Open Prison anyway because he steals television sets. Well, bully for him!"

I could have kissed the Dragon. The bit of sniggering around the darkened ward ceased when two prison officers and a policeman arrived and poked around the empty single room. When I was about to set off home that morning they were openly laughing about the incident.

"We knew straight away you was a Green One, Nursie! Sorry! We wanted to do a little party an give 'im a good send off!"

I told them they were very naughty boys and I would be watching them.

My second night on the ward was to become a real test of my nursing skills. An elderly lady had been admitted for an unknown cause of pyrexia. Her temperature becoming worryingly high. Antibiotics hadn't been prescribed because the consultant wanted to see laboratory culture results first so he could determine the best antibiotic for her.

I wasn't convinced the patient would survive a three-day wait for the culture results but who was I to question this new way of treating infections? I moved her into a side ward in case she was contagious or was developing septicaemia and asked my student nurse to special

343

her and take half-hourly temperatures. The patient became increasingly delirious in the early hours despite our tepid sponging and a bedside fan. I spoke to Night Sister Dodd on her rounds about my concern and said the houseman had so far not responded to my calls.

"Very good, Staff. Try him again. I'll leave it in your capable hands."

The houseman eventually decided it wasn't necessary for him to come up to the ward. I made a note and suggested to Day Staff first thing that this patient needed urgent attention. They said the consultant would be in within the hour and I should not worry any more about it.

I had four days off and was not on that ward again for a couple of weeks. By then I had forgotten about the patient.

The night staff at the Medway were a friendly, hard-working bunch and good to work with. The auxiliaries too were the heroic hard-working mothers and grandmothers I had come to know who would slog away at night getting by on little sleep in the daylight hours because of other important things. There was no us and them culture here.

Because the hospital was the main A & E hospital for the Medway Towns it was often extremely busy. Sometimes it felt as if the non-stop banter between staff members was the only thing preventing us from sinking to our knees. On a couple of occasions I had to sit while going through my night report with Day Staff because I knew my legs would buckle if I didn't.

One night, Hilary, our very proper young Night Sister with whom I shared many a laugh in adverse moments came to do her round and took a moment to tell me about an incident in A & E the week before. The 'phone had rung several times during the evening but whoever it was ringing said nothing. Finally a young woman asked if it was alright to bring her husband in because he had something "stuck up his bum."

He came in with a blanket around him supported by his wife, Hilary said. He had a distinctly bow-legged gait and there was a whirring sound coming from under the blanket. It was all the more obvious because the ward was very quiet that night. Staff put the couple into a cubicle to await the doctor.

344

The husband had asked his wife to insert an active vibrator into his lubricated rear end. Sod's Law meant she pushed it too far and lost it. The casualty doctor attempted to retrieve it and described it as like trying to dislodge a rat by its tail determined to get further up a drainpipe. It had to be removed surgically with the unfortunate man's predicament ensuring heads turned all the way to Theatre. The exhausted vibrator was returned to the ward along with the embarrassed patient. Exhibit A disappeared within minutes of Day Staff coming on duty Hilary said. With that incident, she had seen it all.

The story was retold during our break and a male nurse said he had been helping a drunken lady brought in from sheltered accommodation back into bed when he couldn't believe seeing the bottom of a milk bottle poking from her rectum. She told him smartly to leave it alone because it kept her warm. Another nurse said they removed a milk bottle from a woman's vagina while she was under anaesthetic for a different procedure. They got a mouthful from the woman afterwards about minding their own business!

One of the auxiliaries chipped in that the matron of the Nursing Home her old dad was in rang her up indignantly one day requesting she make arrangements for her father to be moved because he had Venereal Disease. Matron admitted he had caught it from one of the cleaners who had been selling her favours for fifty pence a go. At ten bob, as they would have known it in those days, that was cheap! The auxiliary stood her ground, she said proudly and insisted it was the cleaner that had to go.

Regarding sex having no upper age limit I remembered nursing a lovely old chap of ninety-two who had been a guard, he told me, on the Duke of Windsor's bedroom door out in India. Every night the same cry from the old chap would resound around the Nursing Home, "quick! I'm coming now, Bertha, Love ..."

I wasn't sure what it was all about but his fellow patients said he seemed to be enjoying himself, one way or another.

One November afternoon in 1973 after I had been working at the hospital six months, there was a knock on our door in Windmill Road. A very polite young man said he was a solicitor and there was a management meeting going on at the hospital to which I might be able to contribute. Curious, I agreed to accompany him. I left Lilly with Lady. The meeting was about the elderly woman patient on my second night on duty admitted with a very high temperature. She had died that day and the solicitors were acting on behalf of her family.

Circumstances like these are every nurse and doctors' nightmare and I was anxious even though it was an informal meeting. A member of management asked if I recalled that night. I remembered it well, I said. My ward report along with temperature charts and other notes were on the table. My presence was simply to verify that the paperwork was mine and that nothing was missing. The matter would be going to tribunal.

The case for medical negligence, fortunately not directed at me, was held at All Saint's Hospital in Chatham a couple of weeks later. I took the stand in the boardroom which had been laid out like a court room. The first questions were how long had I worked at the Medway Hospital, how long had I been there at the time of the incident and in response to my answer of two days, had I received any induction or training?

My actions, including the half-hourly temperature observations and attempt at getting the houseman to come up to the ward were praised. This was commended in the light of my being unfamiliar with hospital policy and practices. I breathed a huge sigh of relief. The outcome was that the consultant was found negligent, along with other staff for not prescribing antibiotics after admission and for not addressing Staff Nurse MacFarlane's concerns about the patient while she was on the ward.

It was a sharp reminder of the need to keep immaculate records, charts and notes at all times, no matter how tired you might be. Lives can be at risk. It bolstered my confidence once again and made me pleased that my training had not let me down even after an absence of some years from NHS practices.

Chapter Twenty-four
#Working at the Coal Face ...# (Men of the Deeps)

Our tutor at The Royal did not let us forget we are entrusted with the most intimate aspects of people's lives. The need for hospital treatment is worrying for patients and relatives. Patients are vulnerable and tolerance and open-mindedness is essential.

There was occasional light relief on the ward. Nursing and humour, even black humour are inextricably linked as it helps in coping with the more difficult aspects of the job. My new best friend at Medway, an auxiliary named Bernice was certainly one to have a laugh with. She was from the Emerald Isle, blessed with a soft Irish face and voice and a figure like a little Sophia Loren. Male patients were always eyeing her up, if not chatting her up.

Both of us were on Women's Surgical through the Autumn of 1973. We were as busy as ever at night, particularly on a list day. The two- and six-bedded bays in the ward would be full with post-ops' hooked up to drips, drains and catheters. There was non-stop observation of patients' temperature, blood pressure and pulse and checking for pain, potential shock, haemorrhage and infection. We had patients undergoing treatment and in recovery and new admissions with anything from a head injury to appendicitis. My student nurse or auxiliary would look after new admissions and I would do spot checks as often as possible.

One night in December will be remembered by Bernice and I as Mad Night. On top of what I have described four women needed preparing for emergency operations. We had thirteen intravenous infusion drips and two blood transfusions when six would have been work enough. Ensuring each patient had the correct infusion with the correct dosage of drugs was a head-aching task. IV Drips were tricky in the 'Seventies without today's clever monitoring machines. Being the only nurse on the ward that night qualified to deal with them I felt like a Drip Conductor from a manic episode of On the Buses.

Infusion orders are written up by the medics for the solution to reach the patient's arm vein at a specific rate. Rehydration is a complex calculation relating to body chemistry. A patient's drip arm is inspected regularly to make sure it isn't inflamed and susceptible to bacteria and infection. Drips can also pack up or start racing as you turn your back. If a drip runs too fast it can drown a patient's lungs. If they run through completely they are hard to re-start and a dreaded air bubble, an *embolus,* could reach the vein. That night it was like tinkering with fifteen dripping taps endeavouring to get them exactly right.

Two of my patients were keen to help. They watched every drop from fluid bag to drip chamber when they should have been resting. Most people loved television hospital dramas in those days. The new ones were M*A*S*H if you weren't squeamish and General Hospital, a twice-weekly daytime soap. This was like Emergency – Ward 10 that everyone had grown up with.

"They didn't do it like that on Dr. Kildare, Nurse. I mean, the bloke died didn't he? 'Cos the nurse put the wrong drip up and his kidneys failed because it weren't checked properly!"

"Thank you, Mister Smith. Yours is spot-on."

"It is O-positive in the bottle, Nurse? I've got pain round me kidneys. And that guy opposite, his drip's got lots of bubbles in it ..."

"Yes, Mister Jones. Everything is correct and running properly and you're not due your pain medication just yet."

Post-op' patients are likely to be in pain and we had to be on top of that. Narcotics take an age to check and administer. All opiates and sleep or relaxation medications were kept in a double-locked drug cupboard. Items could only be checked out by a nurse or doctor with one other nurse or auxiliary present. Usage of all medicines was entered in legal records and on a patient's prescription sheet and signed for.

On Mad Night we also had two confused ladies shouting their heads off. The other patients on the ward were soon fed up and we wheeled the ladies to the nurses' station to keep a stricter watch on them. Such patients are easily roused by events around them from a telephone ringing to a porter rushing a trolley down the corridor. The arousal can be anything from singing and ranting to outright violence.

To complete the night a twenty-stone-plus man with the worst case of diarrhoea I can recall was wheeled in. The male ward was full and we had to place him in a bed screened off from the other women. I wasn't happy because we didn't know how contagious he was and mixed-sex wards are unacceptable in situations like this one.

Neither Bernice nor I managed a break and by five o'clock that morning we were close to collapse. I began my complex night report while trying to keep the deranged ladies from falling over their fragile cot sides. Bernice had to clean up the new admission again on her own.

"Nurse, nurse ..." he was hissing, "I has had an accident, I've shit myself, again ..."

Greatly overweight patients are a problem because of the strain on your back. Goodness knows how nurses cope today when people are on average considerably heavier than in 1973. Bernice, as small as an Irish Pixie, had gone beyond the call of duty with this man even in just rolling him over to change sheet and draw-sheet on which he was lying in his own *excreta*.

"That's it, Rose," she snapped eventually, grabbing the cup of coffee I made for her. "That was gross, gross, gross. I'm handing in my notice today, if I don't die of exhaustion first ..."

"What's up?" I asked innocently. "We're not being fattist, are we?"

"No, Rose, not that way gross. He groped me while I was cleaning him then said I should do myself a favour and go out with him!"

"It's just diarrhoea! Perhaps you should be flatulent-ed ..."

We began to cry with laughter at how tired we were just as one of the fighting ladies started up again.

"Send me some nice blue cabbages, Dear ... twenty-two ... SHUT UP, BLOOMING THINGS! Lah-di-lah-di-lah ..."

The other responded with an excruciatingly tuneless Silent Night and we finally had to call for a porter and the houseman. He gave the most animated patient an injection that put her out cold. Her combatant went to sleep with an angelic smile on her face. When at last we signed off I was almost too tired to crawl the few hundred yards home. Bernice gave me a lift. Then I was worried she would fall asleep at the wheel on her way to nearby Rainham.

She didn't and we were back on the ward again that night, mercifully a quieter one.

Early in 1974 after a long period of three nights a week on medical, surgical or orthopaedic wards at Medway Hospital, I was sent to ICU (Intensive Care Unit).

Working in ICU requires a different mind-set from general nursing. It feels like a meld of church and sci-fi set when you walk in the first time, eerily quiet with a click-click of ventilators and beeping of various monitors. The lighting can cast an ethereal green sheen around the walls. Dim tungsten bedside lights make the patients look more sickly than they are. Large curtainless black windows add the final touch to a Last Hope Saloon look. What it needed was Hilda Ogden's flying ducks up the wall and some soft music. I understand the need for plenty of light but it vies with that all-important rest at a critical time.

Staff communicate in hushed tones and often I couldn't wait for a break from the claustrophobia. ICU units didn't exist during my training years so I was learning on the job. Observation was continuous. Drug regimes, charts and reports are more complex and my brain ached from reading and analysing lab reports and case notes. It was especially hard to sustain at night. ICU folk were known to go a bit queer, start twitching, take on a haunted look and age quickly!

The plus side was an extraordinary variety of cases that my grey matter responded well to. Learning is ongoing in such a unit, even for senior staff. Patients here will be in a critical state from a wide range of trauma including serious physical damage and major organ failure. The brightest nurses and medics are attracted to these complex and sometimes puzzling cases that need to be assessed, diagnosed and treated quickly. There is no room for error.

On the wards you saunter in with cloak and shoulder bag containing snacks, knitting or sewing maybe and a couple of magazines. You might be rushing around a twenty- to thirty-bed area dividing your time between poorly and recovering patients. You might be lucky and have a quiet night. Wards are familiar territory and there is none of the daytime hospital cut and thrust.

ICU Night Sister, Sister Mason thrived on the pressure and satisfaction. On a high-octane night, anaesthetists, consultants and registrars could be buzzing in and out relying on everyone being up to speed. A complex lab result in the right pigeonhole, a peritoneal kidney dialysis machine in its right place and everything needed for open heart massage within minutes of the request, were typical of what was expected. I was regularly left in charge when Sister was on breaks knowing, with my three-day week regime and relatively tender age, I was not experienced enough to take full responsibility.

There will always be downer moments in ICU, Sister Mason said and the feeling you could have been more sympathetic or done more to ease a person's suffering. There would be days hijacked by gremlins, hissy-fits, lab result mix-ups, lost notes and misplaced X-Rays.

Sometimes we have to accept the day, warts and all she said, knowing we did our bloody best. Tomorrow will be a better one.

A skeleton night staff on the wards is bad enough. For the nurse in charge of ICU it can be seriously stressful. Staff she can call on might not have ICU experience. It's a matter of keeping all the balls up in the air all night long. In my first week I did not expect a burst aneurism spattering the doctor and wall behind him bright red, a patient with end-stage liver failure and the remaining staff running to a patient going into cardiac arrest all at the same time. Along with the heavy work load, patient turnover is high. They perish, or they stabilise and are moved onto the wards.

On many occasions, Bernice who was frequently with me in ICU was too tired to laugh as she drove me home. Always I was worried about her making it back to Rainham and got to thinking that, like most night staff with families, we should be more aware of burning the candle at both ends. It did nobody any good.

On one particularly busy night similar to Mad Night on Women's Surgical in December, I put my head in the cubicle where she was monitoring a patient badly injured in a car crash. She was so tired at four that morning she looked like a zombie. She was about to take her patient's blood pressure once again when I stepped in and put my arm around her.

"Bernice, Hon," I whispered, "your patient has died. Sister will be back from her break in a minute. Tell her you would really appreciate a short break. You did your best and he wasn't expected to live."

I couldn't take over her charges as I had my own deceased patient I was in the process of laying out.

The after-effect of being cool and controlled at work was that my mind began seeking solace elsewhere, usually in dreams and it left me feeling like a skinned rat on waking. I started to experience some anxiety at getting back to work after my four days off each week.

I had a friend years later who loved her work as a hospice Nursing Sister. She and her colleagues are known as 'deathniks.' She seemed not the slightest bit affected by a one hundred per cent death rate in the patients under her care. The work was too depressing for me. Cancer wards are also a sombre experience. Not all medical personnel handle these disciplines well.

Were the Victorians more in tune with their departed loved ones

351

in keeping them at home before burial? Lisa Presley spoke of the calming effect of being able to talk to her late father Elvis, as he lay in his coffin. She said it was "strangely comforting." Paul Burrell also wrote of praying at night by the late Princess Diana's casket because he did not want her to be alone. Most would be unnerved nowadays at the thought of keeping a relative at home until the funeral.

That a patient might die on a dimly-lit ward without our noticing, as had happened to Ellie Kane in our student block when Sister Bubbles accused her of being a murderer, was every student nurse's nightmare. Some nurses admitted to using a small mirror to see if a patient is actually breathing. It is a time-honoured way of checking there is life in a patient and you hoped the patient didn't wake up and wonder 'what the bloody hell' you were doing.

One shambolic nurse and her antique auxiliary at The Royal were said to have wheeled a cold, stiffening corpse into the bathroom on a Women's Geriatric ward at dawn. She had died at the beginning of their shift and they didn't know because they had forgotten about her in a side room. They were hoping after a hot bath Night Sister and the houseman would think she had only just passed away. Hospital legends, like urban legends are probably based on real incidents.

Not every dying patient has a relative or loved-one present. However, it is a solemn duty to endeavour to advise next-of-kin that a relative is in a critical state and you hope you are not ringing the 'wrong' kin at home or work. On the night on ICU when two patients died Night Sister made the important calls. This is not a job for part-timers or juniors.

Last Offices is an exacting process and I half hoped Mrs. Mac and Martha from Pye-Smith Ward in my student days would appear and guide me through my first death as Nurse Newbie-in-Charge on a Medway ward. Night staff are duty-bound to finish laying out anyone who has died before the day staff come on duty. All newly-deceased patients must then be left alone for an hour so their soul may depart. It was hoped the entire process would be complete by the end of the shift.

Once the soul had hopefully winged its way like Tinker Bell's shadow to eternal rest, we bathed the body and shaved a gentleman's face if necessary. We finished by tying the gentleman's penis with a piece of bandage in a neat bow to prevent leakage. The hospital issue plastic shroud is then placed over the corpse should there be a need for a post-mortem. Bagged and tagged the corpse would be wheeled over to Rose Cottage by the Porters' Lodge. An inventory of the deceased's belongings had to be ready for the relatives to take away after the issuing of the Death Certificate.

It was still common in the 1960s for older citizens to keep a starched white shroud and two pennies in neatly stitched covers to place on the deceased's eye-lids to keep them closed. Doing it properly meant there would be a set each for husband and wife in the bottom drawer where the bride's trousseau had been kept. Some relatives brought bereavement clothes for their loved ones to be buried in.

When a patient will actually die is never easy to ascertain. It can be very important where a Rabbi or Imam, or priest or pastor needs to be called for last rites or prayer. Comforting a dying person when no relative or loved one is present is as deeply moving as is birth. Where relatives are present the stress or shock can evoke surprising reactions, including violence.

Some relatives were remarkably stoic, even humorous and a help to us. Some very sick patients too, especially children were an inspiration in the way they were dealing with their demise. It took a while for me to get used to life and death situations throughout my working day.

Today, some amazing recoveries occur because of skilled medical staff and hi-tech equipment. Not all patients are grateful, however. One elderly man admitted to Medway ICU had stabbed himself with two large kitchen knives. He was resuscitated and his first words to me on regaining consciousness were that if he had wanted to live he wouldn't have stuck a pair of knives in himself. There is no ready answer to a patient in this state.

Other awful nights include that in which a young woman named Sadie was brought in from a motorway pile-up in which her husband and mother-in-law were killed. Only Sadie and her little boy survived. The bewildered but otherwise unhurt child was taken to the children's ward. Sadie sustained a head trauma and for three months was not aware she was moaning her husband's name K-e-i-t-h constantly, except when asleep.

She had probably screamed his name at the moment of the accident and it was as if her brain had stuck there. For the staff in ICU and the ward she was transferred to this cry became a nightmare because there was almost nothing we could do to ease her mental state. A singer friend of my daughter terms it Head FM when she can't get rid of a tune in her head. Sadie's was the worst case any of us had experienced.

It was equally sad she become a compulsive masturbator during the weeks she was semi-conscious. We kept her in a side ward and had to warn doctors and visitors that it was not total inhibition. She was still very poorly. Dealing with her grief while recovering was another challenge. She would talk non-stop and there was little we could do or say in her despairing moments. She became like a recalcitrant teenager with mood swings from really sweet to difficult.

Her little boy was sent home with his maternal grandmother. Sadie went home for weekends until she was fully fit. I hope this likeable young woman managed to re-invent her life for herself and her child. I was learning to drive at the time, though not in a Jaguar, of course. Sadie's tragedy and having to attend to other road traffic accident victims finally put me off driving.

Another ICU patient, the memory of whom stays with me also was a young woman called Jenny. She had endured a year of repeated resection surgery on her colon for Crohn's Disease. I had nursed her several times on Women's Surgical and always admired her courage after surgery. Crohn's Disease is a venally debilitating condition that in serious cases is like unrelenting food poisoning. High doses of steroids are often prescribed in the form of enemas, along with strong sulphur-based drugs. Patients become pale, anaemic and thin.

It isn't surprising that young people with chronic diseases become world-weary before their time because they are often too ill to enjoy a normal social life. Self-image problems also feature where they have long been too weak to enjoy the high-energy vitality of youth.

On this occasion in ICU Jenny was intubated and in a ventilator, having relapsed in theatre. She was still under the effects of anaesthetic and the antidote and could not be sedated and must have felt as though she was drowning. She was alert but unable to speak or move while her lungs were being pumped. The look of terror in her eyes was deeply upsetting. How could this have happened? It didn't take Night Sister a moment to realise I was probably too involved. Her look and response was a neutral but telling reminder of the First Commandment of Nursing "thou shalt not ..."

Several thoughts came into my head that I could have done without that night; ICU staff could become too detached and are more interested in the grey matter aspect of care than bread-and-butter nursing; anaesthetists chose the discipline because patients didn't answer back; plastic surgeons liked the money; the more extrovert surgeons referred to themselves as high-class butchers.

Returning to Jenny's bedside I said "Sweetie, blink your eyes twice to answer 'yes' and once to answer 'no.'"

I asked her if she was frightened and she blinked twice. She also blinked twice to confirm she was cold and in pain. I explained she had a lot of anaesthetic in her and it was too risky to sedate her until a little later and she would have to tough that one out. Hot water bottles aren't permitted in hospital, I said but I would find an electric heat pad. I did this and in every spare moment through yet another busy night I held her hand and talked to her until I went off-duty. She died later that morning.

Bedside nurses today are encouraged to undertake terminal care courses outside hospices because you can never stop learning how to care for the patient. Dame Cicely Saunders began her lifelong campaign to radicalise terminal care in the latter half of the 20th Century with the aim being the terminally ill should be alert and pain-free and retain their dignity to the end. Almost forty years on since my time at Medway I believe the medical profession still has a long way to go before every doctor, nurse and carer in the UK is a proficient terminal care practitioner.

On another Wooden Spoon Award night at Medway, the senior Night Sister asked me to special a girl of seven with meningitis in ICU's side-room. The GP had missed the early signs, a rash on her lower limbs. She was now unconscious and in crisis. Her consultant said the early hours were the latest she might "turn the corner." Concentrating our efforts on nursing this very sick little girl helped stop thinking the unthinkable. I had first contact with her on admission without knowing what she was suffering from and the danger I was now in.

It was about three in the morning when her parents requested she be christened as a form of last rites. The impromptu service at which our Anglican vicar sprinkled water on the child's forehead was almost unbearably sad but his belief that such ritual can lead to miraculous healing gave some comfort to the parents. When he had gone I was unsure of what to do with the water. It wasn't Holy Water the Catholic Church specified should be returned to the earth. Priests have a basin that leads out to the garden specifically for the washing of hands after baptism and for the disposal of Holy Water. The water used that morning had been consecrated so I waited for the automaton of a Night Sister's round to ask her advice.

"Oh, throw it away, Dear. It might be contaminated!"

She may have been correct as Holy Water in churches has been proved to carry bacteria but she could have shown a little empathy towards the importance of the christening to the family.

The girl's paediatric consultant prescribed antibiotics for Lilly and me as a preventive measure against meningitis developing. I gave Lilly her first dose when I got home before taking her over to the hospital nursery she now loved. Sally in charge had become "Auntie Tally" and when I wasn't about, Lilly would hang on to Sally's skirt. She had also befriended a tiny tearaway called Sonny. His mum Greta became a good friend as she was a Nursery Nurse at the hospital's Baby Unit.

My 'phone rang at lunchtime, waking me after only three hours of fitful sleep. It was the nursery asking me to come and fetch Lilly because she had developed a sore throat and stiff neck. I nearly went into a panic as my sleep-deprived brain told me these were surely signs of meningitis.

Our grandfatherly GP Dr. Hughes came over straight away and said in his opinion Lilly had nothing more serious than swollen glands. He was not impressed I had been asked to special the child in ICU when I had a small child of my own and said he would make sure the hospital understood his concerns. He rang me later with the sad news the girl had died. He was kind enough also to arrange the night off for me not least, he said, because of the sleep I had lost that day.

Lilly was fine the next morning and I was satisfied I

had not behaved like a neurotic mother. I told my father about it a couple of days later when visiting my parents in Bayswater. He said that meningitis occurs in cluster groups that are prevalent in certain areas, the Medway Towns being one at the time. My GP concurred and advised me to return to adult ward work. My father maintained that nurses make fretful mothers because of what they are confronted with through their working lives. I agreed, to a degree.

The following week I was back in the relative calm of D Block Orthopaedic wards. With a week to go to Christmas Eve 1973 I also learnt I would be on duty over the Christmas holiday. Back in D1 we could sometimes almost put our feet up on night duty, though somebody was usually up to something. It could be pinching a plant-cutting, sharing their birthday cake or slipping a saucy present under the ward Christmas tree. It was over tea and a mince pie I agreed to join in on some fun at A & E's expense. It was usually A & E that copped it and invariably the auxiliaries that were up for a laugh.

The next night, when Sister had finished her midnight round, I piled up my hair, dusted it with talcum powder, donned a white coat and put on some passion-killer specs. I went striding down to a quiet A & E as Dr. Deidre Plunkett from the Post-Graduate Centre to do an assessment of A & E practices at night.

Every six months for their first three years, rooky Housemen and Women are allocated new posts. This causes the wards, theatres, A & E and ICU to groan since the newest newbies could be helpless prats until they got themselves sorted. With the first intake of first-year doctors at the beginning of August, experienced nursing staff are on their toes. They have prevented many a dire consequence at this time.

Doctor Kiljoy in A & E still on his first six-month stint was in for a Christmas he would remember. In preparation, the porters had sneaked into the Doctor's Rest Room beer bottles, cigarettes, girlie magazines and a vibrator. One of the porters made *papier-mâché* cartoon figures with fairy light eyes. He placed one of these beautifully-crafted heads in an examination cubicle with blankets and tested the lights. The effect was, well, like a Christmas spoof!

So the young doctor didn't think we really had it in for him, a petite blonde nurse from Men's Surgical was happy to change into a nurse's play uniform, red 'Scrooge' hat with pom-pom and balloon bosoms. Nurse Dolly Parton tested the effect in her ward to great appreciation and wolf-whistling then hot-footed it down to A & E's Resuscitation Room.

Dr. Kiljoy was bleeped to return from the Medics' Dining Room to A & E. I held out my hand stiffly and presented myself as Dr. Plunkett, the 'New Medics Night Inspector from Post-Grad. My first check, I said was that he was able to relax during breaks. He was after all, in charge of an important area of the hospital. The doctor was suddenly a little jittery.

His orbs on opening the Rest Room door were like Catherine Wheels and his reaction was swift. He pulled the door shut. He knew I had seen everything and muttered he didn't know what that was all about ... I started making notes on my clipboard. A moment later A & E Staff appeared and said they had an admission, a nurse from elsewhere in the hospital. How she kept a straight face I do not know.

"Excellent! Some first-hand observation!" I said in my best Joyce Grenfell voice, "I'll just shadow you, if you don't mind Doctor, as you interview and treat the patient."

As we headed for the trolley on which "Nurse Parton" was now wriggling and moaning about how she needed a doctor, the houseman caught sight of the head in the examination cubicle, darkened, except for the fairy lights. It was a moment of pure Carry On but didn't need a Sid James dirty laugh for the doctor to twig. As our Dolly slipped off the trolley her chest thrust forward and latex uniform now half-way up her hips, he burst out laughing.

"Alright," he said as I took off my specs and white coat, "I've been had! Where's the Candid Camera!"

I handed him a card saying he had passed the inspection and wishing him a less traumatic Christmas. He got a hug from all of us. Nurse Dolly's bosom popped. She squealed, then concentrated on getting her tiny uniform down to a more modest level.

"I think I'd better run!" she exclaimed, blushing. "Christmas or not, Sister will go bananas if she catches me looking like this!"

My GP's remonstration was not fully taken on board because my Christmas period shift was back on Children's Ward. I gave the benefit of the doubt to Admin that they must have been desperate. I didn't really mind, even though I'd had no paediatric training apart from a three-month block in Sheffield many years earlier. Night Sister would be on duty to make sure everything went smoothly.

With my having to work on Christmas Eve night, Jo, Lilly and I decided we would walk over to the hospital that afternoon to hear the Day Staff carol singers. Just as we were leaving the house the telephone rang. I handed the 'phone to my young daughter, then nearly three and said with my eyes wide open "it's Father Christmas and he would like to talk to you!" She took the receiver, nodded a couple of times and said "yes" and "thank you" very faintly and handed the receiver back to me.

In the entrance hall Lilly spotted Father Christmas, alias Bernice's husband Terry with a huge sack over his shoulder. Her beautiful hazel eyes widened as Terry in his red costume and curly white beard came over, knelt down and opened the sack.

"I'm so glad to see you, little Lilly, before I ride off with my reindeers!" Father Christmas said, knowing her, of course. "As I promised over the telephone, here's a little present as I expect you're too excited to wait until tomorrow!"

Lilly was so overwhelmed she couldn't speak and I didn't feel too bad being away from them that night.

Sister reassured me that none of the children on the ward were contagious and warned of a problem with little Billy recovering from a tonsillectomy. He was recently fostered and had been screaming at night because of bad dreams. It was an unfortunate coincidence that his younger sister was admitted because of a chest infection. She was still living with her natural parents and her mother, their mother, brought the girl in. Mother and sister had steadfastly ignored Billy all week. The staff had not got to the bottom of it.

When Night Sister did her first round that Christmas Eve I told her of Billy's mother walking straight past him and dropping several presents on her daughter's bed. Sister was aware that Staff had received abuse from the mother after asking that her son at least be acknowledged. There was little we could do because the foster parents were elsewhere over Christmas. Sister said all she could do was make sure Father Christmas left him something special that night.

Aside from the psychological trauma Billy was going through the ward looked really nice. It had been decorated by children from the local school. Two impish boys cheered me up by saying I looked like a model and drew effigies of me on a Christmas card. Student nurses ramp up the party atmosphere best with paper hats or flashing reindeer antlers. Even the more sedate staff adorn their hair with tinsel. All wards are decorated and a side-room is set aside for a mini-buffet and soft and boozy drinks.

Doctors, medical students and nursing staff trundle round to each other's wards during breaks. They don't touch the alcohol if on duty. There is good *bonhomie* and usually weary smiles especially from those already tired from having rushed around getting everything ready for their own family festivities.

It proved to be a pleasant Christmas in the hospital without further drama, on Children's Ward at least. For staff, a break from the family Christmas can be bitter sweet. My quiet time would not last long because I was back on at New Year's Eve, in A & E. My D Block days were numbered as it was the hectic emergency wards that tended to need experienced staff.

Thinking back over the previous months I remembered Sadie and her little boy, Jenny and the girl with meningitis. They were but three of a few that stay in my mind out of the thousands of patients I have nursed over the years. Some were beyond brave and an inspiration. All were extra-special.

Chapter Twenty-five
#Baby Mine ...# (Bette Middler)

It was about nine 'o clock one night in January 1974 when I was reading through the ward report at the nurses' station. Night Sister had done her round and left me with a pretty Singapore Malaysian student nurse named Putri. Her name translated as "daughter" she said. She was a tiny little thing, keen and awaiting instruction.

"Staff, you have lovely smile!" she complimented.

It was as though her remark triggered a demon behind us. A male patient leapt up from his front row bed mad-eyed. He had completely lost it. Fitfully asleep when I had done the round with Night Sister he was now uraemic, naked from the waist down trailing a drainage bag behind him and tearing at his post-op' dressings. His threatening stare and unshaven appearance was unnerving enough. What really worried me was the heavy glass urine bottle he had in his left hand.

"Call the porters ... and Night Sister ..." I yelled as the patient's right hand clamped on my throat. He pushed me into the corner between the drug cupboard and ward entrance doors and raised the urine bottle above his head. My student stood there stunned.

"Porters ..." I managed to gasp once more, using a sudden superhuman strength to prise his fingers from my throat. This time my student responded.

It was pure luck that the patient's demeanour changed suddenly from manic to dismissive. He let go of me and strode off down the corridor smashing windows in the private side-rooms and a fire alarm on his way to the far doors. The trail of blood showed he was in urgent need of attention.

"Call the Houseman too and keep right out of his way ..."

I followed him briefly then decided to heed my own advice and returned, crunching broken glass, going from bed to bed reassuring a ward full of highly vulnerable patients that the situation was under control.

Only when I remembered I was confirmed pregnant a few days earlier did I start shaking. Putri asked if I was okay. She was still trying to get an answer from the Porters' Lodge. We swapped roles so I could sit down for a moment and just as I began to calm, the men in blue burst through the far swing doors sporting axes, air bottles, visors and gauntlets. As they came striding down the corridor, boots crunching the glass into ever smaller pieces I didn't know if I should laugh. It was only minutes since my patient disappeared and here were the firemen. There was no sign of dozy hospital staff.

"Sorry gentlemen," I stuttered over the loud and persistent fire bell, pointing to the blood on the floor, "no fire, just a patient gone loco. He's carrying a heavy glass bottle and is losing blood. Is it possible you could bring him back to the ward?"

"No trouble, Nurse," began the Leading Fireman, "we saw him on our way in."

Five firemen, four porters, one of the Night Sisters and a harassed doctor eventually returned with the patient wrapped in a white blanket looking as blameless as a choir boy. Night Sister made a beeline for me.

"Are you okay, Staff?" she asked looking carefully at my throat which was probably showing bruising.

"I'm worried about miscarrying ..."

"... the Angels will look out for baby!" Putri chipped in. "She'll just have eight lives left now!"

Night Sister tried to make light of the situation but I came close to having my skull crushed. A build-up of body urea as waste toxins affecting the kidneys can give an emaciated old boy manic strength, let alone a fit middle-aged man. The doctor sedated the patient and set up the drips and drains again. It was the same symptoms suffered by Prime Minister Harold Macmillan when he was being treated for prostate problems, according to my father.

I didn't miscarry. A week later, however, I had a show of my own on the same ward. Student Nurse Putri was with me again. She went off to supper at midnight and returned to find me in the side ward. I had managed to stagger there and collapse on the bed. She said her introduction to British nursing was not what she expected! The doctor ordered me to stay put until morning.

It was hard to believe I felt so ill that night when my first pregnancy had been problem-free. My GP called at home later in the day and prescribed hormones and bed-rest for a week. The hormone was stilboestrol which he said would counter a possible miscarriage. Taking such a medication didn't feel right and I flushed the tablets down the toilet.

My father tutted. They had not been prescribed for miscarriage for a decade and a couple of years earlier, he said, a link with vaginal cancer in some daughters from their late teens on had been proven. From this incident came my life-long habit of researching all medicines proffered.

Social problems are reflected in A & E intake. At Medway in the early 1970s and in hospitals I had worked in up to then, drug and alcohol-related violence was there but not on the scale it is today. Friday nights were the busiest in Medway Casualty with incidents sometimes leading to it being called a Hell Hole. The Police would be in and out. Ambulance crews were back and forth and people would stagger in off the street with blood all over them.

Friday was pay day, when cash for a week's work was still handed over in a little brown envelope. Off they went to the pubs with it. The terms lager lout and binge-drinker hadn't been invented but elements of it were there. We certainly knew about pub closing time but staff were able to get on with their jobs without being attacked or abused by patients or their relatives or friends.

A large part of A & E work for me was calming neglected cubicle patients. Facing a full house of fifty or so minor injury patients could be a brave act. To help us deal with an increasingly frustrated intake on a busy night we were advised to acknowledge their feelings, give reasons for them having to wait and thank them for their patience. If it had been that simple.

They could be drunk and unpredictable, silent and in shock or moaning like porn stars. The hope was an addict in withdrawal or alcoholic with a grudge would not set upon us. I also had to learn how to appease and dodge irate and potentially violent relatives demanding to see a doctor. My diplomatic skills became well-honed.

It reminded me my sister Jane had a bedside locker thrown at her by a Sheffield Mooney gangster on a ward ten years before I qualified. My maiden aunt when Matron at the Darlington Memorial Hospital in the 'Twenties had one drama I know of. The husband of one of her patients walked in to the ward and shot his wife dead.

I felt particularly for passive, obedient older people all but abandoned on hard examination couches or trolleys in a corridor, or who might have suffered hours on a hard chair in a draughty waiting area. I don't think French and Germans for example, put up with it and wondered why our older people should. Unfortunately it was something we became hardened to. A & E doctors too become immune to lines of sick and injured patients but might achieve this only by cultivating a defensive M*A*S*H-type humour.

Errant behaviour is not one-sided. Shamefully, some of the medical and nursing staff during my career were abusive and punitive to troubled teenagers admitted to Casualty for over-dosing, self-harming, glue-sniffing or attempted suicide. Cheap aerosols and products containing butane were the rage in the early 'Seventies. Such kids can be stroppy but extended counselling and support rather than a heavy hand is now recognised as the way to go.

Abysmal role models in those days, as Hendrix, Keith Moon, Jim Morrison and Janis Joplin didn't help. A & E nurses today are often in the front line dealing with damaged young adults. It was endlessly frustrating in my day having to cope with senior staff who would give these kids, "time-wasters," short shrift. Nurses nearer my age whose teenage years coincided with the 1960s were more likely to want to understand hopelessness and despair and sympathise with these vulnerable youngsters.

Another aspect of Casualty that affected me was the waste of life from motoring fatalities, particularly those involving motor cycles. Casualty was so full one Monday morning when I was about to go off shift, a motor cyclist was put onto a spare bed in the adjacent Orthopaedic Ward. He had been hit by a car on his way to work. He was slipping in and out of consciousness but kept apologising for being a nuisance as I inched his helmet off. I had to stop him trying to help me. I didn't expect to see a fresh-faced lad of about eighteen, a determined character who even managed a smile. I don't know where his energy came from. He was blue from internal damage and had so many broken bones it looked as though only his leathers were holding his body together.

The exhausted doctor appeared briefly. When I went off shift Casualty were desperately trying to find space to get him hooked up to monitors and drips. It didn't happen, sadly. He lived only another half hour. The suddenness with which life can be snuffed out haunted me after this. I still fear for bikers and am not backwards at coming forward in advising people not to ride these machines.

Casualty units like the Operating Theatre suite, Intensive Care and an Outpatients Department operate in a bubble in every hospital. Night shift in Medway Hospital Casualty could be anything from tediously slow to a frenetic adrenaline rush. It did seem to be my shift when the maimed would stampede through Casualty's portals and fill all cubicles with every mishap to a body you could think of.

For the early part of the night there might be a wino slipping into oblivion in relative warmth, clutching an empty sherry bottle. He would lie along the back row of chairs blissed out under soothing neon lights etherised by a porter's Lysol and vomit-fragranced mop swirling and bumping impatiently around the chairs. How could I turn these men and occasionally women away, often great characters happy as slugs in a beer trap waiting for Godot?

Suddenly there might be a succession of ambulances bringing in a cardiac arrest, an abortive train-track suicide or head-on vehicle collision. It could also be a serious burns case, a hand crushed in machinery, a broken nose from a lovers' tiff, a toddler having swallowed a drawing pin or an outbreak of meningitis. Hospital dramas on television have endless gory material to draw upon.

Vital equipment would have to be wheeled in and primed up for stressed doctors. Blood bags would need fetching. I would frequently have to run what seemed miles down spooky corridors through cold, darkened labs to the blood bank. Running back I would be clutching it to my bosom under my cape, warming it if it was to be infused immediately. Mad rush emergencies are high-risk scenarios. Errors can occur and giving a wrong blood type to a patient is a serious one.

It was under these circumstances part-timer Nurse Dogsbody was likely to be used and abused and her status sink to its lowest. Full-time staff didn't worry too much about getting on with me since we might not cross paths again for months. I only had to draw a sigh of relief at the end of my shift and exit.

My first crossing of swords occurred at Medway. It was with a Senior Houseman, a doctor with grey hair and a neat beard. I was sufficiently concerned about a patient's deterioration to seek permission from Sister to call the houseman. He was not suited at being summoned in the early hours and told me sharply the patient was not having a stroke.

"My experience told me it could have been a stroke," I snapped, without thinking and obviously a little tired. "It needed a doctor to confirm this one way or another."

The doctor flounced off. An hour later I was called to Sister's office and knew immediately it could only be on a disciplinary matter. The swine had indeed made a complaint, about me doing my job. Sister barely looked up from her paperwork.

"This complaint ... most unlike you, Nurse ..." she said and waved me away.

There were lighter moments that elicited plenty of comment at break times around the hospital, though they would have been extremely embarrassing to the patients. One young couple were brought in from an ambulance clutching each other on a single trolley. The girl's vaginal muscles had clamped her boyfriend's penis and it was only after the doctor injected a muscle relaxant that the boyfriend could withdraw. It wasn't funny at the time. Serious damage to the vaginal wall has been known to occur if the male panics and tries to tear himself free.

The condition, *penis captivus* was rare I was told. One doctor suggested it was not so rare, rather, more discretion was used in its reporting. A nurse said she had heard of a couple dying of hypothermia locked in a cruel embrace one winter's night up on the Great Lines behind us at Gillingham presumably because they had been unable to make anyone aware of their plight.

I had my own penis story, one not quite so traumatic but seriously embarrassing. A lad of about fifteen had to be prepared quickly for theatre one night on Men's Surgical because of an inflamed appendix. There was no male nurse or porter to hand to shave him and the doctor asked if I could do it even though this was against the rules.

Shaving a man's face was not a problem, this part of the anatomy I had not done before. He and I were fine with the situation until my kneeling on the floor in front of him caused an erection. Many a young lad in bed would get an erection with young nurses walking about. This I could understand. This was an intimate situation and the best I could do to afford the boy some modesty was place a green paper towel over his member. I then found it extremely difficult to shave him with minimal handling and without nicking skin that can risk infection in theatre.

The clumsy depilatory exercise was one of the most awkward moments of my nursing career and double agony for the young lad suffering dire embarrassment and pain from his appendix. I made my displeasure known to Staff once the boy was under anaesthetic.

"Oh, we could have done it while he was under, Rose! No probs!"

Before the nationalisation of health care in June 1948 in the form of the National Health Service, people self-managed injury and illness with a range of remedies, including prayer, in ways largely unchanged since the 19th Century. For more serious conditions and operations they had to scrimp and scrape to pay. Suddenly there were 5,000 consultants and almost half-a-million beds available at apparently no cost.

It was not before time, with sub-standard housing, malnutrition and endemic diseases including tuberculosis all around. Into casualty departments they hopped, skipped and tumbled with bee stings, rashes, cuts, headaches and colds. No wonder there was a serious shortage of nurses for many years until recruitment caught up and the service stabilised.

Even in the 1960s and 1970s there were many older people who would still be popping in to casualty to try it out, even try it on. There were regulars who would sit quietly snoozing the night away because it was warmer or more comfortable than what they called home, a post-war Jerry-build or condemned back-to-back. This applied particularly at Christmas and many a performance was put on by wily old folk to get them a place at the Inn.

Obvious hypochondriacs and time-wasters did annoy staff who would hear every reason for the patient coming in; she had lost her contraceptive pills; did he have a brain tumour because he couldn't remember things like he used to; she could hardly walk and wondered if a week in a hospital bed and regular meals would help.

Hospitals had a list of people with Munchhausen's Syndrome to try and prevent them sneaking into hospitals to be examined or even operated on for their favourite illness. Add this to the drunks, homeless and ghouls who would wander in and hope the night staff would not notice them.

Many believed it was a stigma to call the doctor and relied on time-honoured remedies like sitting on brown paper to cure car sickness and getting a good whiff of rank cow shed smells for breathing difficulties and general well-being. Milk maids did not, after all, catch the pox ... Mother remembered people spreading straw about outside their house in the 1930s after being diagnosed with tetanus. It was believed it would prevent the onset of lockjaw.

One of Pa's patients died relatively young from a lung complaint. Her father, a navvy, was so convinced of the health benefits of tar he took a small bottle of it, probably carcinogenic coal tar, home every day for his children to inhale deeply.

Meal times are when hospital staff get to hear or share the worst. A couple were brought in to Casualty at Medway after a car crash. The man was dead and the woman unconscious. The woman was identified by the police and they called at her house to speak to next of kin. Her mother-in-law answered the door because she was babysitting. The police told her that her son had been killed in a car crash and that her daughter-in-law was in a coma.

"Well whoever that is" the woman began, "he ain't my bleedin' son, 'cos he's in jail in bleedin' Turkey for drug smugglin'. Me bleedin' daughter-in-law told me she was going to bingo ..."

The police had the good sense to warn ward staff that the patient's mother-in-law was coming in and was not likely to show much sympathy. It was unfortunate the accident victim remained in a coma for years in a long-stay geriatric hospital.

Reading about coma patients who came alive after being given certain medicines, including sleeping potions, only to fall back into a coma presents a dilemma. How hard it must be for a relative to give permission for a life-support machine to be turned off. How can it be that we still have so little knowledge of what consciousness is and how the brain can become permanently unconscious in a living body? It is of even more concern when CT scans monitoring brain activity show clearly they are conscious.

A railway line suicide victim was brought in to A & E one evening as a DOA (Dead on Arrival). Staff told us these can be particularly

368

difficult to put back together again because of the massive damage done to the body by being hit by a train at speed. It can disintegrate. This one was very easy, Staff said. The person had been sliced neatly in half by the wheels. Some of us wanted to go off and be sick.

One of the most difficult incidents was an A & E night duty SEN brought in after setting fire to herself at home because of marital problems. It upset all of us because we couldn't use our normal emotional distancing mechanisms, including black humour, to deal with it. We also felt a great sense of sadness in having failed to notice and help a colleague in distress.

It was very difficult seeing people, children, admitted in extreme pain, especially if they had to wait for pain relief. I felt I was failing them as we waited for the doctor. I am a ward nurse at heart who sees patients coming in for treatment and being sent home feeling better. Terminal care can be fulfilling as well. Each to their own in nursing.

Ditzy Delia much preferred theatre work because she was not really a people person. She liked the challenge of the cut and thrust on patients who had been knocked out cold. No small talk here that might get in the way of an interesting medical or anatomical problem.

Working every weekend through the Summer of 1974 became too much as my pregnancy advanced. Jo and I needed my income to pay for food, household items and clothes in the main and I started thinking about alternative ways of helping the finances. Besides, I needed to tackle my daughter's illusion that I stayed in bed all day. Reading in her school diary how she spent her weekends I learnt "Mummy stays in bed all day while Daddy takes me out to play ..."

Easing up a bit on weekends I visited friends in London. A girls' night out was a relaxing reminder of what it was to be footloose and available. Being a wife and mother with a young child is give, give, give to the point of forgetting who you were pre-mum and pre-wife. Pregnancy was not so bad. When seven months' gone with Lilly, Celia insisted I come to an art student party. I felt really ungainly but my condition was of great interest to the males and I was danced off my feet the night long.

The high point of my second pregnancy was a Stones' concert at Olympia. I was right at the front, three feet away from Mick and tiny Bianca as they wandered by inspecting something at the foot of the stage between sets.

One topic of conversation with my old school friends was a growing awareness of the shortcomings of our education. For me, even after attending two grammar schools, it was partly due to my over-riding wish to be a nurse and partly to years wasted in dead-end religious study. In general it was a lack of stimulation through all my schooling. Some of us felt we had spent years underwhelmed in the classroom. I have yet to get to the bottom of why secondary education today looks so much more interesting, more fun today, yet fewer students can read or write to a level we considered basic.

The answer for me in my late twenties was to enrol in the Open University. This would, I reasoned locate my brain again, it having been encased in cotton wool from kiddie-speak in recent years. Jo said he would support me in any path I wanted to take, as I would him. He was far better at ironing than me anyway!

I was anxious about baby and birth during my final two months. In the days before scans, antenatal tests were for weight and blood pressure. Urine was tested to detect symptoms of eclampsia. The midwife would listen to the foetal heartbeat through an ear piece and determine by feel the position of the baby. That was about it. No one wrote or talked about how lonely a pregnant woman can feel. Partners may do all they can to be reassuring but there is only one person in the driving seat on a bumpy one-way ride. Pregnant mothers will suffer endless platitudes, with the most perverse empathisers eager to tell their horror stories.

When my labour started, Bernice drove me to All Saint's Hospital in Chatham. Lilly loved her and her two young children so I knew she would be in good hands. Jo was on his way back from London. Lilly's birth had been so well-managed at St. Mary Abbot's in Kensington I naturally hoped for a similarly positive birth experience with Kitty.

That evening early in September 1974 began well with a warm and friendly Malaysian midwife. In sharp contrast, the behaviour of Night Sister was disgraceful. She was hostile and distant from the start. An auxiliary with a face like a dead cod was no better. She flounced in to my room at about eight in the evening offering me two Mogadon sleeping tablets. Now banned and probably stronger than a bottle of horse pills I refused them, fearing I would be knocked out until the Second Coming. When I questioned my ability to push if full labour was to start soon I was told I could suit myself.

After Sister's rounds and another cold once-over, Jo and I were left to get on with it. My contractions in the early hours became excruciating and when I asked for some pain relief I was told it was my fault for not taking the Mogadon. I was desperate to move around also but could not do this. The policy in those days was that women in labour should be confined to bed. The auxiliary even managed to slip in a dig about my keeping my husband up all night when I "should" have been asleep.

Poor Jo sitting beside me looked haunted, as he had no idea how to deal with the sadistic staff. I didn't have the strength to defend myself against this treatment and wondered if I was being punished because I was a nurse. Normally our colleagues are exemplary with us as patients. When Sister Merciless did push a gas and air mask on my face I felt sick and could not continue with it. I was given short shrift for this. Jo, was desperate, seeing me in agony with no sympathy or assistance from these nurses but we had no alternative but to endure my labour alone for the rest of the night.

Things changed when Sister came in to see my progress at about 5.30 am. She examined me briefly and exchanged a look of great concern with her auxiliary. Her tone was considerably softer when she said it was imperative I push very, very hard.

I did, with a loud scream. My big baby, Kitty shot out on her back "face to pubes." Even then in the difficult circumstance I saw the auxiliary's eyes roll upwards with my undignified yell.

"You did very well," Sister Penitent said.

She knew she had boobed in not detecting the baby's position and being ready for possible complications. I had done very well. A face up baby often requires forceps delivery or even a Caesarean section. It is why she took so long to deliver, poor lamb.

I felt anger for a long time. It was upsetting to think that the first sound Kitty heard was her mother screaming. With Lilly's birth the staff were so on the ball I was able to sit up and gently pull her on to my tummy. I thought about complaining but feared being labelled as a troublemaker. I was still not learning.

In the late '60s I could see a difference in the way patients in private clinics were treated compared with those under the NHS. The attitude that NHS patients did not matter so much was subliminal in some medical staff. It frequently left me upset, moving between the different levels of care patients were receiving. I was not aware of the concepts of profit or making money in those days but it was there.

Watching consultants greasing up to private patients was nauseating because at my old training hospital, quality of care for all was the goal. There should have been the same level of courtesy in the NHS, a service paid for by the patient after all.

"... you see a different one every time ... they don't know anything about you, looking at them computers all the time ... they tell me it'll be three months before a specialist can see me ... I waited hours on them rotten seats and the doctor didn't seem interested ... we're treated like blooming cattle ..." are comments I heard a hundred times in outpatients and A & E departments from the 1970s onwards.

My father was one of many GPs wary of the Health Service. This I found strange for an intelligent, caring man. If a patient couldn't pay he didn't charge and his inability to make a living under the old regime will have contributed to his exhaustion. Charity is no way to run something as fundamental as the health of a nation.

His 'principles' were partly the reasons he sold his practice and went to sea. Strange again, since he would often tell me of the huge benefits the NHS was proving to be to the population at large, including to thousands of women in the early days whose prolapsed womb conditions were at last operated on. No longer did these women have to suffer their womb poking out through their vagina. His brother-in-law with whom he trained in medicine in Cork bit the bullet, stuck with his NHS practice on a council estate in Sheffield and retired on a reasonable pension.

Private clinics, like private schools do have a higher staff-patient ratio and you would hope this situation would win hands down over an understaffed NHS ward. I would say the private sector's people management policies relate to business and shareholder profit before altruistic concern for the patient.

There is always room for a cross-over of ideas. In the dark days of unacceptably long NHS treatment waiting times I paid to have an urgent procedure done at a private clinic. I was sent a follow-up survey asking me to comment on the quality of care received. This should be standard practice in the NHS.

We should not forget we have all paid into the Health Service. Management should be made aware daily by patients if their hospital is not up to the mark. They in turn will have everything they need to look at procedures and if necessary approach their paymaster.

The Jessop Hospital and the Children's Hospital in Sheffield in the 1960s were the only NHS hospitals I worked in where all patients were treated holistically, as private hospital patients tend to be. Although care at The Royal Hospital was ultra-efficient the patients' emotional welfare was not considered as important as at the other two hospitals. To my mind they lose a mark because of this.

Should senior NHS nursing staff have some sort of star rating? The efficiency of wards in NHS hospitals depends on the Sister or charge nurse. Something is going wrong in wards when we keep reading about failings in service, care and hygiene. Should any nurse lose her initial passion and sense of dedication because she feels mistreated, overworked or undervalued, good ward managers will spot the warning signs and help prevent a downward spiral. If they don't, then they are not up to the job. Not in the way it used to be done, anyway. I think all staff should have access to and be encouraged to attend counselling, problem-solving groups and relaxation sessions. Twelve-hour shifts are too long.

Small is beautiful and more likely to be better run. Unfortunately, in this day and age it is not cost-effective. There can, therefore, only be compromise between care and cost. I am not alone in being apprehensive about the care I can expect from our National Health Service.

In the late 1980s I was admitted to the Kent and Canterbury for a hysterectomy on a ward recognised as a centre of excellence and run by an intelligent and responsive Sister and staff. A few months later I was admitted to a different ward in the same hospital with vomiting and dehydration and the care was dire.

The ambulance attendant was rude and impatient; A & E Sister barked at me to imagine a nice picture, to help me stop my intractable vomiting; an auxiliary instead of a trained nurse changed my drip; the beds were too close together and reminded me of budget airline economics; all-day visiting in the cramped ward was a nightmare; the sloppy staff sat on the ward eating their packed lunches. I was eventually sent home at an hour's notice with no outdoor clothes or shoes to an empty house.

To compound my feeling ill at ease about the NHS as a patient on my last admission during the 1990s I was put on a mixed ward with mainly male patients. I was expected to use a commode because of my stomach problems which would have been embarrassing enough on a women's ward. The only other woman, opposite me, was also mortified at being on a mixed ward.

"I bet the bleedin' management have private health care," she remarked. We were moved after making a fuss.

At last, no longer an NHS employee, I was standing my ground and demanding better service.

Since the 1990s my problem remains a spinal injury and chronic pain. I was let down badly with dismissive, patronising interviews from NHS management and senior medical staff. I was also subjected to an almost Philistine level of care. I have to hope that medical staff who made statements like "the pain is all in your mind" and "you've got to learn to live with it" are wiser and better-informed now.

I spent most of my time getting to grips with my problems over the following decade as well as setting up a self-help charity for many, many others in intractable pain. The issue with the Health Service became more one of lack of interest in my well-being and pain management and about keeping me informed of new surgical techniques. Pain is still not being addressed by the medical profession. I have researched the subject for almost thirty years and regret I am now looking at health services around Europe for more satisfactory interventions than those offered in Britain.

I wondered recently (in 2012) about new priorities. My husband's GP sent him a letter reminding him he had not taken up her prescription for statins for his slightly "higher than she would wish for" cholesterol level. It is the only letter he has ever had from a GP. Through a slight change in diet and a supplement of natural plant sterols over the year his next blood and cholesterol tests, done elsewhere in the country (charmingly at the tiny health centre in Florence Nightingale's village of Holloway, Derbyshire), showed he was back to 'normal.' I note the same Health Centre has not written to me in twenty years about my pain and the fact I am on the same continuous and dare I say it, inadequate medication.

Chapter Twenty-six
#Prelude No.1# (Villa-Lobos)

Towards the summer of 1975 when Kitty was six months old, Jo and I agreed it was time I finished at the hospital. I had been working nights for much of every week for two years. Irregular hours and broken sleep during the day could not have been doing me good. It was not satisfactory for Jo either on his precious time off at weekends.

The calibre of night care was high during my time at what is now Medway Maritime Hospital. It was an incredibly busy emergency admissions hospital and I remain full of admiration for the efficiency and good nature of the Night Sisters and nurses, my friends and colleagues, pulling together to deal with crisis after crisis, night after night. They gave me a touching send-off with a big party and stack of presents for me and my daughters.

It was back to days at Family Planning. My lodger Sheri had been a great help in looking after the children in recent months and we had become good friends. Going back to the FPA for three-hourly sessions three times a week suited all of us.

My previous work at the FPA in the centre of London had been enjoyable. It was a grown-up, even anarchic working environment. The centre dealt with the reality of birth control, protection against cervical cancer, STDs and the sexual health of young women. Breast checks and regular smears were offered. Nobody moralised or patronised the client. Religion was irrelevant. Thoughts on underage sex and sex before marriage remained personal.

We preferred young females attending with their mother but it was not mandatory. It was hard sometimes, not wanting to be protective towards these youngsters embarking on a sex life, especially when we believed they were not emotionally ready or they were being coerced, or exploited. A thirteen-year old girl who wanted to take the Pill was treated in the same way as a thirty-year old, though many of the pale, pinch-faced mini-adults hadn't a clue about how much more complicated their lives were about to become. There never seemed to be enough time in which to explore all issues with them. The girls' mothers could be pathetically passive. Many hadn't a clue themselves or were only concerned their daughter didn't bring home a baby.

All of us respected our colleagues' areas of expertise and everyone was trusted to do his or her best for the benefit of the client. In the main it was much easier for girls to discuss practical matters with FP doctors than with hospital medics. The client undoubtedly benefitted from lengthier female-to-female discussion.

How different it was from the hearsay of my early teenage life with a mother excommunicated by the Catholic Church because of her insistence, after her eighth child, my father use condoms. I am not surprised discussion about sex in my family was rare and invariably negative. My two sisters would have had the same blanking. I only remember my otherwise enlightened eldest sister joking it might be expedient to begin dropping the Pill into her blossoming thirteen-year old daughter's Rice Krispies.

Along with part-time work in Family Planning conveniently at nearby Rainham, I undertook child-minder training so I could look after extra children with confidence. Friends made among other mothers while caring for small children can be sanity savers. There is a common understanding of juggling of family matters, sleeplessness and the toll of the incessant, frequently inane but essential "why?" Toddler prattle should not be ignored. Neither should mischief, squabbling and ear-piercing tantrums that can arise from cuties being disciplined. There was constant support from all mothers within our group in looking after children for the day, sometimes at very short notice. There was also humour and adult conversation so we did not forget how to communicate with our tired husbands at the end of each day.

Lady was my Fairy Godmother. She continued with her gifts of sweets and cakes over the garden wall, now to the children I was looking after. Her constant praise and encouragement was not wasted on them either. They loved Lady. A research study from the USA at the time found young children were assailed with negative interjections and put-downs from adults a staggering ninety per cent of the time. This did not include sibling rivalry and derogatory slanging matches from aggressive peers.

We all recognise these:

"Shut up! ... Go away! ... Stop! ... How dare you! ... No! ... Go to your room! ... Do as you're told! ..."

And these:

"Stand still while I'm talking to you ... You're a disgrace ... Don't be cheeky ... How can you be so stupid? ... Why do you always? ... You'll sit there until it's finished ... You'll be very sorry ..."

My mother was autocratic throughout our upbringing. Her discipline was from the top down and non-negotiable. We were a pack of little beings to be trained, as puppies are. She did not have to work beyond running a family but had few labour-saving devices and simply did not have time for dissent or argument. She kept a thick bamboo cane in her bedroom and we never dared answer back.

More shocking to me at ten years of age was learning it was given to her by brother Pascal. The policeman instinct in him surfaced early. I remember her using it once on Simon and me after we had been arguing. Twice actually, because we laughed and she was not amused. She did not moderate her views with her grandchildren. A soft or gentle approach to any misbehaviour was regarded as a rod being created for our own backs.

By contrast, all of us younger mothers in my Gillingham days were happily surprised and disarmed by our bright, loquacious kids who didn't feel self-conscious about arguing points of unfairness or adult hypocrisy. We certainly had no intention of smacking, as our teachers and some parents had done. We didn't like to put children down either, individually or in front of others.

One of my best friends Greta at the hospital crèche, was whole-heartedly with me on implementing creative play for the younger children. Thankfully, Lilly was always well-behaved away from the house, if an entrepreneurial bossy-boo at home. She was not slow in organising the children with dancing, make-believe circus, Guy Fawkes Night penny collecting, carol singing at Christmas and so on. For my group sessions we had tambourines, drums and triangles and would sing, play, dance and rah-rah the afternoon through to a tiring but very satisfying end-of-day for the little ones. Those a little older would be taken to dance, judo, skating and other sport activities and more formal music lessons. I was determined to introduce mine to a wide range of music from Britten's A Young Person's Guide to the Orchestra to calypso and steel drums.

Jo was a practical husband, cleverly making trolley carts, miniature shop fronts and a Wendy House with table and chairs for the lucky little monsters. In the garden were swings, a slide and a climbing frame. If the weather was not so good there were powder paints brought home from work to experiment with. Greta and I sat in the

kitchen one afternoon watching her wee treasure and Lilly take the paint outside with great purpose. It was not long before just about everything from the swing to the garden gate had been transformed with a rainbow of colour. We had no wish to interrupt them.

"Turner Prize-winners in the making!" Greta laughed.

Not limiting ourselves to garden and living room, two or three of us adults and a dozen children would troop to the Strand Lido on the River Medway about a mile away from Windmill Road. The new Black Lion swimming pool was an attractive alternative. On the best summer holiday days we would take advantage of free train travel, courtesy of London Transport, with trips along the North Kent Coast for excited children to the beaches of Westgate, Margate and Broadstairs. In those days Punch and Judy, the bucket and spade, shell collecting and donkey rides reigned supreme. There was plenty for the children to see and explore. I think we were all more comfortable now with Winnicot's "good enough" mother.

Freed from working nights I began to remember what an adult social life was. At weekends we might get together with Greta and Bernice's families and Jo's old friends. He was a Gillingham man. It wasn't the most exciting of places but his native friends were a lively bunch who more than made up for it with outdoor pub lunches, outings and dinner parties even though we were all on tight budgets. Medway Hospital's new child-friendly Social Club was a haven.

My auxiliary pal Bernice had older children of eight and ten whereas Greta's little son was Lilly's age, four-and-a-half in mid-1975. Named Sonny, this angelic golden-haired bubbles was actually a little devil. I was the only mother who allowed him into her house. Greta's creative play principles extended to no discipline, whatever he got up to. He was constantly scribbling on walls, dismantling toys to see how they worked or testing them to destruction.

"But I was only ..." he would protest when I suggested something he was doing was perhaps not a good idea.

"Little Darling ..." his mother would comment, smiling.

It was not so funny when my responsible four-year old hurried down stairs and said "Mummy, Sonny has eaten your pills from the cupboard."

There were aspirin and contraceptive pills in the cabinet.

"Did you eat the big ones or the little ones, Honey?"

"The little ones," he replied helpfully, "three!"

Lilly contradicted him, offering a more worrying "no, eighty!"

It was time for us to leave that afternoon anyway, me in one direction with Lilly late for an eye test and Greta and Sonny in the other towards Casualty. Sonny was wailing his angelic head off, complaining he didn't want to be made poorly again at the hospital. He was fine after gastric irrigation, Greta reported later. I locked all medicines away and reappraised everything else that could cause a drama on his next visit. We were dealing with Terminator Sonny!

My constant support while at home with lots of pre-school children was my lodger-cum-*au pair* Sheri. She moved in with "smiley eyes" baby Kelly two weeks after I gave birth to Kitty. Naturally they became playmates, though Kitty was always a head taller than other children as both Jo and I are tall.

Sheri came from a tough background and at twenty years old was proving herself to be a good mother. Her adored father died when she was fifteen and her bereft mother left her traumatised daughter to fend for herself. Sheri also had to deal with her older brother, Buster, being the centre of their mother's new universe. She kicked Sheri out when she became pregnant but it didn't stop her getting on the 'phone when she was depressed expecting Sheri to drop everything and listen to her litany of moans. My heart went out to Sheri, along with some occasional tart but unheeded advice. As with my own needy mother there was much take and little give

Buster I knew before Sheri because he was our first lodger. He left the young mother of his first two children at the age of nineteen and asked if he could bring his new girlfriend with him to his room. He was a good-looking, likeable rogue, a hard-working painter and decorator. Jo, my mother-in-law and I were not prepared for their love-making marathons.

"Is that the elephants frolicking again on the trampoline, Dear?" he asked me innocently when Buster and his girlfriend got started for the evening just as Jo's white-haired mum called with some lemon curd and wondered what the noise was all about.

Lady was more worldly but was embarrassed *in extremis* at the reaction of one of her family. He had seen me in the garden heavily pregnant one afternoon and heard Buster and Co. going at it during the evening with the French windows open. He thought Jo was a monster treating me so roughly and was going to come over and sort him out.

Bonking Buster found himself a flat soon after but was back shortly afterwards desperately hoping I had not let his room. His sister was about to be out on the street. Their mother went on holiday the day Sheri returned from hospital with Kelly leaving a note she wanted her daughter out by the time she returned. You couldn't have made it up.

I had no trouble with Jo on matters like this. He was tolerant and easy going to whatever I wanted to do, though I wondered sometimes if he would notice if a team of astronauts bound for Mars were temporarily billeted with us. We did discuss the situation and with foresight and a little smile he wondered what else lay in store for us with people from that end of Gillingham!

The only time I ever saw him lose his rag was when he returned from an afternoon walk with Lilly. I was still in bed after night duty when he strode in and said he was going to 'phone the police. His cross voice sounded so odd I propped myself up on one elbow.

"I am phoning the police," he repeated, "because we were nearly kicked by a horse on the Great Lines …"

I whooped with laughter. He sounded like the Prime Minister, not the then Harold Wilson who could be fractious but John Major twenty years later in one of his "the Three Bastards are out to get me" rages. He and Lilly were obviously fine and Jo couldn't do anger. His head, as far as I could ever tell, was preoccupied with things like photography, steam engines, vintage cars, trams and 'mothology' as I thought it was until corrected politely. He would have been more comfortable in the 19th Century with his interests. Tricky modern things like emotion and bad behaviour passed him by.

To be so in control was incredible. He refused to be drawn in whether kids were fighting, someone was being rude or tempers were frayed. I don't believe he has ever been rude or unpleasant to anyone in his life either. This was such a contrast to my dramatic Irish-Scottish *persona* that, stupidly when younger, I let get the better of me in ramping up some drama because I thought it would be a better way of making a point. Only-son Jo did suffer a God-fearing Mother's regime with its required early rising. I don't think he would have preferred a big bruising family driven by drama and tantrum.

Sheri, for all her traumas when she arrived on our doorstep was a quiet beauty with thick, waist-length hair that reminded me of Disney's Little Hiawatha. She was a gracious girl with a no-messing air about her. I admired her getting to grips with her situation from the start. The thought of living with two "posh" strangers she admitted later, was almost as stressful as anything that had occurred in her life. To Sheri and her Council Estate mates, posh people, any Middle class bods, I suppose were interfering do-gooders. Fortunately we clicked on first meeting and our matching sense of the ridiculous caused us to ache with laughter more days than not in 1975. I am pleased to say we can still cry with laughter over the 'phone to each other nearly forty years on!

When I was still working at Medway and about to leave for work one night Sheri had an upsetting 'phone call.

"Rose, me mate Reggie, is in Casualty across the road. He was in a crash coming back from work in London and was thrown out of the van ..."

"Don't worry, Sheri, I'll go down to ICU as soon as I can and find out how he is."

"Friend of yours, Staff?" Night Sister asked, pulling the sheet back to reveal a tattoo just below the good boy's navel that read "It's all yours!"

Reggie survived the accident but sustained permanent brain damage. He returned home for a short while and did odd things like make tea with gravy powder and urinate on the Hi-Fi to turn it off. His wife could not cope and he had to live away because of her concern about the safety of their little girls.

Before I started my child-minding I was already indebted to Sheri, irrespective of Jo's caution. On many a fraught weekend in Casualty, when young men were being particularly hard to handle I resorted to playing the lodger card. I threatened them with Sheri and her mate Mo. They all knew them and fancied them and magically they would start behaving, even laugh.

The maternal instinct is intriguing. Sheri's daughter is now in her thirties, balanced and happy with two children of her own. Sheri's mother is in her nineties and as demanding as ever, knowing her daughter, another unsung, unpaid heroic carer will do her bidding until the day she dies. Neither Sheri nor I had maternal mothers yet we had strong bonds with our babies. Neither of us suffered post-natal depression despite having our first babies in difficult circumstances.

Sheri's comfort for her many stresses, including feelings for her baby's father, was smoking cigarettes. It was not until we had to take Kelly to hospital with bronchiolitis at six months old that I realised the effect this was having. We gave Kelly her own fag smoke-free bedroom and Jo put an extractor fan in Sheri's bed-sitting area. Anti-smoking had yet to become organized but it opened my eyes about children and passive smoke inhalation. Smoking was not banned outright on London Underground trains until 1984. Millions of us still had ten years more of this toxic stink when we travelled around London. Only when it had gone did we realise how bad it had been.

Related health issues are well-known now but in those days some hospital consultants still smoked in the belief it protected them from catching infections from the grubby patients while on their rounds. Patients with smoking-related illnesses weren't judged for bringing it on themselves as so many men, including doctors, smoked. Unbelievably, patients were still allowed to puff away on the wards.

Taking Sheri in as a lodger introduced us to her mates who took pride in challenging the social mores of boring, law-abiding do-gooders, like Jo and I! Sheri and her two close pals Mo and Meg became known as the Three Missketeers on the back of Bad Boy Oliver Reed's films The Three, and Four Musketeers.

Meg gave birth at fourteen, something almost unknown then but she was responsible enough to work out parenting duties with the father and complete her schooling. The child would be with her and her parents during the week and with the father and his parents at the weekend. The lad is an engineer in the Middle East today. Whatever befell these kids they got on with it to the extent that all three were almost too responsible and too sensible as mums.

Off these three Misses would troop on Friday nights to Rochester's favourite Rockers and Heavy Metal pub The Nag's Head, committed denim chicks heading for a night of 'Seventies Rock that slapped your face and dissolved your grey matter. It was in this notorious pub swirling with whizz (amphetamines) and wacky baccy smoke that their past continued as the present. Sheri would canoodle with Kelly's errant dad and Mo with similar rogues.

"Me Ex is goin' down for muggin' an old lady. Sad bastard!" Mo would report.

"And our mate Chaz is runnin' the prison library. He's in for selling whizz and dope from his ice cream van. Sad git!" Sheri would add, screeching with laughter.

If ever there were two girls who had been there and done that, from drinking themselves silly at thirteen, long before it was easy with Alcopops, to experimenting with LSD and magic mushrooms in the woods at fourteen, to being smacked about by boyfriends at fifteen from whom they would bounce back without resentment. They were Birds of a Feather, only funnier and prettier. Bosomy girls both, Mo blonde and Sheri dark.

One evening Jo and I called in at our local pub, the Tam O'Shanter on Chatham Hill to find Mo and Sheri sitting at the bar. They were rabbiting away as if they hadn't seen each other for weeks and we left them to it. They wised me up later on a Chatham ploy.

"Oh, it's only our chat, Rose, 'cos we don't want to look like doughnuts at the bar, do we, Sher? We didn't want the guys there to think we were interested in them in any way whatsoever, but at the same time we can't appear boring. Right, Sher?"

"Yeah! It goes like this. I say 'bananas' ..."

"... an I say 'a pound of apples,' like we're talking about something amazing!"

"And we go on, all animated like, listing every fruit and veg we can think of, giggling on some! Course, it's only when we run out of real gossip!"

Mo also moved in with us for a while and we really became a mad house. It was a revelation for Middle Class me getting to know these talented resilient girls who could have had brilliant careers, if only. It wasn't that they had low expectations, they had no expectations. Teenage Mo made her own wedding dress and those of her bridesmaids without using patterns. She also had a beautiful calligraphy hand. I saw this waste of talent with many of their friends. The secondary school system let them down almost immediately they walked through the school gates and they were on the scrap heap long before they walked back out for the last time.

"'Av you noticed, Sher," Mo began, watching me doing some housework as we chatted, "'ow Rose dusts around them ornaments 'cos she can't be arsed to pick 'em up!"

That gave me a complex for the whole day. It could have been something to do with little time for things like cleaning. Looking at Sheri and me with squalling babies Mo swore she would double her pills rather than fall pregnant. That was until she met a Heavy Metal biking Jehovah's Witness. They soon had gorgeous girl twins, followed by two more children. They moved in to a house in old Windmill Road in the early 1980s, because of Mo's happy memories of when we lived there, I am told.

Then there was Polly, another local mum who would bring her child to the morning playgroup that Lilly, Kitty and Kelly attended when Sheri and I were working. It was held in the Methodist Church

Hall where Sir David Frost's father was once minister. It is now a Sikh temple.

Polly was a tiny, fair-haired Cockney who couldn't say her 'r's, like Monica Rose. Her two boys were like pixies from a Noddy book. Polly soon became known as the Fourth Missketeer with her infamy based on her thieving. To me it was more kleptomania. It was manic and she was proud at how enterprising she could be about "lifting" stuff. It often left me speechless.

For a while she worked in a canteen. I might have expected her prowess to extend to half a Battenberg, for example but Polly was in a very classy league. On one occasion she turned up on our doorstep with a cheese as big as my hips, a hundredweight of spuds she could hardly drag along the pavement and two catering-size tins of instant coffee. They were a present I had to decline. When she worked in a wallpaper shop her house was soon transformed with the most expensive of wallpapers. Nice it looked too!

She was also interested in her boss's hobby of making fishing rods. One evening when she called to pick up her Pixies, lo! she was carrying two of his most exquisite creations.

"But Polly, you don't fish, Darling!"

"I know, Rose but they are so bloody beautiful I 'ad to 'ave 'em!"

She spent the weekend with a new boyfriend, not fishing but looking for a rowing boat they could 'borrow' to go fishing in. She was miffed when they didn't come across anything suitable, as it was something new she looked forward to. There was some compensation that Sunday afternoon courtesy of Butlins at Margate, or some tots holidaying there, two neat little bikes she thought her boys would enjoy more.

At yet another job as an evening cleaner in Outpatients at Medway Hospital she dropped the kids off as usual for me to mind. When she returned later she was in a state, shaking and sweating. I started to make fun of her.

"Nah, Rose, it ain't funny," she said seriously. "I 'ad the fright of me born natural! You've seen me Mum's big staring eyes?"

"Yes ..." I began.

"Well, I've hated staring eyes since I was a little girl. When Mum lost it wiv us, her scary eyes would stick out of her head in rage, like frog's bleedin eyes, y'know!"

"... and ..."

"Well, I had to clean the Eye Doctor's clinic today. And you know what was in his bin staring at me ..."

I burst out laughing. A glimmer of a smile returned to Polly's face but I believed her when she said she wouldn't be looking in his bin again!

She eventually divorced her children's miniscule father. He was a homely Irish lad with a sweet, handsome face who couldn't read or write. The real problem was his gambling and Polly having to treat him like an errant child. She couldn't trust him with money for fish and chips for their supper. She certainly couldn't trust him with money for Christmas or birthday presents. She did meet another man, a good guy, another divorcee and they eventually married. They were still together thirty years later and had two more children. She told me she had given up her "wicked past." I smiled when remembering her as the Fourth Missketeer.

I wasn't disappointed when she said with a little grin they planned, saved up for and talked about nothing else but their two annual trips to do Las Vegas. You couldn't make that up either!

Polly's discomfort reminded me of the pretty identical twins training as nurses with us in 1965. We could only tell them apart by Clare having a glass eye. She had glaucoma when a baby and was defensive about her false eye because of her perfect twin. She was with a group of us in uniform at a crossing on Sheffield High Street. As we began walking, her eye popped out as it occasionally did. Four of us scrambled between pedestrians, some of us on our hands and knees looking for the eye while Clare stopped the traffic from moving on. The eye was returned to her and she waved it triumphantly at the irate bus driver at the front.

I heard when in Medway that clever Clare, overall top in our qualifying year ten years before, did follow her vocation of nursing nun in a cloistered world that did not stigmatise her appearance. Most recently I heard she is doing missionary work in East Africa.

Sheri left Windmill Road in 1978 when Kelly was nearly three and moved into a small council flat in Chatham. They were extended family and we missed them deeply. Getting to know Chatham's under-class through Mo and Sheri showed Jo and I that although their choice of fellers was abominable they and their siblings and friends were real, rock solid and would rise again. Their BS Geiger Counter and street savvy were as sharp as a nark's snout.

I didn't miss gullible boys telephoning after Mo and Sheri had been spinning all sorts of nonsense on their naughty nights out. I once had to pretend they were undercover police officers in the pub staking out villains in advance of an international drugs bust. Another time a boy asked politely "can I speak to Mo please?" When I said she was not in he replied she was probably out riding or at the races.

Mo's last tease was for the new gawky teenage neighbour. Green-eyed, busty twenty-three year-old Mo tied her hair in bunches, squeezed into her old school uniform and asked me to pretend to be her mum. Plain, spotty, Timmy had plucked up the courage to ask her out.

"Er ... I was wondering ... er ... would you like to come out with me, Mo?"

"Well, I'd like to but Mum says I've got to do my homework, like!"

She shouted to me in the living room stifling a giggle. "Mum, Timmy would like to ... can I go out with Timmy ... p-l-e-a-s-e?"

"Certainly not, Mo!" I responded, "Homework comes before ... anything else ..."

Sometimes I would wonder who the grown-ups were but their take on life was to live each day to the max and not be hampered by navel-gazing. They were not at all concerned at leaving such stuff to us do-gooders. Most of them were streets ahead in other ways, well-qualified in Life Adversity Science, for example, when teenagers.

Sheri and I had much in common as female offspring regarded and treated as inferior, with needy mothers and favouritism driving deep wedges in the family. We didn't know how much our emotional futures would keep failing us in blindly reliving our past, seeking out 'love objects' that would ultimately kick us in the teeth. Robin Norwood's Women Who Love Too Much published in 1990 was written for Sheri and me and millions of other women who were struggling to get it right.

Money became tight after Mo and Sheri left and I took in five lads from one of the last Chatham Dockyard intake of apprentices. They boarded with us between Monday evening and Friday morning, good-natured, amiable Kentish lads who trailed in and out of the house as part of their treadmill. They provided a steady income and my girls enjoyed their brotherly teasing. They were also very polite about my cooking that was still not my strong point.

My Family Planning sessions continued and I did occasional weekend agency work in London. The pay in town was much better than for local NHS work and an ongoing education. At a few hours' notice I could be pitched in to a busy ICU or ward anywhere in London. It was always stimulating, if nerve-wracking. Permanent staff were too often overtly rude as if agency nurses could not possibly be as qualified or experienced as themselves. Part of the problem must be the difficulties agency nurses face when left in charge. You have to get to grips with the hospital's regime and learn where everything is very quickly.

One night in 1977 I was sent to staff on a women's medical ward at University College Hospital. It was a large, thirty-bedded Gothic monstrosity of a ward for patients who were very sick or who had rare or unusual illnesses. The environment was rank and Day Staff gave me a cursory report without showing me where anything was, not even the emergency resuscitation trolley. The two auxiliaries were lazy and monosyllabic. It was a nightmare from the start.

Staff's report showed a quarter of the women were very poorly and needed specialist care through the night with but one nurse, me. However, not all their medicines were on the drug trolley and I couldn't find the intravenous equipment I would need. Here I was in a 'top' London hospital where no-one could be bothered.

I didn't get off the ward for an hour after I should have because I was ignored completely by Day Staff when they came in at eight. The auxiliaries had bunked off at six and I had been on my own since. Only when Day Staff appeared was I able to start my report. I told the agency I would never go back to such a run-down hospital with the most demotivated, apathetic staff I had come across. It was an ugly example of how a busy London inner-city NHS hospital can go into a downward spiral.

That UCL ward was not my only wretched experience agency nursing. Working in many nursing homes in London and in Kent over a fifteen-year period was similarly unedifying. Solicitor Sarah Harman and I contributed to a Television South-East programme in 1984 about our concerns. Things improved but thirty-five years later the charity Elder Abuse continues to report serious misgivings about the standards of care on behalf of distressed relatives of Rest and Nursing Home residents, private and NHS.

Any patient, place or situation can present a challenge. Nursing in private houses was similar because core personality shows when people are ill, whatever their status. People don't have the energy to keep up a façade though illnesses such as Alzheimer's, tumour cancers, electrolyte imbalance, hypoglycaemia, thyroid imbalance and mental conditions, things can cause alarming personality changes. Whatever the challenge, nursing should remain consistent.

My last agency assignment was in the early 1980s at the independent Wellington Hospital in St. John's Wood, London. My remit was to look after a Libyan police official recovering in his private room from neurosurgery. A male agency nurse with a strong Northern accent handed the report to me and said through his teeth to the patient "sure to let Staff know how many poor bastards you've tortured recently, won't you ..."

I held my breath. The thin, wiry peasant with a neat black moustache and bandaged head nodded in response, grinning happily. This was just after the killing of WPC Yvonne Fletcher in St. James's Square in April 1984 supposedly from a shot from the Libyan Embassy during a demonstration outside the building. Gaddafi's regime did not have the best of reputations regarding the way dissenters in Libya were treated. His cronies were clearly treated well.

The patient behaved like an angel that night.

It wasn't my last private patient's job. Naughty George rang me with a job that was more a favour for an old friend on his last legs than actual nursing. We occasional spoke over the telephone since he had been living with his brother in Chelsea. I asked him to tell me about it before I agreed.

"Oh, it's a piece of cake - actually strawberries! I reckon the Old Boy would like to be fed strawberries by his nurse before he expires. The trouble is the two nurses looking after him at the Dorchester are a bit prim and looked at me as though I was, well, a Naughty George when I asked them! It's worth, erm, fifty quid?"

I began chuckling and said I was up for it. The following Sunday evening I dressed up in my best jeans and casual top and walked up a sumptuously carpeted staircase at the Dorchester Hotel in Park Lane. This was something I would not be doing in uniform. The evening nurse was just leaving as I arrived and looked at me without smiling. The suite was amazing. The man was very frail and barely acknowledged me. I sat on the bed and did what had been asked, fed him strawberries I had brought with me in a paper bag. It was not the erotic experience for the man that George thought it would be. He was very tired and said eventually he would like to go to sleep. I was there for less than half an hour. More easy-peasy cash but another job I would not be doing again.

Chapter Twenty-seven
#Just Another Woman in Love# (Anne Murray)

By early 1979 Jo and I had been married six years. I was surprised. Jo was a good and kind soul but I had fallen for the eldest son of Claudette, our French neighbour three doors away and had begun an affair with him.

It was New Year's Eve 1975 when Claudette, new in the street, knocked on our door to invite Jo and I to pop in later and celebrate with them. She was adorable, an Earth Mother who cast sunbeams over you when you entered her house. Three of her four children were still at home. Ross, the eldest son at twenty, an English Literature undergraduate, I could not take my eyes off.

Though a little tipsy that night I had one more call to my colleagues on duty at the hospital across the road. Ross walked me over and brought me back. An American Air Force bomber pilot's fleece-lined jacket and boots with heels, though he was already tall, completed his Brando look. Blasts of ships' fog horns resonated along the river at midnight. There was laughter and music all about and some fireworks.

My next meeting with Claudette was outside stick-thin, red-haired Macey the artist's house two doors away. She was gallantly trying to pull Macey out of a dustbin, drunk as a skunk and well and truly stuck after trying to deposit her empties quietly I guess. Tears of laughter ran down our faces. As a penance we agreed to help Macey clean and tidy her big Victorian house. Dark and gothic with David Bowie posters on the walls, unfinished artwork lying about and dried cat excreta everywhere, it bordered on squalor. We felt sorry for her two children fending for themselves. They were great kids but we soon picked up they were ashamed of a mum who looked like a rag doll and smelt of alcohol.

Claudette and I, the do-gooders of the moment, laboured all afternoon while Macey sat watching, slurping cider and smoking. When we ventured into her kitchen cupboards we were taken aback on seeing pots, pans and cutlery looking as though it had just come out of a display cabinet. It was all cleaner than mine.

I spent the year avoiding Ross except at meet-the-neighbours-down-the-pub evenings and the occasional crossing of paths at the shops. The attraction had been immediate and mutual and it was a tricky situation. He had that X-factor. He was very bright but I could not become involved with him. The only ground not common to us, apart from him being a student, my being eight years older, married and with two small children, was sport. Certainly not cricket, nor a footballer called Glen Hoddle whom he claimed to have discovered. No rhapsodic element there for me, in fact, so there were times I was not receptive.

When we were together socially Ross and his switched-on student friends, a humorous bunch on top of what was current in the arts, were a breath of fresh air in dullsville Gillingham. Because of the poor job market at the time Ross had started an undergraduate course in English Literature at Hull University as a mature student. He was sharing a house with John McCarthy who, ten years later as a journalist in 1986, would be taken hostage by Islamic Jihad in Beirut and held captive for five years.

It was a passion for music that drew Ross and I together finally. I was in awe of his knowledge of '60s and '70s music in a social and historical context as well as in his appreciation. The band he played in was pretty good too.

Love is blind, as they say, or was it desperate? In the UK, in Gillingham, since 1973 we had lived through an international oil crisis, three-day week and plenty of power cuts. There was a world-wide stock market collapse through 1974 and 1975. Unemployment went over the million mark in Britain. To top it all Prime Minister Callaghan was forced to call in the International Monetary Fund in March 1976 to bail the country out of its financial misery. The winter of 1978-1979 become the Winter of Discontent.

My husband had a job and was the regular, responsible type of man who would always have one. Perhaps I should have been more of a grown-up and seen the problems of taking up with a young man dreaming of being a poet and writer and getting a record deal.

When eventually in 1978 I told Jo I was in love with Ross he was ever practical.

"Well, as Ross is still a student, I'll stay at home for his last year and then leave. Is that okay?" was his considered reply. No row, no raised voices. I was grateful because this was hard for both of us.

He had been a good dad to Lilly whom he had formally adopted.

On reflection it was a courageous act, taking on a ready-made family, or at least a Mother-Child unit. He was also generous in telling me he didn't blame me for our split. I still regard him as the better man and one whom I have great affection for to this day. My girls are lucky ducks to have him as their significant other parent.

It was as hard for Lilly to adjust to. Adapting to another adult suddenly, one who would vie with the limited time in which wife/ mother was available would not be easy. There was also the question of a new home, new life, new routine and the making of new friends. Tolstoy's words that happy families are all the same, whereas unhappy ones will be suffering in an infinite number of ways are heart-achingly difficult to read if you were brought up in the latter.

When we talked about our family life years later Jo said he recalled lots of shouting and noise, although some of it was us lot howling with laughter. The house was full of rumbustious kids most of the time. His memory failed him in thinking Sheri was a calming influence! Endless groups of five lodgers followed, so we did not really have much time in our seven years together as a family unit. He also cannily remarked I would have felt less guilt if he'd been a bastard to me.

Ross and Jo were better able than I to cope with such things as divorce, living in sin, limbo and the like. They weren't Catholic and were therefore spared sitting on the public hot seat for sinners. Jo suffered deeply but he was sided-with by friends, not moralised against. He was after all, the victim in our break-up. Ross's friends were totally on his side, even pleased for him, which gave me some comfort. He had no issues to deal with. Viewing himself as a writer he was immune to petty gossip. He laughed at my guilt-trips and said I shouldn't let the negative opinions of smug moralists get to me.

Mothers tend to take the rap in family splits, don't they? I was probably my own worst "hang 'em, flog 'em" as well. He didn't know how bad I felt at times. In the end it was a matter of me making my own bed and keeping my head, indeed keeping my head above the emotional swamp.

As much as I enjoyed the norms of family life, I had a horror of a repeat of my mother's lacklustre marriage. Sleeping in her bed from the tender age of eight I was a sorry captive to the outpourings of a moaning, resentful woman. Her feelings towards my father were of thinly-disguised hatred. He was the typical benign patriarch of his time; she clearly felt she had wasted her life as a burdened mother with no opt-out. She would have embraced Feminism had it not been for the War and the Catholicism she had been drawn into that would regard any feminine stand with distain, even anathema.

I took note of my favourite author at the time, Simone De Beauvoir, particularly her 1949 book The Second Sex, the first enlightened 20th-century text for women. She insists it is our duty to live every second of our one life to the absolute maximum, without being misinformed by religious or societal dictates because there is neither hellfire nor eternity.

Jo didn't stay long in the house because there was almost no point. He removed his personal things that Autumn of 1978 and went to live with a solicitor friend in London. He told me not long after, she asked him if he wanted Ross "knee-capped." I was flabbergasted hearing such a thing from mild-mouthed Jo. His friend eventually became a judge.

Ross rented Macey's attic room during his vacation periods from Hull and we would meet there. When these two men crossed paths, perhaps when looking after the children, they were cordial, if guarded. We were all so busy with commuting, work, studies, school, child-minding and lodgers it was as though my two girls did not notice Jo was less time at the house and Ross more, though he never formally moved in.

It pained me one weekday morning when my six-year old marched two doors up to Macey's and shouted up to Ross "it's okay, Daddy's gone ..."

We still had lodgers at that time and I still had an income from child-minding so I was able to pay my way, though Jo would not have seen me in financial distress. Despite feeling invigorated and more positive than I had been for a long time, years of religious dogma still hung over me, the black cloud on my low days ensuring I felt like a fallen woman. Our mutual friends, even Sheri and Mo were not shy in offering opinion, even judgement, on our separation, sometimes even in the street. It did not make me feel any better around the neighbourhood that Jo was the favoured one. Brickbats were hurled from all quarters, except from Claudette.

I was the Scarlet Woman, the first in my crowd to work abroad, to be a single parent and now to be heading for a divorce.

Work, my lodgers and my girls of course, kept me occupied and we still managed to have some fun. One of the lodgers was Dave the Bouncer. He had been kicked out by his wife and lamented the fact their house would be sold. He had got the décor just right, he said. It included onyx telephones. Sheri and I loved this and it remains a bench mark for lifestyle aspirations.

Dave was shaving late one afternoon before going off to the club when my neighbour Sue over the alleyway at the bottom of the garden popped in. Her daughter Weeny was Lilly's best friend. Sue was a prankster and was delighted to learn it was Dave in the bathroom. She hammered on the door yelling "you know it's your kid ... when are you goin' to own up and start payin' me some money?" She then made herself scarce.

Dave emerged cautiously and asked who the ... was that. I said it was a woman who came in the back door. Sue in the distance giggling had not made herself scarce enough. Dave picked up a bucket, half-filled it with water and marched down the garden. He tossed the water over the alley but slipped and most of it splashed back off the fence wetting his shirt and jacket. He subsequently became known as Slippery Dave because of this incident and recently slipping on dog poo and breaking his wrist one night when chasing troublemakers from the club.

Because Sue was so mischievous, my lot, including Dave thought it a great idea she had a prank pulled on her. One evening I sat pretend-typing while one of the lads telephoned her saying he was from the local police station. We knew Sue had abandoned her broken down Mini the day before at the top of Chatham Hill.

The 'Police Station' told her the car's handbrake had failed and it had careered down Chatham Hill damaging property and cars and had all but disintegrated. Could she come and collect the bits? It was hard not laughing at questions coming back like "how am I supposed to pick it up" and answers like "Madam, do you have several strong plastic bags ..."

My weekly Family Planning Clinic session at Rainham with occasional filling in at Gillingham continued to be a stabilising factor when so much else was going on. We had a new Sri Lankan Head Doctor and the calibre of the team and its working practices was exemplary.

There were occasionally difficult days. One morning our receptionist said quietly to me someone had rung several times but hung up without speaking. Eventually the caller plucked up the courage to speak and the receptionist put her through to me. I was concerned enough at the distress in her voice, at her bad experience as a child, she said with great difficulty, to tell her I would see her immediately.

Alice was in her mid-forties, slim and well-spoken and reminded me of the actress Claire Bloom. It was with great pain Alice told me that as an evacuee aged seven at the outbreak of war she had been raped. She had never spoken about it and never been able to have a sexual relationship. She had been engaged three times but had to break the relationships off.

"Now I've met someone I really care for ..." she said, on the edge of tears, "and it's my last chance. I mean, I know it's too late to have children ... but I hope it's not too late ..."

I said I would make her a cup of tea and asked if she would be more comfortable talking to a psychosexual specialist. There was panic in her voice when she said she couldn't and I was concerned she would run from the building. When I went for the tea I asked the receptionist to divide my list that morning between the other nurse and the doctor.

"Alice, why don't you come and see me each week and we'll work things through at a pace you are comfortable with. Have you thought about bringing your new friend with you?"

"Oh, I couldn't ..." she said, with a look of terror.

She may have thought I was rushing her and I apologised. Such a scenario was new to me, though I knew my older siblings Morris, Billy and Jane had not had an easy time with their evacuation to Ireland. Most of us have seen the 1939 Pathé News clips of tearful children and mothers parting on coaches and railway platforms on an "adventure" and how it was "best" for them. Operation Pied Piper was the largest ever social upheaval in Britain. Alice and my sister and brothers were but four of three million children relocated in the first four days of September 1939.

I read a lot about it on the 60th anniversary in 1999 and felt once again for Alice after the comment from a clinical psychologist that it was a paedophile's charter. The words "I'll take that one ..." still haunted many of the children herded against the wall in a town or school hall to be eyed by complete strangers.

I was shattered when I got home, barely able to get to grips with a little girl's trauma. All I could do was advise Alice it was all about controlling her recovery, that she would experience an overload of mind chatter about our conversation for several days and that she should try and let it pass over her. She hadn't done anything wrong and everything right in speaking about it.

She never returned to the clinic. I had done my best but for a long time thought it was not enough. It reinforced my belief that teenage boys and men could surely also benefit from having a Well Man and Family Planning advice centres they could drop in to. It was not just women with serious problems. Men tend to be bottlers in that they aren't used to opening up about themselves, about their life and health issues. They are more likely to build avoidance anxiety.

Most men that is, apart from the lorry drivers we hitched lifts with in our student nurse days. They couldn't wait to begin their Confessions of a Decent Truckie "being as you're nurses, like ..." and tell us Vestal Virgins, Ditzy Delia and me, all about their problems with their in-laws, wives, children and sex life.

It was partly from meeting Alice that I began training at the Citizen's Advice Bureau in Gillingham in November 1978. It was a fascinating part-time volunteer post and good for my self-improvement. Many of our Family Planning patients used the opportunity at the clinic of having a friendly ear over their concerns without their husband or partner around. All of us had issues we were coping with to varying degrees. My young lodgers had worries and woes and the need for good information, remembering this was in the days before computers and the Internet. I was always looking things up for them at the CAB office, points of law, where they could find financial help, adoption, who they could talk to about property rights and so on.

It was at this time I realized I needed to see my doctor about my own mental and physical well-being. He seemed to think my situation was stress that would be sorted with a prescription of a new "no side-effects, guaranteed" benzodiazepam drug called Ativan. I should have known better. It had a disconcerting effect making me feel semi-detached and seeing my situation as surreal. I suffered the guarantee for a few weeks, to the day I decided to stop taking the drug. As with Valium this was not easy. The withdrawal symptoms I endured when eventually I had to be determined about stopping taking the drug, were greater than the worst PMT.

At the beginning of December I thought my stress had gone but began to suffer bouts of tachycardia and breathlessness that led to me needing to get out of the room, or faint. At their worst they were terrifying attacks and I felt as if I was going mad. They came upon me when I was outside as well. Freud would surely have had a field day with my compulsive urge to bolt.

An acupuncturist in London was recommended and it was no surprise learning my stress levels were high. A consequence was the over-production of adrenalin, insulin spikes and a swollen pancreas. He was concerned, telling me my pulses indicated the need for immediate action. I was ordered to give up caffeine and all sugars, even those in fruit and particularly that from the lager I was quaffing regularly. I had to hydrate with water.

We are used to people walking around with bottles of water today. It was unknown in the 'Seventies and swigging from a bottle looked and felt a very odd thing to be doing in public. It was distinctly uncouth before the American habit of drinking directly from a bottle or can took over in Britain.

Apart from the acupuncturist I did not divulge these strange, nervy attacks to anyone, afraid I would be labelled a neurotic or even lambasted with a "what did you expect from the way you've behaved?" My dietary regime was not entirely successful and I was still having problems venturing into the street. One bus ride I had to make one afternoon, now desperate for information was to the local WH Smith. It had the tiniest Self-help section but there I found a book that put a name to my palpable angst, Panic Attacks. I flicked through it and *voilà*!

My mother 'phoned me two weeks before Christmas to say Pa had been admitted to Rotherham Hospital. I learned from the Ward Sister it was ostensibly for rehabilitation because of muscle wasting from Father having been in bed for a prolonged period with Bulbar Palsy. The symptoms of the palsy are a degeneration of the cranial nerves and therefore difficulty in chewing, swallowing and talking. Mother was at the end of her tether and asked if I could come up to Sheffield for a few days. She knew she would not be able to cope if he came back home and needed some moral support.

His bed had been in the sitting room for weeks and my poor mother had exiled herself to the garage because of his erratic behaviour, his interminable playing of his cherished opera records and his weeping. I wasn't feeling particularly charitable but he was my father and I obliged. I was still technically banned from home from becoming pregnant when unmarried. It still galled me he had met Farid and liked him. Or he liked the fact Farid was Catholic, public school educated, a lawyer and came from a very good family. I was still banned. I wasn't sure either if I was strong enough to face all this just then.

I was concerned at the hospital that he had resigned himself to staying in bed and no doubt to dying. He had no intention of, or was incapable of discussing his condition with me and it was clear on my second day at his bedside his cantankerous behaviour was being exacerbated by uraemia caused by malfunctioning kidneys. When I did things for him on the ward the words "bitch" and "prostitute" emanated from his lips.

He did go back home and a private nurse came in to help Mother. Sister Jane was able to come in for the week before Christmas. When I spoke to her over the telephone I remembered all those years ago, back in the late 1940s she had been Pa's favourite, until she had seen him kissing the maid. After that she got the same silent treatment I had always endured.

"So, any paternal embrace, the filial forgiveness?"

"Huh!" Jane snorted. "He was sweetness and light to the private nurse, calling her Darling. His last words to me were 'get out you whore ...'"

Fortunately, Jane and I had long experience of nursing people with uraemia and other conditions that changed their behaviour and were able to see Father as a patient. I said goodbye to him in hospital on December 15. He died on Christmas Day. The 'phone call I got on Christmas Day some twenty years later to tell me my beloved sister Jane had died unexpectedly was far more upsetting than the one I received from Jane about Father. It is not a time of the year, a day, that gives me any joy.

During 1979 Claudette and her husband Evan sold up and moved along the North Kent Coast to Whitstable. This was then a timeless seaside town with a small harbour handling enough wet fish and shellfish to keep it smelling authentic. I took to the town immediately when visiting with Ross because it reminded me of Cornwall. The shingle banks were worth writing home about because they were not the broad sands of Par beach or even Margate. The town's alleyways, narrow streets, sailors' cottages and Dickensian shops along Harbour Street are occasionally used as a film and television set. It had a pleasing shabbiness, flaking paint, old lobster pots, discarded rope and long-abandoned boats rotting in corners.

The decision Ross and I made to follow his parents to Whitstable later in 1979 was because the kids had taken to him. Lilly was much better behaved than she ever was with Jo. From the age of two my Little Darling had frequently tried to rule the roost, sometimes to an exhausting degree. Jo almost never countered, or responded to her occasional over-the-top rudeness to a parent. Kitty's arrival aggravated the situation. I was asked to put her in the dustbin when I brought her home from the maternity unit. Jo was just too placid about all this. Children need guidance and guidelines. They need to be loved while being made aware of the feelings of others around them. A self-centred child does not make for a balanced adult.

Our Windmill Road house was sold in Autumn 1979. A more than fair settlement from Jo and financial assistance from Claudette helped Ross and I buy a two-floor flat in a sought-after row of houses on Whitstable's beach front known as Wave Crest. This "rare opportunity" to buy an almost uninhabitable abode cost us a little over nine thousand pounds. It sounds cheap when, thirty-five years later such apartments are pushing half-a-million to buy but the purchase of a house or flat has never been easy for anyone at any time. We were all very excited about our new start, right on the shingle,

with the Thames estuary and Isle of Sheppey in front of us and skies
that Turner trekked from London every Autumn to paint.

Looking across the grey waters and the very skies from our
second-floor-to-be while Ross and the girls were exploring the shingle
below I picked out Southend-on-Sea and Shoeburyness on the far
side of the estuary. The Maunsell Forts were visible from the floor
above us. They are the four-legged crab-like defensive structures
named after the Second World War engineer who designed them.
Pirate radio including Radio Caroline, Radio City, Radio 390 and
Essex Radio operated from some of these forts until the 1967 Act. I
could almost wave at Celia and me in our little sailor suits on the
Queen of the South paddling around Sheppey on our way to Herne
Bay, busy, busy with serving drinks to passengers. I was young then,
in 1967.

The estate agent told us that Oliver Postgate, author of the Ivor
the Engine books and Bagpuss had lived in the maisonette above.
Was it a good omen for Ross, who wanted to write? Andrew Motion,
the last Poet Laureate and one of Ross's tutors had consistently
awarded him top marks through his final year at Hull. Ross's mates
had no doubt he would become a worthy scribe. They plodded off
to work for the BBC. He should have as well.

With winter already coming down the North Sea, across the Essex
Marshes and knocking on our door the move would not be easy. Ross
had finished his studies and was without work. We had no money with
which to make essential improvements to the flat. The leasehold
property was un-mortgageable in its current state. Fortunately, Ross's

brother Pat had offered to do basic work in the tiny basement scullery.

He would also line the old bathroom with pine cladding so we could concentrate on decorating the girls' room. There was a real possibility of burst pipes and we had to hang blankets over the windows for a while.

With Kitty five and Lilly eight, relocation to the seaside here was entirely positive. It was a more affluent area than the Medway Towns with better schools. The beach front was a wonderful place for them to play in. Having enjoyed roaming Lostwithiel with my pal Jenny I was gratified my own children would be able to enjoy a similar freedom and fresh air. The difficulties of the previous two or three years were beginning to be worth it, though I would miss all my Medway mates.

Adding to my discomfort at leaving Jo was the new one of living in sin with Ross, with my children, until such time as we married. This particular 'sin' wasn't as common as it is today. I took some comfort in reading Victorian novels in which the idealised family unit was rather rare. So many children were orphaned or abandoned or put into the care of relatives because of the much lower life expectancy. Step-families resulted through tragedy rather than the divorce of today that still has the taint of immorality about it.

The fact that Jo and I remained on amicable terms on his regular visits to see the children in our last few months in Gillingham and that I never talked badly about him puzzled some. There is nothing bad you can say about the man anyway and it was important for the girls that our separation was as smooth as possible.

It took a while to realise in my new relationship I was as much in love in the mumsy sense, with Ross's mother as I was with Ross in the love-bird sense. She didn't disappoint in being a wonderfully patient and loving step-granny. My mother had remained in Sheffield and did not feature in this new stage of my life. Jo's mother, suffering from early Alzheimer's was living with her daughter in Cambridge. Thankfully, she never knew about our splitting up.

Witnessing both Jo's and Ross's mums being one hundred per cent loyal and uncritical of their children was a learning curve for me. Theirs was simple, unconditional maternal love in the way I loved mine. Non-stop family dramas, hysterics and fall-outs were the norm through my childhood and will have had a bearing on my seeking out placid partners from happier families. Is there any point too, in blaming parents who lack the parental gene?

As we prepared to up-sticks from Gillingham, hippy artist Macey, unable to let go of the 1960s, was near the bottom of a downward spiral after years of Free Love and alcohol and substance abuse. She was a highly intelligent but self-destructive narcissist, a spoilt only-child to elderly parents, one who could not adapt to the responsibilities of having children. She had at least one "drying-out" after which her friend Big Mick was a stabilising influence on her and her two children. He loved my two girls as well and I have fond memories of this gentle man in an otherwise slightly fraught but friendly neighbourhood.

Our immediate neighbour whom Sheri named Garth because she was the one who did the practical things around the house was also a bit of a handful and, I found out years later a rather better-disguised alcoholic. She marched in to Macey's one day screaming for all to hear about the seduction of her dozy taxi-driver husband, "you can have him but not the dog ..." She apparently threw down her husband's pyjamas and snatched back the terrified retriever.

Ross and I befriended Macey's eldest in the months we were in and out of her house and were saddened to see him become a recluse in his mid-teens. His younger sister was eventually fostered because of their mother's alcoholism.

Macey had also seduced one of Ross's friends, bespectacled George. He was chuffed that an older hippy chick had sorted his virginity problem to the point where he didn't mind a red rash all over his penis. "Doctor, my lad!" I ordered. He was even more pleased to be seen next time with two large tubes of cream for treating thrush, as though this was part of his rite of passage.

When her fine three-storey house was eventually sold it became the infamous "Nappy House," The Gentleman's Nursery. Proprietor Nanny Hazel was featured many times on television. Producers couldn't get enough of big lorry drivers, lawyers and company bosses in oversize rompers and baby dresses regressing into the comfort of their childhood. Nanny Hazel would even feed them on camera sat in high chairs before tucking them up for an afternoon nap in big cots.

Contrary to what many assume there was strictly nothing sexual about the Nappy House and the big babies were certainly not allowed to soil their nappies. Mo and her future brood of kids lived down the road from Nanny Hazel in what rapidly became a predominantly Asian area. She reported regularly on seeing gentlemen toddlers being pushed around in a large pram and playing on toy trikes and swings in the back garden with dummies in their mouths. We wondered what the Asian community thought of this. Sheri and I are just miffed The Gentleman's Nursery was not there when we were!

Liking men, particularly husbands, two Gillingham Jezebels had already had a go at mine. One Sunday morning after Ross and I and others had been to a wedding in London I came downstairs, fortunately before my children. Ross was on the pull-out sofa bed, Julie who should have been in the spare room, was lying next to him. After dressing she stomped out of the house, her ego well bruised, muttering she didn't know what was wrong with this one who "didn't want to know." Ross said both women, Julie and Macey, terrified him.

I had served my time in Gillingham and wouldn't have missed any of it but it was time to move on.

It was goodbye to the Great Lines and spectacular steam engine rallies, Jezreel's Tower, Medway Maritime and her great 'Seventies night staff, nursery staff and Social Club; goodbye 'Lady'; *au revoir* Sheri; 'bye for now Mo and her super-chav mates; cheerio Lilly's and Kitty's little friends including Weeny, also many mums including Sue and Macey; farewell the Strand and Black Lines swimming pools, Nanny Hazel's Gentleman's Nursery we almost knew, Rainham Working Men's Social Club, The Pentagon and all Medway's doolally citizens; farewell Byron Road Playgroup and Primary School and Summer holiday train trips to the beaches at Westgate, Margate and Broadstairs.

Chapter Twenty-eight
#Heart of Gold ...# (Neil Young)

Much of my guilt about my girl's lives being disrupted disappeared when both children started bringing home little friends whose families were also newly split up. One of Kitty's doe-eyed buddies from playgroup proudly showed me a drawing of her three daddies. There were plenty of nice children at the schools and my girls took readily to a new extended family in windy Whitstabubble as they had rechristened the town after hearing this on television.

Kitty had never been any trouble in Gillingham, being placid like her father. Now she said she loved Whitstable.

"Mum, it's all I ever knew," was her response many years later on my breaking up with her father and moving on.

Her ambiguity showed the same determination of when I was young, in hoping to reinvent the marriage wheel and live happily ever after with the same husband, lovely home, no sickness or financial worries, job satisfaction all round ...

For the moment I was happy enough enjoying watching my daughters growing up, even with elements of "do you remember when Ro said ..." My Miss Malaprop, a little cutie in Heidi plaits with honest blue eyes exclaimed one day on a crowded bus in Whitstable, "Mum, it's packed jam in here!" On another occasion at her junior school she was clearly impressed with lessons on the Egyptian Pharaohs and the pyramids. We had popped in after school to see my mother.

"Granny ..." she drawled, sucking her index finger,

"Yes, Dear."

"... w-h-e-n y-o-u d-i-e ..."

"Ye-e-e-s ..."

"... will you take your jewellery and your Slow Cooker with you in your tomb ..."

Lilly settled down quickly also. A lively and enterprising child she always had plenty of energy when it came to making extra pennies. In Gillingham when a whim took hold she was not afraid to set up a stall outside our front door with a hand-painted "Kiddiewinks Boot Fair" sign. Lucky passers-by could be offered almost anything from grotty apples and pears from our fruit trees, to luke-warm cups of diabolical tea.

They both did well at their new schools. They hadn't taken after their mother who, instead of revising would have been poring over mags in her bedroom puffing on a Woodbine and fanning the smoke out of the window.

Money or no, Ross and I began getting our dwelling into order with input from our brothers. I was grateful Pascal and Morris came down from Putney to measure up and supply double-glazing for a nominal sum. Younger brother Simon fitted the units for pocket money. It was a relief when the blankets came down and there was no longer wind whistling through the old place, through your bones.

That first winter of 1979-1980 was raw. Sometimes it was difficult to turn the corner at the end of Wave Crest by the tennis courts with the breath sucked out of you. Soon the cold was matching that of the 1962-1963 winter. It snowed on and off for months. Essex across the estuary looked to be at a standstill from sheer grey cold.

Jo eventually left Gillingham and bought a flat a few miles away in Faversham. He sorted out our divorce on which neither of us set conditions. We agreed open access for the girls at all times and he seemed happy seeing them many, if not most, weekends. He joined a group of newly-divorced dads including two who had condemned us, particularly me, until their own divorces.

It gave Ross and I a chance to be 'a couple.' We would walk along the shingle to the Old Neptune pub and meet his friends, bright young things without, as yet, children. I enjoyed hearing the younger women talking confidently about careers and equal opportunities and children having to "fit in." At Saturday night parties we gradually got to know Whitstable's Yuppies and the occasionally 'downwardly mobile' trendy.

Although many of my friends allied with Jo and quietly slipped out of my life, I was not going it alone. A 2006 report in the Daily Mail suggested modern woman was choosing a different man every

decade as her wishes and needs evolved. Wow! That made my 1978 stand for a more fulfilling life look pale. Moving on with my children was my decision. Ross turned out not to be the better man and that was maddening but I don't regret meeting him.

There were many exciting moments to come, such as when the actor Peter Cushing, best known for his roles in Hammer Horror films walked past our window. He lived next to Wave Crest at Seaway Cottages. He referred to himself as MOG, Miserable Old Git, my neighbour informed me. She said all his neighbours protected his privacy by diverting fan-seekers and autograph hunters. When we eventually exchanged pleasantries we found him a gentleman, charming, with a wry humour.

My neighbour, Kay, a feisty seaside landlady with a foghorn of a voice was best friend and bingo partner to the actor's housekeeper, Maisie. Being partial to a bevvy after bingo on the High Street, Maisie would often crash out at Kay's so she stood a chance of getting to Mr. Cushing's house the following morning for the daily doings.

The actor kept a low profile, particularly after his wife's death in 1971. He walked by every day for lunch at the Tudor Tea Rooms in Harbour Street. He also walked or cycled the considerable distance to his wife's grave side every day, because he felt he had neglected her and for other reasons during their marriage, Maisie intimated.

Soon after we arrived in Whitstable I began looking for daytime shift work. Not having worked days on wards since I was a student I was daunted at the prospect of the Kent and Canterbury Hospital. Much more convenient anyway was the Cottage Hospital in Tankerton within easy cycling distance. I had a choice of approaches including one along the sea front, through the yacht club and harbour, past the shingle bank uncovered at low tide known as The Street, Tankerton Slopes and beach huts galore.

It was a curious feeling when shown around the wards with the lights full on and being watched by patients, doctors and colleagues. It's not like this at night. Miss Marlow, the Nursing Officer (a title replacing Matron) in charge of Whitstable and Tankerton Cottage Hospital, the "Whit and Tank," offered me thirty hours a week as a staff nurse on a thirteen-bed male geriatric ward. I had always been in charge of a ward on nights. Now I would be joining a team of Ward Sister, SEN, another part-time Staff Nurse like me and three auxiliaries.

Got me a bike, got me a fob watch and new surgical scissors on a chain! Way to go!

"Well, Mum," began Big Ears Lilly who had heard me fretting to Ross about being back at work with new regimes and practices, "Kitty and I had to start at new schools, so you'll have to be brave, like us. Don't worry, nurses are nice ladies because they make poorly people better!"

A little later she asked more thoughtfully if it meant I didn't have to sleep during the day any more. I promised I would have more time and would take them to Canterbury to buy some new clothes and go to the cinema.

Miss Marlow was a dream for someone like me who had been out of the loop for a while. She was a kindly Minnie Mouse and so different from frosty Matron Welburn at The Royal. Miss Marlow's ten-to-two feet raised particles at the speed with which she went around the corridors. She had a rat-a-tat-tat voice to go with it. Unfortunately, her office was next us on William Ward, Male Geriatric, though we soon got used to her squeaky voice with its mix of instruction, woe and occasional pantomime.

Ward Sister Montague was small and serious with an elegant Tudor face with high cheek bones. Neatly uniformed in Sister's navy blue with a silver-buckled belt and white frilly cap she had perfected a girlie pose for doctors walking into her office. I thought she was in her mid-twenties but was ten years out, Polly the senior auxiliary informed me.

Sister Montague, Rachel, took me on a tour of her ward of four and nine beds. I was working opposite her with an SEN and one or two auxiliaries in the mornings and one auxiliary on afternoon and evening shifts. Extra staff were usually brought in on theatre days.

The patients were mostly older fellows with age and lifestyle diseases including strokes, heart attacks, terminal cancer, respiratory disease, Alzheimer's, multiple sclerosis, diabetes and arthritis or rheumatoid arthritis. Some were admitted for respite care to give their exhausted wives a rest. The younger men had back problems usually and would be on traction in the four-bedded side ward that was also used for Op' Day admissions.

It was a GP-led hospital. The doctors would call in on their patients after morning surgery. The weekly theatre list on Wednesday mornings and Friday afternoons was consultant-led from the Kent and Canterbury. The hospital buzzed on these days, Sister Montague said. Anaesthetists first, then the surgeons. They were somewhat flirty Polly warned, like a rugby team on a day trip to the seaside. My tour with Sister Montague was a pleasant surprise and I was sure I would quickly get the hang of things.

Ross was pleased that I was pleased and even suggested to his mother she might like the cottage hospital rather than the Nursing Home she helped out in for a pittance. He looked so young and fresh-faced while carrying such a world-weary expression he made his mother and I laugh.

The togetherness of Claudette and her children had a lot to do with years of wanderings during hard times, Ross said, after his parents lost their pub in the East End. The locals tried to keep it going by buying in the beer then drinking it. They were fighting a losing battle with a landlord slipping down the corkscrew of alcoholism, through beer barrels. It was an era a very young Ross had all but blanked.

Kindly though Miss Marlow was I soon realised she would be hard going. She postulated from first thing in the morning, when beds were undone and awaiting new sheets and elderly gentlemen were being bathed or were sitting on commodes behind curtains. It was usually about her blood pressure, or someone else's in her family and how they would be in a sorry state if she went first with a stroke or something. Such talk was not good when patients were very poorly, even dying. If she was "on one" and could not "zip it," as lovely Polly noted, we would hum quietly to ourselves.

Polly was a ballroom dancer with the look of Bette Davis and deportment of a ballerina. When the mood in the ward was good, we were on top of our chores and Miss Marlow ('Monte Carlo') was not about, Polly would twirl our ambulant patients round and round demonstrating the Fox Trot, Waltz or Gay Gordons. I was soon joining in. They loved it, the Old Boys, dancing with their nurses before bed time and would clap and cheer and just smile. That was the idea.

I learnt to dance at the vicar's weekly gathering at the church hall in Lostwithiel, though that was not our prime reason for being there. I wanted dancing lessons when young and piano and singing lessons for that matter but Mother, fairly, I suppose said if she had to pay for one of us she would have to pay for all. Polly danced well and we all picked up tips and technique from her. Then it was back to reality.

"I mean, Staff," Miss Marlow would twitter, "blah, blah ... my blood pressure ... blah, blah ..."

"... Yes, Miss Marlow."

As experienced nurses and because we were not training others, we didn't actually need an overseer. We quickly refined practices and policy and the ward ran efficiently in spite of her presence. It was a pity because she was a sweetie.

Whitstable was, on the face of it genteel and churchy with a liberal arty clique patronising a music club, social club, art club, golf club, cricket, tennis, football, a theatre, photography club and umpteen art galleries. It was reminiscent of Cornwall. My concern when I started was how some of the older ancillary staff might react to my marital status. Personal lives would come up for discussion.

I needn't have worried. Nurses and doctors tend to be conservative and traditional. A cardiac surgeon remarked it is quite fitting they were viewed as dull, plodding perfectionists, as patients wouldn't really want a Jack the Lad over them with a sharp knife. Nevertheless, there was plenty of gossip about plenty of "goings on."

It was a bonus that William Ward staff were friendly from the beginning, though Ward Sister and SEN Sarah did stick together. Polly in particular was wonderful to me and the patients. She thought she must be very boring because she did not gossip but it was a joy to work with someone so positive about everything. It was also interesting that the auxiliaries were posher than us trained staff.

Geriatric care is not every nurse's favourite. I enjoyed the Old Devils on these wards. They were in the main polite and well-mannered, a generation brought up in the days when people were more respectful to each other. As I have said about my own parents, they had survived one or even two World Wars, a Depression and other untold hardships. They were mostly dutiful innocents. Up to the 1970s I found them generally unselfconscious, uncomplicated, sexually undemanding and often sexually deprived.

Work on my new ward also reinforced my belief that male patients are easier to nurse. Men behave themselves because they are generally nurtured, cared for and loved by females throughout their lives. Nurses also theorise that female patients are so pleased to be looked after, some take advantage, even play up. Some are so exhausted on admittance they make the most of having a rest. I have always enjoyed being a patient for this last reason.

During my nursing I endeavoured to put myself in my patients' shoes. Some therapists call it "getting into state." Labouring up the many hills to the Whit and Tank on my old bicycle was my preparation period for the Old Boys. Twenty minutes was also enough time in which to put domestic things aside and I felt good walking onto the ward. It was not so for all of my colleagues. Black clouds brought in are clear to all and having to tiptoe around colleagues is a trial.

My main focus was on how it is to be elderly and what fears and worries these gentlemen had. They may be losing, or had lost once taken-for-granted abilities, faculties and responsibilities. We had to be aware of trauma the spouse was experiencing, especially after bereavement. Few of the older men could cook or clean or even knew how to use a washing machine. This could be a real worry for a surviving husband.

One elderly man, distraught at his wife's death during the evening came in with me to the chapel attached to the hospital after we had laid her out. How peaceful she looked, as if she had departed for a nice holiday. To her husband the practical side of things suddenly struck home and he blurted out "oo's gonna make me tea tonight?"

One of the long-stay patients in William Ward admitted because they were unable to look after themselves properly was Jim, a recent double amputee. He was an ex-Royal Navy diabetic smoker. Double trouble here for the arteries and circulation. Jim was a "don't mess with me" ex-boxer but really a softie.

His second leg had only recently been amputated and he had returned home to his disabled wife Bet, also a diabetic. Unfortunately he was back with us just after Christmas because she died unexpectedly. They had a nice Christmas night watching television, Jim told me and he had gone to bed at midnight. Bet stayed up to tidy up and because there was no one keeping an eye on her she wickedly scoffed a whole box of After Eight Mints.

"Anyways, Staff," Jim continued sadly, "it was freezing cold and the neighbours saw Bet dancin' around in the snow in the early hours 'cos the chocs must have made her all excited, like. Then she must have just fallen over. By the time she was found it were too late. Who'd 'ave thought it, death by After Eights ..."

John Bull, one of life's observers, knew how to look after himself but his circumstances were not ideal. His dwelling was a rotten caravan on the edge of Blean Woods and the cold and damp affected his toes. Dr. Montague admitted him every Autumn for up to six months to prevent gangrene.

Our weekly list patients admitted on a Tuesday evening for a Wednesday operation offered some light relief from the regular patients in the main ward. One such was the manager of a local squash club. He swaggered in with his sports bag, highlighted hair and perma-tan, flirting, blagging away to a bemused bunch of older patients. He hadn't a clue how much his haemorrhoidectomy would take the wind out of his sails.

"Can't you give me any more painkillers, Nurse ..." he pleaded the morning after his operation.

"Sorry, Peter, you're on the max," I said and asked him to roll on his side. I told him for the last bit of procedure he must push gently but not clench his buttocks.

Hot-to-trot Peter yelled, calling me all sorts of names. I held up the large yellow sponge, the type you wash a car with, the surgeon had placed in his rectum as packing.

"Wot the bleedin' ... you're taking the ..."

The true pain after a piles operation was yet to come, going to the toilet. I did feel sorry for him, simpering away despite strong pain killers. At least he didn't faint at the sight of a hypodermic needle, as men do at a ratio of 20:1 with women! His macho image had well and truly deflated by the time his similarly orange-looking girlfriend came to pick him up.

In my career the reaction of a spouse or close relative to death ranged from calm resignation, to hysteria and shock, to withdrawal. I was screamed at on three occasions, with one woman directly accusing me of killing her husband.

In contrast was the reaction of an elderly neighbour whose wife was taken by ambulance to the Nunnery Fields Ward at Canterbury. They were a Diamond Wedding Anniversary couple who had lived in Wave Crest since the 1920s. A couple of days later I asked no-nonsense Mr. C. who had received two medals for valour and bravery from the Queen, how his wife was.

"Oh, she's a goner ... thank you," he said and shut the door. He was managing, even at 96, though his daughter was arranging a place in a Home. A few weeks later I knocked on his door again, this time with condolences for his wife's passing.

"Thank you ... goodbye," he said and shut the door again.

I also learnt about Wave Crest from one of our revolving-door patients, Mr. P. However hard we worked on his shin ulcer with skin grafts, dressing and re-dressing, resting it, exposing it, oxygen therapy, honey, egg white, zinc and vitamins he would be back taunting us about his intractable wound. It could have been deliberate aggravation, one of the District Nurses suggested. Keeping chronic leg ulcers going was a favourite with some patients to ensure daily visits from a nurse, or repeat hospitalization. It cost the NHS a small fortune in those days.

It was while giving Mr. P., a local man, a pre-dressing analgesia and trying to calm him that I mentioned living in Wave Crest.

"Oh, I remember them being built, around 1910," he said brightening up. "My dad was a carpenter on them and I would take him his lunch. I tell you, even though they've been flooded out, especially in 'Fifty-three when the sea reached the High Street an earthquake won't shift them! My dad said we wouldn't believe how much beach shingle was shovelled into the foundations!"

Inevitably there are more deaths on a geriatric ward. It bothers me greatly that District Nurses no longer lay out their deceased patients unless they are present at the death. This 'saving' along with the demise of Home Helps came about during Virginia Bottomley's tenure as Secretary of State for Health between 1992 and 1995 in John Major's government. The Local Authority Social Services Act of 1970 and the years after 1974 when there was more liaising between local authorities and the NHS was a time of better services for elderly people.

Home Helps, for example was a comprehensive service that included light cleaning or tidying up, essential shopping, bathing and washing of clients' hair and cutting nails. They were in the elderly or mentally disabled person's home for perhaps a couple of hours. The idea was to extend the time people who needed care could remain in the community, preferably in their own home.

Those of us who do not subscribe to the dogmatic axing or re-organising of social services, cost-cutting under the guise of improvement, knew what would come next. Such cutting back most likely to affect poorer people has not been limited to Conservative governments. Like the metalepsis "customers" for patients, introduced in Thatcher's era, elderly people became "cost units."

On the wards the now-extinct SEN was a known quantity. Nursing journals are frequently blunt about SEN replacements being cheap labour, as I am about auxiliaries and juniors carrying out procedures I trained years for. Trained nursing staff are tied up with administrative responsibilities and I don't think this is an appropriate use of their skills. Those of us who trained during the 1960s put in a minimum forty-four hour week mainly at the bedside and are proud of the thoroughness with which we learnt our trade. Study blocks were for three introductory months and then for four weeks each year thereafter. Hands-on experience like this gave me confidence in what I was doing.

I endeavoured to be aware that if a patient irritated or offended or made me doubt reported pain, nausea or anxieties, it was my problem, not the patient's. It was my immaturity or tiredness or low mood. I wonder how many nurses who tread the academic path to nursing are aware of such things?

As a student I did see myself as a dedicated angel and handmaiden and know now that an almost divinely-ordained and passive supplicant to nursing belongs to yester-year. The perception today with modern nursing theory and degree status goes the other way in looking like a career profession re-jigged by modern independently-minded women. Laudable, maybe but with it comes less compassion towards the patient than there was with old-style nursing.

Medical staff the world over welcome innovation and improvement in methods and practices. It was a pity we had no students at the Whit and Tank. They would have been a breath of fresh air, particularly those not afraid of questioning things we were doing that had been superseded. Outdated practices for dealing with wounds and pressure sores, for example were carried on often for no other reason than they were a Ward Sister's preference. Zinc and castor oil cream, or plain soap and water were typical lingering treatments. Soap can be any number of things.

Anecdotal evidence and "good enough in my day" remedies are not acceptable, particularly when it is known they can also cause harm. Degree-trained nurses will be more up-to-date. The issue is not to ignore the intimacy of old-style nursing in favour of analytical, research-based nursing. There will come a balance and the kudos of being a nurse will surely, once again ride high.

In such a small unit I got to know Ward Sister Montague and her husband well. Dr. Montague was an agreeable, grey-haired gentleman, one of the local Health Centre's senior doctors. Rachel worked there before starting at the Whit and Tank. At that time she was married to a local butcher who had the same surname as me. This freaked her when I arrived. The much older Dr. Montague was married with children. Nevertheless, Rachel was determined to take him away from his wife and elevate herself from her lowly background, something she later admitted was the driving force in her quest for status and property.

All sides suffered from the outset. The doctor's teenage son pleaded with her to leave his father alone. His distraught wife was telling people in the street about her husband's affair, indeed, affairs and his drinking. Her husband had her sectioned. Rachel became paranoid knowing this could befall her but still she would not let go. The stress she was causing herself led to a breakdown.

When they finally set up home in a big country house not long before I started at the Whit and Tank, Rachel had a new problem, the good doctor's increased drinking. Within months of my arriving she would be on the 'phone to me during the evening often in tears about the associated problems.

My little situation with Jo and Ross was inconsequential by comparison. Single-minded I may have been on occasion but a pussycat compared with Ruthless Rachel over the years. She was needy and vulnerable and it did not surprise me she adored Princess Diana, associating herself with the Princess's feelings of being a victim and patronised. She felt she was enduring the same at the hands of her husband and of "the suits" at the Health Centre.

In those early days I was interested in how she coped with the step-children over school holidays, for example, as she had no children of her own. Ross was also learning about being a full-time stepfather and I could relate more to his difficulties by hearing about Rachel's.

At times through 1980, Rachel's traumas with her husband affected the running of the ward. On one theatre day Sarah and I were trying to prepare pre-med injections from the drug cupboard in her tiny office while she sat blubbing. Sarah's normally pale poker face on the edge of an outburst herself was a classic. Polly, ever kind offered to take our distraught Ward Sister to her house nearby. We telephoned Dr. Montague who was in the middle of his surgery and he called at Polly's house to give his wife a sedative. His passive, almost detached demeanour on these occasions did not look right to us.

Incidents she could not cope with included the younger son deliberately trapping his dad's hand in a door, setting fire to their house when on a visit during school holidays and the worry he would stab her. Her placid hubby, she said, was caught in the middle and would take to the bottle rather than take charge. The children were all clearly in great emotional pain. Doctor Montague had no idea how to cope with his young wife. I couldn't take sides because I liked both them.

We got through that Op' Day seriously under-staffed. Ross saw how tired I was and began to wonder what I had landed myself in at the hospital. We were not having a hard time like Rachel and her husband but we did have differences that needed resolving.

It was interesting listening to Rachel's entrenched views about the children, perhaps because she was young and inexperienced. She would not give an inch. Ross's take was uncomfortably similar. Both were unable to put themselves in the shoes of traumatised children. Both harped on about them being demonic narcissists, savvy little brutes who knew how to twist the knife to bleed their guilty parents for toys, designer clothes and anything else they fancied.

Becoming a stepfamily was harder than I had envisaged, one with a learning curve that included emotional turmoil when all I intended was to love and be loved. I was fortunate in having Claudette as a mother-in-law. Her anxious-to-please brown eyes and chuckle lines were endearing to an insecure soul like me. She was also a wonderful step-grandmother who eased the family through many a blip and niggle. She had been married before and dealt with Ross's father turning intractably against her bewildered daughter by her first husband. She compromised by sending her daughter away to boarding school at the age of seven seeing it as the lesser of two evils.

During 1980 Ross was accepted by the University of Kent at Canterbury to study for his MA. He also won a small grant. He would be working from home mostly, studying structuralism and the work of the poet J. H. Prynne. This British teacher and librarian at Cambridge University Ross held in awe as an experimentalist and one of the most influential poets of the time. He read me some of his work. Here was a wonderful use of language but I found it obscure even after several readings. Ross faltered while reading one of his favourite pieces and said, grimacing, it would not be an easy ride.

I had a brush with structuralism and "the end of language" as part of one of my OU modules and we would have conversations about not having conversations. It was fun for a while but structuralism became a forgotten science, like twelve-tone, serial, music. I liked Foucault, the French philosopher associated with structuralism. His thinking encouraged me to question the status quo of the norms, institutions and hypocrisies we live with.

His questioning of what is madness, for example and how each culture is selective and even cynical about it was of great interest. The labelling of nuisance and difficult patients is too easy when blame is shifted onto them. It is much more likely to be a problem of society or the blamer rather than that of the labelled, as I wrote a couple of pages back.

The splendid Open University course material was awakening and expanding my thinking. I had been working at it rain or shine since 1977; history, philosophy, literature, poetry and music. I managed to submit monthly assignments and follow the lectures on radio and television in the early morning or after midnight. I took time out during one subject only, psychology. I wanted something more immediate than what was offered at the time.

Ross was a great help in motivating me because three part-time jobs in Gillingham left little time or the inclination to open study books when I was able to sit down quietly. From leaving school I had only ever studied nursing and was all too well aware of what being an ignoramus is around clever or informed people. Both Jo and Ross had good brains. The OU Foundation Course quickly came into its own.

Ross's closest university friends settled in at the Beeb. He found a part-time job. It's possible he could have joined them and it might even have been the making of him. On the other hand I didn't want him to commute to London as Jo had done all the time we were together. He didn't want to do it either. It is a killer journey from Whitstable that would have meant five hours commuting a day.

Living now with Ross was similar to sharing the flat in Earls Court with Celia as he, like she, continued to raise my critical awareness. He was years younger than me but "born old" as they say, like Prince Charles, like many eldest sons. I was almost the youngest in a big family and much younger and lighter in outlook and behaviour. Maybe Ross, serious, bespectacled, his blue eyes weighing up the world was a reincarnation of his handsome French grandfather, a *chirurgeon* who died at a young age during WWII.

Taking on board the poet Wallace Stevens' edict that sentiment was a waste of feeling, out went heartbreak Wings-era girly stuff that had come with me into adulthood. My scratched Beatles and Stones albums were superseded by the complete Bob Dylan and many examples of the giants of '60s and '70s music. Ross also spent much time sharing his knowledge and interest in poetry and books as part of my catching up.

After every heartache and drama through my life as well as through every period of calm and joy, music, my guitar and song books have been with me. Recently I was delighted to discover the anarchic Rubber Bandits and be able to reappraise Irish folk music in a nightly two-hour feast on Clare Radio's The West Wing.

Into my sixties now I still like to "catch up" on television and radio with MTV, Jules Holland, jazz sessions, the Performance Channel and The X Factor, fascinated by new talent. I can happily turn up the volume of music playing on a radio and can wail along at full volume with my favourite songs with the best of them. Perhaps I missed my real vocation.

Chapter Twenty-nine
#Something in the Way She Moves ...# (George Harrison)

The book that inspired the 1982 film Blade Runner, Philip K. Dick's Do Androids Dream of Electric Sheep comes to mind when I look back at the time Ross and I were together. Not post-apocalyptic Whitstable, more the issue of empathy, different views on animals, different levels of intelligence, even the religion of television. We came from entirely different planets except for our love of poetry, music and initially, each other. We both miscalculated the matter of bringing up a family together. Maybe I saw myself as the victim, Rose the Blessed Masochist trying to squeeze love out of a stone.

My pampered, head-in-the-clouds twenty-two-year old partner found it hard to move on from his easy student life and house buddies that included the personable John McCarthy and Nick Toksvig, irrepressible brother of comedienne Sandi. In his muso-fantasy head Ross was Lou Reed and it was only a matter of time before he and his band hit the road to live a dissolute lifestyle for all eternity. His much 'safer' alter ego won the day as thirty years on he is, I believe, still doing the same job.

McCarthy exclaimed that I was the Snow Queen when we met at Hull, because of my pale face and the snowflakes settling on my hair. He reminded me of a beautiful lost poet, an emotionally screwed-up victim of the public school system. When you're older you see more in a group of youngsters than they are aware of, or give you credit for.

The economy and job market continued to be dire through the early 1980s. I did my bit financially for the family enabling Ross to continue on his path to enlightenment. It was unfortunate he was soon to become an introverted Peter Pan, happy for me to be keeping him in the style he was accustomed to. The pre-programmed taker needs the pre-programmed giver ...

"Why are you knocking yourself out every day and Ross is on the tennis court ..." are a neighbour's words that rang in my ear.

"I never saw why I should provide for a woman ..." came directly from the horse's mouth some time later.

This sentiment rang far longer in my ear, especially when I had left a solid husband from an era of responsible providers, a man who would not have dreamt of sitting on his bum while I worked myself raw. But then, the matter of equality between the sexes was growing and it could work both ways. Ross had plenty of allies in his stand against a treadmill existence from a generation cynical about their fathers' main aspiration being to make their 65th birthday and pick up a gold watch, perhaps with a family along the way being the burden.

As is often the case, family upbringing is behind such aberrant thinking. Claudette kept the kind of home and hearth only mothers of her era knew how to. It was always perfectly tidy. There was a tier of cake tins. She was unable not to nourish and cherish her visitors. My mother and I would scold her frequently about giving, giving. She hadn't a notion that she deserved time for herself.

Her problems stemmed from her pre-War upbringing at the hands of an autocratic *mama* who made mine look tame. Her first marriage ended in tragedy. Her second was an ongoing tragedy. The result was to lavish everything on her children. The consequence was a brood of blissfully happy Chunky Chicklets, mouths and hands ever open and in no hurry to leave the cosy nest. Father and eldest son certainly were not uncomfortable in sending their soft mares to the coalface. This Rosie the Riveter was a perfect next step in a seamless transition to easy adulthood for the eldest son.

Dad, Evan was an additional burden to Claudette. He lied about his age in 1940 to get called up and ended up with the "forgotten army" in Burma, a veteran of the Burma Railway. Traumatic flashbacks could only be dulled by alcohol. He was not an ambitious man and remained a clerk in the Dockyards all his life. His drinking turned to alcoholism and he would only ever be a liability to the family being a minimalist when it came to handing over any wages. Claudette never made an inappropriate remark about anyone except her Brezhnev look-alike husband. Here is where her pain showed.

In our first years in Whitstable, Claudette and Evan lived close to us and to the girls' Primary and Junior schools in an elegant three-storey Victorian house. This was great because she loved the girls and was happy to look after them when required. They were an extension of her "babies," her three strapping sons and needy daughter.

In January 1983 my mother decided she wanted to live near me. She was lonely after losing Pa and most recently Nuala in Sheffield.

Whenever she was distressed or depressed I was the one who rescued her. Once again, I did not feel too charitable especially with the distinct possibility there would be consequences. There was a Black Hole of need within her that generated mischief when not being fed.

An artisan-style house off the High Street was actually an ideal project for a woman who could, we joked, have re-organised Post-War Britain. The house's renovation and furnishing kept her occupied for a while. The tiny back garden was soon planted up to attract butterflies. An accomplished *trompe l'oeil* of a Venetian staircase viewed from the kitchen window and leading the eye up the wall was a reminder of her considerable skills.

Whitstable's housing stock needed improving, though its timeless air of neglect was a major charm. It is more trendy today with the old rope, pots and pebbles decorating gardens of new 'quaint' cottage terraces and ill-proportioned shiplap-fronted apartments that can only be afforded by fishermen who lift fishing tackle out of the back of a Land Cruiser. Along with the improvements came property price rises on par with the capital.

Londoners still cram into the town during the Summer perhaps for an exorbitantly-priced weekend in one of the converted netting sheds. They are mostly Yuppies, if this income group still exists, having a look at, or revisiting a town the Sunday Supplements dubbed Islington-on-Sea. One thing townspeople are consistent about is that there is still no love lost for "DFLs," those Down From London.

My nephew Henry, Billy's boy came down from university for the

Summer to paint hers and our house. Ma, whom he called "G-ran" put him up. He brought a piece of the new Humber Bridge which he presented to his second home for the duration, the Old Neptune pub along the beach. He was a laugh from beginning to end, unfortunately most of it related to overdoing it with the beer.

He was particularly late back to G-ran's one night and didn't fancy the dried up Shepherd's Pie she had left him. He didn't want to put it in the bin in case she saw it so he wrapped it in a plastic bag and placed it on the front wheel of his Mini to remind him to take it away. He forgot about it, of course. Ma was waving him off next morning when she and the front of her newly-painted house were splattered with pie. He put it down to the Herring Gulls and 'kindly' cleaned it up for her.

Not so funny one afternoon was a social worker calling at Wave Crest asking if we had seen Mrs. B. in the maisonette above. I didn't know our neighbour well but knew from Rachel she had a history of depression. The young man had several other calls so I said I would go next door to landlady Kay. She had keys to all the flats.

"You go in first," Kay rasped, pushing me forward. The flat was empty but the rear attic room door was closed. I inched it open. Mrs. B. was lying on a bed with a bright orange Sainsbury's bag over her head, her hands on the handles holding it tightly around her neck.

"Oh, my God!" began Kay. "We have to call the Police."

We were sipping medicinal whisky when the police turned up minutes later, a gangly PC and a cadet. I had to comfort the youngster who was almost sick.

At the Inquest I said I knew the neighbour only to say "hello" to and it was only hearsay that she suffered from depression. This prompted a sub-heading in the following week's Whitstable Times I could have done without, "Nurse Ignores Depressed Wave Crest Neighbour who Commits Suicide." I suppose they juiced up things where they could, a newspaper that local resident Janet Street-Porter has long jibed over its more usual "Man's Hat Blows off on High Street" features.

The Whit and Tank became my rock. It was the same for all the regular staff there I believe. Sister Montague's marriage had settled into a routine she could cope with. Polly, our oldest auxiliary but youngest at heart had a new diversion for the ward patients, providing none were too ill. This was an evening sing-song from song sheets that were before my time. All our patients knew them, classics from Ivor Novello, Irving Berlin and Cole Porter.

She did have the occasional drama, one being about her dancing partner.

"Oo, there was a right carry on at last night's class Mirabelle," she began while we were making beds.

"Oo, that's news!"

"Well, Minxie, the one who has a hotel in town lost it with Albert because he insisted on doing the Cha-cha-cha with me, our third dance in a row!"

"What did she do, snatch his toupée off!"

"No, Mr. Wheeler. Just lie back, Dear, while we finish tidying the bed," Polly said to our patient. "She threw his dancing shoes in the bushes outside when we left the hall. It's all over. That was Albert's marching orders!"

When Mr Wheeler left us a week later he said to Polly he hoped things settled down at the dancing club and that Minxie would reconsider! We knew how beneficial it was to recovering patients to involve them in some aspects of our everyday lives.

Just as important was Reminiscence Therapy. We would try and work this every day into our mix of locals and Londoners, usually East-enders, who had retired to the seaside, remembering times through their lives, good and not so good. The Day Room built by the local League of Friends was the ideal venue. Rather than see the elderly patients dozing off after lunch, one of us would strike.

"... Right, chaps! This afternoon we want you to tell us about your favourite films when you were lads!"

So often when they chose the topics, it was the Second World War. Occasionally, for those born just before 1900, it was the Great War. To have lasted into their eighties was quite something for that generation. It was a privilege sitting in on the reminiscing. I have been to the Somme and Passchendaele and back with these gentlemen and been introduced to their families and sweethearts. My over-riding sense of that war was it being a matter of survival so they could return to Britain and marry.

While being bathed they would recount more private or personal moments. Lenny, for example had sold jellied eels and pie 'n' mash all his life in the East End. His party piece was an unaccompanied rendition of Yiddishe Mama that brought tears to many in the ward. It moved him, he said, because it brought back memories of his mum and the hardships they endured between the wars.

He was born in the East End Maternity Hospital and was impressed I had trained there in the 1960s. Of course, I had walked down his street! That started him off, sitting in a steamy bath looking as though he had gone back into the mists of time.

"Well, Nurse, see, me mum was a prostitute on the boats and me dad was the captain of a jute boat, like. Anyways, I could only stay on the boat until I was five and then I 'ad to leave and go into an 'ome, like, in Befnal Green. Then this gentleman come and took me out of the 'ome and it was 'im, about 1900, what taught me Music Hall and I did it wiv 'im on the stage for years, like, until he passed over ..."

Then there was the cheeky chappy from Barnsley who would talk about his childhood during the Great War.

"Me dad perished when I were young, Nurse, at the Somme and I 'ad to be me Mam's right 'and. As we 'ad very little money, everyday int' winter after school, I'd take wheelbarrow down t' goods yard to shovel-up any coal and coal dust, 'owt like. It were better 'an pickin' on the waste tip. You got more in the yard what we could use to cook

wi' and heat scullery. Then I'd go t' shops to ask for cheapest end of day scraps from t' butcher, an' that, bones an' all for stock. It were bread and drippin' and broth what kept us alive, Nurse."

It was not all tales of sadness or high emotion. One Christmas in particularly bad weather we admitted Mr. Mott, a bilateral amputee. Perched on his bed like an elf on a toadstool he was non-stop entertainment. He had been a copy writer and claimed "a Mars a day helps you ..." was his, stolen by someone else. His catch phrases, ditties, limericks, repartee and jokes had us smiling for weeks.

I warmed to him because I had long written nonsense verse and poems often illustrating them with Scarfe-type images for my children, though of course I didn't

424

have his talent, or Edward Lear's for that matter.

"So, what's with this 'vegetarian' food?" Miss Marlow asked in a quiet moment, her arms folded and sounding a touch too supercilious. This was something I had joined Ross with because it was easier than having to prepare two lots of food. I wrote out a couple of 'recipes' illustrated Scarfe-style for her next day that I said would be good for her blood pressure. She walked off reading and I heard her muttering "that sounds odd ..." She didn't bring up the subject again.

When we didn't need the four-bedded side ward for theatre cases they were used for overflow from the main ward. On one occasion we put four gentlemen in to recover from bowel cancer and chronic bowel disease surgery. Their rectums were sealed to prevent normal defaecation and they were learning how to manage their new colostomies.

A colostomy is an incision on one side of the lower abdomen. People are usually uncomfortable with the thought of such a bag but patients adjust to them. They soon learn how to clean themselves and re-fit bags that resemble polythene lunch bags over the stoma hole. A former colleague Dr. X., told me he actually found it a relief after his difficulties with advanced bowel cancer.

Flatulence can be a distressing problem but specialist colostomy nurses, sometimes nurses who are paid for by the companies that supply the goods, come in to teach patients and offer follow-up care.

One morning early in 1984, first shift's staff were in Miss Marlow's office for Night Sister's report for all wards, including the general Women's Ward. This was routine in case we were needed elsewhere in the hospital during our shift.

"Well," Night Sister began frostily, "does anyone know anything about the authorisation of the private colostomy nurse deciding yesterday evening to try her 'super-dooper,' 'odour-correcting' bags on all four of our patients in the side ward at the same time?"

There were no takers.

"I have had some nights to write home about during my many years on the wards," Night Sister went on, "this one was Big Bang night ..."

It was hard not to laugh because we knew what was coming!

"We spent the whole night reapplying them as they kept blowing off. And I mean blowing off ... My poor nurses had to clean mess after mess. It seems our tried and tested bags had been removed. I had a good mind to call the company nurse up in the middle of the night ..."

I went to see our weary colostomy patients in the four-bedder and began innocently, "morning, Gentlemen!" They were a bit sullen, telling me they would have something to say to the colostomy nurse if she showed her face again. I told them Night Sister's comments would be pertinent. Some old-style bags were on their way and we would tiptoe around during the morning so they could snooze a bit.

One of these patient's sons was a nursing professional, an innovator not afraid of speaking out against outmoded nursing practices in the NHS. Thanks to Sister Montague's relaxed running of the ward and her known dislike of militaristic ward management the consultant was impressed with his father's care. We were proud to be mentioned in an article he wrote for the Nursing Times extolling Sister Montague and her well-run ward.

The regime was quite different downstairs. The Ladies Ward Sister was a traditionalist, like those dedicated spinsters I had trained under. I did feel for her knowing how relaxed we were upstairs. Of the five Sisters at the hospital she was the one who could not, or would not bend. Everything was by the book. It was a well-run ward but staff were not allowed to sit with or chat to the patients whatever the circumstances.

I have to say she did make a difference to the overall running of the hospital when standing in for Miss Marlow. Efficiency and a high standard of cleanliness were already there but she put an edge on things, in a positive sense. It was really only gilding the lily.

It only reminds me how standards have slipped over the years in the way wards are run when patients and relatives are moved to complain or write to newspapers about it, about cleanliness in particular. How bad it would become to the extent of serious outbreaks of infection and loss of life among patients, is shocking. I remember the usual political rhetoric of justification, "efficiency," "savings," "improvements." Once again it is probably of little concern to those who are able to afford private health care, where there has been no cutting back on standards of cleanliness and hygiene. In came contractors whose aim was profit rather than cleanliness.

How many of us know teenagers who know all about cleanliness and hygiene? The question sounds facetious but bored, occasionally hung-over students were soon being employed in hospital cleaning. I listened to one speaking to Edwina Currie on her Radio Five Live spot in about 2000 on the state of hospital wards. He said he received no training and was expected to clean three thirty-bedded wards in a morning.

Ironically, advances in medicine are part of the problem. In Florence Nightingale's pre-antibiotic days battling with bacteria and dirt was a priority. This aspect of early nursing regimes was still being ruthlessly adhered to during my training. That reassuring whiff of Lysol with Mrs. Gimlet-Eye making sure you did your bit in maintaining her scrupulous cleaning should not be history book stuff.

We were fortunate in the early 'Eighties on William Ward to have the continuity of the same two pearls, Placid Pauline and Militant Mary. Pocket-sized Mary was an intense sweeper and mopper with a Silent Film-era face, short wavy hair and rosebud mouth. She was a Greenham Common Girl and her husband was a Unison rep. Pauline and Mary were part of the ward team and took pride in keeping their patch spick and span. They did not hold back in barking about sloppy nursing or too much of a cavalier attitude towards Sister's hard-fought hygiene regime.

All the ancillary staff were a joy to know, working their socks off so that patients could enjoy well-cooked meals in a fresh, clean environment. They were better than many nurses at nattering with the patients. Worries that a patient didn't feel able to confide to trained staff were sometimes passed on to us by these gems. There wasn't a week that went by without Mary baking us a Madeira Cherry or other deliciously light cake. They are still the best Madeira Sponges I have ever tasted.

It sounds odd of a caring profession that through my career, nurses were not taught communication skills. Chatting is one thing, though people are rarely naturally good at this. Listening to and reassuring patients on sensitive issues they may have with their diagnoses or treatment or about the delicate issue of sexuality and illness, is another. It becomes even harder when an illness or surgery is fundamental, as with multiple sclerosis, motor neurone disease and commonly, cancer.

When I began working at the Whit and Tank we had a multiple sclerosis patient in his forties named Trevor. His MS was at the stage where his limbs were contracted and in spasm and his speech was heavily slurred and laboured. He was an intelligent, thoughtful man who had become cynical and bitter about his deteriorating, terminal condition, particularly after his wife left him. His only visitor was his father-in-law. It got harder communicating with Trevor especially after he began to lash out.

"Whassyourfirstname?" he asked me sourly one morning when we were washing him. Not wanting to insult him or set him off on a rant by pompously replying we didn't use first names on the ward, I invented one.

"Mirabelle!" I said brightly, without a clue as to why a French-fried nickname had popped into my head. I burst out laughing and said I didn't know why I should be a *leetle French plum* hoping I had remembered correctly that's what they were. Trevor responded with a smile. From then on I was Mirabelle.

At first it was Trevor who would bellow my new *nom de nursing* whenever he needed attention. Soon it was the rest of the staff and visiting doctors, even Miss Marlow. I became programmed to it on the hospital air waves whether in the washroom, or skulking in the ward's tiny kitchen eyeing left-over puddings, or downstairs in the main kitchen waiting for the lunch trolley, chatting with Dulcie the cook and Millie her assistant who was always scouring saucepans. Wherever I was, "M-i-r-a-b-e-l-l-e ..." would seek me out.

It was the briefest respite for Trevor. He was a wearying patient to look after who eventually refused to be placated or soothed by anyone. He just wanted to die. His last year was spent at a long-stay unit for younger people with MS and other long-term diseases. A nurse I later met on a Marie Curie study day for cancer awareness training worked at the unit and I asked if she knew Trevor.

"I nursed him to the end," she said. "He went quickly downhill after he arrived but he wouldn't bloody well die! He finally went into a coma for a week and it was just awful looking at the poor sod. I kept saying to myself, come on Trevor, let go. Go and meet your Nan you were always talking about. Bloody well die ..."

She wasn't being irreverent or unkind. Paul McCartney spoke movingly about giving his first wife Linda "permission" to go. He told her quietly while holding her in his arms that she was riding her favourite horse.

Terminally-ill patients do cling on to life for special events of loved ones, special birthdays or Christmas, or even the anniversary of their spouse's passing. Gloria Hunniford spoke of her late daughter asking to be driven home to England from Switzerland so she would have her family and her mum around her. She survived a difficult journey long enough to have her wish fulfilled. It was different with my brother, Damien. He asked to go into hospital to spare Mother seeing him die.

Death is by no means as sensitive or as touching as in these instances. Terminal patients were admitted most weeks to the Whit and Tank and sometimes we were in disbelief at the attitude of relatives, or flummoxed about how we would manage what is known as a "good death."

A local café owner in his late thirties admitted with a brain tumour was one such patient. We were told his wife had recently left him, which probably explained why his two teenage children would visit on their own after school. The man was soon drifting in and out of consciousness. When his wife eventually appeared with her gormless lover it was to get her husband's signature on a will. She came in most evenings after this, always with her lover, until her husband's death.

I felt for the distressed and disoriented teenagers. Nowadays we have the support of the hospice movement and teenage cancer charities. It was not so in the early 'Eighties. We did our best for our terminally-ill patients but it wasn't until after Sister Montague returned from a three-month course in terminal care at the St. Christopher's Hospice in South London brimming with new knowledge and praise for the hospice movement that we felt more confident about doing a better job. The hospice was founded by Dame Cicely Saunders in 1967 and remains at the forefront of palliative care for patients, and their families, who have terminal illnesses.

It was with this new sense of openness I asked the wife of a patient with advanced cancer if she would like to give him his dose of liquid morphine. She would after all, be doing this if he was at home. She followed my instructions lifting the small glass to his lips. It was unfortunate that her adored husband coughed suddenly, brought up bright red blood and died. We had no indication this would happen and the woman was understandably distraught. She began shouting at me, one of three instances I mentioned.

Grief is said to happen in stages; denial, anger, disbelief, bargaining and finally acceptance. All stages need to be worked through. If left unresolved, some like Miss Havisham in Dickens' Great Expectations may remain locked in with their grief. I saw this woman occasionally in the High Street for years afterwards and was blanked every time. I don't believe, on his death in 1984, she had hospice support or counselling. We were aware of such things but in our little ward were unable to provide such a service. Thanks to our Sister, Rachel, we had made a start.

My opinion of the Health Centre changed when Claudette developed serious pain in her abdomen. Her GP said she might have to wait two months before seeing a consultant. This was in the Tory administration's first term, when waiting lists were the longest they have ever been in the NHS. Her distress got worse until Dr. B. came out during the night and pronounced she had a stomach upset. We had to call an ambulance at dawn. She was admitted to the Kent and Canterbury as an emergency with a burst ovarian cyst.

Claudette's traumas continued when she was examined by the registrar. This beautiful woman with a heart-shaped face framed by cropped white, wavy hair whispered to me before going in to theatre that the examination had been brutal, that she felt as though she had been assaulted. She tested positive to ovarian cancer, known as the hidden cancer until recently. Hidden or not, she may have lived much longer had the cyst been detected before bursting.

She and her husband were living in the maisonette above us at Wave Crest by this time in 1983 and I was looking after her. Her family was in denial. Claudette herself did not help in referring to her cancer as "the nasty thing." There was still a culture of trying to keep the "shame" of having cancer quiet. Evan walked off if you brought the subject up. Ross could not discuss it with his mother or her GP.

All the time I was at the Whit and Tank I thought about running a private Care or Nursing Home. Tory Government privatisation steamed ahead from 1983 after the Falklands Conflict brought Thatcher back somewhat artificially for a second term. The Griffiths Report of 1983 that laid the framework of an NHS run as an internal market in which trusts would be in competition, made uncomfortable reading for those of us who wondered where the patient fitted into this grand scheme. However, a relentless increase in unemployment that peaked at 3.3 million in 1984 prompted many of us to think about starting a business.

Claudette was my main ally. One of the staff in the Nursing Home she worked in had taken the plunge. I knew of another entrepreneur in Folkestone who had so many clients, mostly alcoholics from the London Boroughs he bought a second property within a year. They were as "good as gold" he said, easily managed and very happy living in a bedsit arrangement supporting each other.

In the two years up to Claudette's death she and I looked at several large properties around Whitstable. We got more excited about the idea. Morris did also, approving of his sister thinking of joining the real world, that of business. As I could have guessed, when Mother heard of my plans and that Jane, being the senior nurse in the family, would be Matron in this mooted Home, she kicked up a fuss. The telephone was red hot as she elicited support from everyone else against the idea, as if it was Mother's business.

Jane knew nothing of this until years later and it was a rare moment she was lost for words. She had no idea she had not been in favour for years because of dramas mother had disapproved of. She had no idea at all that Mother had, on her own admission, only ever loved Damien. When I told Jane her face looked as though it had just been smacked.

The motivation for starting a business was simple. I wanted to do better in life and not be a slave to a brown envelope. Others had taken the plunge with support from their husbands and family and bought properties. Within a year they were doing very well. I popped in frequently to see one of them, Mildred in Tankerton, sometimes covering an evening shift for the elderly patients in her care. They were a happy bunch, particularly with the home-baking Mildred had made of feature of her establishment.

I met tall SEN Mildred with ostrich-thin legs at Medway Hospital. Her older husband had died of cancer and I got to know her four children well. She rang me one day and said she had cancer now and was moving to Whitstable, actually to be near me.

"I am going to a clinic in Switzerland for cutting edge treatment," she informed me, after asking if I would look after her affable brood at weekends when she was away. Ross wasn't too happy. Our beach-front location meant we were a magnet for children of all ages and now we were over-run.

Mildred started part-time work at a nearby Rest Home and found a bungalow in Tankerton. She was very interested in the information Claudette and I had on the boom in the Residential Home business. The next thing I knew she had poached four residents from the Rest Home she was working at and set up on her own from her small bungalow.

"Oo, they 'ated it there, didn't you my Loves?" she cooed to her elderly charges. "They were half-starved and shouted at as well. I had to do something!"

When I asked about sleeping arrangements in the tiny house, Mildred said one of her children was sleeping in the garage, the other two were in the old caravan in the garden and she was in the loft.

A friend from Medway who knew Mildred burst out laughing when I told her of Mildred's problems.

"Oh, Rose, you are a dumb cluck ... She ain't got no cancer. Everyone round here knows she's a fantasist. You've just been lumbered at weekends. She gets as close to Switzerland as the nearest chippy!"

This was the first time I had heard of someone claiming to have cancer for gain and I was very upset on her children's behalf as she had also told them she could die at any time. My District Nurse friend confirmed from medical notes Mildred didn't have cancer, just "psychological problems."

I could have forgiven her if it hadn't been for a whopping telephone bill in her name British Telecom somehow seemed to think I was responsible for. It was just as well one of Ross's friends worked at the BT office in Canterbury and was able to route it back to Mildred before legal action started against me. I didn't see her much for a couple of years, until 1983 when she insisted I come and see the big house in Tankerton she had converted into a full-blown Rest Home. Two years later she had bought the property next door and incorporated it.

Here was a complex woman, kind and generous on the one hand, full of "thou shalt nots" on the other, largely from her only reading being the Old Testament. She told us matter-of-factly how one of her ladies had misbehaved and was locked in her room on Christmas Day. Her children paid the price for her ambition. One of her blind residents said gently she thought it was Mildred's youngest child stealing money. When the girl was questioned she shouted out "I hate the old smellies, anyway ..." The child had a toyshop-full of toys and didn't need the money.

The pieces that made up this woman's life were not pretty ones. I am not the only person shaking my head at wills being written in her favour and property left to her. I became concerned about other more insidious whisperings and had to break off all contact.

Needless to say regarding my own aspirations, I was fighting a losing battle on all fronts. Ross cringed at the idea of looking after elderly people, or people with disabilities or social problems. He also said he had no talent for, or interest in business. He was horrified at the thought of us putting up our flat at Wave Crest as collateral. As he had contributed nothing to our small mortgage I considered over-riding him, except his signature was on the papers and his mother whom I adored lived above us. The moment was lost.

True to form after causing an upset, Mother sold up soon afterwards to stay, somewhat perversely, with Jane in Staffordshire. She moved into her garage. My idealised view of Care Homes waned over the next few years when it became clear vested interest and the profit motive brought out the beast in many of the entrepreneurs. I was soon comfortable only with those places that continued to be run by the NHS and County Authority.

Back on the ward later in 1984 I had a moment of shame, one that all nurses dread. It is usually about falling below your own cherished standards. I still shudder when I think about Howard who at the time, drove us to distraction.

Divorced and in his fifties, Howard was tall and slightly stooped with a sad hollow face. He was admitted to William Ward with a suspected stomach ulcer. Perfectly able to walk he would hardly be in his bed, preferring instead to follow us around looking like Munch's painting The Scream repeating "Nurse, I'm in pain ... my stomach ... I am in pain ..."

His GP Dr. S. was competent and thorough and test after test came back marked NAD (Nothing Abnormal Discovered). Howard was receiving strong four-hourly analgesia but would be begging for pain relief only an hour or so after each dose. GP and nursing staff began assuming the craving was an addiction issue. What was confusing and weakened his case was his ability to wolf down huge meals with no apparent effect on his stomach. To my shame as I say, this was the evidence he was hamming or shamming.

"N-urse, n-urse ... I am in p-ain ..." his haunting voice echoed around our top floor ward. Only opiates relieve brain-burning pain and he was not permitted them.

Our ignorance concerning non-malignant pain was woeful, punitive and judgemental. We were trained to believe we knew our patients' invisible pain levels better than they did and became increasingly impatient with Howard. His family were also hard on him, saying he had always been a problem. I wasn't unkind to him but was exasperated over the lack of progress. Over the weeks it was Polly, the epitome of kindness, who reminded us how we should be treating patients, however cantankerous, offensive or difficult.

The Nobel Prize for Compassion went to Dulcie. A self-deprecating Mother-Earth who had, she told us, been beaten as a child. "The poor sod is in pain, Mirabelle. I've seen a lot of it in my time in hospitals ..." She was taking him little treats left over from meal times, as she did us. Now her empathy with Howard made me feel like a rat. It wasn't long afterwards that he died.

A few days later we were dishing out lunches when the fire alarm went off. 'Monte Carlo' shot out of her office squeaking "where's the fire?" like a mad macaw. I continued plonking food onto plates at speed for Polly to distribute to the patients in the Day Room.

Miss Marlow didn't wait for a reply. She was off down the stairs to check it out for herself. I said to Polly I could manage the rest of the serving and perhaps she should follow Miss Marlow just in case we did have to evacuate. Our Dancing Queen set off down the stairs like a gazelle.

"It's okay, Mirabelle," she said on her return, "Dulcie broke the fire alarm glass in the kitchen with a mop handle. She and Millie are taking turns holding it down until the caretaker gets back from lunch. It's a little Dutch Boy job because the alarm goes if they take their finger off it!"

As we were telling the gentlemen in the Day Room all was well and they could enjoy their lunch a sombre Dr. S. appeared.

"Hi Doc!"

"Mirabelle ..."

"Yes, Doctor ..."

"... Howard's autopsy report. He did have cancer, behind his stomach wall. Poor sod. The scans missed it."

"So he was in considerable pain ..."

Chapter Thirty
#Oliver's Army ...# (Elvis Costello)

I enjoyed my stint at the Whit and Tank except for several weeks late in 1984. Vinny, Dr. Montague's one and only private patient was one of the most unpleasant people I have ever nursed. He was a property development millionaire who tried the ward staff beyond endurance. It was the only time I took time off to avoid nursing someone. At ninety years of age he was still running his business with his son, Lemmy. Paranoia prompted an aggressive four-times daily interrogation about every tablet and liquid prescribed to him.

"How do I know you're giving me the right tablet ... these are different ... this liquid doesn't taste the same as yesterday ... are you trying to poison me?"

He was the same with his food and drink and every procedure and test we administered. He was slight in build and would whine without shame if he thought something was going to hurt but his combative energy and a *persona* that swung between the charismatic and demonic would have floored Margaret Thatcher.

There was also constant invective.

"... why do I have to put up with this dump ... call my doctor, I want a real nurse, not an idiot like you ..."

He didn't waste an opportunity to insult others, as with our St. John's Volunteer, Dougie.

"... Mirabelle, how can you respect a dope like him who works for nothing?"

He would only go to the toilet when kitted out with oversize Wellington boots and pink Marigold gloves. I might have understood it at a time of MRSA outbreaks in hospitals but this was when the toilets positively sparkled at the hands of our Mary and Pauline. They refused to go anywhere near his bed when he was in it.

After weeks of this intolerable behaviour several members of staff were about to petition Miss Marlow when our saviour, Dr. S. arrived in urgent need of a bed. He looked through our list in the office at the end of the ward and said loudly "what's a bloody private patient doing blocking a bed when he should be on a private ward? And by the look of it it's a case of hypochondria ..."

He got the bed and to universal relief Vinny was despatched the following Saturday despite his wife pleading that he remain in until Monday.

"Lemmy and I booked him lunch with us at the Savoy," his daughter-in-law explained, "to cheer him up after his ordeal. It's our weekly treat. I mean, where else can you get a decent Sunday lunch?"

The only person he did not insult was Sister Montague. She in turn fawned over him to the extent that one midnight after heavy snow she prepared some smoked salmon sandwiches and made her husband walk with her to the Cottage Hospital from the far side of town. Vinny wanted a snack.

Night Sister was furious but it made no difference to Rachel's obsession. It related partly to Vinny being her husband's private patient. It didn't explain why Rachel kept a picture of him in her bedroom for years afterwards superseded only by one of Princess Diana. That was in 1992 or 1993 at about the time the Prince and Princess announced their separation and Diana started kicking off.

It wasn't until we heard of Vinny's death early in 1985 I took issue with Rachel. It wasn't the first time. She defended herself by saying she loved him like the father she never had. I told her she had crossed an ethical boundary and had not supported us when we were under duress from his tyranny. His obsessive attention-seeking had undermined the standard of care of our other patients. I also told her tartly a canny old man like that would not leave her a penny in his will. She fell silent.

Vinny had boasted he would have the equivalent of a State Funeral in the East End, one better even than Violet Kray's in 1982 which 60,000 people attended out of deference and curiosity. He was actually carted off to London wrapped in a sheet in the back of an old van. Only his close family were present at the funeral the following day. Rachel's request to attend was ignored.

It was a moment of disquiet, learning of Lemmy's death a few months after his father's. He always brought a box of Cornettos with him for staff when visiting his father. He would also insist on showing me his tongue.

"Nurse, I am worried about my tongue. Does the colour look good to you ... surely it's an odd colour ..."

I began fobbing him off as I wanted to do his father. The slight yellowing of his tongue may have indicated a liver problem but I assumed his doctor was on top of things. His death was due to cancer and his tongue colouration was likely a sign. I think he was an extension of his father's ego and on this earth solely to do his father's bidding. He was his *raison d'être* so when his father died there was no longer a reason for him to live.

At the same time we were struggling with our Patient from Hell a paraplegic Patient from Heaven named Ken was admitted. I had a moment of great concern when the night report was read out in Miss Marlow's office. I made the point we really did need some lifting equipment now. This was in the days before such equipment was mandatory, or that porters were on staff specifically for this task.

Our backs were taking a hammering enough, lifting or turning some of our heavier gentlemen. It is estimated that nurses on a geriatric ward can lift the equivalent of a tonne in a morning, more apparently than industrial workers on average.

On my first round I was embarrassed about my remarks on the extra problems of lifting immobile patients. Ken was on his way to the toilet unaided except for calipers and sticks. I stared in disbelief. He had managed like this for more than twenty years to his retirement since falling down a lift shaft at the offices of a national daily in Fleet Street.

"You just get on with it, don't you?" he said. "I had my wife to provide for and two nippers and didn't fancy being confined to a wheelchair. I started by walking from the bed to the door, then down the stairs, then to the garden gate, the first lamp-post, the bus stop. It took a while but as I saw it, I had no choice."

When I asked him how he managed public transport he said he sometimes fell over when trying to grab the pole but the bus drivers got to know him and would wait. People were very kind as well, if a bit uncomfortable sometimes, he said.

Ken's worry-thin wife Irene was as stoical and as admirable. No self-pity, no bitterness, they just dealt with their difficulties. Ken was eventually referred to East Grinstead for skin grafts because the skin was breaking on his buttocks. He recovered from that and depression but then lost an eye after another medical problem that should not have happened. He returned to the Whit and Tank on the new long-stay ward after I had left.

More MBEs and OBEs should be issued to the Kens and Irenes

of this world.

We endured one more traumatic period after Dr. Montague's private patient. Student nurses and junior staff learn quickly about bullying in the workplace as they are obvious targets. Auxiliaries ramping up their power can be the most vile because if the standard of care in the ward suffers it is usually the nurses that are bawled out.

The extent of suffering through bullying in the workplace should not be under-estimated or ignored in the hope it will ease off. Bullies get away with their pleasure because people are either not prepared for, or are emotionally unable to face the problem. A clique can be harder to deal with.

If colleagues are being bullied then so are patients. Bullying is an addictive power trip. When the bully is sugar-coated in the presence of 'the boss' on the ward and a Machiavellian monster when she is not it is almost impossible for newcomers to deal with. Ploys include moody game-playing.

I learnt over the years that bullying by management is as prevalent and that management can be poor because of the mistaken belief bullying is managing.

When I arrived at the Cottage Hospital, mention of senior auxiliary Beryl was in hushed tones. She was off sick at the time. Some of her auxiliaries tested me from the start by trying to get one up on me or trying to put me "in my place." Madge, beefy with cropped red hair, behaved like a sulky child when I stepped into her territory. She was a big girl with a booming baritone Cockney voice that could be heard throughout the hospital. Her speciality was 'toileting' timorous, tottering ladies.

"Have you finished on the toilet, D-e-a-h? Do you want a wipe?" she would broadcast down the ward smirking. I cringed ever time. It was unfortunate because she was a box of surprises, particularly in her love of jazz. It seemed no one had been strong enough to stand up to her, except perhaps Beryl.

Beryl's return was not what I expected. She did not make eye contact with me, or anyone I realised immediately, unless it was absolutely unavoidable. She huffed and she sighed continuously, these being control mechanisms in themselves. She had zero humour and she bossed and bossed and bossed. The first time we worked together as auxiliary and Staff Nurse in charge of the ward she completely

438

ignored me. This is, of course an intolerable situation where peoples' lives are at risk, never mind the rudeness and disrespect. It quickly became clear she would continue with this regime until I became subservient to her. Along with her working mode was an arrogance that undoubtedly got her good results, from patients in particular wanting to keep the peace.

In one shift I saw her *modus operandi*, her colluders and the passive bystanders that kept her power going. I was grateful to have been primed, otherwise I would probably have been wrong-footed.

Within a couple of days I had a week's holiday and all but forgot about Beryl. When I returned I learnt that the wife of tiny, frail Percy had died and I started my round by offering my condolences to him. His condition had deteriorated noticeably and I asked him if there was anything in particular I could do.

"I hate that milkman's wife," was all he said tearfully.

Polly filled in the details. Percy and his wife were admitted at the same time for their individual problems but his wife took a turn for the worse. Percy wanted to go down to the women's ward to see her. It meant a wheelchair trip and Beryl, with collusion and keeping quiet about the importance of the request, made every effort smiling sweetly, for this not to happen. Percy's wife died in the meantime.

I let one more incident pass with Beryl still not having communicated with me before requesting an appointment with Miss Marlow. When she asked me cautiously what it was about I told her in one word, Beryl. The outcome was that Miss Marlow, who hated confrontation, hastened Beryl's retirement.

I couldn't have made a stand without the help of Sister Pear Drops who ran Women's Op' Ward down stairs. In return I supported her with a formal complaint against an older SEN whose thieving was getting worse. It was another example of kleptomania because the woman did not really want or need the food she took from patients' plates, chocolate bars from lockers, or flowers that mysteriously disappeared on their way to being put into water. Her early retirement was also hastened.

Sister Pear Drops, Barbara, was about my age and we became friends. On duty she smelt of acetone from sucking these sweets in her ongoing battle with smoking. Alas, the fags got her and she died quite horribly twenty years later in an oxygen tent when only in her early sixties.

Neat little Ruby, one of our senior cleaners and demon in disguise was yet another problem. New cleaner after new cleaner wept over their mops because of Tyrannosaurus Ruby. I confronted her on the basis that standards were slipping in the ward and that patients were picking up an "atmosphere" among normally jolly cleaning staff. It surprised me how sweet Ruby was about it, probably an attempt to disarm. She brought in a peace offering of sweets the next day and said she would be good to the next new lady.

She wasn't and was warned. It was a pity because it seemed to be a habit rather than part of her character. She admitted she did not need to bully her assistants to get good results. She just knew she could and they would not answer back. I think that is the key.

With all this going on I was surprised to receive support from her one lunchtime. She was outside our tiny office scrubbing the floor when one of the most unpopular GPs at the Health Centre drifted in. We referred to him as The Snurge. As too many doctors believe is their right with nursing staff he began haranguing me at the doorway. On this occasion it was about sending a patient home and that his condition had deteriorated and he was likely to be back as an emergency.

Taken aback at being dressed down in public my brain went into overdrive.

"May I remind you, Doctor F. you gave permission to his daughter to take him home. You have forgotten I was standing right behind you."

The Doctor hesitated, aware his attempt at sowing the seeds of blame on someone else for a possible fatality had been rumbled. Having had enough of his haughty unpleasantness for more than four years I lost it.

"How dare you accuse me of putting a patient at risk, in front of a ward full of patients," I said, raising my voice, gesturing down the corridor to several elderly men agog at their nurse losing her temper. "I am sick and tired of Tin-pot Gods down at the Health Centre expecting us to give medication and treatments ordered by 'phone because you can't be bothered to come up here and write them up and knowing we would carry the can if anything went wrong ..."

Very upset, I burst into tears which was a very rare thing. At least I had showed him up. At my lowest ebb a tiny voice just two feet away piped up,

"That's right, Love, you tell 'im, Doctor Snurge!"

"I am so s-o-r-r-y, nurse. I didn't mean to, to question your judgement ..." the doctor stuttered.

A few days later I was making a bed with our new male staff nurse Arran and asked him if he was being leaned on to be part of the hospital's entry in the Whitstable Carnival. Miss Marlow had sportingly agreed to be a 'star patient.' A dozen of us, including Ruby would be cross-dressed as hospital staff pushing a Nil by Mouth Monte Carlo through the town on a hospital bed.

The Snurge hovered by his patient whose bed we were just finishing.

"Will you be appearing in the carnival, Doctor?" Staff Nurse Kitson asked, friendly as ever. The doctor gave me a sheepish look and said he didn't think he would be welcome.

I told Arran about the earlier incident during our break. He was dismayed to learn patients had referred to this doctor by name for his poor bedside manner in complaints in the local press about hospital treatment. Letters on government policies, about the NHS and waiting lists in particular were coming in thick and fast.

Arran was surprisingly empathetic saying the man may have problems at home, perhaps with a relative and his behaviour should be understood in this light. It was nice to hear but "problems with the wife" wears thin when you are at the butt end of it for years.

Our working relationship with the GPs at the Health Centre was good. However, we considered one as dangerous because he was a lazy and lousy practitioner; two others were woeful under-performers and another was judged to be a nasty sadist whom we feared. In 2010 three out of the four were still practising. The last, Doctor Nasty had been promoted. Lazy lousy Dr. B. who had demonstrated incompetence over Claudette's serious condition had only private patients on his list. Good luck to them.

On the whole, standards at the Health Centre were high, though it was not to reach the standards of excellence some of the senior GPs were working towards. I had insider knowledge and was disgusted, in those pre-Shipman days, it was *de rigueur* that they covered each other's backs, even after serious professional mistakes.

I also learnt the newer doctors were not interested in working the long hours of the dedicated older gentlemen. Dr. Montague, for example would often be in the building at midnight working on something or other. They were taking their salaries, later very large salaries and perks for far fewer hours and knocking off on the dot.

Arran was a breath of fresh air. This good-looking boy arrived for work on a Harley-Davidson and proceeded to blow everybody's preconceptions about male nurses to the wind. We were impressed with his endless patience with even the most cussed old buggers. They thought he was wonderful and we all fancied him, of course!

Male nurses were non-existent during my early days and if they worked in the NHS they were usually from Ireland and tended to be in our mainly deplorable mental hospitals.

Having just completed my Feminist Course with the OU was bad timing for Miss Marlow to announce that "a recently-qualified male nurse" had requested a transfer to our male ward and I would be booted downstairs to the women's short-stay surgical ward with Sister Pear Drops. I was damned if I was to be ousted without a say because, as I perceived it, I was female and therefore dispensable. I liked my colleagues and the old geezers! SEN Sarah was moved instead and didn't mind.

Arran had just been diagnosed as a Type 1 diabetic, though he was managing it as if a minor issue. Naturally, it upset him knowing he would develop health problems. I did warm to him, a man who, on the day John Lennon was shot dead in 1980, went into Canterbury Cathedral and wept. My husband was a species away from such tenderness. We became good friends and sparring partners until he left to travel and work in Steiner schools.

He looked me up about ten years later and visited with his adored little boy. He looked careworn and a good deal older and I was very sorry his health was deteriorating. It was a spooky moment learning his partner was Austrian. Our "psychic" Polly had told him when he worked on William Ward he would marry an Austrian!

The staff at the Cottage Hospital in my last year there, 1985 became a well-bonded unit. Even Madge refrained from sulking and picking on newbies after we had joked her out of it. She had a raucous, good-natured laugh that could have blasted the bats from the rafters of Canterbury Cathedral. Once the serial bullies were eliminated the day and night staff were probably the best bunch I have ever worked with. Polly, Sister Pear Drops (Barbara), Sister

Montague (Rachel) and I became good friends off-duty as well.

Sarah was happy with her lot downstairs. She and Barbara were a formidable team, two of the best nurses I have known. Barbara was inclined to be a worry-guts due to her heartbreaking upbringing. Abandoned by her society beauty divorcee mother, she was sent away to boarding school at the age of six. Many nurses confess to having had a far from ideal childhood. It has prompted New Age counsellors to ponder their motives for entering the nursing profession. Were they seeking to heal themselves, or were they concentrating on the needs of others at the bedside as a means of keeping their own emotional baggage at bay?

I do remember enjoying feeling good as a child when pretend-nursing my sick dolls and teddies and when opportunity presented itself, I could care for grudging siblings and parents. It was to gain 'strokes,' affection, when there was precious little of it to be had otherwise.

As you get older and gain experience in life, in your profession, fulfilment grows in knowing you are on top and ahead of situations rather than being led, surprised or caught out by them. It was a pity I didn't use my commonsense during a routine Sunday situation at the Whit and Tank just after my fortieth birthday in March 1985.

We had fifteen patients on the ward, a mix of convalescent and high-dependency. One gentleman was dying. I was on my own with Dougie, my *aide-de-camp*. His valued role was to put out light suppers, do the toileting and fetching and carrying and chat to the patients. He had been a ward stalwart for years.

Our seriously-ill patient Tom died at seven that evening. It was a straightforward death whose laying out we managed with ease, largely because there were no relatives present. It is not meant to sound uncaring. When there were relatives at the bedside we would offer them tea in a side room and stay while they talked, or wept. It was not often as straightforward as this because of a particularly distraught relative or perhaps because of other emergencies on the ward, or even because of colleagues who are not as sympathetic as they might be.

Our shift ended at eight-thirty and as was customary, we would allow an hour or so for the 'departure of the soul.' For many of us this was more about allowing reflection on the life of the deceased than the passage of *anima* in a spiritual or religious sense.

When an hour had passed Dougie and I rolled heavy Tom onto a trolley to take him to the lift and down to the little mortuary chapel at the side of the main building, actually a much added-to Victorian pile. Porters were not employed on Sunday evenings so we had to do this ourselves. I 'phoned Barbara to ask if she would be kind enough to listen out for bells from my patients. They were particularly busy downstairs with post-op' patients she said but she would, of course, oblige.

With the pressure of an unattended ward and only twenty minutes in which to take the deceased to the mortuary and return and finish off our tasks for the evening, my caution was forgotten. The trolley was too heavy for us to lift over the step into the mortuary as Dougie was smaller than me. We managed one wheel but the trolley stuck firmly in the doorway with me in the mortuary and Dougie on the step. Now very anxious about my unattended ward full of patients I had the idea I could lift the corpse off the trolley. Dougie could then climb over to me and we could lift it on to the mortuary table.

With sheer will power I lifted Tom over the end of the trolley and carefully on to the floor. With another supreme effort we lifted him again, laid him on the table and hurried back to the ward. Everything was fine there. We finished our chores, I thanked Dougie copiously for his help that night and cycled off home along Tankerton sea front with a welcome cool breeze in my face.

The next morning I could hardly move. My lower back felt as if it had been steam-rollered. Nevertheless, I limped into work as Mirabelle the Magnificent informing Miss Marlow of my wrenched back and the mortuary trolley debacle. She tutted and twittered as she made a record in the industrial accidents book.

I could still hardly walk when I called in at the Health Centre and was not amused at being told I had strained my back. I was advised to take a few days off for bed rest. Short staffing drove me back after two. Rachel was not at all sympathetic with the comment my job was at risk if I started taking time off. Her husband, visiting one of his patients overheard.

"That's a bit harsh, Darling ... let me demonstrate something."

He stood over the nearby sink to show that he did not have to bend because he was not tall. The risk of back injury in tall people, especially when lifting is significantly greater, he said. He stooped to demonstrate this and show how, with the centre of gravity much higher and further forward, considerably more strain is transferred to the lower back. I could have hugged him.

Rachel's ominous words stayed with me, being the bread-winner, even though every patient I helped lift or turn over the next few weeks hurt my back more and more. Sister Pear Drops was in the ward one afternoon and noticed I was putting the cot rails up so I could lean on them to get more leverage. She had recently become our Lifting Instructress. The expression 'pardon came too late' comes to mind here.

Into the Summer I had to take more time off. My GP arranged X-Rays and consultations and ordered me to rest. I appreciated this and was able to visit an old friend along the beach on Island Wall at the very edge of Whitstable. She was dying. Her District Nurse had hardly distinguished herself over the months and a Wave Crest neighbour and I eventually camped on our friend's floor to prevent a repeat of her getting up in the night and falling down the stairs.

Her younger daughter took over from us the following day with no idea of procedure. Her mother died during the night and her body remained curled in the same position in a soaking bed for seven hours while the distraught daughter tried to find out what next to do. The undertaker could not come until the afternoon.

On ringing the senior District Nurse to complain about the non-appearance of the regular nurse, for what her visit was worth, I was informed they were no longer involved in Last Offices. This is progress, I asked? She admitted Health Service cut backs were beginning to bite. Anyone dying at home and who had not been laid out by family members was placed in a black bag, a body bag, in whatever state and position and "seen to" by the undertaker.

Their team may be skilled at their job but to me the moment of dignity had passed. There would be no love involved and how the deceased looked immediately after death would be of little concern. Time allowed for the departing of the soul had been dispensed with.

Claudette's health deteriorated during July. It had been two years since her ovarian cyst problem and cancer diagnosis. This was a remarkable remission considering she continued smoking and had been cavalier about taking her chemo pills, for what they were worth. The moment of realisation of the inevitable came when this dignified woman had a serious bout of shingles across her abdomen that caused her to crawl around her bedroom floor trying to cope with the pain.

She didn't want to die.

The Whitstable Carnival in August gave us all a brief lift. Gallant Kitty dressed up as a nurse, her Mum became the hospital's Witch Doctor in a grass skirt. Miss Marlow thoroughly enjoyed being pushed up the High Street on a heavy hospital bed by her minions past crowds that made their support for their local hospital known. She was dressed in a pink mop cap and nightie and clutched a hot water bottle all the way, swigging regularly from it.

My ten-year old was tired and thirsty that August evening as we arrived at the railway bridge at the top end of town and I asked Miss Marlow if she could have a drink from the bottle. "Certainly not, Mirabelle," our chief hissed, her cheeks glowing, "it's gin and tonic!"

I was still on my Summer break and moved Claudette into our flat where I could more easily look after her. Ross all but disappeared with discomfort. Callously, I thought as she had grown weaker, none of them upstairs had sat with her over the weeks to talk quietly and laugh and remember better days. I was just preparing supper when her daughter came in to the kitchen white as a sheet.

Amber, a District Nurse I knew ignored new procedural rules and came over immediately to do the honours. It was with a deep sense of gratitude in the short time I had known Claudette that I was able to assist Amber in performing Last Offices. She completed everything with great sensitivity, dignifying the life of a woman who had given her all to the end. My enduring image of my mother-in-law is of a beautiful white lace counterpane, a single rose in a slender vase and a woman at peace.

Amber's experienced professionalism re-energised us to cope with the emptiness that followed. Claudette's bereft family said their goodbyes fortified by Rescue Remedy and brandy plied by Evan's sweetly bonkers opera-singer sister who had appeared like the Good Fairy. A much-needed Auntie of the moment she bossed and busied a whole group of exhausted people until the undertakers arrived.

A day or so later I was off sick again, this time with excruciating sciatica in my left leg. My GP confirmed I had a prolapsed disc, a condition I knew nothing about and had to look up. Within days, being my own worst enemy I was back on the ward. It was the day after Claudette's funeral and I thought if I could get up to attend that, then I should be working.

It was a strange feeling looking around a ward full of sick people and thinking I can't do this anymore. I was grieving for my mother-in-law but something else was telling me it was time to stop. It hurt to sit down, to walk, to do almost anything. I bent down to lift a vase of flowers off the ward floor and heard a pop in my back. That, finally was it.

I managed to get in the bath that evening. Ross came in and sat down. He had something to say and it wasn't words of sympathy. He was passing blood and wondered what I thought. It has to be taken seriously, I said. It could be colitis or even the beginning of Crohn's Disease. He should see the doctor in the morning. My mind began racing. The pair of us out of action would be a tough one to get on top of.

A drug company trial was about to start for patients with bowel problems the GP said and Ross agreed to partake. I spent the next week in bed in no fit state to look closely at his regime but struggled every afternoon to get up before my girls came home from school to prepare their supper and give the semblance of normality. Ross moped about.

To keep this façade up until I got to grips with the situation I would need help and I telephoned my mother to ask if she could come down for a week or so. Her reply was blunt, she couldn't spare the time.

A couple of weeks passed before I realised Ross's health was deteriorating with the drugs Ceptrin and Sulphamethazine he was taking. He was sometimes faint bordering on comatose, he had trouble getting up in the morning and he was losing weight. Now he was unable to work. Uncharacteristically he shouted at me about my being incapacitated. I had started a Rage Diary on the advice of a colleague and after dwelling on things wrote that my husband was a third child in the family to whom 'Mummy' would not be able to carry the family responsibilities as before. It reminded me too he had shown no compassion in March when I had first strained my back. He shouted at me then.

Very worried about his soon rapid deterioration, I accompanied him to the Health Centre. From there he was taken by ambulance to the K & C for a blood transfusion and was in for two weeks. He returned home hairless. The effect of the drugs had given him more problems than he started with, including alopecia. Kitty was frightened because she had never seen such a thing. She didn't get

used to it for a while and did not want her school friends to see him.

One morning she came into our bedroom saying she couldn't breathe. Poor girl. It can't have helped that I was trying to get Ross to start an action for compensation from the pharmaceutical company that had almost killed him. He did not want to know. Kitty's breathing problems were the start of asthma that she suffers from to this day, approaching her fortieth birthday, when she is under serious stress.

The weeks and months became a haze. On the first of many visits to the Royal Sea Bathing Hospital at Margate in the Autumn for a variety of therapies for my condition including traction, physiotherapy and general prodding by a merry-go-round of specialists, I was put into a plaster jacket. It relieved the pain for the first time in months and I wept. However, I knew as I stepped carefully down the stairs my life had changed forever.

As I crept back along Canterbury Road to Margate station, Rachel pulled up in her car and asked why I was crying. The screeching of the Irish Orthopaedic Ward Sister, "your pain is all in your mind ..." was still ringing around my head. Rachel got the idea of the state I was in when I tried to get into the passenger seat without doing myself more damage. She calmed me down and took me home. Seeing that I was unable to bend to sit on the toilet or recline on the sofa without a palaver, she appeared the next morning with a raised toilet seat to make life a little easier. She no longer talked about my coming back to work.

When the plaster came off some time later I felt good but it was only temporary. Nevertheless, I said to the doctor with a big smile I would like to go back to work.

"I think not ..." was his grim reply. I was eventually signed off work forever.

"What an absolute criminal waste," commented a caring orthopaedic consultant at St. Thomas's Hospital, "killing your career and permanently disabling yourself from having to lift too heavy a corpse because the hospital wouldn't pay porters Sunday overtime."

On another occasion I was interviewed by a consultant at Bart's who had the manners of a boar and decided after five minutes I was suffering from Compensation Neurosis. My solicitors referred me to a psychiatrist in Harley Street.

When the psychiatrist heard I had started a nationwide charity encouraging self-help, in which I was singly handling calls at night from people around the country in serious pain, he said he would support me in court as a matter of principle. He thought it was outrageous the NHS were closing ranks and making such statements with impunity to one end, an aggressive and amoral determination not to compensate a dedicated nurse for a serious injury sustained in the workplace, loss of career and livelihood.

If only ... If only ever-obedient Naked Nurse had refused, as she should have done, the heavy lifting. It was easy to see after the event I habitually took on too much in an under-staffed male geriatric ward. That night I was charged up to get everything done as an unquestioningly obedient bedside angel.

From allowing ourselves to be dumped on over the years by senior staff, terrifying sisters, arrogant doctors, snotty physios, occasionally bolshy cleaners, brusque porters and some bullying, even physically

449

aggressive patients - you name it - we were profiled from our first day of training to be amiable and efficient passive nurses.

My behaving like a mutt was also reflected in my personal life. It was something realised only after some sanity-saving counselling relating to my coming to terms with the collateral fallout from the accident, to my marriage mostly.

A legal battle for compensation from my employers, the NHS began. That was a disgraceful episode in itself that included statements from slick solicitors and aggressive consultants conjuring up paranoia in their favour. I lost the action ultimately on the NHS case that I had an inherent weakness in my back because "I had been to the doctor about back ache in 1973." That was soon after giving birth to Lilly. The doctor did not think it problematic enough at the time to prescribe anything. Obviously I should have had better support from my union and legal representative. A dedicated nurse was dispensed with a paltry financial settlement that didn't pay the bills I had incurred to date.

We had to sell up and by 1988 when I started getting really busy with my charity, Ross and I had been separated a year. One of many interviews was with Liz Hodgkinson for the Independent. She quoted me about wanting to kill myself after the accident because the pain was so bad. That trauma I now have under control. I won awards also, all moments that kept me going along with things such as Peter Cushing agreeing to become a patron. He even joined one of my sponsored walks after needing a hip replacement after falling off his bicycle. He knew what pain was all about.

Punishing as it has been on occasion for almost thirty years, now in 2013, the accident pushed me in a direction I would not have considered and which has probably been more fulfilling than a slow edging up the short nursing ladder. Fulfilling in all but a financial sense. With support and encouragement I have travelled more than I ever did before. Just like Sleeping Beauty, I was going to wake up sometime.

Almost by way of a post script, Claudette's will was a classic. What her children had not bled her of, she left to them. This included the maisonette. She left nothing to her husband except a note saying exactly what she thought of him. The children exited the defunct nest but reassured their father he could remain in Wave Crest, as long as.

He went into a silent rage after copious expletives about his step-daughter in particular, inheriting and months later had a stroke. It was not the reminder of Claudette Ross and I wanted to hear night after night, his father dragging his left leg around muttering ever more drunkenly.

It was most upsetting when fifteen-year old Lilly went to live with Jo in Faversham. It was understandable as Evan spent most of his time in the room above hers.

Christmas of that year, 1985, was a thoughtful one for me, out of work, unable to work or to sit down because of the risk of my back flaring up and making me bed-bound for days. Financial help in the form of Supplementary Benefits was grudging and eventually nilled for the sake of two pence I was receiving over DHSS limits because of my nurses' pension.

In 2005 and living on my own I was hovering on the point of blubbing again at the Christmas dinner table at what will always be a sad time for me, as I have written. Now my daughters were with me. Lilly, a freelance film business journalist had flown over from LA. Kitty had come over from France where she lives and works in publishing and fashion.

"Mum, why is it every older lady you love, dies?" Kitty asked. She was referring to Jean, Nuala, Claudette and most recently my nursing friends and colleagues Barbara and Rachel.

Rachel's marriage was doomed from the beginning. She eventually evicted her husband from the house he had paid for because of his alcoholism and started an affair with a terminal cancer patient at the hospice she worked at after leaving the Whit and Tank. He didn't leave her anything contrary to what she had planned. Dr. Montague married again, someone on Benefits this time and was conned out of every last thing he possessed. He had just died of cancer. Rachel did also in 2005 of cervical cancer she was convinced she had contracted because of her philandering husband. I counted myself comparatively lucky.

Kitty raised her glass and went on, grinning,

"... to the Old Tarts!"

How could I not smile!

45859636R00248

Made in the USA
Charleston, SC
05 September 2015